WILLIAM HARDING CARTER AND THE AMERICAN ARMY

Campaigns and Commanders

CAMPAIGNS AND COMMANDERS

WILLIAM HARDING CARTER
AND THE AMERICAN ARMY

A SOLDIER'S STORY

Ronald G. Machoian

University of Oklahoma Press : Norman

For my Parents

and,

like everything else in my life,

for my daughter, Maddie

Library of Congress Cataloging-in-Publication Data

Machoian, Ronald Glenn, 1965–
William Harding Carter and the American Army : a soldier's story /
Ronald Machoian.
p. cm. — (Campaigns and commanders ; v. 9)
Includes bibliographical references (p.) and index.
ISBN 0-8061-3746-0 (alk. paper)
 1. Carter, William H. (William Harding), 1851–1925. 2. United
States. Army—Officers—Biography. 3. Generals—United States—
Biography. I. Title. II. Series.
U53.C38M23 2006
355'.0092—dc22
[B]

2005052987

William Harding Carter and the American Army: A Soldier's Story
is volume 9 in the Campaigns and Commanders series.

1 2 3 4 5 6 7 8 9 10

Contents

Illustrations

Acknowledgements

My study of William Harding Carter and the developing American military profession was completed only with the gracious help, advice, and expertise of numerous individuals and agencies, each of whom have earned my sincere thanks and appreciation. My doctoral study, from which this book is derived, was accomplished under the sponsorship of the United States Air Force Academy. For this great luxury, I am extremely grateful. It is a singular tribute to previous generations of military scholars that our armed services continue to recognize the great value of graduate education.

The staff of the National Archives in Washington D.C. was very helpful in guiding me toward pertinent materials and ensuring the wise use of my time. Mike Musick, Mike Pilgrim, David Wallace, and Trevor Plante were patient and indulgent as I peppered them with questions and asked for their help at the most inopportune times. Mitch Yockelson of the National Archives in College Park, Maryland, is an invaluable resource who manages to make all patrons feel as though their work is of great personal interest to him. This description is just as true of Bradley Gernand at the Library of Congress Manuscript Division, whose suggestions and guidance made my visit there a valuable and rewarding experience. Suzanne Christoff, Susan Lintelmann, and the entire staff at the U.S. Military Academy

Archives and Special Collections showed me the greatest hospitality during my visit to West Point. Their collective expertise and obvious passion for their work is a credit to the academy and its storied history. David Keough at the U.S. Army's Military History Institute (MHI) at Carlisle Barracks provided great insight into the historical development of the general staff and gave me unlimited access to his knowledge of MHI's extensive holdings. Dr. T. R. Brereton, whose recent study of Col. Arthur Wagner in many ways provided a model for my work, read my manuscript and offered very useful suggestions. To each of these individuals as well as countless others, I offer my sincere thanks and hope that I can someday return the favor.

My dissertation committee was a tremendous asset to my growth as a historian. I owe a special debt of gratitude and friendship to Prof. Herman Hattaway for his constant encouragement and guidance. Dr. Hattaway truly fulfilled his role as committee chairman, intellectual mentor, and friend. Prof. Jerry Cooper also was instrumental in my development as a student of American military history, encouraging my work and guiding me toward important themes that lay hidden in my often-cloudy analysis. I am equally indebted to Professors Stuart McAninch, Russell Doll, and Douglas Toma. Through numerous seminar hours, Dr. McAninch taught me to think critically, looking beneath what is merely said and done to the contextual elements that influence human constructs. Similarly, Dr. Doll showed me the value of recognizing a subject's philosophical underpinnings, and Dr. Toma helped me to understand the army's developing system of professional education as part of a larger evolution in civilian higher education. All of these gentlemen offered numerous hours of limited personal time while sharing their experience and insights. I hope that each of them can see some reflection of his unique contribution in my work.

I also want to recognize several others who have prodded me toward fruition in this endeavor. At different points in my professional career, Dr. Jerry Martin, Col. Eric Ash, and Col. George "Barney" Ballinger each encouraged and supported my ambitions when many (perhaps most) others would simply have shown me the door. Dr. Elliot Converse, Dr. John Farquhar, Dr. John Higgs, Dr. Kurt Schake, Lt. Col. Phil Lasala, Maj. Dave Cochran, and Lt. Col. Mike Peterson of the U.S. Air Force Academy; Dr. Ethan Rafuse of the U.S. Army Command and General Staff College at Fort Leavenworth; and Dr. Charles

Krupnick and Dr. Clayton Chun of the Army War College all offered me their time, advice, and friendship, while gently pushing me toward higher achievements in the study of military history.

I owe a special thanks to the Carter family. Although individual members of this family shall remain nameless to ensure their continued privacy, they offered me unprecedented access to the rich historical resources left by their forebear, inviting me into their homes and lives with absolutely no strings attached. Their dedication to an objective record of William Harding Carter's contributions and military career has made this study a very rewarding and satisfying pursuit. My simple and heartfelt thanks can never repay their trust, generosity, and kindness.

Finally, I want to thank my parents, John and Sherry Machoian, for showing me the exciting panorama of our nation's history. As elementary educators, they understood the importance of hands-on learning, taking my brother and me to countless historical sites and museums from a very young age, and in the process, imparting to us a passion for the study of history. But most of all, I want to thank my wife, June. She has endured the presence of William H. Carter in our home for many months, and without her love, patience, and support I could never have finished this project. At this point, I undoubtedly owe her a nice vacation, someplace far away from this record of Carter's struggle to build a new American army.

WILLIAM HARDING CARTER
AND THE AMERICAN ARMY

A TIME FOR REFORM

W hen William Harding Carter retired from the army in 1918, he
was the last officer remaining on active duty to have served
during the American Civil War. From the day he volunteered to carry
Union dispatches as a young boy in war-torn Nashville in 1864, his
military service continued with only brief interruptions during a career that lasted almost fifty-two years. During that period, he rode in
search of Geronimo, took part in the Indian Wars' tragic final chapter
during the Pine Ridge Campaign, served on the U.S. Army's first General Staff, battled *insurrectos* in the Philippine Islands, twice prepared divisions for intervention in Mexico, and oversaw the training
of thousands of American troops during mobilization for the First
World War. When he finally left active duty as a gray-haired veteran of
so many campaigns past, the army had become a vastly different,
more complex, and distinctly more professional organization than
the one into which he was commissioned so many years earlier.

His adult life was quite literally defined by America's transition
from a relatively isolated nation bent on westward conquest to one
transfixed by global commercial interests and imperial adventurism.
Rather than merely watching this process as a bystander, pushed
along by unseen forces, Carter seized the opportunity brought forth
by change and worked tirelessly to ensure that the U.S. Army kept

pace with a dynamic world. Understanding his pivotal role in bringing the American military into a new era broadens our knowledge of
both the institution and the nation that he served.

Carter's service spanned two American military traditions that
are most often referred to as the "Old" and "New" Armies. These ill-
defined terms have been applied to various chronological points of
departure between the early American army and the latter-day army
of an industrialized nation. The army's transition to a new institutional paradigm slowly gained momentum during the nineteenth
century's last decades, setting in motion a series of cultural shifts that
continued fitfully for several years. Edward Coffman's seminal study
of American military culture set the Old Army's end at the Spanish-
American War's onset in early 1898—a useful terminus for Coffman's
examination of the frontier soldier. The dawning of a new century
marked the beginning of an era that was highlighted by the United
States' entry into the race for international prestige and economic
dominance, levying new and difficult demands on the nation's military establishment.[1]

The war with Spain also proved a watershed moment in Carter's
own professional life. By the time Elihu Root was appointed secretary
of war in 1899, Carter had become an important figure in the War
Department's adjutant general's office (AGO). Already recognized by
peers and superiors alike as a forward-looking officer with an enthusiasm for institutional progress, he drew Root's attention as a soldier
with big ideas matched by skills and persistence to carry them to
fulfillment. As Root looked to redeem a military system that was
apparently out of touch with the nation's needs, he found in Carter an
able ally whose thoughts and expertise complemented his own. For
three years, the two worked side by side to lay the foundation for a
New Army, characterized by a graduated system of professional education, a coherent command structure, and institutionalized strategic planning and direction.

An amateur historian in his own right, Carter grasped the historic
changes in the world around him and considered the nature of the
terms "old" and "new" as they applied to his beloved army. The words
themselves, he concluded, had only relative meaning, but more importantly, implied a departure from the comfortable practices of the
past: "After each war the progress of knowledge in military affairs and
the active presence of new leaders of heroic mold tend alike to mark a

distinct line between the old and new armies." Memories of the camaraderie of hard-fought campaigns brought forth warm feelings for
the "old army" way of life, but just as modernization brought changes
to the broader American society, the army had to evolve with the
times. Accordingly, Carter believed, with the advent of a new century
and an industrialized world, forward-looking soldiers had to transform the army by paralleling the course taken by the era's developing
civilian professions.[2]

An important backdrop for Carter's insight was American society's expanding perspective of contemporary issues. The citizenry's
previously local or parochial outlook gradually widened to embrace
the nation, the hemisphere, and soon enough even large parts of the
world. After the Spanish-American War, a broadened sense of national
purpose—manifested in an imperialist foreign policy—expanded the
military's role and placed new demands on its antiquated practices
and organization, stretching the War Department's resources and
overburdening its structures. The pleas of Carter and his sort attempted to bridge the gap between the army of the past and the army
that was needed to secure the nation's future. In addition to broader
institutional concerns, this endeavor at its core was wrapped in a
subtle but nonetheless important self-defining motivation. Military
intellectuals saw professional reform as a distinct avenue toward
group security and prestige in the larger society—what was good for
the army was also good for them as members of an officer corps and as
individuals. Understanding Carter's efforts in a context of dynamic
social currents is essential to grasping the essence of his work to
transform the American army into a more professional force.[3]

Late nineteenth-century America—a period known derisively to
contemporary observers and historians alike as the Gilded Age—
experienced a trend toward occupational organization and definition. In a manner rooted in traditional republican ideology, a nascent
"middle class" celebrated competitive opportunities for material success and social prestige through higher education and hard work.
The climb that assumedly brought such rewards required specialized
skills and abilities to differentiate "professional" from the less able
amateur. Professionalism, with the internal organizational control
and expert achievement it implied, developed into a powerful socioeconomic force that left adherents and admirers alike with a comfortable sense of order. Individuals with shared expertise in a variety

of undertakings began to exert themselves collectively through publication, conference, and correspondence in the name of common
interests.[4]

Although middle-class America was a diverse segment without
easily defined borders, its members shared a confidence in the ability
of trained expertise to bring order and direction to a society that was
increasingly fraught with disorder. Many looked toward professionalism for "a basis in universal and predictable rules to provide a formal
contest for the competitive spirit of individual egos." The educated
professional became the Gilded Age hero of the American Dream,
assuming authority and autonomy in a manner consistent with the
era's spirit of Darwinian competition. These conditions constructed
a framework conducive to similar developments in the U.S. military
profession. When Carter and his colleagues pursued professional reform to heighten the prestige, security, and efficiency of the U.S.
Army, they did so as part of a greater social construct. Quite simply
put, "the American soldier's bond with the society that produced him
was not lost on nineteenth-century army officers."[5]

In sum, this departure from the past produced a different kind of
warrior, with different characteristics, experiences, and functions to
define his responsibility. "Gradually, at least among reform-minded
soldiers," wrote Carol Reardon, "a new image of the model army
officer of the future emerged. He would be equally comfortable in the
field or in the classroom." William H. Carter was an archetype of this
new breed, a leader who wielded the pen and podium as skillfully as
he sat a horse or deployed a skirmish line. During the fifty-year period
following the Civil War, the officer corps as a whole gradually—and
for some grudgingly—left behind notions that the battlefield was the
realm solely of natural-born warrior-chieftains and moved toward a
more sophisticated concept of martial leadership that incorporated
educated expertise, formal training and preparation, and deliberate
strategic planning.[6]

Military reform and its related process of professionalization
were certainly not new phenomena that appeared in the post–Civil
War army. Although it was previously theorized that American military professionalism grew from physical and cultural isolation suffered by the late-nineteenth-century's Frontier Army, more recent
scholarship has convincingly revised this conclusion. In *An American Profession of Arms*, William Skelton posits the emergence of

professional characteristics in the U.S. military much earlier, during the years immediately following the War of 1812, when a group of younger officers who had risen to wartime command sought to enhance the prestige of their newfound occupation. Under their leadership, the officer corps gradually adopted definitive standards that set its activities apart from the citizen-soldier's similar but much cruder martial undertakings. This marked the birth of an American military profession that for several decades struggled toward maturity with only limited success.[7]

The army's institutional culture during the immediate post–Civil War years did very little to foster any sort of further professional development. The war produced many officers of widely varied backgrounds and abilities who lacked West Pointers' corporate identity as well as their relatively high standards of education. A large number of such men remained in the army following the war, and in a Jacksonian vein, were more likely to espouse the amateur's traditional concept of natural or innate soldierly ability. As a group, they often resented talk of formal military education or theoretical expertise as a tacit indictment of their own "homespun" battlefield leadership and provided a cultural foil for colleagues who espoused such ideas. Serious efforts to bring lasting professional reform to the army would require visionary ideas tempered with pragmatic leadership and no small amount of political support to overcome such resistance.[8]

But at least a modicum of professional interest began to reemerge during the decades following the war's end. A new generation of young West Pointers followed the lead of forward-thinking veterans such as William T. Sherman, John M. Schofield, and especially Emory Upton—an officer remembered as the "major prophet of American professionalist thought." Dissatisfied with the army's onerous postwar missions and inspired by Sherman's conceptualization of the regular officer corps as an educated cadre, a small but dedicated group embraced reform as an avenue by which institutional influence and prestige might be restored.[9]

It was through their tireless efforts that a simmering sense of professionalism was not completely lost among widely scattered frontier outposts and left to the efforts of some future generation. Carter and others such as Arthur Wagner, Theodore Schwan, Tasker Bliss, and Eben Swift carried the army's intellectual torch as a self-appointed cabal of true believers. These soldiers are most often remembered simply as "Uptonian" or "professionalist"—useful and accurate categorizations insomuch as each of them evinced Upton's overarching goal of a stronger and more professionally prepared U.S. Army. But in the quest to sort intellectual strains into neatly generalized constructs, historians sometimes inadvertently lose sight of what was a very human effort. The reformers' individual and sometimes divergent contributions, opinions, and motivations are easily overlooked or downplayed in the attempt. Although common denominators are readily apparent—such as a West Point education, an association with the Leavenworth schools, and an enthusiasm for critical reflection—each participant is a historically significant variation on the greater theme and deserving of biographical study.[10]

Carter emerges as one whose career metaphorically reflects the greater chronicle of an army in transition. He was an exemplar of the "professionalist" mindset, while at the same time a singular and imaginative actor on the stage of military reform. For four years, from a unique position near the secretary of war, he placed his ideas before the nation's senior leadership and thereby played an important role in setting the army on a course toward modernization. His story is the record of one man's contributions to shaping a distinctly American military profession.

Despite Carter's very public efforts in the Root war department, his exact capacity has heretofore been misunderstood or entirely discounted. The credit given to him at the time by Secretary Root supports the central role that Carter later claimed for himself in *Creation of the American General Staff*. But some have doubted the authenticity of such claims, emphasizing instead Root's supposed Progressive principles as the true locomotion behind military reform. One historian unceremoniously painted him as Root's Uptonian lobbyist, a "palace soldier" who was adept at little more than chasing the next higher rank. Others, like Philip Jessup, have merely assigned him a technician's supporting role, noting quite simply that he was "invaluable to the new Secretary in working out the details of the reorganization plans." If he is remembered at all, it is as a legislative draftsman whose larger substantive impact is unfairly neglected. Carter remains an unknown quantity—familiar in name but still undeveloped as to the real character of both his person and role.[11]

Few realize that Carter became a leading professional voice of his generation through prolific publication on contemporary military topics and issues. Active until his death in 1925, he left an extensive literary record that is unparalleled among his peers. In addition to numerous articles that appeared in professional journals and popular magazines, he authored several books, the most important being *The American Army*, a study that summarized his professionalist perspective of American military policy and national preparedness. His achievements with the pen are all the more impressive when it is remembered that, only a few years earlier, he had entered an army in which intellectual activity was not only uncommon but frowned upon and even ridiculed. It is in large part through his own perseverance that by the time he retired, professional participation had become one of the standards by which an officer proved his mettle for higher command. Carter's efforts were absolutely vital to this shift, and thus equally important to the founding of a twentieth-century army.[12]

In 1915, on the occasion of Carter's first retirement from the army, then-Senator Elihu Root wrote in a private letter of

> the passing of a period during which we worked so hard together . . . to put our army on a better footing. . . . I know of no one retiring from active service who leaves a record of more valuable achievement than you. . . . It is a satisfaction to feel that through some of the things we did, notably bringing about the detailed administrative staff, the general staff, and the system of militia conformity and training, we made it possible for steps to be taken towards a more adequate military system which would have been wholly impossible before.[13]

This sentiment echoes the more public praise that Root had offered years earlier in his last annual report as secretary of war. Despite modern skepticism that a young cavalry officer might have played such a critical part in achieving reforms that were decades in the making, there is much about Carter that prods the historian to look further. He was a transformational leader with visionary ideas and the skills to articulate them before a sophisticated audience. As Americans find their way through a similarly dynamic and sadly tumultuous period at the opening of a new century, it is hoped that readers may find in Carter an example of the great influence that an individual can have in steering the future of a seemingly immovable institution.

2

GROWING UP AMONG SOLDIERS

On 19 November 1851, William Giles Harding Carter was born to Samuel Jefferson Carter and Anne Vaulx, the eighth of fourteen children in a family whose American lineage claimed roots among the earliest English colonists to settle Virginia. William Carter's antebellum childhood was spent on his family's modest farm just three miles outside of Nashville, Tennessee. The Carters were of a sort of middle-class status, lacking any real financial means or powerful social influence but nonetheless comfortable and respected by their affluent and yeoman neighbors.[1]

The Carter children enjoyed a reasonably secure environment, spending most afternoons outdoors with few worries beyond a mandate that they return home in time for supper. Like many southern boys of his day, William spent much of his childhood playing with the son of one of the family's slaves, with whom he remained in contact during his adult life. Willie, as family and friends knew him, attended a local grammar school and obtained good reports for his "deportment," but received only average grades in reading and arithmetic. His first ten years were rather quiet and unremarkable when compared to the turmoil that would mark his adolescence. Rural Tennessee provided a tranquil setting for a healthy little boy who loved the outdoors and was surrounded by siblings near his own age.[2]

Nearby Nashville was a growing regional center with a population of thirty-seven thousand and was among the most modern
cities in the South. By the end of 1860, its citizens could brag of gas
street lamps, brick sidewalks, a widely acknowledged university, and
a noted system of free public education that taught two thousand
schoolchildren. The area's agriculture flourished and Nashville was a
bustling trade center with regional influence. It was by all accounts a
shining example of the traditional culture that so many southerners
deeply revered.[3]

The Carters lived near the prominent plantation of young William's formal namesake, William Giles Harding, whose Belle Meade
estate was a sort of local landmark known for some of the region's finest thoroughbred horses. Harding's blooded racing stock had gained a
national reputation by the mid-1850s, and Samuel Carter, who operated Walnut Grove, a local track, imbued his children with a love for
fine horses and equitation, which in William's case developed into an
adult passion. As Carter later remembered, he had grown up "under
the daily influence of those interested in the breeding and development of horses" and quickly became quite at home in the saddle.
Certainly little Willie could not have known then that his skills on
horseback would lead him very quickly into a profession that would
define the rest of his life.[4]

When Carter was not yet ten years old, he, like many thousands
of other American children of his generation, became the innocent
witness to war's inhumanity on the homefront. Although too young
to properly understand the complex social and political meanings of
civil war, he was subjected to its local effects, even within the seemingly secure confines of his own family and home. Nashville was
quickly swept onto the war's stage and the Carter family became a
microcosm of its shattering impact. Like many parts of the Confederate South, middle Tennessee's populace was never of a single mind on
the secession issue, and exuberance often carried support in one direction and then another. One observer noted "there was much division of sentiment even among members of the same family and shifts
of opinion . . . were frequent and illustrated the confused state of mind
among the people." But the luxury of indecision was soon lost as
events accelerated and open rebellion against the federal government
became reality.[5]

The area had voted strongly in favor of a Unionist delegation to a proposed convention in early February 1861, but by the end of the spring, after events made further violence a foregone conclusion, a vast majority had become rabid secessionists. After the attack on Fort Sumter and President Abraham Lincoln's subsequent call for seventy-five thousand Union volunteers, "many men who had been strong for the Union the day before . . . were 'among the first to raise the standard of resistance.'" A secession ordinance was submitted to Tennesseans for ratification on 8 June, and most of Nashville's white population became quick converts to newfound Confederate sympathies. A tide of martial fervor gripped the city, turning it into the "great storehouse and arsenal of the western Confederacy." Carter's boyish emotions must have teetered between excitement and fear as he watched the upheaval and turmoil build around him.[6]

Like the nation itself, the Carters were pulled asunder when many relatives joined the Confederate army, including the husband of one of William's older sisters. Samuel Carter was placed at bitter odds with neighbors and relations when he steadfastly maintained Unionist beliefs in the face of growing ostracism. "'As martial ardor increased," observed Peter Maslowski, "the plight of the few remaining Nashville loyalists became proportionally worse." At first, young Carter was caught up in the emotional energy of Tennessee's secessionist spirit, and he "'saw nothing wrong in the frequent assertion that each of them [his Confederate neighbors] was the equal of five Yankees." But as his father's loyalties drew increasing resentment and even physical threats from a neighborly "vigilance committee," William's support quickly returned to "the righteousness of the cause of the Union."[7]

As the child of a known Yankee sympathizer, William was prevented from attending the few school classes that remained open. But this temporary loss was the least of the family's concerns during the summer of 1861, as Nashville's Confederate government soon began enforcing acts aimed at harassing the city's remaining Union men. Perhaps the Carters were saved some of this heartache by their rural location, but others did not fare so well: "Hounded, closely watched, and persecuted, it is not surprising that only a tiny handful of Unionists endured the harassment and remained in the city." The ardent hatred that motivated such actions was transparent to a ten-year-old child. While his family worried about their continued existence in their own hometown, Carter often visited Confederate relatives in nearby encampments, not understanding that his father's sentiments might conflict with his enjoying the strange sights of an army preparing for battle. A few months later, on 23 February 1862, following Confederate losses at nearby forts Henry and Donelson, Nashville was surrendered to the advancing Union army. As one of the few loyal families remaining in the city, the Carters became host to a series of federal officers, and William was treated to an even closer look at the workings of an army at war.[8]

Writing over a half-century later, Carter remembered watching Confederate cavalry on the bluffs overlooking the Cumberland River as they carefully eyed Yankee troops who gathered on the opposite bank for the crossing into Nashville. Walter T. Durham described the same unfolding scene in almost poetic terms:

> Across the muddy river in Edgefield, a clatter in the streets signaled the arrival of Federal cavalry pickets. On the Nashville side, inquisitive crowds lined the river bluffs to get their first glimpse of Yankee soldiers while Confederate stragglers rushed to get out of town.[9]

The exchange of authority over his hometown equally fascinated William, and the sight of the city's mayor, Dick Cheatham, crossing the Cumberland in a rowboat to treat with the invading Federal army was firmly etched in his young memory. Unlike most of Nashville's populace, Samuel Carter and his family welcomed Union General Don Carlos Buell's army as liberators. The elder Carter by this time owned the St. Cloud Hotel, a modest establishment that played host to some of the first Union officers to enter the city, and for a time even served as Buell's headquarters.[10]

When William's sister Laura married a Northern officer serving on Buell's personal staff, the Carter family was permanently split by war's misfortunes. Eliza Carter, the oldest of Samuel's daughters from a previous marriage, whose husband served in the Confederate army, grew so embittered that she never again spoke or communicated to family members who remained loyal to the Union. As Carter appropriately noted in his memoirs: "Women are the last to surrender." Certainly the horrific concept of civil war was revealed in short order to the people of Nashville as the pageantry and excitement of the conflict's first weeks gave way to the hard reality that followed.[11]

Despite the measure of adventure it undoubtedly brought to William's life, the war's terrible destruction was driven home to his lasting impression. The "ills and dangers" of military occupation were played out at neighboring Belle Meade plantation when Yankee foragers continually plundered the estate, shot one of their slaves, and even threatened the Hardings' young niece with an axe. After the Battle of Stones River was fought just south of Nashville in Murfreesboro, Tennessee (31 December 1862–2 January 1863), several wounded Union officers convalesced in the Carter household.[12]

In his own parlor, William overheard graphic descriptions of the battle and specifically remembered an account of the gruesome death of one Colonel Garesche, whose head was "shot off by a cannon ball." The recuperating houseguests explained that Garesche's body was identified by the U.S. Military Academy (USMA) class ring that remained on a lifeless finger—a macabre story that, in an indirect manner, provided the army with one of its future general officers. Carter remembered that he later announced to his family that he too wanted to be a West Pointer "so that I could have a ring and be identified if my head was shot off." This simple memory illustrates a ten-year-old's absurdly innocent perspective of battle.[13]

Despite witnessing the war's devastation, constant exposure to Nashville's Union garrison proved irresistible to William and he yearned for a soldier's life. In 1864, at the age of only twelve years, he entered government service as a volunteer dispatch rider for the Army of the Cumberland's Quartermaster Department. This work combined his love for horses with his newfound enthusiasm for all things military—an association that would happily accompany him for most of his professional career. Years later, General R. W. Johnson remembered that even as a boy, Carter was admired for his "brave and manly conduct." His duties were apparently serious enough to last until the end of the war, and this experience stirred his desire to someday become a bona fide cavalryman.[14]

During the battle of Nashville, Carter captured an even closer view of the war. For several weeks, Federal fortifications around the city were strengthened by feverish work performed by the quick impressment of all available hands: "Quartermaster's men, Veteran Reserves, fellows convalescent, and darkeys under arms" all were pulled into the lines to prepare for the arrival of John Bell Hood's Confederate army. When Union troops returned to the city on 30 November following victory at Franklin just twenty-five miles south, Nashville's families fretted as a battle in their midst appeared to be imminent. But young Carter could think only of the coming spectacle, and he remembered that he hardly slept "for fear the big battle would come off hurriedly," causing him to miss the action.[15]

Once the fighting began on 16 December with Union General George Thomas's attack on Hood's line, Carter joined his Negro barber at a prearranged rooftop vantage point, obtaining a panoramic view of the carnage by use of a telescope belonging to his older friend. The developing battle kept him at this self-appointed post until late into the night when the firing finally began to die down. William likely did not realize how close his own home had come to becoming part of the bloody battlefield, just as his relatives' farm had two weeks earlier on nearby Carter Creek at the battle of Franklin. The twin defeats at Franklin and Nashville ended Hood's foray into Tennessee and dashed Confederate hopes of taking the war westward. But more than any grand strategic outcome, it was the battles' horrific human costs that were plainly evident to the citizens of Nashville. For a long time thereafter, "few families of Middle Tennessee appeared in other than garments of deepest black."[16]

Beyond its more immediate impact on his home and community, the war profoundly affected Carter's future. As he later put it, "for four years during the Civil War I was never out of sight of armed men, and had grown accustomed to interest myself in their affairs." War's terrible spectacle left him with deep respect for men who offered their lives for abstract notions of duty and country, and it is little wonder that he burned to follow in their footsteps. The U.S. Military Academy at West Point, New York, was the obvious path for a young man seeking an army career, and it was this path that Carter determined to follow.[17]

When the war finally drew to a close, William's family sought a return to normalcy. Making up for the wartime interruption of their children's education became a primary concern, and William was sent to Frankfort, Kentucky, to study under B. B. Sayre, a regionally well-known tutor. When Sayre shortly thereafter accepted a position at the Kentucky Military Institute, Carter naturally followed and was enrolled as a cadet—his first encounter with the disciplined life that would accompany him into adulthood.

At the Institute, William was introduced to a course of instruc-

tion that was very similar to that of contemporary West Point. Private
military schools of the period often patterned their practices, curricula, and regimented student culture after that found at the USMA.
But the war had taken its toll: the four-year hiatus of the nation's
already-rudimentary primary training left its glaring mark on the students' preparation. As Carter observed, "there was too much difference in the standards of education among the boys and young men
coming from the war worn districts to hope for immediate success."
But this brief approximation of cadet life only strengthened William's
hope for a military education, and thoughts of attending West Point
were not forgotten.[18]

The South's destruction and the poorly concealed resentment of
many neighbors and even relations convinced Samuel Carter that it
would be best to move his family north, away from the war's constant
reminders. Reconstruction efforts in postwar Nashville, as in much
of the South, did very little to melt wartime rancor, and most Confed-
erates continued to display the utmost disgust for Federal institutions and Unionist neighbors. In 1866, keenly aware of this pervasive
bitterness, the elder Carter moved his family to New York where
the war's legacy was less vindictive and commercial opportunities
abounded in an industrializing nation. William moved with his family leaving behind Mr. Sayre and the Kentucky Military Institute at
midterm, his education once again interrupted by the misfortunes of
civil war.[19]

When he arrived in New York City, Carter was reluctantly swept
into the period's enthusiasm for capitalist venture. Postwar New
York was enthralled with its position as a marketplace for burgeoning
industry, as evidenced in its bustling urban streets. Carter's father
was convinced that his sons should apprentice in the business practices that might eventually provide an avenue for social and economic mobility. Even though he admittedly lacked "the inclination,"
William began an unpaid work-study at Justice & Co., a local retail
business, in a half-hearted attempt to mimic the ambitious course
taken by so many of the eastern-bred city boys around him. Far from
Tennessee's rolling landscape, he found the work dull and monotonous and quickly concluded that he lacked a mind for business. Carter chafed for the vibrant outdoor life he had left behind, making it "a
physical necessity . . . to seek another career." Dreams of becoming a

West Pointer remained strong, and he began to campaign actively for the opportunity.[20]

Shortly after his failed acquaintance with the business world, Carter submitted his name to President Andrew Johnson for an at-large appointment. Johnson was a staunch Unionist Democrat who had ruled wartime Tennessee as military governor. There is little doubt that he was acquainted to some degree with the Carters from the war years when Samuel's politics placed him near the inner circles of Tennessee's federal governance. William's service as a Union dispatch rider must have also helped his petition and set him apart from many other boys his age. His application began while he was still only fifteen years old—a year younger than the minimum age at that time for an entering cadet. But like most boys his age, Carter longed to begin adulthood, and burned for the adventure that he was certain would accompany an officer's commission. While eagerly awaiting the much sought-after appointment, Carter attended a school under the direction of Mr. Thomas Hunter, whose educational outlook was similar to that of Sayre at the Kentucky Military Institute.[21]

Beyond Hunter's coursework, New York City provided ample opportunities for a young student to experience the arts and sciences at numerous exhibits, libraries, and other public forums. Carter was intrigued by the pursuit of knowledge, and took full advantage of the city's offerings to satisfy his newfound appetite for learning. He became almost amusingly convinced that he was a budding intellectual, and his diary entries during the few months spent in New York reflect this growing self-image. Carter began to record the titles of books he read, and often added short critical reviews of their relative strengths and weaknesses. On New Year's Day of 1868, in an obviously solemn mood, he wrote of the opportunity "to gain knowledge, and to do all to relieve the wants of others, that is in our power." Looking back, modern observers might find such a proposition naively romantic as the foundation for a career in the Frontier Army.[22]

William acted on his interests and attended several of the city's public lectures, such as "Cities" given by Richard O'Gorman, which he described as "flowery" but nonetheless "very well given." This was followed by Rev. Dr. Chapin's "Building and Being," a lofty-sounding topic for a fifteen-year-old's digestion but one that Carter enjoyed very much; and lectures on scientific subjects ranging from

"Steam" to "Electricity." His attraction to scholarship and public discourse was further piqued by frequent visits to the Aston Library, the New York Historical Society, the Tract Society, and the Academy of Design. At such places, he was treated to some of the period's finest exhibits of literature, science, and art—and the experience imbued him with an enthusiasm for knowledge and contemplation that matured in his later professional life.[23]

Finally, on 15 April 1868, Carter received the treasured letter for which he had been waiting. President Johnson appointed him at-large to the Class of 1872, which entered that June, one of only ten such appointments offered by the president under existing regulations. Accompanying the nomination was a "Circular to Persons Receiving Cadet Appointments," a summary of the physical, mental, and legal qualifications necessary for admission to the academy. This sobering decree played heavily on Carter's anxious mind, and years later he recalled it as "the most depressing, nerve-racking document" he ever encountered. Worried about his physical aptitude, he sought reassurance from local physicians who, probably amused by his concerns, offered opinions that he had none of "the serious defects to be avoided by those who would offer themselves as food for powder." Thus satisfied, Carter looked forward to beginning what was to be a very long relationship with the U.S. Army.[24]

By the time he actually appeared before the academy adjutant that June, Carter had read so many books on the place that he had already absorbed some of the feeling which graduates often referred to as "the Spirit of Old West Point." The institution's culture had changed very little since its early wholesale reorganization under Sylvanus Thayer's leadership as superintendent. From 1817 until 1833, Thayer had molded West Point into a scientific and technical school that was the envy of its contemporaries in civilian higher education. In the image of European military academies, cadets learned in a highly disciplined environment that rewarded performance and frowned on deficiency of any sort—whether in the classroom, on the parade ground, or in the barracks. The mood was one of overwhelming expectation, with cold stone memorials and ramparts constantly reminding young cadets that failure would breach their solemn obligation. Carter was thrilled to become a part of this austere life, and after enduring his first day as a new cadet wrote: "I have looked around the Point, and think it is the most beautiful place I ever saw."[25]

Despite politically fueled wartime controversies attacking its purpose, West Point's academic prestige remained largely intact. The school stressed the sciences and mathematics as subjects that would prepare cadets for the analytical details of their careers. Cadets were expected to recite daily lessons and were examined twice yearly under the threat of being found deficient and eventually expelled if they failed to meet grades.[26] Although the academy has been faulted as "stagnant" for not accompanying civilian schools into an era of revolutionary educational progress, West Point rationalized its academic traditions according to the peculiar needs of an officer's professional responsibility. Thus, the culture that greeted Carter on the bluffs above the Hudson River was very much the same as that encountered by previous generations of West Pointers. This shared experience was an important professionalizing factor that did much to develop an enduring sense of camaraderie and continuity within the officer corps.[27]

Cadet education certainly did not end in the classroom. Summer encampments, military training, and other extracurricular duties helped define West Point's singular culture. Hazing or "deviling," as cadets called it, was commonplace despite regulations against the practice, and provided upperclassmen with a welcome distraction from the daily routine. New cadets were subjected to numerous traditions and "games" that, for better or worse, acculturated them in a manner that went well beyond the gray wool uniforms and constant drill. Other forms of recreation also found their way into the cadets' daily regimen—some of them sanctioned by the school's ever-watchful authorities while others, such as drinking and gambling, were wholly outside the prescribed diversions.[28]

Carter and his new classmates quickly became a part of this larger West Point experience when they reported that June in 1868. Perhaps the single most dominant aspect of a cadet's four years on the Hudson was a total immersion in a unique culture that imbued deep respect for institutional solutions to both public and private challenges. Carter's own developing outlook, as later demonstrated in his professional career, certainly reflected this propensity. Although particular frustrations often sorely tried his patience as a cadet and officer, he never doubted or lost faith in the validity of the institutions he served—whether the federal government, the Regular Army, or West Point.

3

A SOLDIER'S EDUCATION

After passing the daunting entrance examinations, Carter set about the business of becoming a cadet and beginning his pursuit of an officer's commission. The summer weeks spent in "plebe camp" seemed to amuse more than discourage him, and initiation into cadet life was followed by a somewhat more sedate but perhaps even more demanding academic year in the barracks. He remained solemnly focused on his chosen profession, and already wrote of a desire to continue his personal study after graduation, so that he might offer the country the "full benefit" of his abilities. Even during academics when, like most cadets, he found preparing for daily lessons a difficult enough undertaking, Carter continued an ambitious personal reading schedule, concentrating on topics that might apply to his later career.[1]

The first semester passed with little trouble, and by the time semiannual examinations took place in January, he was gaining confidence in his ability to complete the four-year program and graduate. But this confidence could hardly be mistaken for arrogance. He was already reconciled to the fact that he was not going to graduate at the top of his class, and his general standing as number forty-three in a class of seventy-seven at the end of the fall semester certainly supports this conclusion. But Carter also found that he was not so "out-of-place" as previously feared, and eagerly looked forward to the spring semester when he and his classmates would be within sight of the end of their first year.[2]

The disciplined atmosphere agreed with William, and although he naturally grumbled about such things as the quality of meals and the lack of Christmas leave, his letters and diary entries as a cadet generally exuded optimism. Yet it is also clear that he lost some of his boyish enthusiasm for academy life. He now chafed at the constant regulation and observed that such discipline could backfire if overdone: "The consequence of confining young men to the house too closely is the same here as everywhere; card-playing, smoking, chewing and very frequently drinking." Such an observation was itself a lesson learned and, carefully filed away, became one of many blocks in Carter's foundation for future leadership.[3]

The exhausting schedule of classes, formations, and inspections took its toll, and he noted that a cadet's life invariably dampened "the ardor of the youthful 'aspirant to military glory.' " Carter received his fair share of demerits, and marched a number of punishment tours or "matinees," as he called the Saturday-afternoon version of this disciplinary tool. The spring thaw brought promise of a better life as a third-classman, and when the academic year ended in June, he once again passed examinations with neither fanfare nor distress. After surviving their first year at the academy, Carter and his remaining classmates eagerly looked forward to the summer as "yearlings."[4]

With the tribulations of their first year now behind them, the new third-classmen were able to enjoy some of the adventure afforded by summer training at West Point, and Carter described the transition from plebe to yearling as "like ushering us into a new world." He found the summer thoroughly rejuvenating and remembered enjoying it "more than any other of my life." But the next fall's return to barracks also brought a sobering return to academics, and Carter's performance in analytical geometry gave him cause for worry almost right away. By the time the end of the semester rolled around, his future as a mathematician was certainly in doubt, and even the Christmas season did little to lighten the weight of impending semiannual exams.[5]

Shortly after the New Year, examinations hit the battalion hard—twenty-seven cadets failed at least one course. Carter was found deficient in geometry just as he feared, and faced reexamination shortly thereafter. The failure did not panic him, although he admitted that it "was not very pleasant news considering that I had been boning very hard for some time past."[6] But he succeeded on the second attempt and put the episode quickly behind him. The promise of a summer furlough was a guiding light, and William, perhaps taking after his sister Laura, an aspiring poet in New York, wrote the following short rhyme:

> For a while we'll cease
> to bone,
> Forget all we ever knew
> Of "the intersections of
> the cone"
> While sporting Furlough
> Blue.[7]

The spring semester could not pass quickly enough, and he was counting the days until he might finally break away from the academy's daily grind. Unfortunately, before the much-sought-after leave became reality, examinations once more proved a daunting obstacle that this time almost put a premature end to his army career.

At year's end, Carter again failed mathematics, but fortunately was saved from expulsion by a merciful decision of the Academic Board. He was held back a class, and although this entire sequence of events was wholly unnerving, he avoided the fate of dismissal suffered by five of his classmates. When he returned in the fall of 1870 after summer leave, it was as a member of the Class of 1873, and he spent a year repeating the coursework that had given him so much trouble. Carter vowed to graduate despite the disappointing setback, and perhaps realized that the extra year's study might prevent yet another failure, when the outcome would undoubtedly be more severe. As it was, his dream of becoming an army officer was delayed but thankfully not entirely lost.

The year 1870 was important for both the institution of West Point and the nation. For the first time in history, two African-American men were appointed as cadets, and when one of them actually gained admission, it was a watershed moment that might have had momentous implications for American society. That summer, the two candidates were placed in William's cadet company and he quickly formed an opinion that one, the young man who eventually passed entrance exams and gained admission, was "the most unworthy fellow ever backed by misguided supporters," while the other was "a real man." The latter was Michael Howard and the former was undoubtedly James Webster Smith, whose four-year stay at the academy was filled with private and public turmoil. Smith's conduct confirmed him in Carter's mind as "a tattler who runs to the com'd't [commandant] for the slightest thing which is done to him," and one who "demands much better treatment than his classmates." This first attempt at racial integration of military education was played out before Carter's eyes, with results that were in the end unsatisfactory for all concerned.[8]

Carter's witness illustrates that West Point's experience with the admission of African-American cadets must be considered in the broader context of the times. When Smith and Howard arrived at the Military Academy in 1870, the nation was still in the throes of Radical Reconstruction—a period that pitted congressional Republicans against southern politicos. The latter were intent upon revitalizing the postwar South in a manner that closely resembled the antebellum culture of racial and social deference. As emancipated slaves struggled to gain a foothold in American society, the promise of freedom and equality was quickly diluted—first in practice and later under the law. By the time Democratic "redemption" restored political terms friendly to the South's old guard, very little had been achieved in the way of true social reconstruction. Outside of a handful of traditionally integrated colleges, such as Oberlin and Bowdoin, very few civilian schools even attempted racial integration at that date, and those that did endured resistance and turmoil. Racial prejudice was still a pervasive force across the entire nation; many whites—both north and south—steadfastly refused to acknowledge racial equality in fact even as it now existed in constitutional theory.[9]

Accounts of the treatment of Smith and Howard run a spectrum from accusations of harsh physical abuse to simple ostracism and isolation. The reality may have been somewhere in the middle, their presence drawing varied reaction from a diverse group of cadets. Howard was quickly disqualified when the entrance examination was administered four weeks after the plebe class reported, but Smith passed the exam and entered the academic year with his class. A reporter for the *New York Tribune* wrote that both Howard and Smith "have been treated with uniform kindness at the Academy, and the tricks that the boys usually play upon new comers have been omitted in their cases, because the cadets thought the people would say they were roughly handled because they were colored boys." The situation was clearly charged with political overtones that loomed much larger than the mere presence of a new cadet.[10]

That summer, Carter, and several other southern-born cadets were placed at the same mess table with the "unworthy fellow"—an arrangement that no doubt issued from some malicious mind. As Carter put it, "I never knew who plotted the thing, but I do know we were better friends of the negro race than he was." The white cadets apparently requested to be reassigned to different tables, but were quickly rebuffed by the new commadant of cadets, Emory Upton, a Union war hero and later a prominent voice in military reform. From this vantage point, Smith's turbulent stay at West Point became a singular illustration to Carter, not only of the powerful changes at work in American society, but also of the pervasiveness of politics in military affairs—a lesson that would be repeated many times over during his career.[11]

Over the next several months, Smith was twice brought up on charges of fighting and making false statements, and each time met a court-martial as per cadet regulations. In the first instance, he was found guilty only of fighting and escaped serious punishment, but in January 1871, he was convicted of all charges, including lying—a very serious offense under the still ill-defined cadet honor code. Later that spring, President Grant, although in agreement with the court, abridged Smith's impending dismissal to a reduction of academic class by one year, stating that lenience was necessary to reflect "the policy of the government—of which the presence of this cadet is a signal illustration." The cadet corps was outraged, and political interference only deepened cadets' resentment of the situation. Anger aimed at Smith was rationalized with a cloak of concern for the institution itself, with little acknowledgement or even recognition of the issue's larger moral significance.[12]

It was in this vein that Carter expressed his own serious verdict: "It has come to a disgraceful pass, when liars are kept in our midst contrary to the advice of military courts convened on him. But politics, that bane of an honest man who enters the public arena, has its influence upon the Sec't'y of War."[13] A few weeks later, after an unrelated disciplinary situation was also manipulated by outside interest, he complained that

> Every country congressman, politician and editor seems to think his duty to his constituents, God, his country and himself, to give some advice concerning the management of West Point; while in fact [they] have no more idea of the workings of the academy than a hog has of music.[14]

This introduction to politically burdened decisions was received with painful clarity and Carter remained keenly aware of the public's sensitivity to military matters—an insight that would later become a valuable tool in the struggle to build reforms in a highly charged political environment. Apparently for at least one cadet, an important part of West Point's education took place outside the classroom.

The 1870–71 school year was a difficult one for all associated with West Point. But despite the year's controversies and disruptions, Carter repeated his "yearling" courses with no further problems and ended the spring semester ranked number twenty-five in his class. His disgust for the political face of academy governance was not easily forgotten, and at first, he failed to grasp the very public nature of his chosen profession. But his initial reaction—"I believe in letting this be a strictly Military Academy, run by the War Dep't and Army, and not allow its control to come in as political spoils"—would in time be tempered by experience and supplanted by a more mature understanding of the Republic's civil-military relationship. When the long year finally ended, Carter advanced to the second class—twelve months later than planned, but nonetheless still wearing cadet gray and looking forward to becoming a soldier.[15]

The next two years at West Point shaped Carter into a young officer, identifying his personal strengths and weaknesses with sometimes brutal honesty. The classroom continued to demand his full attention, and when academics again threatened his very existence at the academy, he bore down and found the motivation to rally from despair. He sought extra help from old classmates who had already prevailed in the chemistry and physics courses that he found so difficult. Their encouragement helped lift him through exams, although never creating any lasting affinity for these subjects. "I love reading and literature," wrote Carter, "but mathematics and all its applications have been the bane of my life as a scholar."[16]

Demerits and confinements were a cadet's reward for minor sins and transgressions, and Carter joked in his letters that marching "extra" punishment tours was not an unusual activity for him. But military regulation and constant discipline, though often the target of his disgust, never discouraged him. He respected West Point and its traditions, even as the daily grind sometimes bordered on the ridiculous. Through this shared endurance, cadets generally developed a very high sense of loyalty to one another as well as to the institution, and it was this same feeling that was later transferred to the army and nation at large. The academy defined a sort of microcosmic military culture, and for the astute observer, events at conservative West Point signaled the army's coming transition from old to new.

In the fall of 1871, after many of the older generation of academy faculty had either resigned or passed away, Carter wistfully noted venerable Professor Dennis Hart Mahan's tragic death as symbolic of a passing era. Mahan, who had joined the permanent faculty as a young officer in 1831, handpicked by Thayer himself, had fallen or perhaps jumped overboard into the paddle wheels of a steamboat after several years of worsening health and depression over impending retirement. The announcement left Carter in a pensive mood, and he reasoned that "perhaps it is sympathy for the sad remnant of that honorable old Corps of Prof's, whose ranks have again been depleted by the suicide of Prof' Mahan." A prominent foundation of the "Old Army" had passed before his eyes. Certainly those cadets who took part in Mahan's funeral could not have missed the event's poignant significance.[17]

As his final year as a cadet neared, Carter began to find a few more minutes for himself and spent as much time as possible on horseback. Equestrian training was part of the cadets' military curriculum and his boyhood love for horses was whetted but never satisfied. He excelled in the riding hall and relished opportunities to take longer, more enjoyable rides to such places as nearby Fort Putnam. During time alone, Carter sometimes reflected on the fortunes and misfortunes of cadet life and debated his choice of occupations. Despite increasing resentment of the political nature of military decisions, the answer was always the same. He remained convinced that an army career suited him and was the best hope for any sort of adventure beyond the drudgery he had seen in New York City. "Why not . . . stay in the service," he reasoned. "It is hard but is the only profession where frightful reality is clothed with a garb of romance." After passing final examinations in the spring of 1872, he saw his old classmates accept their commissions and bid each other an emotional farewell—an occasion that also meant he and his new classmates were only months from saying their own good-byes. By the time he started his last academic year, Carter was already coming to the realization that graduation would bring a bittersweet departure from West Point.[18]

He anxiously wrote in his diary that "four years and a half [have] nearly passed since I donned the grey and oh for the end which in eight more months will come." But on the same page, he already lamented having to leave behind the close friendships built at the academy. With mature wisdom, he noted an ironic twist in the cadets' constant longing to escape their seemingly severe environment: "How we look forward to the time to doff the bob tails! And yet I dare say that with all its trouble and work; our cadet lives will be the happiest part of our existence." But despite this tinge of sadness at leaving West Point's somber stone walls behind, Carter's last months at the academy were spent in keen anticipation of finally beginning an army career.[19]

On 2 April 1873, William's life was tragically interrupted by news of his father's death. Although Samuel Jefferson Carter had been seriously ill over a year earlier, he had since recovered and seemed to regain his health. Thus, his passing was by no means expected and came as a devastating shock to a young man who proudly looked forward to graduation in only a few weeks. Unable to attend the funeral due to intense preparation for final exams, Carter could only pray for his family and hope to visit his father's Nashville grave at some later date. The fact that he was unable to be with his family made the moment all the more difficult, but he had to press the loss from his mind and continue to prepare for the very last hurdle of his cadet career.[20]

As June approached, the graduating class was preoccupied with receiving their first assignments, ordering Regular Army uniforms, and planning their all-important graduation leave—the first taste of true freedom that most had enjoyed for four or more years. Carter's affinity for horses and youthful experiences as a Civil War dispatch rider guaranteed his wholehearted desire to enter the cavalry as his first and only choice. "I do hope I shall get in the cavalry," he had written two years earlier, "for I enjoy so much to be on a fine horse who is anxious to run and can jump anything." With commissioning day rapidly nearing, he could think of little else than the hair-raising adventure he was sure would accompany service with a troop on the frontier. The equestrian instructor had recommended only Carter and one other cadet for cavalry duty, and granting this fervent wish seemed all but assured.[21]

West Point graduates of the period requested assignment to a specific opening in a given regiment. Once assigned, an officer usually remained in that regiment for an entire career, gaining promotion to the next rank only when a vacancy occurred within their organization. Thus, a graduate's initial assignment was indeed an important one, and often foretold the nature of the rest of his professional life. It was not until almost twenty years later that promotions became competitive across an entire branch of service, and officers were thus able to progress from a position in one unit to a vacancy in another. The seniority system that existed in the Old Army, although supposedly discouraging internal politics and rewarding longevity, only created a standard of mediocrity whereby an officer's performance had little impact on his career, save some disaster for which he was cashiered from the army. As Edward Coffman put it, such a system "made it impossible to control standards of competence, much less reward merit." Justifiably then, cadets were highly interested in claiming one of their top choices for assignment.[22]

Carter finished the academic year and graduated without further setback, after trudging through a four-year program in five years—thanks to an abundant helping of mathematics for which he had little capacity and even less affection. As he philosophically noted, perhaps such a feat rendered his diploma even more noteworthy than that of the top men in the class. In later years, Carter suspected that the great amount of outside reading he undertook at the expense of his assigned studies likely undermined his classroom achievements. The long lists of book titles entered in the back pages of his cadet diaries lend support to this notion. Nevertheless, it was not his class standing that caused him one final frustration as he prepared to begin his army career, but a wholly unexpected and rather unfortunate turn of events. The adage that "the best laid plans sometimes go awry" certainly applied to Carter's dreams of finally taking his place as a dashing cavalier.[23]

For some unknown reason the vacancy to which he requested assignment remained unfilled, and with all other cavalry vacancies already requested by other members of his class, the newly commissioned Lieutenant Carter was assigned to the U.S. Eighth Infantry. He was momentarily devastated by the news, but kind words from Secretary of War Belknap during a chance meeting at the Jersey City railroad depot a few weeks later gave him some hope for future reassignment. In the meantime, he joined the rest of his classmates in a hard-earned vacation from the academy, the army, and any thoughts of discipline or regulation. The sacred weeks of leave taken by graduates before reporting for duty were spent, as Carter later remembered, "in doing everything I had not been required to do, and in not doing anything which I had to do."[24]

The years spent at West Point developed Carter's penchant for serious reflection on the issues and events of the day. He already kept a critical watch not only on the army but also on the diverse world that lay beyond the academy's walls. Perhaps in this disposition a careful observer might have noted a harbinger of his eventual rise to prominence as a leading mind and voice of his profession. Yet a new lieutenant's immediate obligations were of a more technical nature, strictly focused on adapting to the daily realities of a frontier post. There would be time later for thoughts on a higher plane, but for now, Carter had much to learn about becoming a soldier in the Old Army.

4

Experiencing the
Old Army

On 30 September 1873, newly minted Lieutenant Carter reported to the U.S. Eighth Infantry at Fort D. A. Russell in Cheyenne, Wyoming. Typical of the period's officer corps, the Eighth's commander and many of his subordinates were living reflections of the army's past. Their conversations and personal habits recalled experiences of the Civil War, antebellum Indian wars, and even the Mexican War of almost thirty years ago. By the early 1870s when Carter reached Wyoming, such men must have seemed rather anachronistic to a young lieutenant only recently removed from New York City's bustling streets. Their presence at Fort D. A. Russell and dozens of other army posts dotting the American West only underlined the larger cultural transition that was then being imposed on the region itself. To many Americans, the western frontier was just an inconvenient obstacle on the march toward a brighter future, and the Regular Army was merely a blunt instrument against such obstacles—given the unsightly task of controlling and removing the last vestiges of America's simpler but savage past.[1]

The soldiers that Carter met on the Plains were an accurate reflection of the demographic changes at work in the officer corps at large. Young postwar Military Academy graduates were joining older colleagues who were deeply imbued with antebellum traditions and perspectives. Carter was personally struck by the Eighth Infantry's seniority, and noticed with ill-concealed disappointment that "the chance for promotion looks very bad. The officers here are all about ten years my senior except one. There is only one [other] young graduate here; Robinson of '69'." Such men shared a professional outlook that was defined by their common past and tended to be very skeptical of any talk of forward-looking reforms or new ideas.[2]

Many of the Civil War's volunteers-turned-regulars saw attempts to professionalize the army as merely the work of young overly-ambitious newcomers too infatuated with textbooks to be of much use to a real regiment. "Rare was the officer who actually studied his profession," concluded T. R. Brereton, "and the more thoughtful among them were ridiculed as eggheads or bookworms." The archetypal traditionalist believed that a combination of natural ability and field-worn experience was the only source for true warrior-leaders— book learning or idle talk of one's profession was only a distraction that offered a true soldier little or nothing of value. Such views also served to defend personal egos from implied attack. Progressive measures undoubtedly loomed as an indictment for those officers who lacked the requisite education or intellectual skills to participate.[3]

Carter's first impression of frontier life was shared by many new officers reporting to their regiments. Boredom prevailed at most western army posts. "The monotonous routine in tiny garrisons bored one within days," summarized Edward Coffman, "and the future offered little hope of anything different." Fort D. A. Russell was certainly no different in 1873, and although occasional bands of hostile Sioux and Cheyenne's posed a degree of physical danger, the daily life that greeted Carter on the rolling Wyoming plains was anything but adventurous. "The duty amounts to nothing," he wrote, likely wondering when he too might have a chance to earn the martial glories of which he had read and daydreamed while a cadet.[4]

Carter endured his first months of duty with no small amount of astonishment at the stagnant culture that had developed among soldiers lacking professional stimulation or reward: "The number of men available for drill was so small as to make progressive instruction out of the question. . . . Promotion was so slow as to give no hope to men who had surrendered high commands in the volunteers to accept lieutenanties [sic] in the regulars."[5] From a young, aggressive

West Pointer's perspective, these circumstances seemed at once full of despair and a sort of noble selflessness:

> The whole situation was hopeless from the point of view of ambitious officers looking for a future of military usefulness, and yet those men went patiently about the duty of the hour, the guarding and protecting of the settlement and development of a great empire where still the Indian and the buffalo held sway.[6]

This "whole situation" sparked the desire for something vaguely better in Carter and at least a few of his peers. The Old Army that they witnessed firsthand was, in many ways, very much like the frontier and its gritty inhabitants. For better or worse, each was destined for eventual extinction before Americans' steady march onward and upward toward a vaguely defined notion of modernity. In Wyoming, as elsewhere across the American West, this march was played out in the ongoing cultural and physical conquest of the Indians by the United States government.[7]

Soon after joining the Eighth, Lieutenant Carter very wisely began to seek out opportunities to accompany more experienced officers into the field. He befriended Major Frank North, a soldier who had raised companies of Pawnee scouts and understood the Indian culture. Carter credited North with introducing him to the eccentricities of the region and the various tribes who lived there. Thus began his long-standing interest in the ethnological aspects of the Indians who were often both friend and enemy to the frontier soldier. This deeper interest returned practical as well as intellectual rewards, imparting valuable insights into tribal peculiarities and customs that proved useful knowledge during both peace and war. Open to suggestion, Carter viewed the frontier and his more experienced colleagues as a sort of graduate practicum in which a passing grade meant staying alive. Only months after his arrival in Wyoming, he served as a pallbearer for another young officer who unfortunately failed to take precautions and paid for a shorted-sighted mistake with his life.[8]

In February 1874, Carter and Lt. Levi H. Robinson were each placed in command of separate wagon trains ordered to make short supply trips within the region. Carter's train left Cheyenne and moved through Fort Laramie to Fort Fetterman, a post situated to the north on the Bozeman Trail. Robinson, of the U.S. Fourteenth Infantry, led a similar train from Fort Laramie to retrieve lumber from a government-run sawmill near Laramie Peak. At each and every stop, Carter judiciously parked the wagons in the forested creek bottoms and set up strong defenses under the advice of two frontiersmen who had warned him of "impending trouble" among the Sioux at the nearby Red Cloud Agency. These astute actions may very well have saved him and his train from disaster, but Robinson's column was not nearly so fortunate.[9]

Lieutenant Robinson, who likely never received the frontiersmen's warning, failed to exercise such caution. On 9 February 1874, Robinson's tiny command was ambushed by a Sioux war party while the young lieutenant and two troopers were separated from the main body, hunting antelope within plain sight of the wagon train. Robinson and one of the soldiers with him were killed in the short fight, which proved to be one of the opening events of the so-called Sioux Expedition of 1874. When Carter arrived back at Fort D. A. Russell, he was ordered to accompany Robinson's corpse to Cheyenne, where it would be placed on a railroad car for the last journey east. He remembered this brief exposure to soldierly "adventure" as "the first of a never-ending series of tragedies which I was destined to encounter during my service on the frontier," events that must have underscored the value of educated vigilance. Enduring endless months of monotony in garrison was clearly the more healthful activity, and Carter's eagerness for action was surely blunted by the tragic fate of his young contemporary.[10]

This attack was only the most recent and grievous incident in a series that signaled a general outbreak among the Sioux at both the Spotted Tail and Red Cloud agencies. In response, Gen. Philip Sheridan, commander of the Missouri Division, ordered a general assembly of available troops for immediate field operations to secure the agency employees and preempt further hostilities. Sheridan's orders placed Carter in the thick of his first real military campaign. As he prepared to take the field, he likely did not have time to consider the complicated issues that prodded the Lakotas to desperation. But like other soldiers tasked with enforcing a distasteful policy, he had already adopted a sort of hardened paternalistic attitude that required

their peaceful subjugation. The army's interpretation of its constabulary mission on the frontier was an important facet of its developing
self-image.

Many frontier officers believed the only viable alternative to the
Indians' eventual annihilation before advancing white settlement
was their wholesale detribalization and acculturation. They realized
that the lure of western lands and their untapped resources was too
great a prize to be ignored by a commercially driven society, and that
voracious pressures on the aborigine tribes would only increase with
the passage of time. Yet, collectively, soldiers also believed that the
American public was obligated to offer some sort of viable future to
the conquered Indians. Thus, regulars found themselves in a morally
trying role as the physical arm of a nation determined to exercise its
adopted right of Manifest Destiny over the entire western half of
North America. Soldiers did not question the act of conquest itself so
much as the often-harsh manner in which it was executed.

Recent studies have found that army officers generally believed
in a policy of moral fairness undergirded by the threat of military
force. Although recognizing the need for physical coercion, officers
usually stopped short of advocating extermination or even brutal reduction. Instead, most held "that it was their nation's moral obligation to provide some means of survival for Indian people," usually
in the form of cultural assimilation. Soldiers often voiced some degree of disapproval for the manner with which whites dealt with
the American Indian, but remained convinced that the irrepressible
forces of modernity dictated the Indians' ultimate cultural demise.
This tension left many in a moral quandary. In their failure or inability to address the fundamental immorality of Indian relations,
officers "increasingly portrayed themselves as detached instruments
of public service," an approach that may have mitigated individual
and collective feelings of guilt as the strong arm of the government's
Indian policy.[12]

Soldiers lived and worked close enough to the Indians to understand that circumstances often gave tribes little choice but to fight or
abandon their own culture and lifestyle. "The Indians," lamented
Carter in matter-of-fact commentary, "found their treaties were mere
scraps of paper, and since they could not go further towards the setting sun, they were given the privilege of relinquishing their last

hunting grounds and adjusting themselves to the limits of reservations with annihilation as the only alternative."[13]

The army, with Carter as one of its newest subalterns, was left with little choice but to implement the edicts of elected civil government. Federal policies pursued a sort of bipolar course of "benevolent conquest," that to some degree mirrored the army's own interpretation of the "problem." As Sherman himself summarized the situation, it was a "double process of peace *within* their reservations and war *without.*" Though the army's very presence was founded on the premise that frontier morality was best adjudicated from a position of strength, soldiers "saw merits in both nature and civilization. If the military men and women viewed Indian warfare as an inevitable aspect of progress, they did not delight in that prospect." In this conclusion, the army was not only an instrument of society but also its very reflection. The only difference was that young officers like Carter—and his recently departed colleague Lieutenant Robinson—came face-to-face with the stark reality of westward expansion. But unlike their eastern counterparts, they could not merely turn the page of a daily newspaper to find a more pleasant story. Their professional mores sometimes dictated objective detachment from the severe work at hand, leaving moral distinctions to the American people and their elected policymakers.[14]

The Sioux outbreak which pulled Carter into the field that winter of 1874 was not the result of any single event, but rather stemmed from boiling dissatisfaction among young braves who resented the white man's increasing interest in the region. Young warriors had become irate when tribal leaders at the reservation declared in favor of cooperating with an Indian Bureau census—a contentious issue for its effect on government subsidies. Feeling spurned, they rode away to wreak havoc in all directions. A Minniconjou brave had already murdered the acting agent at the Red Cloud Agency when Lieutenant Robinson's train was attacked, and the agency employees and their families were holed up in blockhouses, fearing for their lives.[15]

On 23 February 1874, an expedition of cavalry and infantry departed Fort D. A. Russell to relieve the agency. Carter was attached to a company assigned to guard the supply train. Bitter cold gripped the region, leaving many soldiers with frozen and frostbitten hands and feet. "It seemed unpardonable to start soldiers on the march. . . . the snow was deep, the wind sharp, and the thermometer 30 degrees below zero."[16] The miserable conditions inflicted severe casualties in the most painful manner. Carter remembered a young recruit who carried his rifle in one position for so long that his hand was nearly frozen stiff:

> I got a bucket of cold water from the stream and had him put his hands in it. The water in the bucket commenced to freeze, but as he moved his hands up and down he kept an opening in the center. The sharp edges of ice forming in the bucket cut his hands to pieces, and we desisted from the fruitless and painful efforts. . . . We learned later that it was necessary to amputate all but one thumb and one finger.[17]

The all-but-impassable conditions focused thoughts solely on survival and Carter quickly developed an awed respect for those Indians who had dared to break from the reservation in such weather. But the slow-moving column finally reached its destination and fulfilled its mission, lifting the de facto siege in early March.[18]

Carter spent the rest of his first winter at Red Cloud encamped outside the reservation stockade, enjoying little protection from the elements and doubting his ability to defend the agency or even himself. This predicament was painfully obvious as he looked out over the hills and realized that his little detachment was an almost laughable deterrent to the overwhelming numbers of well-armed Sioux. His matter-of-fact description is an apt commentary on the army's tenuous presence across much of the West:

> On my graduating leave I had grown solicitous for fear all the Indians would be killed or captured before I could see them in their wild state. Now I found myself one of two hundred and fifty white men left on the outside of a stockade to protect the supplies and employees from Indians whose lodges covered the neighboring prairie in compact masses, each containing bucks armed with magazine breech loaders, while we had single shot Springfield rifles. It all seemed like a pretentious joke.[19]

These same tribes were becoming very aware that white America had no intention of giving up designs on the Dakotas, and thus were increasingly committed to waging a final battle of bitter resistance.

The weeks spent camped near the Sioux villages proved a benefit as Carter gained an insider's view of the Indians' way of life. While a cadet, he had read as much as possible about the American West and thought that he understood the Indians and their culture. But the experiences of his first year as a commissioned officer opened his eyes to the chasm between literature and reality. Later that spring, after the soldiers encamped outside the Red Cloud Agency had moved to another site nearby (a place that would eventually become Fort Robinson, Nebraska), Carter experienced military combat for the first time. Anger mounted following the arrest of an Indian who had escaped from jail after a murder conviction, and it became obvious that trouble was imminent when Sioux lodges nearest the little outpost hurriedly broke camp. That night, Indian braves attacked and in the ensuing skirmish Carter took command of a firing line and helped drive the attackers back into the night.

This brief baptism of fire had its humorous side as well. When running through the darkness with revolver drawn, Carter fell headlong over the camp's Irish cook, who in the excitement had "put his belt on upside down . . . and spilled his cartridges in the grass." As Carter cocked his pistol and readied for the desperate struggle that he was sure would bring his earthly demise, the frightened trooper quickly screamed, "Don't shoot—it's Finnerty the cook!"—undoubtedly to the great relief of both men. "I don't know which of us was most scared," Carter later admitted with candor, "but I was always prompt to admit that I did not like being astride an Indian in the dark." Although this first encounter with battle was hardly the stuff immortalized by West Point's storied annals, it still must have come as a great relief to a young officer who had spent years preparing for the event. Carter's first year on the frontier, insignificant as it was, taught him the difficulties of leading men under the most trying circumstances, and also gave him the opportunity to observe the starkly human side of his Indian adversaries.[20]

When the Eighth Infantry departed Nebraska for the Arizona Territory on 29 July 1874, Carter left with them, much wiser than when he had reported fresh from the academy a year earlier. He was experiencing the Old Army first-hand, listening to veterans' nostalgic stories of long-past glories while enduring the frustrations and hardships shared by generations of his comrades. "There is no other life," Carter reminisced, "in which may be encountered greater extremes

of comedy and tragedy than in that of the old frontier garrisons."
The Frontier Army was given a thankless job and pressed into action
amid harsh environments without proper resources or preparation.
Its efforts to meet this task lie somewhere between the East's pious
morality and the West's brutal savagery. To reconcile the two extremes required strict adherence to an unwritten professional code
that demanded objective service under the worst conditions. The
next twenty years would expose Carter to these ambiguities with
greater frequency and vividly illustrate the glaring inadequacies of a
military policy that was ill-fitted to its purpose.[21]

The Eighth Infantry's journey to Arizona began with several days
awaiting railroad transportation in nearby wild and woolly Cheyenne. While there, Carter met the famed William "Buffalo Bill" Cody,
a childhood friend of one of the regiment's officers. Apparently Cody's
celebrity did not impress the young soldiers, who already considered
themselves frontier veterans. "Bill was dressed in a short velvet coat, a
red shirt, close fitting trousers, and a broad brimmed hat," remembered Carter. "I made a quick survey and formed the very erroneous
opinion that he was a fraud." But this impression was soon revised
once they had spent several hours with Cody at McDaniel's Variety
Theatre, a locally prominent venue for the arts. "I soon learned that
those who knew him best, esteemed him most," Carter observed,
"and that his theatrical dress was part of his advertisement for the
western play he had been presenting on the stage in Chicago."[22]

An evening on the town with Buffalo Bill must have been a memorable occasion for young men who had spent several months with
very little in the manner of commercial entertainment. Cody wisely
rushed Carter and his comrades from their box seats at McDaniels'
and led them through a private exit as other, less-cultivated the-
atergoers became rowdy and threatened open violence. From there,
he took his guests to a nearby saloon, where none other than "Wild
Bill" Hickock was engaged in a losing game of faro. Carter noted that
Hickock, a sometime-lawman, pistoleer, and gambler of dubious reputation, was already down to his last chip but quickly borrowed another stake from hapless bystanders, which he proceeded to lose as
well. The episode only reinforced Carter's aversion to gambling, a
distaste that may have grown from his early exposure to the "turf
culture" that surrounded Nashville's Thoroughbred racing farms.
This cameo appearance by Cody and Hickock, already two of the

West's most recognizable characters, highlighted the Eighth's otherwise uneventful and often uncomfortable trip to Arizona.[23]

After departing Cheyenne, the regiment headed by rail to the Pacific Coast, delaying in San Francisco for several days before sailing
through the Gulf of California. But while the Eighth moved on toward
Arizona, Carter stayed behind in the city to appear as witness in a
court-martial proceeding. His prolonged visit lasted several weeks
and apparently gave him enough spare time to mingle with some of
the locals. It was during this stay that he first encountered Miss
Ida Dawley, who had moved to San Francisco from Connecticut with
her mother and sister. Carter began a sort of long-distance romantic
friendship with her. He was not so favorably impressed by the city's
soaring cost of living, which chagrined many other soldiers who
passed through the area. "With a steadily mounting hotel bill," noted
an annoyed Carter, "I thought the population of the slope, as the Cali-
fornians called the coast, was decidedly unpatriotic." After this brief
detachment, he continued his journey down California's Pacific coast-
line, leaving San Francisco and Miss Dawley temporarily behind.[24]

The change of station would prove significant for Carter, not only
in the dramatic contrast in climate and scenery, but also for his army
career. Of course, the move's positive aspects were not immediately
so apparent as he headed overland from San Diego by springboard
wagon in the desert's excruciating heat. "I never really knew what
dreary traveling was until I entered that country—the Department of
Arizona," Carter later bemoaned, recalling his introduction to the
new post. "Had anyone suggested that I was destined to have a tour of
duty on that border lasting sixteen years, I think I should have either
committed murder or suicide, yet that was my fate." Despite initial misgivings about his new surroundings, he quickly dedicated
himself to the job at hand and set about learning the region's many
peculiarities.[25]

Shortly after arriving at Camp McDowell, located near present-
day Phoenix, Carter began campaigning for transfer to the cavalry—
his branch of choice as a cadet. He wrote earnest letters to both the
secretary of war and the army's adjutant general requesting assignment to a company-grade opening in the U.S. Sixth Cavalry, a regiment that was due to be parceled among several southwestern posts
in the coming months. His petition was "based on a very decided
preference for the cavalry arm," and he betrayed a growing sense of

desperation to leave the infantry behind. A year spent as a foot soldier on the plains grated on the young horseman's pride, turning his initial disappointment upon graduation into a burning desire to take his rightful place as a cavalier.[26]

When Carter wrote to Secretary James Belknap, with whom he had spoken informally after receiving his original assignment from West Point, it was with an air of presumption that risked overstepping the army's traditional chain of command:

> In accordance with verbal permission granted by you shortly after my assignment to the 8th Infantry, I have made application for a transfer to the cavalry, which I hope may meet your approval. . . . My great love for the cavalry makes me feel that my life would be wasted when this dissatisfaction continues. I understood you sir, to say that I might let you know when an available vacancy occurred, and hence this letter; other wise I should not have dared to trespass on the official channel.[27]

Such brash action was certainly a gamble, but fortunately paid off without retribution, for he was transferred to the Sixth Cavalry on 28 November 1874. Carter's association with this proud regiment would confer a lasting self-identity as a cavalryman of the "old school" and place him in the thick of some of the era's most notable and notorious military events.[28]

The army's work in Arizona consisted primarily of administering the several reservations of Navajos, Yavapais, and Apaches that spread across the region. Military and civilian authorities had finally reached a working (if still woefully inadequate) understanding concerning the government's Indian policy after several years of intense debate and a great deal of costly trial and error. Consensus grew from both political expediency and a fundamental shift in Americans' outlook on the nagging "Indian question." In an attempt to alleviate the public's growing consternation after failed efforts to "pacify" western tribes, the Grant administration articulated its so-called Peace Policy. This plan, although on the surface well-intended, became tragically confused in its application, leaving Carter as both witness and participant in the perplexing and dangerous frustrations that resulted.

Simply put, Grant's policy was founded on the basic premise that advancing Anglo-American society had pressed native cultures into a deteriorated state, leaving them mere wards of the federal govern-

ment who lacked the means to act and treat as sovereign nations.
According to Robert M. Utley, this approach was motivated by an odd
combination of self-serving, idealistic, and pragmatic factors:

> For years reformers and policy makers had called for 'con-
> centration' of the Indians on reservations, for their 'civiliza-
> tion' through education, Christianity, and agricultural self-
> support, for a cleansing of the Indian Bureau of corruption and
> inefficiency, and for replacement of the treaty system with
> something better suited to the actual status of the Indian.[29]

Despite efforts to consolidate control of Indian affairs under the War
Department, Grant eventually transferred administration to various
pacifist groups who shared a basic belief in "conquest by kindness"—a
shrewd move that placed a somewhat paradoxical moral face on his
policy of forced concentration.[30]

The Peace Policy reflected a belief that the only alternative to the
American Indians' eventual extinction was "a system that would
place 'all the Indians on large reservations, as rapidly as it can be
done,' and there give them 'absolute protection.'" This contention,
though undeniably framed by ethnocentrism, appeared nonetheless
downright humanitarian when argued alongside westerners' calls for
the Indians' virtual annihilation. A deep chasm separated regional
perspectives on the Indian issue—eastern cities were "hives of pro-
Indian activities" from which emanated philanthropic pressures that
"westerners dismissed as naïve sentimentalism." Both outlooks were
skewed toward extremes by their proponents' vantage points—east-
erners remained physically remote from the issue while westerners
were influenced by their proximity. Soldiers privately espoused variations on each theme, often vacillating somewhere between the two,
perhaps dependent on the day's events.[31]

Arizona was a grand example of the fatal quandary that resulted
from a collision of disparate cultures. The territory had been rocked
by bloody violence since the spring of 1861 when the foolishly conceived "Bascom Affair" provoked Cochise and his band of Chiricahuas to declare war on white settlers. Since that time, brutal depredations committed by both sides created a hateful environment in
which rational thought figured very little in the search for solutions.
Violence was followed by revenge in kind, and the area had known
little peace for more than a decade.[32] Finally, in the fall of 1872, Gen.

George Crook was given free rein to bring the situation under control. Crook brought energy and initiative to operations in Arizona, qualities that were clearly lacking in previous attempts to pacify the region. A strong believer in principled justice supported by the threat of credible force, he quickly proved that he could fight the Apaches on their own terms if required to do so.[33]

By the time Carter reached Arizona, the hostiles had already surrendered before Crook's almost constant military pressure, and accepted, at least temporarily, the more sedate confines of the reservation. After a decade of destruction, the region enjoyed a very tenuous respite, although still seething with cultural hatred under the pressure of increasing settlement. Measures now turned to an attempt to "civilize" the Apaches into an agrarian lifestyle. When the Sixth Cavalry arrived from Kansas, Carter was sent to the San Carlos Agency, home to many of the same Apaches who had only recently come in following Crook's successful Tonto Basin campaign. Here, just as during his earlier days among the Sioux, he was given an opportunity to become acquainted with his wards close-up. His observations reflect an acute awareness of the cultural travesty that was consuming not only those Apaches who lived just outside his tent flap but also the many other Indian tribes spread across the shrinking frontier. "I remained in contact with these bands quite intimately," remembered Carter years later, "until the wire fences of the cattlemen and the increased population of the mining districts began to operate in connection with the army to seal their doom as nomadic tribes." Clearly, he had not missed the moral uncertainties of the "civilization" process in which he and the army were active participants.[34]

At the several reservations that dotted the region, the army began to methodically implement Crook's plan of benevolent paternalism, a philosophy founded on a distinct conceptualization of cultural progress. Crook's ideas were not left in the abstract, but were related directly to specific outcomes. He afforded the Apaches an opportunity to gradually build a personal interest in the rewards of individual labor, thus instilling material values and teaching the traditional Puritan work ethic. This purposeful transformation also had a more practical side—Indians kept busy tilling the land and preparing crops for market were much less likely to be roused to hostile action by malcontents who remained in their midst.[35]

Carter's first months in Arizona were very much like those of dozens of other army officers across the West. "Do nothing but hunt, read and paint," he recorded. "One's own society may be ever so nice, but it grows exceedingly tiresome." Sometimes picnics, parties, and dances staged by either a nearby settlement or a fort's own military community provided welcome distractions, but more often, soldiers looked for entertainment by gambling, drinking, or whatever else passed the time. Just as in the Dakotas, the extreme boredom of garrison duty in Arizona was broken only occasionally by the very real dangers of field operations.[36]

On 22 November 1875, only three days after his twenty-fourth birthday, Carter was given command of a company of Mojave Apache scouts at Fort Verde, Arizona. This assignment took him into the field almost immediately, and proved an excellent learning laboratory for a young soldier who was still relatively new to Indians and Indian fighting. On 10 December, Carter's scouts were ordered to pursue a band of recalcitrant White Mountain Apaches who had stolen livestock in the area and attacked a nearby wagon train. His patrol followed the band's trail through Arizona's Tonto Basin under the guide of Al Sieber, a renowned scout who figured prominently in Crook's later Geronimo campaign. The scouts surprised the assumed perpetrators in camp and killed fourteen of their renegade kinsmen as they headed toward refuge on the White Mountain reservation.[37]

Carter was impressed by the Apaches' willingness to fulfill their soldierly obligations, even against their own tribal relations. "These scouts pursued their own kindred with the unerring instincts of the bloodhound," he noted with some amazement, "and when overtaken killed them as remorselessly as they would have done their white enemies." Although many officers kept their distance from native scouts and only employed them with reluctance, Carter had no qualms about his assignment, even if somewhat unnerved by their propensity for brutality. Other patrols ended in frustration when the hostiles escaped into Mexico or back onto one of the agencies. In such instances, Carter often "turned the scout into a hunt," and spent many enjoyable days pursuing deer, antelope, and wild turkey with his Mojave troopers, gleaning a multitude of invaluable lessons from them in the process.[38]

Arizona's reservation system was far from an effective solution for the region's violence, and it certainly did little if anything to promote the long-term well-being of its subjects. But it did offer Indians and settlers alike some relief from the almost constant hostilities of earlier years. Carter described the months spent at Fort Verde as "about as quiet as any within my experience on the frontier." Although sometimes sent out after small bands that committed isolated depredations, operations were hardly of the intensity that had previously kept so many troops in the field. His time was more often spent hunting the area's plentiful wild game—sometimes even making good use of a pack of greyhounds that was left behind by officers of the Fifth Cavalry. When it was decided to disperse the Chiricahua Apaches at Fort Verde to other locations in response to increasing clashes with local settlers, the garrison's troops were also moved, and Carter was sent to Fort Apache, at the southeastern base of the Mogollon Rim. Arizona's short interlude of relative tranquility would soon come to a crashing end.[39]

Even at this early stage of his military career, Carter, like many of his brother officers, recognized the fatal shortcomings of the nation's lack of a coherent military policy. Rather than the result of any coordinated strategic vision, it was often merely reactive to widely disparate political demands. As a frontier constabulary, the army was spread so thinly that its efforts were of little consequence, and only the pragmatic cooperation offered by many tribal leaders prevented constant warfare. Carter blamed parochialism for these shortcomings, believing that more nationally-minded "statesmen" could have overcome myopic regional interests to provide a successful conclusion to frontier violence. Long months spent at the receiving end of an ineffective policy gave him pause to consider the political realities of representative government: "Recognition of these essentials of party government early in life preserved me from illusions later when called to the seat of government." Clearly, the sage lessons imparted by his experiences among the Apaches were not limited to the wiles of hunting in the desert.[40]

5

THE ARMY, THE MEDICINE MAN, AND CIBICU CREEK

In Arizona, just as in many other parts of the American West, officers' lives were almost completely defined by the garrison's military subculture—an environment that strengthened identity with regiment, branch, and the army itself. At a place like Fort Apache, Carter's social and professional interaction was almost entirely with the few other officers with whom he served. He quite naturally began to interpret and evaluate local, regional, and even national issues from an institutional perspective. If frontier service did little else to engender military reform, at least in Carter it nurtured an awareness that he was a member of a distinct group with distinguishable values, issues, and needs. This created a framework for what modern scholars have termed a sense of professional "corporateness," an institutional bond that seemed to mature and strengthen in Carter during his service in Arizona.[1]

In the Sixth Cavalry, Carter was rapidly given increased responsibility that sometimes went beyond his time in grade and certainly his experience. Although rank was at a premium due to continued reliance on a strict seniority system for promotion, junior lieutenants often found themselves at the head of a detachment or even a company, replacing more senior officers who were away on extended leave, court-martial duty, or other such diversions. Many frontier regiments could claim only a small number of their assigned officers available for duty. In a report destined for department headquarters, one of Carter's contemporaries in the Sixth complained that "a young officer just joining a post, must be put in responsible positions before he has experience." In Arizona's unforgiving environment, this condition demanded that young officers quickly learn to exercise sound judgment "on the march" or else suffer the consequences. While still new to the cavalry, Carter was placed in command of various patrols and details that ordinarily would have been led by someone more experienced. But despite obvious hazards, such responsibilities also offered accelerated professional growth: "Active service in the Apache country demands youth and vigor," declared Carter, "and the juniors were given opportunities not accorded where large bodies of troops operate together." These circumstances stemmed not only from the period's deep cuts in army personnel and appropriations but also reflected the very nature of the Southwest's environment and its particular brand of warfare.[2]

Apache warriors moved fast and fought in small bands, requiring close pursuit by equally small cavalry patrols to achieve similar mobility across unfriendly and difficult terrain. As Carter observed, "One acquired self reliance and learned woodcraft rapidly in such service." Acting on initiative without hope of immediate support was an accepted facet of even the greenest lieutenant's role in Arizona. Young officers who failed to exercise judicious caution could easily find themselves facing dire straits, not only in the relatively infrequent engagements with hostile Indians but also in battling the singularly harsh environment. This point was driven home when two of Carter's West Point classmates (one a former roommate) were drowned while attempting to save rations and equipment swept down a rain-swollen creek. The desert could be an unforgiving host.[3]

Life among the Apaches made Carter a daily witness to the inhumanity of conquest, an aspect of military service that was not lost on his thoughtful mind. Like many of his comrades, Carter was indignant about the immoral manner in which government contractors often took advantage of local Indians—reaping even greater profits from an already shameful equation. On one occasion, he accompanied an Apache scout who wished to finalize his accounts at the fort's trading post before departing to another reservation. Saltoun, the scout, was due the balance of a credit for time served, an account that was kept open by the fort's contracted sutler. "I was astonished," Carter remembered, "when the trader's clerk handed him $20.00 as payment for the account, saying it was the usual discount [under payment] charge to Indians. I resented such a shameful transaction and reported the matter to the post council."[4] Attempts to reconcile the injustice met with temporary defeat when the post council ruled that the army had no legal authority to act against a contractor except on the quality of goods provided. Rebuffed, Carter concluded that he would simply have to change his tactics if he was ever going to make the matter right.

If, as the council found, the only way to correct the trader's crooked practice was to find something amiss with contracted goods, then the steep path to righteousness was entirely clear. Carter acted with presumption that reached beyond his lieutenant's shoulder straps: "I immediately put before them [the post council] a charge that the liquor, alleged to be whiskey, sold by him [the trader] crazed the men and was unfit to drink"—a clear breach of contractual obligation. The amused post council simply could not argue with this self-evident assertion, and the trader's contract was summarily terminated. Although the story ends there, one can only assume that Indian scouts at Fort Apache began to receive their full credit shortly afterward, compliments of one Lieutenant Carter's somewhat audacious but inarguably effective sense of moral justice. His intervention in this instance reflects a strong sense of fair play that might just as easily have been lost or forgotten amid the frontier's drudgery and violence.[5]

Soon thereafter, Carter's assignment as regimental quartermaster forecast the direction of his future military career. On 20 August 1878, he received a telegram urging him to delay a planned leave of absence in order to accept the new position immediately. He had served for a very short time as quartermaster with the Eighth Infantry, and the job seemed to fit his natural abilities. This position increased his responsibility, placed him near the regiment's leadership, and gave him a taste of the difficulties of combining staff considerations with operational concerns. The move also introduced him to the intricacies of the Old Army's system of promotion—a system that many officers loudly despised even as they became willing participants in its intrigue.[6]

In a regiment, the quartermaster position was filled by a first lieutenant, and thus the job should have promised Carter promotion to that rank. But although records do not provide the details, it seems that promotion was delayed until the next summer due to the actions of Lt. James H. Sands. Sands held onto his billet as a first lieutenant in the Sixth pending the outcome of his application for retirement. Officers of the time were promoted strictly according to seniority within their assigned regiment, unless somehow able to gain permanent reassignment to one of the staff bureaus. Thus, Carter's promotion to a first lieutenancy commensurate with his new position relied on Sands's retirement. Apparently, Sands was in no hurry to speed along the process, likely hoping that he would be promoted to captain in the meantime and thus garner retirement benefits at the higher rank.[7]

This impasse prompted Carter to begin a letter writing campaign in an effort to hasten Lieutenant Sands's departure and open his own opportunities. He appealed at least twice to the adjutant general's office, pointing out that Sands's only possible motivation was the desire "to hang out long enough to get to be a captain ... hardly just to those doing the duty." Sands's actions, or in this case inaction, diminished the already-small chances for promotion within the regiment and threatened to close the narrow window that existed for Carter personally. Carter's efforts for remedy, unashamedly self-interested, reflected a growing disposition to confront institutional wrongs that he witnessed around him—a somewhat brash proclivity that grew stronger with every small victory. This particular situation was reconciled when he was promoted to first lieutenant in July 1879.[8]

Several months after assuming his new rank and position, Carter's life underwent another significant change. He had continued to correspond with Ida Dawley, the Connecticut native whom he had met a few years earlier while temporarily assigned to court-martial duty in San Francisco. Little is known about their meeting and subsequent long-range courtship—perhaps Ida was an acquaintance of one of William's brother-officers or a relation of a West Point classmate. In later years, the couple demonstrated ample propensity for correspondence, very likely the sole romantic avenue between San Francisco and Arizona in the 1870s. Whatever the circumstances of their introduction, the two were apparently confident enough of their match to set a wedding date for sometime in September of 1880. As the day approached, Carter anxiously plotted to take advantage of a suspended leave of absence that had been granted two years earlier. But as a soldier's luck would have it, the wedding plans were interrupted by orders to take the field in pursuit of Victorio, perhaps the greatest of the Apache war chiefs.[9]

In late September, several converging U.S. Army columns attempted to push Victorio and his Mimbreno Apache warriors to exhaustion. The Sixth's ten-troop expedition, commanded by Colonel Eugene A. Carr, pressed forward into Chihuahua, Mexico, running low on rations and suffering from a shortage of water. Carr planned on moving with all possible speed, and since provisions were carried for only two days, it fell to Carter as quartermaster to keep the troops supplied with rations and forage while on the march: "In the matter of rations we had never started with less. Before we got back we had to disperse hunting parties and, as commissary, I issued antelope meat instead of beef." In the desert, water was a priceless commodity and its supply was a constant concern, even shortly after it sometimes appeared in the form of violent downspouts. Carter declared that on such occasions men could almost be washed away by intense storms one minute only to suffer from wretched thirst a few hours later. Despite such hardships, the Sixth pressed on with little rest and helped push Victorio and his warriors toward their ultimate demise in an ambush sprung by Mexican troops led by Col. Joaquin Terrazas.[10]

Although careful to point out that eighteen Apache women and children were also killed in the fighting, Carter applauded the cooperative effort as a complete success. Victorio was a master of guerrilla warfare and "came nearer to forming a coalition of Apaches, Comanches, and Navajos, against the whites, than any other chief," an alliance that surely would have brought death and anguish to both white and Mexican settlements. From Carter's perspective, Victorio's string of violence rendered his "destruction necessary to prevent the enforced abandonment of the whole frontier"—a somewhat one-sided conclusion in a war of cultural conquest, but one that plainly expressed the soldier's role in westward settlement, whatever the larger issues at play. For his part, Victorio had inflicted a great deal of human suffering across the region, and his defeat was a major milestone in the settlement of the Southwest.[11]

When the Sixth returned from the field, Carter finally obtained the long-awaited leave and departed for San Francisco where he and Ida were belatedly married on 27 October 1880. The summer's events had already inaugurated the new Mrs. Carter to army life's uncertainties, but nonetheless, the couple began a marriage that always took prominence in both William's private and public life. His family was never forgotten or pressed aside, even later in his career when professional obligations demanded his utmost attention. Although likely horrified by Arizona's severe landscape and Fort Apache's "modest" accommodations, Ida quickly adjusted to army life in the Southwest and became a supportive partner in her husband's military career. Her mettle was soon put to the test by an episode that shocked the country and established Carter as a bona fide hero of the Old Army.

Less than a year after the wedding, Carter was thrust into a series of events that signaled the beginning of a very long end for the military struggle against the Apaches. Arizona's seething hostilities boiled over after the army attempted to arrest an Apache medicine man at Cibicu Creek. The ensuing skirmish and its violent aftermath drew national attention and became a stark illustration of the failure of federal Indian policy in the region. But more importantly, Cibicu was a sort of defining preamble for Carter's later professional life. His actions there permanently associated his name with Old Army lore, and from that point forward, he carried laurels that footnoted his every endeavor with a soldierly credibility.

Although there had been an uneasy lull in violence across the territory following Victorio's defeat, there certainly had been no change in the underlying conflict itself.[12] Later, various quarters would be blamed for the violence at Cibicu, but real blame for the ethnic friction that created the tense conditions fell squarely on the federal government's attempt to confine—both culturally and physically— indigenous peoples who quite plainly did not wish to be so corralled. The Peace Policy became such an unbearable burden to the Apaches that in despair they looked to their spirituality for relief. The events that placed Carter in the field at Cibicu Creek on 30 August 1881 were only the most local manifestations of this fundamental miscalculation.[13]

That summer, the preaching of Nockay-del-klinne, a Coyotero medicine man, stirred emotions that erupted into physical confrontation. Rumors circulated at Fort Apache that the old man was promising he could raise the Apache dead from their graves if only their living kinsmen would rise up against the whites. Carter and others believed that, rather than envisioning a brighter future, Nockay-del-klinne was simply inspired by a lust for tribal prestige and power—a conclusion shared by at least some of the Apache elders. A "Ghost Dance" was the medium for Nockay-del-klinne's professed spirituality, and with its growing popularity came increasing tensions that threatened an already-tenuous peace.[14]

An Apache account describes a more benign version of Nockay-del-klinne's medicine, claiming that he never called for violence but only reminded his people that Ussen would "rid the country" of their enemies in his own way. But while the prophet's promises may have started out more innocently, it seems that he soon began calling for the whites' departure as a smokescreen for his failure to produce spirits. After he demanded and received material gifts to perform such deeds, the chief came under increasing pressure and even threats to bring results. Desperate, Nockay-del-klinne quickly upped the ante for the fulfillment of his prophecy: "He had been promising to raise the dead for some time," Carter recalled, "and he was growing rich through the largesse of his foolish patrons. When he announced that all the dead Apaches were risen, except that their feet were held down waiting for the whites to be driven from the Indian country, the time for interference had arrived."[15]

Perhaps the old man was shrewdly trying to "save face and his own life by tying the [unfulfilled] resurrections to an unlikely event." Carter, who watched the unfolding saga from regimental headquarters as Colonel Carr's adjutant, believed that the Apaches were growing "impudent from brooding over racial wrongs" at the hands of an "aimless Indian policy," and were all too ready to indulge even the most fantastic promises. As the summer progressed, Apaches listened with rapt attention to Nockay-del-klinne's calls to action, and a harmless tale rapidly grew into cause for real concern.[16]

Perhaps most disturbing were reports of Navajo interest, fanning fears of an intertribal alliance that would likely require thousands of troops and years of arduous campaigning to defeat. The situation thus took on a terrifying undercurrent that was far out of proportion to the odd ranting of a single old medicine man. At San Carlos, Agent J. C. Tiffany—a man disliked by Apache and soldier alike—worried that Nockay-del-klinne would soon spark open violence. By the end of August, Tiffany was urging Carr to take military action to somehow preempt the trouble. Carter later testified that the feeling had become almost unanimous "that a general uprising of the White Moun-

tain Apaches and possibly the Chiricahuas was about to take place."
Whether the danger was real or imagined or somewhere in between,
Nockay-del-klinne clearly had become a source of great anxiety for
the cavalry at Fort Apache.[17]

By the end of August, Carr felt increasing pressure as Tiffany
prodded him to arrest the medicine man. Carr maintained—and in
retrospect, wisely so—that any such attempt would precipitate rather
than prevent violence. But it appears that Carr then began to doubt
his own judgment. He equivocated in correspondence with higher
headquarters, fishing for definitive orders that would relieve him of
responsibility. After finally receiving explicit directions from General Orlando B. Willcox, commander of the Department of Arizona,
to "arrest the Indian doctor, who you report as stirring up hostilities,
as soon as possible," he even then attempted to mitigate his previous
estimates of the situation. From his vantage point on Carr's staff,
Carter looked on with a degree of bewilderment, wondering if a decision would be reached before violence erupted or the Apache dead
actually rose from their graves.[18]

Finally, on 29 August, Carr took action as ordered. Troops D and E
of the Sixth Cavalry, a packtrain, and a company of Apache scouts
mounted their horses and departed down the Verde Trail toward a
fateful meeting with Nockay-del-klinne. Much discussion had focused on the question of whether to take the scouts, who, although
"hitherto of unblemished character for fidelity," had become as
strongly fascinated as their tribal kinsmen with the Ghost Dance
craze. Their reaction to the Prophet's planned arrest was a genuine
concern—a point that would later be examined in great detail. The
scouts' ammunition had been taken from them a few weeks earlier,
and it was only after a day's march, in camp on Carrizo Creek, that it
was reissued. Carr attempted to convince the scouts that no harm
was intended, and that the old man would be released after promising
not to foment further unrest. For his part, Carter spent the first night
on the trail nursing an excruciating headache, and his attention was
fixed solely on getting rid of it by wrapping wet handkerchiefs around
his head—an inauspicious beginning to one of the most memorable
events of his adult life. Early the next morning, Mose and Charlie,
Apache scouts, departed camp with Carr's permission to ride ahead
and reassure the Indians on Cibicu Creek that Nockay-del-klinne
would not be hurt.[19]

The next day, as the column approached their destination, the remaining scouts became agitated when Carr chose to take a second trail that forked from the Verde about three miles from the Cibicu village. Their odd irritation at this decision was later looked on as evidence of their part in a preplanned ambush—one that was narrowly foiled by Carr's unknowing but very fortunate choice of routes.

After stopping briefly to rest, the command crossed the Cibicu and rode straight to Nockay-del-klinne's lodge, where he stood with Mose and Charlie. Following introductions, Carr told the medicine man through an interpreter that he would be treated as a friend until the charges against him could be sorted out and then released. Carter remembered that after first attempting to negotiate his way out of the arrest, Nockay-del-klinne then appeared "to surrender so readily that our suspicions seemed unfounded."[20] Carr instructed Lieutenant Cruse with the scouts and Lieutenant Stanton with E Troop to wait while the prisoner quickly gathered a few personal belongings before bringing him along. The rest of the column, including Carter, then departed down Cibicu Creek to make camp for the night.[21]

As Nockay-del-klinne prepared to leave his lodge and accompany the soldiers, a number of armed Apaches gathered and began to edge closer to the remaining troops, leaving no question as to their view of the old man's arrest. Carr and his half of the now-divided force had left the village and were already well out of sight when Cruse, the escort, and their new prisoner finally rode after them. Though this complacency likely signaled Carr's relief that the situation seemed well in hand, to Cruse and those who followed, the Apaches were quite clearly more than casually interested in their prophet's well-being.[22]

With the hot afternoon sun still overhead, Lieutenant Cruse and his detachment warily made their departure across Cibicu Creek to rejoin their comrades in camp—now followed closely by a throng of agitated Apaches. Nockay-del-klinne, accompanied by his wife, was placed under guard in a circle of packsaddles and other equipage, and Cruse reported the Apaches' growing belligerence to Carr, who now had his own concern that things were not nearly so well as they seemed just minutes earlier. It was sometime after three o'clock in the afternoon when Indians began to enter the campsite, crowding the troops and trying to make their way toward the medicine man. Carr ordered Capt. Edward C. Hentig to warn them away, and told Carter, who had been placing the guard and organizing the encampment, to move the scouts' campsite farther from the main body. This reasonable precaution triggered a violent explosion that wracked Arizona for almost three years.[23]

While Hentig moved toward the Apaches, yelling to them in their own language, Carter pointed out a position for the scouts to make their camp. The scouts refused and ominously spread out along the crest of a low mesa. Carter worriedly turned away to find Carr, only to hear Apache shouts and an explosion of gunshots. Hentig and a nearby trooper both fell to the ground dead and "the firing immediately became general" as the Apaches began their attack and frantic soldiers scrambled to defend themselves.[24]

The scouts, whose loyalties had been at issue from the very start, joined their tribesmen in the assault, letting go a volley directly from Carter's front: "As they were about to aim, 'Dead Shot' [a longtime acquaintance of Carter's] spoke to them and when they had fired I was amazed to find myself among the living." Carter immediately dropped to the ground and returned fire with his revolver. Colonel Carr yelled an order for Nockay-del-klinne to be killed, and a trooper shot the old man through both legs. He fell to the ground with his "wife falling across him, beginning the death wail," and was later shot again as he crawled toward the Indian line, yelling encouragement to his disciples. Carr's worst fears had become damnable reality—the column had been ambushed by a determined force of overwhelming size and turned on even by its own scouts.[25]

Accounts underscore the brutal intensity of the battle's first moments, opened from almost point-blank range: "It is difficult to describe the first of this Cibicu fight in any detail," wrote Cruse. "Practically all that happened occurred explosively, almost simultaneously." Nockay-del-klinne's sixteen-year-old son was killed when he rode wildly into Carr's firing line in a suicidal attempt to save his father. The medicine man's wife then picked up a discarded pistol and with an anguished scream attempted to fire it at a nearby soldier before she herself was shot down. Soon after the fighting started, Carter took command of Hentig's Troop D and began to press the Apaches at that part of the line back across the creek. The exchange of fire continued unabated as the soldiers recovered from their initial shock and organized a defensive circle around the encampment.[26]

It was at about this time, as lines of battle were drawn, that someone near Carter yelled that Hentig's body, which lay some hundred feet beyond the firing line, showed signs of life. Carter and two volunteers from the ranks, privates Richard Heartery and Henry Bird, immediately ran from behind their scant cover to attempt rescue. Under a withering fire, Bird fell severely wounded while Carter and Heartery dragged Hentig's body back inside the perimeter. Seeing that the situation had now repeated itself, Carter made a lone second trip under fire to retrieve Bird, a courageous act that under the conditions bordered on pure recklessness. The two miraculously made it back to the perimeter's relative safety, but despite Carter's brave effort, Private Bird died a short time later from his wounds.[27]

As darkness fell, the Apache fire slackened and then stopped altogether, allowing Carr to begin working out a plan to extricate his command from its precarious position. The troops buried their dead in a single large grave and pitched a headquarters tent over the site, while Dr. McCreery, the surgeon, attempted to stabilize the wounded. Carr had lost seven killed and suffered three wounded, including one man who would die on the return march. A quick council of war concluded that there was absolutely nothing to gain and much to lose by remaining in position through the night. If successful, a march through the Indian lines would place them near Fort Apache by morning, when the fort would likely be under attack and need their aid.[28]

Preparations were made with quiet haste, rations and ammunition were issued, and the wounded were secured for the march. Carr sent Carter to examine Nockay-del-klinne's body to ensure that he was in fact dead. If the medicine man were to recover from his apparently fatal wounds at this point—appearing to his followers to indeed return from the dead—it would energize an uprising that likely would spread well beyond the region. Carter was shocked to find the old man with a weak but discernable pulse and quickly reported as much. Carr ordered Nockay-del-klinne quietly killed, but Carter demurred from "such work" and the task was passed to a civilian packer, who was only too happy to execute the order promptly. The Prophet's "medicine" was thus ended with brutal finality, but it was his unwanted legacy that now concerned Carr and his troopers. Sometime just after ten o'clock, the column departed in a single-file line with orders to maintain strict silence and close order.[29]

Despite expectations of immediate attack at every twist and turn of the trail, the column miraculously reached Fort Apache early the

next afternoon without further engagement. News of the action at
Cibicu Creek had already made its way to the post via Apache run-
ners who had gone among the nearby villages telling wild stories of
the command's complete annihilation. Throngs of Indians appeared
on the various trails that passed near the fort—excited young men
racing to join those who had fought the bluecoats at Cibicu, and those
desperately wishing to distance themselves from further trouble. The
garrison hurriedly prepared for what they believed was an inevitable
assault while hostile Apaches made their presence and intentions
known throughout the region—murdering four Mormons at nearby
Seven Mile Hill and wiping out a small party of soldiers who were
repairing downed telegraph lines near Black River. On the morning of
1 September, brazen warriors demonstrated on the open ground surrounding the fort and sporadically prodded Carr's defenses. Desultory
attacks followed throughout the day, some pressed farther than others, but none marked by any committed effort.

Needless to say, Ida Carter was ecstatic to find her husband among
the living after listening with horror to the rumors of total tragedy
that preceded his return. She and Mrs. Carr, the only two wives living
at the post, had maintained a positive front during the past forty-eight
hours, steadfastly asserting their husbands' continued survival. But
such events surely took an extreme emotional toll on a young bride
only recently arrived from San Francisco. As troops prepared to defend
the fort upon the column's return, Ida doggedly refused to await the
outcome again, and Carter had a difficult time keeping her out of
harm's way.[30]

After having told Ida—likely without much room for negotia-
tion—to remain in the corner of their sturdy log cabin quarters, Carter was aghast at one point to find his wife standing directly behind
him on the firing line. "The strain of waiting inside while I was exposed outside was too much for her and she walked out and stood,
unconscious of danger, while we [soldiers] lay behind our little forti-
fication." One can only imagine the enormous shock when he realized that his young bride had been standing in the line of fire. The
few months spent in Arizona had clearly turned Mrs. Carter into
a bona fide frontier army wife, somewhat inured (or perhaps somewhat oblivious) to the savage dangers that currently threatened her
new home. Although the skirmishing was worrisome and resulted in
several wounded among the garrison, it ended as the sun went down,

and by the following day, the hostiles had withdrawn from the immediate area.[31]

Relief arrived from Fort Thomas and brought a wealth of overdue telegrams and letters bearing information from the outside world. The Sixth was quite surprised to hear that its complete destruction was widely reported by eastern newspapers. Sensationalized stories that bore very little resemblance to reality were headlined: "Shot Down by Indians: Gen. Carr and His Command Murdered," and "Indian Massacre: General Carr and his Command Said to be Slaughtered by the Apaches." Papers even carried brief obituaries for the supposed "victims" under the mournful heading, "The Slain: Something About the Victims of the Horrible Deed." These highly embellished versions of events extended even to the Fort Apache garrison, and Ida Carter and Mrs. Carr were both reported as taken prisoner and carried off by the hostiles. The dramatic appeal of Victorian pulp fiction was clearly not lost on editors who wasted no time in conjuring up a Little Big Horn–style disaster in order to sell copies. The names of actual places and participants were added almost as afterthoughts to lend some minor air of reality to otherwise wildly fictional accounts.[32]

The Carters certainly were as glad as their relatives and friends that these stories proved less than factual, but the harsh truth was that life in Arizona was about to become even less pleasant for whites and Apaches alike. General Sherman was incensed over the Cibicu affair, and he subordinated both Willcox and Carr to officers brought in from elsewhere to lead the punitive operations that immediately followed. Sherman's sharply worded orders reflected the public's horrified response to the disaster: "What I expect is action, results not speculation. All Apaches outside the reservation must be killed or captured and if any of them take refuge on the Reservation, that must not save the guilty parties who fired on Genl. Carr's command." Public outrage demanded action, and for soldiers in Arizona, that meant little rest for many months to come.[33]

Carr and the Sixth Cavalry returned to the field to pursue their attackers and other Apaches who had fled the reservations. Carter continued to serve as regimental quartermaster, participating in some engagements and watching others from the distance of his headquarters duties. The army brought portions of several regiments into Arizona for the campaign, some from as far away as California, and the presence of so many troops likely exacerbated the situation. A rash of ill-conceived arrests at San Carlos only heightened suspicion and fear among bands that had not participated at Cibicu Creek, pushing them to flee the reservation as well. The Chiricauhua Apaches joined the outbreak, led by prominent warriors such as Juh, Nachez (the son of Cochise), and Geronimo. Both directly and indirectly, Nockay-del-klinne's arrest set off a chronology of renewed violence that lasted until 1886, when Geronimo and his dwindling band finally surrendered to Gen. Nelson Miles after years of unrelenting pursuit. In the interim, Arizona and New Mexico were literally besieged by numerous raids and wanton brutality at an enormous cost in human suffering.[34]

The events surrounding Carr's actions at Cibicu Creek drew immediate criticism from the public and close scrutiny from within the army. Although the casualties at Cibicu were only a small fraction of those suffered by Custer's Seventh Cavalry at the Little Big Horn (25 June 1876), haunting memories of that catastrophe fueled the controversy and heightened public attention. That Carr and other leading participants had lived to face their accusers was reason enough for the army to pursue a formal inquiry into the matter. Even as he searched for Cibicu's fugitives, Carr came under direct censure and was made a scapegoat for the tragedy. His history of ill-feeling with Willcox and other senior officers made him an obvious choice for the part. Early on, many questioned whether or not the army's actions were proportionate to the actual threat (or lack thereof) posed by the Ghost Dance and its influence with the Apaches. In addition, Carr's tactical decisions during the expedition itself were particularly impugned as possibly having jeopardized his entire command. Eager to galvanize his own role in the fiasco, Willcox appointed Capt. Harry C. Egbert, U.S. Twelfth Infantry, to investigate the Cibicu outbreak and attempt to reconcile its circumstances with its terrible outcome.[35]

After a month of conducting interviews, Egbert issued a report on the events leading up to the battle and spent a great deal of time sorting out which Apache bands were actually involved in the various acts of violence and destruction. He concluded that the Ghost Dance had in fact become a credible threat to the regional peace and thus dictated some sort of preemptive government action. But Egbert's report stopped there, leaving unanswered troubling questions that still surrounded not only the propriety of Nockay-del-klinne's arrest but also the manner in which the entire operation was executed.[36]

On 26 January 1882, the Army Judge Advocate General, acting on Willcox's request, preferred court-martial charges against Carr for his actions at Cibicu Creek as well as an alleged failure to follow orders aggressively during the weeks that followed. That October, after reviewing the evidence and wading through a bitter exchange of charges and counter-charges, a court of inquiry found no purpose in pursuing further judicial action against Carr or any of his officers. Although the finding faulted Carr for not taking sound precautions to secure his command following the medicine man's arrest, it exonerated him on all other counts and specifications. An official cloud of censure was thus formally lifted from the operation and its participants, but the action at Cibicu Creek is still remembered as an especially tragic episode.[37]

For Carter, Cibicu Creek proved to be a defining moment in his frontier service. Although the battle itself was really only a skirmish even by Indian War standards, his personal leadership and bravery under fire was widely applauded and he was later awarded the Medal of Honor for his actions. Cibicu may have been a dismal failure as a military operation, but, as a writer for the *New York Herald* later put it, Carter was undoubtedly "the hero of that fight." He quite literally had offered himself as a sacrifice for his fellow soldiers—perhaps the single most admirable feat within any military culture. Although likely not realizing it at the time, this action would become a subtitle for his later endeavors, marking him in some ways as a kind of Old Army relic. The campaigns and events that highlighted Carter's service in Arizona had a lasting influence on his professional persona. His success as a young officer of the line gave him the confidence and credibility to pursue those larger issues that he later became convinced were seminal to the army's progress.[38]

Carter already saw the regular officer corps as a sacred repository of the nation's security and professed disgust with the political wrangling and patronage that he believed weakened this important role. Warfare was the realm of experts, and external interference only undermined regulars' claims to expertise. This perspective was later translated to what he believed were grievous inadequacies in the nation's military policies, guiding his ideas for institutional reform. In short, he was becoming more professional, developing from a technical apprentice into a participating veteran of the officer corps—someone who could voice opinions with reasonable hope of finding an audience. Although this evolution in his professional awareness was only now at its beginning, it was undoubtedly spurred toward maturity by his bittersweet experiences among the Apaches in Arizona.

6

Coming In from the Frontier

As Carter developed into a seasoned soldier, his interests and ambitions matured as well. Prone to reflection even as a young man, as evidenced by his letters and diaries as a West Point cadet, he began to seek a more active role in the army's institutional development. Although Carter's time on the frontier was by no means over after Cibicu Creek, in retrospect the battle seems to have been a watershed for his career—a point of departure toward more serious concerns than the adventures of a young lieutenant. In the years after Cibicu, as he advanced in age, responsibility, and experience, he increasingly sought professional satisfaction in a manner that might leave some sort of lasting legacy.

Now Carter looked for new challenges, and perhaps the changing nation around him suggested avenues and endeavors that might satisfy his ambitions. During the 1880s and 90s, the nascent American middle class began to coalesce into an active social force, exhibiting a unique range of sensibilities and values. For many middle-class Americans, professionalization became a touchstone for the imagery and acknowledgement of success, promising not only material security but also the respect and admiration of one's social peers. It is not surprising that Carter and his brother officers would reach for these same rewards.[1]

Soldiers were at least aware of these broad social developments, even though sometimes geographically far removed from their source. Eastern newspapers were common enough at otherwise isolated western outposts, and books, periodicals, and personal correspondence also kept soldiers aware of the larger social and cultural currents at work in civilian society. John M. Gates establishes strong ties between the contemporary officer corps and developing middle-class America, referring to the period as "a time of continuous interaction between officers and the civilian elite." Carter's own record certainly supports Gates's premise. Army officers were well aware that the nation was becoming more cosmopolitan, and improved methods of communication, more reliable rail transportation, and intervening assignments to the East all helped to draw them closer to American society at large. Obvious signs of emergent professionalism in a number of occupational fields were not lost on Carter. As he matured beyond youthful exploits, he desired more serious participation in the military profession, actively searching for a role in the army's future.[2]

The months following Cibicu Creek were difficult ones for both the Apaches and the soldiers who garrisoned Arizona and New Mexico. Public outrage over the explosion of violence was fueled by newspaper headlines demanding immediate satisfaction. Pressure for decisive punishment was passed down the chain of command, and efforts to find and subdue any Apache not on the reservation were coordinated to a degree rarely seen in frontier warfare. Indians who refused to submit were pushed relentlessly toward exhaustion. Operations held troops in the field for long weeks at a time with very little rest and few opportunities for even the simplest creature comforts.

But a soldier's life during such a grueling campaign apparently left at least a small amount of time for family business. Despite the arduous conditions at Fort Apache and Carter's several deployments into the field, William and Ida's plans for a family did not wait for more peaceful times. On 20 January 1883, Ida gave birth to their first son, William Vaulx Carter, destined to become a soldier like his father. A new baby at a frontier fort must have caused a small storm of excitement, even in the midst of the region's continued turmoil. In typical fashion of the period, Ida kept the family's tiny quarters, took care of their newborn son, and assumed a variety of social duties at the garrison while Carter continued his own role, which often included long hours of exhausting work followed by weeks spent in the saddle away from home.[3]

Troops not in the field stood heightened watch and accomplished extra duties to make up for those on campaign. When in garrison, Carter toiled at his staff work as regimental quartermaster, attempting to keep the various patrols and expeditions supplied as best he could. This job often demanded ingenuity and innovation in order to overcome a procurement system that proved unresponsive to fielded units' unique needs. From the line officer's perspective, the army's staff bureaus seemed to act as powerful fiefdoms unto themselves, protected by virtue of their physical proximity to Washington's policymakers. This proved to be a divisive obstacle to operations, not only at the command level, where cooperation between staff and line was often woefully lacking, but also at the regiment level, where officers like Carter were detailed to make the best of an incoherent system. Petty jealousies, institutional competition, and subcultural disparities marked the uneasy relationship that traditionally existed between staff and line, exacerbating the already-heavy burden for those troops taxed with subduing hostile Indians.[4]

In the summer of 1883, Carter's attention was drawn to the staff system's glaring frustrations when "a critical situation was created among the troops by an order cutting off the issue of bacon in garrison." Although such an action might seem relatively inconsequential from a comfortable historical distance, for the frontier soldier of the 1880s it bordered on near-catastrophe. Bacon was a staple, like the rations of flour, beans, and coffee—as well as an important item of barter for locally procured luxuries such as vegetables and fruits. With righteousness aroused, Carter took pen in hand to do bureaucratic battle with the agencies responsible for this unreasonable action.[5]

To soldiers in Arizona, the bacon ration's discontinuance was symbolic of the much larger institutional issues that clearly separated the staff from the line. From Carter's jaded viewpoint at Fort Apache, the staff bureaus seemed to conduct business with absolute disregard for the needs of the line, resulting in a chasm that shackled the army's ability to fight. "I undertook to show the bureau of the War Department which was responsible for the order that it was ill-advised," he remembered, but "the result was typical of bureau action in those days. It was this kind of action which was responsible for the feeling that the line was only permitted to exist as an excuse for maintaining the staff." Such animosities were based as much on narrow parochial perceptions as they were on reality, but nonetheless ran deep in the army culture and were perpetuated from generation to generation in the officer corps.[6]

Carter's annoyance with this grievance (and to an even greater extent the bureaucracy that sanctioned it) was hardly veiled in the acerbic letter he wrote to the army's commissary general:

> If the present state of affairs continues, the men finding themselves furnished with only bread and coffee for supper, after a day's hard work, will soon be in that condition of mind that desertion ceases to be a crime. So long as the Q.M. [Quartermaster] Department cannot furnish laborers to posts, just so long will enlisted men have to work; the only way to meet the matter is to fill the men's stomachs. I believe that every troop and company commander on the frontier will sustain me in saying that the ration, minus the bacon component, is not sufficient to properly feed the men, whether the bacon be replaced by salt pork or fresh beef.[7]

Once again, just as when he addressed the post trader's unfair treatment of the Apache scout a few years earlier, Carter's response to perceived injustice was somewhat precocious—a perilous stand for a young lieutenant in a rank structure marked by deference.

Carter proposed that if the bacon ration had to be discontinued, it should immediately be replaced by a ration of vegetables. He reasoned that since bacon was most often used by troops to trade for local vegetables and fruits, then this action would be the only sensible response by the Commissary Department. To leave soldiers without means of procuring such items locally would lead to an unfit fighting force in an environment requiring physical exertion and endurance. But despite the endorsement of his one-man letter-writing campaign by even General Crook, who had by this time replaced Willcox as department commander in Arizona, Carter's ideas were, as he put it, "buried in the deadly pigeon-hole" once they reached Washington's bureaucratic maze. He sorely concluded that "the oft-repeated statements of the Commissary General that ours was the best fed army in the world" did not suffice for "young soldiers with big appetites" who found themselves caught between staff politics and line requirements. Carter was already developing the reformer's spirit that would mark the struggles of his later career.[8]

In 1884, the Sixth Cavalry was moved to Fort Bayard, New Mexico, to exchange domiciles with the U.S. Fourth Cavalry. Carter was sent to Bayard early to assume the post quartermaster's duties in preparation for the regiment's arrival. The change of station provided little rest, however, as the department was yet again the scene of a major field campaign that kept its troops working at a fevered pitch. Geronimo had abandoned the stifling reservation life for a second time and, with about forty warriors and ninety women and children, was making his way to the Sierra Madres, committing depredations against unfortunate white and Mexican settlers who happened to be near his trail.[9]

George Crook, already reputed for practical innovation, kept his columns in the field, operating with pack mules to cut loose from more cumbersome wagon trains—a practice that allowed him greater mobility but multiplied problems of logistics. A large portion of this effort fell to Carter and he found that "it was a trying job to keep communication open and deliver rations and forage on time" to units that remained constantly mobile in pursuit of an ephemeral foe. His duties underlined the complexities of large-scale campaigning, giving him a view of command not seen by many officers of his age and grade. Years later, he reflected on this period as a practical education in the military art: "My service of many years in quartermaster work fitted me to direct operations which would have been embarrassing without that experience." As a line officer charged with implementing staff functions at their most basic level, he gained an understanding of the immense challenges involved with meeting the needs of campaigning troops. Frustrations were translated to solemn lessons by one who was ever mindful of the larger organizational and policy issues that underpinned such operations.[10]

When the Apache campaigns finally ground to a halt in the fall of 1886, Carter had been posted in the Southwest for twelve years. This tour was lengthy even by the standards of the day—a point that was surely not lost on the Carters. Their second son, two-year-old Leigh Carter, had developed chronic ear problems owing to a bout with scarlet fever, and doctors believed that an operation was required to relieve the child's almost constant pain. Carter and his family were grateful when a respite was offered in the form of a recruiting assignment in New Jersey. In October 1887, they packed their belongings and headed east, leaving behind New Mexico's desert landscape for the bustle of America's Gilded Age.[11]

Carter was sent to open a recruiting office in Newark, a growing town that was heavily influenced by the increasing urban sprawl of nearby New York City. Although the duty itself did not appeal to him, he recognized that the somewhat stifling atmosphere of eastern cities offered a good source for potential recruits. "I could never understand," Carter pondered, "how any young man could prefer to drive a rivet, or feed a machine, day after day, when a career in the army on the frontier was open to him." In Newark, so far from the desert heat and dusty trail, Carter remembered only the camaraderie and relative freedom of a young officer's daily life and easily forgot the difficulties and mortal dangers of contemporary soldiering.[12]

He had been east only one other time since graduation from West Point—a short trip taken with Ida during the fall of 1882. Urban Newark was a vivid illustration of American society's rapid modernization, and for the Carters it must have been a shocking contrast with Arizona's austere lifestyle. For many Americans, the frontier was by 1886 becoming a quaint anomaly found only in literature and newspaper accounts. Much of the country was undergoing an accelerated process of urbanization—a phenomenon that was changing the way Americans of all social classes lived, worked, and viewed the world around them. Carter was very much in touch with middle-class society and its heightened awareness of public issues. He often made use of free time by visiting libraries, galleries, and museums—intellectual stimulants nonexistent at far-off Fort Apache and Fort Bayard.[13]

It was during this period that Carter published his first professional article, beginning an avocation with the pen that would continue throughout his life. In "One View of the Army Question" (1889), he revealed a perceptive realization of the army's place within an evolving nation. His topic, the future direction of American military policy, is familiar in a genre that historians have since tagged as "Uptonian." The term refers to the pervasive influence of Emory Upton, a post–Civil War crusader for service reforms in the manner of contemporary European armies. Professional education, internal standards of performance, and active intellectual participation were important characteristics of this identity, and the Uptonians clearly sought to define a class of military elites who alone were prepared to lead America's armies in time of modern war.[14]

Such convictions certainly met with a great deal of opposition, not only from external observers—often veterans who had served as citizen-soldiers in the Civil War—but also from colleagues within the Regular Army itself. An anti-intellectual segment existed within the officer corps, especially among soldiers who were commissioned directly from civilian life or the enlisted ranks. These men owed any claims of martial expertise to strictly experiential learning, and thus were apt to view talk of requisite professional education as a tacit attack on their own homespun abilities. Thus, the postwar army's so-called professionalist movement was by no means propelled by a collective mindset. Instead, it is more accurately described as a long-frustrated seed that finally began to show some degree of growth, albeit in fits and starts. Progress came only through the tenacious efforts of a relative few stalwarts who struggled to overcome cultural inertia in their quest to bring about institutional change.[15]

Although Emory Upton is most often credited with popularizing professionalist ideas via his widely read views on American military policy, it was William T. Sherman who truly spurred forward army reform in the post–Civil War era. As commanding general, Sherman not only championed the army as a peacetime repository of martial expertise but also took an important step toward institutionalizing this definition by creating the Infantry and Cavalry School of Application at Fort Leavenworth, Kansas, in 1881. Sherman openly encouraged professional participation by junior officers who otherwise would not have dared to openly support progressive ideas. Upton emerged as a sort of protégé, articulating a set of professional ideals that called for broad changes in the way Americans envisaged their military forces. From this impetus, there developed a small but strengthening voice for army reform.[16]

Carter embraced this impulse by writing "One View of the Army Question." In so doing, he identified himself as one of a handful of officers who actively sought to modernize the army according to a very loosely defined "Uptonian" model. These soldiers, most of them postwar graduates of West Point, were a part of the Old Army, yet not so saturated with its traditions and lore that they were unable to see a growing need for change. They shared many of the social values that spawned new interest in the civilian professions, and they used the same printed media to achieve such ends. Russell Weigley named them Upton's disciples, and in a very broad manner, this title seems to fit. Like Upton, they idealized the professionally educated warrior who operated autonomously at the behest of a grateful society. Even if individual ideas differed among the genre, they collectively reflected Upton's thematic emphasis on professional definition and authority—with his suspicion of external interference. Regulars were the keepers of a specialized expertise, a cadre around which organized reserves and volunteers might rally in time of war.[17]

This professionalist genre looked forward to an army that was marked by professional standards of education, training, and leadership—an obvious departure from traditional warrior-leader concepts that were held so dear by many in the Old Army. Carter began his essay by underlining the nation's "gigantic strides in the onward march of modern progress" as a harbinger of new responsibilities with their accompanying dangers of external embroilment. Expectedly, he then dismissed the notion that in such a world "men successful in other pursuits" could lead modern armies into battle. Carter admitted that particular examples of natural ability were demonstrated even in the Civil War on "limited fields of action," but in true Uptonian fashion, he steadfastly maintained that in modern industrialized warfare, military leadership was "uniformly the work of professional soldiers educated in the art of war." In its absolute implication, this assertion relegated America's citizen-soldiery to a strictly subordinate role—a tenet that would likely doom the entire thought to failure as a foundation for any real policy reform unless moderated. Regardless of how reasonable reform arguments might seem in abstract print, actual attempts to change fundamentally the American military would have to be reconciled with the social and political realities of the times.[18]

Like other reformers, Carter addressed the need to develop and refine such expertise during peacetime, when Americans were not apt to maintain a standing army of the size and expense of a wartime footing. As he resignedly put it, "It may be accepted as a fact that Congress—which must be presumed to represent the people—is not in favor of any increase of the army."[19] Thus cognizant of contemporary democratic realities, he looked to the established cadre principle for an acceptable alternative:

In the absence of a large army it is quite important in this
country to have at hand the largest possible number of officers
educated not only in the theories of war, but familiar with all
the most modern improvements relating to guns, ammunition, and material of all kinds, with all kinds of transport
service, accustomed to handling men, and to performing all
the duties, staff and line, incidental to actual war service so far
as it is possible to acquire them in peace.[20]

This advice reached backward to the "expansible army" concept that
had long been a cornerstone of reformers' arguments for peacetime
preparedness. Since the early National Period, American soldiers had
espoused the maintenance of a corps of commissioned and noncommissioned officers who, in wartime, would become the framework
for a much larger army whose ranks were filled by militia and volunteers. For several generations, variations on this theme had been
heard as the best workable alternative to wholesale cuts to Regular
Army manpower.

Perhaps best articulated by John C. Calhoun's "Report on the
Reduction of the Army" (12 December 1820), this concept cleverly
combined the nation's popular preference for a citizen-soldiery with
the professionals' conviction that armies could only be led by experienced regulars who were carefully prepared for such roles. The idea
had survived the test of time, although never explicitly adopted as a
foundation for national military policy. In 1878, Upton presented his
version of it in *Armies of Asia and Europe,* a book that was originally
written as a report of his observations during an official trip abroad.
He proposed an army structure that could expand from a peacetime
footing to one of wartime readiness through a system of "national
volunteers," a sort of federal reserve that would be absorbed into skeletal battalions led by regulars. This latter point—*led by regulars*—is a
salient aspect of truly understanding the Uptonian mindset.[21]

Although Upton may very well have acquiesced to the need for
amateurs as militia and volunteers, he denied citizen-soldiers a leadership role of any significance. According to Upton's most recent biographer, his true legacy was the articulation of a coherent military
policy that fit neatly into a republican framework. But while it is
certainly true that Upton called for the establishment of a trained

national reserve to augment the Regular Army in time of crisis, he relegated the state militia (or National Guard, as it increasingly became known) to a tertiary role of last resort. Upton's national reserve would be wholly under federal control, "officered and supported by the Government," thereby rejecting the citizen-soldier's stake in wartime *leadership*. Thus, the professionalist mindset failed to accommodate the powerful sense of localism that still existed among the American populace.[22]

In 1889, this was a salient point that Carter also failed to grasp. He dismissed the notion that nonprofessionals could cope with the complexities of modern warfare in any but the most subordinate roles—perhaps a valid technical assumption, but a seminal misunderstanding of the contemporary emphasis on community and locale. Reconciling military policy with the American political and social climate would become a required feature of later reforms, but Carter was only just beginning to recognize this important relationship. Thus, while he made room for the National Guard as a viable resource for wartime mobilization, it was only under the transcendent federal authority of the professional's expertise.[23]

Carter proposed a military organization that founded wartime strength on peacetime preparedness, explicitly relating the army's professional role to the decades-old cadre principle. While lamenting that Upton's work "lies pigeon-holed at the War Department," he advanced similar ideas that carefully avoided Upton's more absolute maxim for a national reserve, possibly already recognizing its political inexpedience. "Each arm of the service should be a working model for the great body of National Guardsmen and volunteers when called into service," he wrote, acknowledging a supporting role for America's celebrated citizen-soldier, "and nothing which can be provided in peace should be left to experiment in time of war." Thus he loosely adapted Calhoun's expansible army concept to justify the Regular Army's increased attention to military professionalism. As a product of his times, he prescribed an intellectual approach to gaining soldierly expertise—paralleling the middle-class practices he witnessed in the changing society around him.[24]

During the Gilded Age, a developing middle class looked to colleges and universities as the road to material opportunity and social influence in an industrialized economy. Advanced degrees were increasingly grasped as certificates of true expertise that differentiated the professional from the mere amateur. Americans sought to re-define their occupational lives through the social status and authority wielded by the professions. Academia became the legitimating factor in this quest, emerging as "the seminal institution within the culture of professionalism."[25]

Occupational groups such as law, medicine, and engineering began to coalesce around standardized paths of hierarchical learning, allowing these self-identified "professional" endeavors some degree of internal control over admission to their ranks. Such groups protected their autonomy by highlighting their "special grasp" of a particular skill, defining their activities according to objective standards of competence. In the military profession, this growing emphasis was already reflected to some degree by the developing role of the infantry and cavalry school at Leavenworth. In 1891, Gen. John M. Schofield applauded Leavenworth as the army's professional icon: "Its opportunities are now sought for by young officers as a means of gaining that higher education which is essential to the satisfactory performance of the higher duties of the staff, and of the command of large bodies of troops in time of war."[26] As in society at large, a widening circle of army officers was recognizing graduate schooling as an important undertaking—not only for the knowledge it imparted but also for its value as a cultural trapping of the true professional. As James Abrahamson summarizes, "Despite the features differentiating the officer corps from other professions, army and navy leaders used education to the same end." It is not surprising then that Carter called for increased emphasis on graduate professional instruction and training as proper preparation for the modern warrior. For many years regulars had sought popular recognition, autonomy, and prestige, and as the twentieth century neared, graduate education clearly marked the path toward social reward.[27]

Carter believed that many of his brother officers exhibited a burgeoning "progressive spirit" and welcomed educational advances. "There is more reading and study of a professional character done in the army to-day than ever before, and its effect is visible in every garrison in the higher standard of perfection and the almost entire absence of many things which were characteristic of the army ten years ago."[28] Although he may well have overstated the degree of acceptance that greeted professional study in the contemporary army, his assessment was accurate insofar as there existed a growing inclination for reform. As Indian resistance to white settlement weakened into a painful memory, forward-thinking officers naturally turned their attention to the army's future.

During Carter's first two decades of service, an increasing number of Indian tribes had resignedly accepted the reservation. Although this sad fate marked an end to the aboriginal cultures as they had existed for centuries before white incursion, it also diminished the pressing need for a military presence of the magnitude required during the height of westward expansion. Circumstances demanded a re-examination of American military policy, and also allowed the army a physical respite during which professional reform might be institutionalized. Carter noted this transition and the distinct opportunity it represented in language that betrayed the modernist tendencies of his time:

> The pressure from the East and from California has narrowed down the frontier until it practically exists no longer, and Indian and outlaw alike find themselves constrained to succumb to civilization. A few years more, and a greater part of the army—all but the cavalry perhaps—may be safely spared from Indian police duty. Is it not time, then, to be up and doing, in order that some clearly-defined policy may be adopted for the future in regard to the army?[29]

This observation certainly seems to prophesy the twenty years that followed its publication. As the Indian Wars wound to a bitter close, the Regular Army struggled to redefine its role in a changing nation.

In October 1889, when Carter packed up his family to leave Newark's recruiting depot and return to the West, it was with a revitalized outlook and sense of purpose. Although not appealing to his personal tastes, this sampling of staff duty on the eastern seaboard balanced his field experience and gave him the opportunity to renew his more reflective side. "I worked hard those two years on recruiting service to improve myself," Carter remembered, "intending to return to the regiment a better man, intellectually, than when I left it." He was no longer merely interested in the technical aspects of soldiering, but instead was beginning to view his profession with a broadened perspective that was concerned with the greater issues of institutional policy.[30]

Carter's argument in "One View of the Army Question" identified him with a cabal of officers who appreciated the necessity for military progress. Like their civilian counterparts, these men met with no small resistance as they struggled to overcome the obstacle of decades-old traditions. After suffering a great deal of frustration in the attempt, they eventually would find that a politically delicate touch was required to gain and secure substantive change. But such insights would have to come later, when the battle of progress and reform was fully joined. In the meantime, Carter and other so-called Uptonians still served in the Old Army, and had only begun to stake out their positions in what would prove to be a long and difficult fight.

After being notified of his forthcoming promotion to the rank of captain, Carter was authorized to take a leave of absence while awaiting formal assignment to command a troop of the Sixth Cavalry at Fort Lewis, Colorado. He spent a few enjoyable weeks hunting with friends at old Fort Supply in the Indian Territory, relishing the chance to once again escape Newark's urban confines. Although no specific mention is made of his family's whereabouts at this time, it is likely that Ida and their two sons remained in the East while he established quarters at their new post. The surgery that little Leigh underwent in 1887 had proven somewhat less than effective, and the child, now five years old, was still plagued by excruciating ear aches. As Leigh grew older, it became clear that frontier posts could not provide the medical expertise to meet his long-term needs, and William and Ida may have realized already that this malady would eventually require a permanent return to the east. But for now, Carter, ever the dutiful cavalryman, looked forward to receiving command of a troop and assuming the rank of captain after seventeen years of service.[31]

Carter's journey westward in 1889 was very different from the one he had made as a green lieutenant so many years earlier. The frontier's uncertainties were greatly diminished and violence was no longer the most prominent feature of daily life. Quite simply, the American frontier—that place of folk legend and ideological myth— had started to disappear before the triumphant march of so-called modern civilization. Industrial power was harnessing much of what Americans found both intriguing and threatening about the West's daunting characteristics of space and geography. The railroad bridged the prairies, mountains, and deserts while the telegraph brought inhabitants almost instant communication. Where formerly mere shantytowns and outposts identified white settlements, full-fledged towns and even cities were growing in their place, offering many of the modern amenities and even luxuries.

The cultural demise of the Indians, now partitioned on out-of-the-way reservations, was already a foregone conclusion. Sporadic resistance would yet grab national headlines, but such episodes were by now little more than quaint reminders of a bloodier past. Soldiers and civilians alike were already beginning to write with twinges of remorse about the nagging "Indian problem" that finally succumbed to advancing white settlement. The army's western role was also changing, and from this transition would rise both new opportunities and uncertainties.

It was still the Old Army that greeted Carter at Fort Lewis, but as he noted with irony, its mission had turned completely on its head: "The calls for troops took another form—that of protecting the peaceful Indians from the encroachments of the frontier whites, who had no regard for the treaty or other rights of the red men." In a manner reminiscent of the social reform efforts of Gilded Age elites, soldiers found themselves trying to protect the very people whose deteriorated condition they energetically helped to create. The next decade would underline the need for a thorough reevaluation of the American military's purpose, and hence also its internal framework. But in 1890, most soldiers still clung to a decades-old professional culture that was rapidly becoming doomed by events.[32]

7

GHOST DANCE OF THE OLD ARMY

When Carter reported to Fort Lewis in the fall of 1889, he relished the long-awaited opportunity to assume company command. Despite the obvious hardships of returning west with a wife and two small children, he was glad to once again be among active troops in the field. Although the post was unpopular among many soldiers and their families due to its isolation and extreme elevation, Carter was so pleased with making captain after years of waiting that he hardly noticed these irritations. As he put it, "I was too contented over having a troop to notice a few thousand feet of altitude." The challenges of field duty appealed to him, and the relatively mundane work in Newark only reinvigorated his enthusiasm for greater professional responsibility. There was little doubt in Carter's mind that the army was poised for an era of great change, and the only remaining question was whether that change would be led by soldiers or dictated by politicians. But before he and his family could settle into their new home, the Sixth Cavalry fell victim to the capriciousness of the latter.[1]

Less than a year after arriving in Colorado, the Carters were appalled to learn that congressional cuts in army strength were sending them on yet another move—once again to New Mexico. A reduction in the 1890 army appropriation demanded that regiments "skeletonize" two troops each, losing outright their complement of enlisted personnel and reassigning officers to detached duty elsewhere. The decreasing threat of Indian attack and the lack of an obvious danger from abroad left the army with little argument against such cost-saving measures. Carter's own formal protest against the legality of such cuts fell on deaf ears in Washington and was merely an expression of frustration. He and his family were victimized by the very expansible army concept of which he was a proponent. The political face of military policy was again made painfully clear as he ruefully grumbled that "the pruning knife of economy is usually first applied to lopping off a few soldiers, who are the lowest paid, and are without votes or influence."[2]

The Carters moved to Fort Wingate during the summer of 1890, likely with some consternation that they were starting over in the very desert they had left only three years before. But any such dismay proved ill-founded as events even then unfolding on the Northern Plains brought swift changes in Carter's career. They had been at Fort Wingate only a few short weeks when the so-called Messiah Craze spread across the Plains, sending white settlers into a panic. For Carter, the Ghost Dance conjured up unpleasant memories from a decade earlier when Nockay-del-klinne's medicine had attracted a similar following among the Apaches. He certainly did not expect a seemingly harmless dance on a reservation hundreds of miles to the north to once again take him from his family and draw him into a series of tragic events.[3]

During a solar eclipse on New Year's Day of 1888, Wovoka, a Paiute shaman in Walker Valley, Nevada, experienced a vision in which he saw living Indians reunited with their dead ancestors. Shortly thereafter, he began preaching a sort of millenialist spiritualism that combined traditional Indian beliefs with elements of Christian salvation. Wovoka rapidly gained a large following as his ideas were spread among the Indian nations by zealous emissaries. Like Nockay-del-klinne before him, Wovoka became known as the Prophet, and held his followers' rapt attention with vivid revelations of a coming world of "blissful and eternal life, free of pain, sickness, want, and death, free, above all, of white people." But although the Ghost Dance may have begun with peaceful intentions, by the time it reached the Dakotas it had taken on a more ominous meaning.[4]

During the spring of 1890, Short Bull and Kicking Bear, two "apostles" of the Sioux nation, brought their tribesmen a somewhat distorted version of Wovoka's pacifistic canons. According to their adaptation, "the millennium prophesied by Wovoka might be facilitated by destroying the white people." Now hemmed in by numerous settlements and ranches, the Sioux had fallen into a dismal condition during the preceding decade. Short Bull and Kicking Bear, like so many prophets before and after, latched onto their audience's needs as fertile ground for a purposeful message—in this case, one that alarmed the region's white population. The Sioux, according to ethnologist Alice Fletcher, "saw little in the future but hunger and despair for themselves and their children. They fell easy prey to the rumors of a coming Messiah, and the Ghost Dance craze was the outcome."[5]

The situation began to deteriorate when the Ghost Dance drew increasing numbers of Sioux. Bands thought to have finally acquiesced to white "civilization" seemed to threaten hostility in their newfound spiritual zeal. By early October, one worried observer estimated that there were almost three thousand disciples at the Pine Ridge reservation alone. At the Rosebud Agency, Indian agent E. B. Reynolds, fretted that the movement was "continually gaining new adherents" who were "daily becoming more threatening and defiant." Others echoed Reynolds' concern, and the Bureau of Indian Affairs soon declared the situation beyond its control.[6]

The government was deluged with public cries for action as "panic-stricken whites in the Dakotas and Nebraska unleashed a flood of telegrams, letters, and petitions for help," and newspapers inflamed the already tense situation with a stream of sensational stories. On 13 November, after parrying appeals from almost every direction, Secretary of the Interior John W. Noble asked President Benjamin Harrison for military action. Soon thereafter, Harrison authorized the army to proceed, and a host of well-armed bluecoats headed from every direction toward the Pine Ridge and Rosebud agencies. Their arrival had an inflammatory effect that more astute onlookers might have expected, and the Ghost Dancing continued with increased energy.[7]

General Nelson A. Miles, the notoriously ambitious commander of the Division of the Missouri, continued to order more troops into the region from Nebraska, Kansas, Montana, and New Mexico. At Fort Wingate, "from a clear sky, on November 23, 1890," remembered Carter, "came a telegraphic order for the regiment to prepare at once to take the field in Dakota." On 9 December, several troops of the Sixth Cavalry—still under Eugene Carr's command—reached the Black Hills to take part in a campaign that has since become a dismal metaphor for the United States' failed Indian policy.[8]

In 1890, the army had at its disposal many of the instruments of modern technology, and telegraphed orders brought a massive troop concentration by railroad in only a fraction of the time it would have taken just a few years earlier. With modern breech-loading field guns in tow, the army faced the Ghost Dancers in a manner only vaguely resembling earlier such encounters. But technology could do nothing about the Dakota winter—a lesson not easily forgotten after Carter's days at Fort D. A. Russell:

> Only those who have experienced the rigors of winter on the northern plains, and in the Bad Lands of Dakota can appreci-ate the necessity of guarding well against disaster. To enable troops to remain in the field and accomplish their work in midwinter, special clothing and equipment are necessary. To meet the conditions, the men were supplied with fur caps and gloves, blanket lined overcoats, heavy wool socks and arctic overshoes. The horses were supplied with blanket-lined can-vas covers. The regiment . . . moved out by squadrons as fast as the winter clothing and tents could be issued.[9]

Carter's experience with the logistics of large-scale campaigning and familiarity with the region's harsh winter climate made his expertise invaluable to Carr's preparation. "I am left here in command of all the odds and ends with my troop," he wrote to Ida from Rapid City. "My quartermaster record got me into this, but I feel I am doing the regi-ment a good turn." Carter set about requisitioning needed supplies and organizing the pack train before following the regiment into the Cheyenne River valley. His frustrations in these efforts only high-lighted yet again the deep gulf that separated the army staff from their line brethren in the field.[10]

Carr had telegraphed an order for Hotchkiss guns before leaving New Mexico on the journey northward. When the Sixth arrived in the Black Hills, Carter was distraught to find that only the guns them-selves had been sent. When he inquired about the location and status of the necessary gun carriages, harnesses, and ammunition, he was shocked to learn that they had not been sent because the requisition expressly stipulated only the guns—the needed equipage was a separate supply item. Fortunately for the troopers of the Sixth, the matter was quickly resolved by the marvels of express freight, and Carter and the all-important pack train soon left Rapid City to catch up to their comrades: "I am fitting up aparajos as rapidly as possible, and will push on with as much for the regiment as I can carry. . . . I will take on rations, so that there need be no turning back until the business is settled." He arrived just in time to take part in one of the most notorious episodes in American military history.[11]

When Carter caught up to his troop, it was encamped near the Cheyenne River, some thirty miles east of Rapid City. Miles had placed the Sixth where it might "prevent Indians from committing depredations or roaming about among settlements" in the area stretching from Battle Creek on the south to Boxelder Creek on the north. In late November, several bands of well-armed Sioux had left the reservations in defiance of government authority. The army's hand was pressed when two groups under the leadership of Short Bull and Two Strike joined together after plundering the empty villages of compliant Indians who had moved to the agencies as ordered. These combined bands, accounting for almost one thousand warriors, holed up on a plateau known as the "Stronghold," situated about twenty miles north of the Pine Ridge Agency. From the white perspective, this move was certainly belligerent, even if it had not yet turned violent.[12]

Outside of the Stronghold were other Ghost Dancers who concerned Miles and the Indian Bureau. A band of Minniconjou Sioux, under the leadership of Hump and Big Foot, was encamped farther north on the Cheyenne River near Cherry Creek. Big Foot's people were rabid converts to the Ghost Dance craze, and he urged his followers to arm themselves and be prepared for a possible fight. But in early December, Hump, who had been an ally of the army since abandoning the warpath in 1877, renounced the Ghost Dance and led his band to the Cheyenne River Agency. Thus weakened, but still adhering to the prophecy, Big Foot and his people returned to their village several miles to the southwest, where they were hemmed in by converging columns of Miles's soldiers. At this point, "Big Foot professed peaceful intentions," but under the spell of his own spiritualism, soon was "hurried unwillingly toward disaster by fiery young men he could not control." When Miles finally assumed field command in person, he shifted to a strategy of increasing physical pressure. The likelihood of a climactic confrontation seemed to build by the day.[13]

Carr and the Sixth Cavalry still patrolled the Cheyenne River valley in the vicinity of Rapid Creek. Thus far, to the troops' immense relief, the weather was unseasonably mild, so conditions remained good for field operations and made rapid movement possible in case of further orders. Carter's own expectations were guardedly optimistic, but framed by a degree of cynicism that came with bitter experience: "I do not expect any hostilities if the Indians are given time, but so much money is being spent on this affair, Gen'l Miles may bring on trouble by crowding the poor devils. We are now outfitted for a winter campaign and I have very little hope of getting a roof for sometime to come."[14] He expected the campaign to continue until severe winter weather settled over the region, weakening resistance and making the Indians more willing to succumb before Miles's pressure. But newspaper headlines continued to stir public fears, prodding the army to take immediate action.[15]

In the early morning hours of 15 December, Sitting Bull, the revered Hunkpapa medicine man, was shot and killed by a detachment of Indian police who came under attack while trying to effect his arrest. News of this event spread quickly throughout the region and darkened prospects for a peaceful resolution even as diplomatic efforts seemed to finally bear fruit. The frenzied Ghost Dancing continued and many of the most faithful in Sitting Bull's camp joined those already with Big Foot, ready to defend themselves from white or Indian interference. This latter point is an important footnote to the story. With the destruction of friendly villages by those who garrisoned the Stronghold and the likelihood of armed intervention growing daily, the religion fell out of favor with many reservation Indians who simply hoped to avoid white retribution. The Ghost Dancers lost much of their support even among their own people, and the Sioux nation became badly divided. Wovoka envisioned a peaceful movement that would unite nations, but the Ghost Dance that Short Bull and Kicking Bear brought to the Dakotas roused only hostility and resentment.[16]

While Carter awaited further developments on the Cheyenne River, Ida and the boys had moved to Fort Leavenworth, Kansas, with several other Sixth Cavalry families. The couple's correspondence during this period, delivered by way of Rapid City, reflects a very devoted marriage in which Ida shared the trials of her husband's army career. Like so many other officers' wives, she had become part of the army culture, and was well versed in current events through the newspapers and post gossip. At Leavenworth's New Delmonico Hotel, Ida did her best to prepare a memorable Christmas for the boys, even as she constantly worried about news from Pine Ridge. "I only hope there won't be any fighting, I watch the papers and yet don't know just how much to believe," she wrote to Carter. "I do wish we were all settled at some post, I don't care where, for with you I always feel perfectly contented." Willie, just seven years old, reminded his mother to tell "Papa . . . not to let the troop get out of cartridges." The painful realities of his profession must have weighed heavily on the middle-aged Carter's mind as he read such letters and considered his family's future. But the immediate prospect of leaving the Dakotas before Christmas diminished as the Ghost Dancers considered their own plight and desperately looked for a way out of Miles's closing cordon.[17]

Like his view of the Indian situation generally, Carter's outlook on the affair reflected a sort of paternal pragmatism combined with an objective dedication to civil authority. "This is the quickest way to settle the matter, and end the hostile attitude of these Indians," he wrote. "I do not believe they would do any harm if left alone, but they have been insubordinate so long that it is deemed best to make them go to the agency." Such an attitude was typical of many frontier soldiers—although the disappearing Indian culture was in itself harmless, federal governance had to be upheld through the application of unwavering strength. Reminiscent of Nockay-del-klinne's demise at Cibicu Creek years earlier, the current Ghost Dance crisis was clouded by cultural misapprehension and fueled by self-serving journalists who preyed on the public's overactive imagination.[18]

Events in the Dakotas gripped the nation's interest in a manner very familiar to Americans today. The correspondents who flocked to the scene hungered for a bloody end with which to fill the telegraph wires, and the incessant waiting brought their wrath on Miles and the army. Frederick Remington, the renowned western artist, joined Carr's camp on the Cheyenne River as a representative of *Harper's*

Weekly, hoping to "illustrate affairs" as they unfolded. A mutual acquaintance had given Remington a letter to pass on to Carter, and he became the artist's unofficial sponsor during the remainder of his stay with the Sixth. Newspapers had contributed so much to the crisis by stirring up fear that soldiers must have cringed at the mere sight of a writing tablet or sketchbook, but Remington, always friendly to the army's interests, was surely welcomed by the men of the Sixth.[19]

During the last two weeks of December, while the eastern press echoed highly embellished stories of Sitting Bull's death, Miles was preparing to move against defiant bands. Big Foot's camp of Minniconjous was high on Miles's list of troublemakers who had to be dealt with, despite the assurances of Lt. Col. Edwin V. Sumner, the local commander, that the chief's intentions were wholly peaceful. While Sumner tried to convince Big Foot to surrender at Fort Bennett, the chief also considered an invitation from the Oglalas to come to Pine Ridge and there declare peace with the whites. Under the prodding advice of his tribal headmen, he started south despite his own concerns that heading toward Pine Ridge would only lead to trouble. Many of Big Foot's young men bristled at his moderation, and their increasing aggression bode ill for a long journey through very uneasy country.[20]

On 24 December, Miles was horrified to learn that Big Foot and his band had broken camp during the previous night and started in a southerly direction, supposing that they intended to join Short Bull's still-defiant disciples at the Stronghold. He had been assured that Sumner had the situation well in hand, and so this turn of events was a very unwelcome surprise. Fearing the consequences if they reached the Stronghold, Miles immediately ordered troops to take up blocking positions across their trail, putting into motion a chain of actions and reactions that accelerated toward disaster.

On that same morning, Christmas Eve Day, Carr and the Sixth were alerted to move eastward to intercept Big Foot, who probably had little idea that he had become such important prey. Only the night before, Carter had returned from a two-day patrol that left him exhausted, but had risen early that morning to try to purchase a new horse at a nearby ranch since his own had balked at crossing the frozen Cheyenne River.[21] He had just completed the deal and arrived back in camp when orders came to take the field:

About 10 a.m. . . . a courier arrived in our camp with a message saying Big Foot was moving south on the Deep Fork trail and would probably pass the head of Bull Creek in the Bad Lands. General Carr had been sending his troop commanders in all directions, scouting for trails and familiarizing themselves with the country, and it so happened that I had returned the night previous from the Bull Creek pass, and had found no signs of Indians in that country.[22]

While buglers sounded "boots and saddles" and troopers rushed to ready their horses and equipment, Carter felt sure that the news signaled the opening of a major campaign, and he wisely issued orders to pack cooking utensils, blankets, and extra rations. As the column broke its way through the icy Cheyenne River, he was silently very grateful that he had earlier left the warmth of his bedroll to procure a new mount.[23]

Carr hit the trail with four cavalry troops and the two Hotchkiss guns, and was soon joined by two more troops that were already out when the action began. The weather had turned, and the Sixth spent a miserable Christmas Eve near the head of Sage Creek, alternately piling wood on their campfires and trying to grab a few minutes of fitful sleep.[24] After spending all of Christmas Day in the saddle searching the Bull Creek valley, the Sixth finally returned to its position on the Cheyenne, having marched over seventy miles in about thirty hours. Carter and his comrades had found no sign of their quarry, were hungry, chilled to the bone, and generally worn out. They thankfully settled down to the relative comforts of their original bivouac and awaited further developments.[25]

Only three days later, on 28 December, a battalion of the Seventh Cavalry under Maj. Samuel M. Whitside finally caught up to Big Foot's band near Wounded Knee Creek, some sixty miles to the southeast of Carr's position. Bitter cold now gripped the region, and Big Foot, who was gravely ill with pneumonia, already intended to head straight toward Whitside's detachment to surrender. Col. James W. Forsyth and four more troops of the Seventh rode out to ensure that Miles's firm orders to disarm the band were fulfilled to the letter. The army, goaded by Miles's own misconceptions, warily eyed Big Foot as a belligerent who had slipped out of Sumner's grasp and was making a bold bid to reach the Stronghold. "Big Foot is cunning and his Indians are very bad," Miles telegraphed, "and I hope you will round up the whole body of them, disarm [them] and keep them under close guard." Miles hoped that Big Foot's capture would signal a successful end to the crisis—Short Bull, Kicking Bear, and their remaining disciples had abandoned the Stronghold a few days earlier and were heading toward the Pine Ridge. But it was a tense situation at Big Foot's camp the next morning as Forsyth attempted to collect weapons.[26]

The act of disarmament provoked a violent eruption that might otherwise have been avoided. As Robert Utley explained, despite the obvious futility of attempting to fight against overwhelming odds, "the actual disarming could be expected to turn loose some intense emotions. . . . One and all, the Miniconjous could not shake the fear that if they gave up their guns they would be slaughtered by the troops. It was an unreasonable and unjustified fear, but a very real one."[27] Forsyth, frustrated by a futile search of the village, ordered an individual search of the men. When soldiers struggled to take a rifle from a young Indian who was later described by his own people as a "crazy man, a young man of very bad influence," the weapon discharged. At the same time, a shaman who had been dancing about, reciting incantations, threw a handful of dirt into the air. In combination, these two meaningless acts sparked the tension-filled moment. Several young men pulled rifles from beneath their blankets and leveled them toward the nearest soldiers. Volleys were exchanged and the encounter burst into a horrific fight at almost point-blank range.[28]

When the brief but intense battle was over, the army's cruel efficiency had taken its toll. The Seventh's response to the warriors' near-suicidal resistance was rendered even more lethal by the devastating fire of a battery of four Hotchkiss guns. Although exact numbers are not known, approximately 146 Indians were killed and another 51 were wounded, 7 of whom died later at the Pine Ridge hospital. Many of these were women and children who became victims of shots fired by both sides in the confused fighting that moved in several directions. The army's own casualties numbered 25 killed and 39 wounded, including 2 civilians who had accompanied the column. The needless tragedy quickly put an entirely different face on a campaign that only a few hours before seemed to be nearing a pitiful but nonetheless bloodless conclusion.[29]

The next day, news of the Seventh Cavalry's fight reached Carr on the Cheyenne River. Few details were known, but rumors were clear that a large number of Sioux were killed and that the Seventh had also sustained casualties. Carter, who was once again in the field with his troop, was immediately recalled as the Sixth began a rapid march toward the mouth of Wounded Knee Creek, several miles downstream from the scene of the battle. At Pine Ridge, the catastrophe also sparked frantic activity, and a large number of Brule Sioux broke from the agency in both fear and anger, heading toward the holdouts with Short Bull and Kicking Bear. Now the number of Ghost Dancers, who previously were so close to surrendering, swelled to four thousand, including almost a thousand warriors.[30]

After a hard rain turned into a driving blizzard on 31 December, the Sixth Cavalry huddled against the cold while continuing to scout the surrounding hills for signs of the now-hostile Sioux camp. Miles had quickly moved his forces into "a solid blue wall along White River and Wounded Knee Creek" in an effort to block expected attempts to rally at the Stronghold. Watching events accelerate out of control, Carter hoped that the miserable weather might prove an ally and yet convince the hostiles to give up further resistance. "The situation does not look as bright to me for a quick settlement as it did a few days ago," he wrote, "but I have hopes that the blizzard now will bring them to their senses, and all those who do not want to be hostile will go in." Like the grievous circumstances that resulted from Cibicu Creek's unexpected violence ten years earlier, deteriorating events in the Dakotas now seemed even bleaker and threatened to become a general "outbreak" that would grip the region for several months, if not years.[31]

On New Year's Day, distant shots were reported by the Sixth's pickets, and Carr, fearing that his still-absent wagon train was under attack, immediately mounted two troops and sent them to investigate. Led by Carter's Troop F, they "went at a gallop through the snow, guided by the sound of the firing," and near the confluence of White River and Wounded Knee Creek, found the Sixth's Troop K in a stout fight with a number of Sioux warriors. The squadron charged across the icy river and deployed into a skirmish line at the gallop, pressing the attackers into a running retreat as Carr arrived with further reinforcements. "The result of this attack was particularly gratifying," Carter remembered, "because the Indians were seeking revenge for their losses at the hands of the Seventh Cavalry, and found the Sixth so fully prepared to give it to them." That he participated in this closing engagement of white America's prolonged war with the American Indian was perhaps fitting for an officer who would later play a vital role in the army's passage toward modernity.[32]

Fortunately for all involved, soon after the skirmish on White River, the Pine Ridge Campaign emerged from the violent spiral that seemed unstoppable after Forsyth's poorly managed encounter with Big Foot's Minniconjous at Wounded Knee. Miles wisely held his troops in check while diplomatic pressure was brought to bear by several messengers sent into the discordant Sioux camp. These efforts, combined with growing internal animosities between the Brules and Oglalas, finally met with success. On 12 January 1891, the last of the remaining stalwarts with Short Bull and Kicking Bear recognized the futility of further resistance and headed toward Pine Ridge. Three days later, the Sioux nation surrendered to the army one last time.

Just as the battle at Cibicu Creek had brought bitter allegations and inquiry, the army's actions at Wounded Knee were roundly questioned as wildly divergent stories circulated and the public demanded an accurate accounting. But even if the larger campaign was tainted by questionable actions therein, Carter himself had performed admirably. Demonstrating his continued high regard for Carter's subordinate leadership, Carr recommended him for the brevet rank of major for his actions at White River. If Carter's essay in 1889 had marked him as one of the army's rising intellectuals, then his career as a frontier cavalryman was equally distinguished by his ability in the field. As at Cibicu, he had proven his mettle as a soldier of the Old Army.[33]

On 21 January, in a scene that in retrospect foretold the closing of an era, Miles ordered his remaining troops to assemble for a formal review. Carter's melodramatic description of this event underlines the symbolism that clearly accompanied the campaign's end:

> General Carr commanded the cavalry brigade, consisting of the Sixth, Seventh and Ninth Regiments, and the mixed squadron which had come from the Fort Leavenworth school. . . . No such body of troops had been brought together since the Civil War, and there could be no doubt that the sight of these well equipped and seasoned soldiers, comprising cavalry, field artillery and infantry, with truly every button and cartridge

in place, caused the Indians to comprehend the hopelessness of any further struggle against the encroachment of the
whites.[34]

Carter applauded the martial splendor that forced an entire culture's
surrender, even as he regretted the "encroachment" of white authority. But in this seeming contradiction, he unwittingly expressed a
salient aspect of the army's emergent professional identity. Soldiers
took great pride in the selfless objectivity that defined their relationship with civilian authority. Thus, Carter was able to note with
some detachment the painful outcome of government policies despite the salient role that he and his fellow soldiers had played in their
execution.[35]

Two years after Carter and the Sixty Cavalry left the Dakotas in
1891, historian Frederick Jackson Turner issued his oft-quoted eulogy
for the American frontier, a proclamation that was decidedly premature even in its most narrow interpretation. But the end of the army's
role as an Indian-fighting constabulary is more easily delineated.
Many contemporary observers—both in and out of the army—realized that the Pine Ridge Campaign signaled a last chapter to a passing
military era. Carter and the more astute among his colleagues were
well aware that the very nature of the army was about to undergo a
fundamental transition. Only a year before he watched the defeated
Ghost Dancers return to the reservation, Carter had forecast this end,
asserting that "although troops will be required for a few years longer
on the frontier, it is time to consider the future of the army." Although the "Indian problem" continued to require military attention
for some years to come, Wounded Knee represented a real cessation of
major violence. In the weeks following the campaign's inglorious
ending, the several regiments at Pine Ridge were dispersed, and, having vacated Fort Wingate, the Sixth Cavalry received orders for a permanent change of station. Troop F was sent with four other troops to
Fort Niobrara on the southern boundary of the Rosebud Agency, near
the present-day town of Valentine, Nebraska.[36]

When Carter and his exhausted battalion reached Fort Niobrara
after marching through a dangerous blizzard, only the roofs of several
buildings were visible above deep snowdrifts. The unwelcome sight
of an entire post nearly covered with snow metaphorically described
the garrison's mundane duty there. At the Rosebud, soldiers were

primarily concerned with ensuring that local contractors did not cheat the agency's wards of their due rations—a mission that certainly reflected the changing nature of the frontier equation. After looking over the situation that greeted him there, Carter declared that the Indians' "fighting days were over, and they settled down to a life quite as monotonous as that of our men in garrison." Clearly, the army would have to refocus institutionally or else, like the frontier itself, risk becoming a mere relic of decades past.[37]

After Carter had spent two years at Fort Niobrara with few highlights outside a memorable trip to the Chicago World's Fair, the nation's changing military needs were finally manifested in his own career. In April 1893, he and his troop were ordered to Fort Leavenworth, Kansas, to serve as part of the small garrison maintained there for the use of the still-developing Infantry and Cavalry School of Application. Rather than any formal recognition of Carter's proclivity for professional study, this assignment was more likely a reward for the fine impression made by his troop of steel-gray horses as they led the dedication parade in Chicago. Nonetheless, the move gave him an opportunity to consider his profession from a somewhat more intellectual perspective. At Leavenworth, graduate military education was maturing, and under the zealous leadership of such reform-minded officers as Arthur Wagner and Eben Swift, the school was becoming a torchbearer in the army's fitful struggle for modernity.[38]

When Carter arrived in Kansas that spring, he was approaching a sort of crossroads in his career. This personal transition is an individual story within a much larger change undergone by the contemporary army as a whole. The end of the army's primary mission on the frontier meant that the maintenance of many small military outposts as pinpoints of government strength was no longer needed or justifiable. As the threat of hostilities lessened, the War Department took practical steps to consolidate western troops at fewer installations. Professional opportunities were an unforeseen by-product of this move at economy. As Carter noted, "The necessity for guarding isolated and exposed points had for years prevented proper instruction of officers and men in the administration and manoeuvres [sic] of battalions, regiments, and brigades." Consolidating greater numbers at fewer places gave the army an enriched environment for professional growth of the kind that would have been impossible only a few years before. Beyond even the formal exercises and training that became more commonplace as frontier operations slowed, consolidation created opportunities for informal interaction and discourse that encouraged professional interest and participation. Like other professional groups, military officers organized to give their collective interests a stronger, more coherent voice.[39]

The founding of the Military Service Institute of the United States (1878) and the publication of its associated journal began a trend that was followed by the army's individual branches. Soon after, the United States Cavalry Association (1887) and the Infantry Society (1893) began publication of their own journals that featured articles of both professional and technical focus. The success of these undertakings is a testament to many officers' increasing desire for a more active role in their institution's direction, as well as their recognition of other, perhaps less tangible, returns. Professional associations and journals were becoming "symbols of authority" for specialized groups, lending an air of social legitimacy to officers' claims of expertise while giving participants a public medium for their ideas.[40]

Widely read organs such as the *Journal of the Military Service Institution of the United States* (*JMSIUS*), *The United Service*, and the *Army and Navy Journal* (*ANJ*) were part of what one historian has called an "explosion of specialized literature on the art of war." The latter two periodicals even brought army and navy officers together on the same pages as both commented on issues that transcended service boundaries. Writing for an audience of one's peers was no longer dismissed as an impractical waste of time, but instead became an appreciated sign of professional leadership. In essays, reviews, and open letters, senior and junior officers alike entered into conversation on issues of institutional importance, providing a national forum for the professional process. More than just a sounding board, the journals served an important function that was closely related to that of the army's developing system of graduate education—"affording an outlet for ideas and studies nurtured at the schools."[41]

As further expression of the burgeoning emphasis on professional thought, soldiers at various posts were required to participate in the army's new lyceum program, instituted in late 1891 by Commanding General John M. Schofield. At Fort Niobrara, Carter participated in the lyceums as both a student and instructor, perhaps piquing his desire to become a part of the Leavenworth experience. Schofield's program, made practicable by the already noted troop concentration and the waning frontier threat, reflected a growing awareness that true professionalism was the product of a continuing process and not merely a static milestone that was attained and held. The lyceums built on Leavenworth's relative success and similarly aspired to "stimulate professional zeal and ambition" among junior- and company-grade officers at operational posts. The program never reached Schofield's expectations, but, as historian Timothy Nenninger points out, it certainly helped imbue "an atmosphere within the army sympathetic to the needs of military education." Although Carter later criticized the haphazard implementation of the early lyceum system, he supported the professional principles that founded such activities and later incorporated this experience into reform efforts on behalf of military education. The lyceums helped frame Carter's professional ideas and fostered a desire to voice his thoughts in a meaningful arena with some hope of instituting progressive change. Assignment to Leavenworth proved to be an important first step in this direction.[42]

The Infantry and Cavalry School had undergone a decade of often-painful evolution since its establishment in 1881. It had at first endured some resistance from the officer corps' tradition-bound rank and file, but gradually received increasing acceptance and even attained some degree of prestige with support from the army's senior leadership. By the time Carter arrived there in 1893, the school had shaken its earlier reputation as merely a "kindergarten" and was making great strides in achieving higher goals as a graduate institution. "Now the majority of young officers are not only willing but anxious to enter the school," Carter boasted, "to test their powers with their many brilliant young comrades, and to profit by the professional training now given." The curriculum emphasized practical application and the syllabus was organized as a progressive pyramid of learning, with each new subject building on the material of previous lessons. Although by no means energizing a grassroots movement toward higher intellectual study, Leavenworth's work was attractive to those officers already disposed to professional activity, and by the early 1890s, it had made great strides toward convincing even its skeptics.[43]

In addition to maintaining command of his troop, which often included leading them in field exercises, Carter was appointed an assistant instructor in the cavalry department. This section was charged with teaching not only the application of mounted troops on the march and in combat but also the theory and practice of hippology—an impressive name for the scientific study of equine care, training, and use. Clearly, his life up to that point had given him a singularly strong resumé for such a position. From the time he was a small boy, Carter had been in close contact with horses, beginning with middle Tennessee's Thoroughbred farms and continuing through his long association with the cavalry. During the years in Arizona, he had made an impressive effort to study equine subjects, reading all available works in the area. At one point, the army even offered to assign him to graduate study at the American Veterinary College. Although he turned down this tempting opportunity, Carter obviously had been singled out as an expert in the field. Later, at Fort Niobrara, he was entrusted with purchasing, inspecting, and training the Sixth Cavalry's remounts—a highly respected job in a frontier regiment that literally lived or died by the quality of its four-legged transportation. Now a part of the Leavenworth faculty, Carter was one of only a few officers specifically charged with intellectual pursuits, and he took the job very seriously.[44]

Teaching the course in hippology made it evident that the subject of horses lacked a knowledgeable treatment suitable for an American reading audience. To fill this void, Carter set about writing a textbook that might become a resource for the general public as well as the army. In 1895, he published *Horses, Saddles and Bridles*, described by a contemporary as "a much-needed . . . manual for cavalry everywhere." It proved to be a work of lasting influence that garnered professional accolades for both him and the Leavenworth school.[45]

Carter's *Horses, Saddles, and Bridles* was not merely a topical study that synthesized extant corporate knowledge on the topic. The book was an attempt to enter the scholarly arena in a subject area that was very important to the period—contemporary interest in the equine species clearly transcended that of recreational enthusiasm. In his preface to a later edition, Carter described his contribution as part of a larger effort by soldier-scholars to carry forward the torch of institutional progress, to "keep pace with modern progress."[46] Like civilian celebrants of higher education, Carter and his peers at Leavenworth viewed formal study as the most effective avenue to a more professional officer corps. In this context, *Horses, Saddles, and Bridles* was more than just a good book about horses—it was a product of Carter's developing belief that a modernizing world required a more sophisticated approach to the military profession.

Only a year after joining the Leavenworth faculty, Carter published his second article, "The Infantry and Cavalry School at Fort Leavenworth" (1894). Written in the same professionalist tone as his first, it stressed the fundamental importance of blending theoretical study with practical application, an assertion that reflected his thorough immersion in the Leavenworth culture. The essay was a clear reflection of the Uptonian ideas that he shared with a growing number of like-minded contemporaries. By this time, Carter had come under the influence of Arthur Wagner, who in 1894 assumed leadership of Leavenworth's Department of Military Art. Wagner was an intellectual who rose to fill a void left by Upton's untimely death. His thoughts on the military profession, as well as his theories of tactics and strategy, were already well known through various articles and books. He emphasized analytical problem solving, and from his education philosophy grew the so-called applicatory method. This approach to military study was drawn from centuries-old ideas on the learning process, but at Leavenworth it was the immediate brainchild of Wagner and his cohort Eben Swift, both instructors of military art. Carter astutely tied this philosophy to the officer corps' professional ascendance.[47]

The applicatory method translated classroom theory to the more practical education gleaned from complex field problems, requiring students to detail various solutions in a standardized format. Thus, Carter emphasized a "happy combination" of theory and practical exercise as the foundation for a new archetype of soldier "who can on the field of battle, with its turmoil and strange scenes, turn theory into practice." For the new military professional, formal study and experiential learning were compatible approaches to the development of more complete expertise. Such conclusions not only demonstrate Carter's wholehearted support for Leavenworth's emergent approach to graduate learning but also offer some insight into his own evolving ideas about the very nature of officership and military service.[48]

As the new century approached, Leavenworth was becoming a sort of cultural icon for the "new army" envisioned by a growing number of forward-looking officers. A professionally educated officer corps was requisite for an army that would enjoy the autonomy and prestige reserved for functional experts. Soldiers of the so-called Uptonian genre saw America's volunteer tradition as a quaint idea with little usefulness in an increasingly dangerous world. Professional education was becoming a celebrated trapping of the expert's social authority, and thus Leavenworth's success amounted to much more than the tangible outcomes of its lessons and exercises. For many officers, it increasingly symbolized the Regular Army's status as America's preeminent martial arm.

Carter's writing reinforced such imagery, portraying the Regular Army and its trained officer corps as a trust for the nation's security. "War has become more and more an absorbing special profession," he declared, "and it is safer for the country to trust its welfare to instructed officers than to leave its fate to the inspiration and patriotism of untrained volunteers."[49] The emphasis on professional instruction differentiated the masterly expertise claimed by regulars from the natural abilities claimed by amateurs. Leavenworth was an important element in this reasoning, as it alone built on West Point's undergraduate experience:

> In the absence of an army of moderate size, it is very important to have at hand the largest number of officers, not only educated in the theory of war, but familiar with all modern improvements . . . accustomed to handling men and performing all the duties of line and staff incidental to actual war, so far as it is possible to learn these requirements in peace.[50]

Carter thus joined others on the Leavenworth faculty who embraced graduate education as a medium which produced soldiers able to think and act with authority in a field that was becoming far too complex for amateur participation.[51]

After expounding the virtues of Leavenworth's role in a truly professional army, Carter offered suggestions for improving its curriculum through a sort of capstone field exercise. This practicum would expand the school's reach by encompassing not only its resident garrison but also regiments assigned to nearby posts, such as Fort Omaha, Nebraska, and Fort Riley, Kansas. In this manner, succeeding generations of student-officers might plan, implement, and critique operations on a scale never before seen in a peacetime army—experiences that would prove a great benefit in case of America's future mobilization for war. Carter argued that the immense advantages reaped from such exercises would far outweigh their fiscal costs, an observation that demonstrated he was acutely aware of the American public's heavily-laden pursestrings.

As he closed "The Infantry and Cavalry School," Carter could not resist adding a short diatribe against the "incessant importuning and wrangling of army officers over staff promotions." Political favor and patronage remained the likeliest avenue by which officers gained assignment to the lucrative staff bureaus, and line soldiers jealously despised this circumstance as an unseemly detriment to army operations. Carter seized the opportunity to advise that staff assignments be made solely from the ranks of qualified officers who had passed examinations for promotion in their respective arm, with, perhaps expectedly, *"due weight being given to diplomas from service schools."* His added emphasis certainly highlighted a conviction that professional education should play a seminal role in an ambitious officer's military career, becoming a discriminator for both promotion and assignment.[52]

Carter believed that formalizing service schools as stepping-stones for career advancement would "popularize" military education in general and "vitalize the perfunctory efforts of many officers with despondent natures." The educated military mind was an important requisite for command in a modern army, and thus institutionalizing its requirement would energize officers' professional participation. By this stage of his career, Carter had little tolerance for soldiers who grew complacent in their technical duties without giving conscious attention to the broader issues that defined their service. These convictions marked him as one of a number of "professionalists" who were gaining stronger voice as they matured in the postwar army.[53]

At Leavenworth, Carter was in an environment that encouraged a critical outlook and allowed him to refine those ideas and observations which had developed over a period of years. The army's continued shift from an active frontier constabulary to peacetime's relative inactivity gave more reflective officers some pause to consider their service's future. They recognized that an army primarily charged with preparedness must by definition concern itself with education, planning, and training. During the 1890s, in an institutional culture that was still defined by Old Army traditions, each of these arenas was alarmingly underdeveloped, and thus Carter and his reform-minded colleagues applied themselves to progressive efforts with no small sense of urgency. From these men flowed ideas that built on Emory Upton's foundation to propose a new army marked by internal standardization, deliberate planning, professional education, and competitive promotion.

In addition to maintaining command of his troop and serving on Leavenworth's faculty, Carter also edited the quarterly *Journal of the United States Cavalry Association* and sat on the central examining board for the promotion of lieutenants in both the infantry and cavalry branches. These positions increased his visible presence as a professional leader and brought him into contact with likeminded peers. "There was much work of an interesting character," he later reminisced about his time in Kansas, "but above all was the value of the opportunity to meet a large part of the young officers of the army." In the officer corps' close community, the assignment placed Carter in an ideal position to absorb the many opinions, complaints, and desires espoused by both students and faculty—discourse that offered valuable insights into the army's cultural disposition. When Carter left Fort Leavenworth in early 1897, it was with a strengthened conviction that the nation was at the threshold of a modern age and that its army required a new direction.[54]

Carter thus developed a philosophy toward his profession that transcended the more traditional outlook of many of his brother officers. For almost twenty years, he had experienced the Old Army in its own peculiar environment, learning about officership from men whose entire personas were defined by service on the frontier as well as in the Mexican War and American Civil War. This culture cared little for formal study and even less for the conceptualization of a more professional approach to military leadership. The Old Army placed a premium on actual experience, for which the majority of officers believed there was no book-learned substitute. But Carter and a handful of other visionaries saw beyond such notions and looked toward a broader definition of military competence.

After remaining at Leavenworth for four years, Carter pursued an appointment to the Adjutant General Corps, a staff bureau charged with administering the army's personnel system and managing its daily correspondence and official records. In practice, the adjutant general's office also gave military advice to the secretary of war, informally carrying on many of the functions that might be expected of a general staff. Although often proclaiming disgust with the staff's lack of field employment, most line officers—Carter clearly included—envied such assignments for their rapid promotion and informal influence. Thus, competition for the comparatively few openings in the staff was sharp and the prize was justifiably considered worthwhile.[55]

Like many of his peers, Carter's application to the staff was likely motivated by a combination of personal ambitions and concerns for his family's well-being. But as he considered his future in the army, the adjutant general's office must have seemed a very appropriate step for one so keenly interested in the army's institutional progress. This inclination was readily apparent to those around him, and endorsements to his application make it clear that Carter already carried a reputation as a thoughtful soldier with an active professional interest.[56] Staff duty promised the opportunity to voice his opinions and even exert some small influence on more senior institutional decisions. But, as Carter himself pointed out in his essay, a competitive application to the staff required not only an impeccable record but also highly placed political endorsements. Apparently not entirely immune to the political "wrangling" for which he claimed disdain, Carter secured the sponsorship of Sen. William B. Bate, a Tennessee Republican and an antebellum family friend who was active in congressional military issues. Bate's influence with the War Department almost certainly played a role in Carter's eventually successful application, but it seems unlikely that his support alone could have overcome the heavy endorsements wielded by many of Carter's competitors. A growing professional reputation combined with his impressive field record set him apart and made him a logical choice for the adjutant general's staff.[57]

Even though it meant leaving behind his beloved cavalry and the camaraderie of a western post, Carter relished the prospect of making some relevant contribution to the army's progress. After serving for almost two decades in the field, he had little desire to play a continued role as the army presided over the disappearing frontier. "We were too busily engaged in getting all the Indians had that any of our voters wanted," he remembered with disgust. "My Indian service had been a long and character building experience for me, but I was glad to go to other duty while the adjustment of the wild tribes to so-called civilization was worked out." The American West no longer held the lure of adventure and glory. Carter looked forward to satisfying his ambitions with another challenge, that of the army's transition to modernity.[58]

8

A New Secretary and an Era of Reform

In 1897, Carter put on the rank of major and reported to the War Department as an assistant adjutant general, embarking on an endeavor that would become the defining legacy of his military career. He was forty-five years old and had served in the army for over twenty years, but the very nature of his occupation was changing. As a line soldier, he had witnessed firsthand the army's struggle with a military system that was still largely left over from traditions that began even before the War of 1812. Now, as a staff officer, he hoped for the opportunity to facilitate progress.[1]

In replying to congratulations from Gen. George D. Ruggles, adjutant general of the army, Carter asked that he be allowed to address the issues of examinations for officer promotion and also the army's lyceum program—areas of personal concern that he believed were of fundamental importance to the officer corps' professional development. His declared "special purpose" was to effect change that better suited the needs of the line: "It is a subject of grave interest to line officers and every step of revision would have to be gone over very carefully. I make no pretense of being better fitted than others but it is a subject to which I have devoted much labor and I sincerely hope to see a change, both as to Examinations and Lyceum work." Although careful to subdue his enthusiasm in deference, Carter's reply to Ruggles left little doubt that he intended to leave his stamp on the American army.[2]

At the adjutant general's office, Carter wisely set about learning the ropes of a bureaucratic system and culture that was just as foreign to him as putting together a supply train of pack mules might have been to a career staffer. He quickly overcame any preconceived notions that he could solve the army's organizational problems overnight. The staff bureaus functioned in a world far removed from that of a frontier regiment, and Carter recognized that reforms of the magnitude he envisioned would require corporate knowledge and insight applied with a subtle touch at exactly the right time.

Just as he sought the wisdom of older, more experienced officers years earlier on the frontier, Carter spent his first weeks in Washington as an eager student of department-wise bureaucrats, absorbing the intricacies of his job while developing relationships that would prove beneficial in the future. He later recalled that the

> time spent in that way was of great moment to me when the War with Spain began, for I had acquired a very good idea of the routine, so often referred to as 'red tape,' of the department, but what was of more consequence, I had made the acquaintance of the officers and chief clerks of bureaus and divisions, and knew where and by whom the different subjects received attention and final action.[3]

He was preparing for his new duties in much the same manner that he had learned about Apache warfare from the Apaches themselves. To Carter, the chasm that separated staff from line was just as deep and perhaps even as menacing as the more obvious cultural divisions he had encountered when first thrust among the Indians.[4]

As he requested, Carter was assigned to rework the system of officer examinations for promotion. This had been a controversial issue almost since the exams were introduced in 1890 at the direction of General John M. Schofield. Previously, officer promotions had wallowed in a stifling system of strict seniority within each regiment. This approach failed to reward merit, thereby encouraging mediocrity. The 1890 act expanded opportunity for promotion to each branch of the line and required written examinations in an attempt to standardize competition. In theory the measure was sound, but in practice it lacked coherence as examinations varied a great deal and were often poorly written. Never missing an opportunity to highlight a perceived misfortune, line officers soon branded the new process as something less than satisfactory. Perhaps spurred by his own frustrations, Carter set out to address the system's inequities as his first effort on the staff.[5]

Up to this point, Carter's own career had advanced at a painfully slow pace. After spending seventeen years as a lieutenant and seven more as a captain, promotion to major had come only by virtue of his recent staff assignment. But his story was by no means uncommon by the day's standards. Many officers commissioned during or just after the Civil War spent years or even decades at junior or company-grade rank with little hope for further promotion. After having led large numbers of wartime volunteers at the head of regiments, brigades, or even divisions, many veterans later spent in excess of twenty years at lower grades with relatively menial duties and responsibilities—a circumstance that gave rise to bitter frustration and divisive intrigue among ambitious men. In 1893, the average captain was already fifty years old, certainly past that age normally associated with a warrior's youthful vigor. Promotion based on seniority within a particular regiment had become an unbearable weight on the officer corps' professional well-being, making it a subject of some importance even to senior officers who had little to gain personally from the system's revision.[6]

Carter believed that the process instituted in 1890 was fundamentally sound and helped to build professional awareness by providing an "impetus to the closer study of authorized manuals and text books." But he acknowledged that numerous complaints of unfair examinations contained a degree of truth, making it evident that promotion practices still required further revision. His investigation into this subject also exposed a related failure: the glaring need for an improved approach to officer education and training.

As part of a proposed solution, he developed standardized situational problems for the use of promotion boards in their examination of officers who came before them. These problems were written in the contemporary Leavenworth mold, integrating theory with practical application. Carter asked the president of the first board that subsequently convened to send him the very best answers he received so that they might be disseminated as examples to aid officers in their preparation. He was astonished when the board president forwarded the submissions but noted that none of them were good enough to serve as a model. After reviewing the work himself, Carter could only shake his head and agree, finding it a sobering commentary on the sad state of his profession.[7]

While he was at Leavenworth, shortcomings in the army's approach to officer education had become disturbingly evident. Though the lyceums and schools of application pointed in the right direction, they still lacked the coherence of a truly graduated system of military instruction. When he reflected on the comments sent to him by various examining boards, Carter realized "that nothing but systematized study would fill the measure of the department's expectations." Like the graduate study that was then developing at contemporary universities, professional military education had to become a hierarchy of learning. Beginning with West Point's undergraduate foundation, each step had to build on the one that came before it, integrating classroom material with the officer's experience and level of responsibility. Convinced that he was right on the mark, Carter continued to turn this concept over in his mind, but the opportunity to champion its cause would have to wait. For now, he concentrated on learning the intricacies of the staff, and was very quickly immersed in his new job by an accelerated and wholly unexpected flow of events.[8]

As the nation rushed pell-mell toward war with Spain over affairs in colonial Cuba, the disjointed military policies that Carter had endured on the frontier were played out before his eyes in the War Department's halls. Like most Americans, he believed that physical intervention in Cuba was merely the final exasperated reply to a history of Spanish provocation. Although frustrated to look on from Washington while so many of his peers took the field in Cuba, he was given an unequaled opportunity to witness expeditionary warfare at its most senior levels of planning and direction. Carter was assigned to the AGO's personnel division, responsible for administering the army's nominations, appointments, commissions, and orders. But the conflict's rapid mobilization quickly drew him into broader issues that went well beyond duties normally undertaken by an inexperienced staffer, giving him a rare view of the complexities of a democracy at war.[9]

The nation's jingoistic newspapers so excited public opinion in support of the war that seemingly every American male clamored for his fair share of uniformed glory. The War Department was inundated overnight with demands for military appointments and commissions, and these were often distributed according to the applicant's political influence with very little if any consideration for actual ability or experience. Carter watched with disgust fueled by personal and institutional pride: "Many elderly men, unfit for grueling war, were elevated to places for which they were eminently unqualified, while trained and younger men were turned away. It was degrading and dangerous to fill military offices as was done at that time."[10] From a senator's son-in-law to cabinet members' personal friends, many dozens of men with few qualifications beyond enthusiasm and a claim to political favor received commissions or special appointments. This chafed Carter's professional self-image, especially when many such men were promoted "over the heads" of experienced regulars whom he considered infinitely more deserving.[11]

The Civil War, extolled as the citizen-soldiery's shining glory, now haunted Uptonian-minded professionals as a reminder of the dilettantism that they had worked so hard to overcome. Carter pointed to President McKinley's own volunteer experience in the Union army as a detrimental influence on current War Department administration: "The President had entered the volunteers in 1861, ignorant of the military profession, as were most of the men on both sides in the Civil War. He emerged from the war as a major, and simply did not have any fear of disorganizing the army by appointments of men no more ignorant of war than he had been."[12] Carter looked on in horror as the army he revered was adulterated by amateurs who enthusiastically put on uniforms with little regard for any notions of professional competence. As the staff bureaus scurried to keep pace with overwhelming demands to organize men, material, and transportation, he became even more convinced of the dire need for fundamental reform at all levels of national military policy. He had arrived in Washington with this opinion already developed, but the war's haphazard mobilization of ill-trained and otherwise wholly unprepared citizens turned it into a consuming conviction.

In early April, only two weeks before formal declaration of war, Carter was appointed, along with Lt. Col. Arthur Wagner and Lt. Col. Theodore Schwan, to a board charged with formulating plans to meet the impending crisis. These officers shared a professionalist mindset and placed little faith in an amateur's ability to become an effective

soldier without prolonged training. Their report opened with the contentious statement that "it is a well-known fact that raw troops can
not be depended upon to conduct offensive operations successfully."
It is not surprising, then, that they recommended an expeditionary
force relying to the greatest degree on trained regulars and only "the
best regiments and batteries of the volunteers." Seacoast fortifications and other garrisons could be depleted to allow as many Regular
Army units as possible to take the field. Volunteers would be integrated into active brigades according to a sort of expansible concept
and led by regulars—an overt reflection of traditional Uptonian-style
thought. Although large parts of the plan were subsequently approved in spirit if not in letter, its application became quite confused
in the ensuing rush to war.[13]

Following bitter debate, legislation of 22 April 1898 created a
volunteer army drawn primarily from existing state and local organizations and led by state-appointed officers. Regulars saw this as a
galling mistake, preferring instead to bolster the existing army structure with federal volunteers. The measure implied that the nation's
defense remained largely reliant on the citizen-soldier tradition then
embodied by the National Guard, a contradiction of the Uptonian emphasis on highly trained expertise. But even if the act was a poor compromise, it reflected the popular values of the time, a point probably
missed by Carter and his cohorts at the War Department. Though
mollified somewhat by the Regular Army's expansion to 65,000 troops
and the later addition of federally led U.S. Volunteers, professionalists
saw the bill as a travesty for the war effort and a triumph of the
militia's powerful political influence.[14]

The war in Cuba brought the nation's lack of military readiness to
the front pages of American newspapers. Although the victory over
Spain was roundly celebrated, the effort vividly demonstrated the
military establishment's inability to plan and conduct operations
against external foes. The small frontier army had barely been adequate (and only arguably so) for the Indians Wars, and its employment
overseas stretched both line and staff to the breaking point. The militia system also proved unequal to the task, and the mobilization of
tens of thousands of volunteers was marked by deplorable conditions
in many of their encampments. Although American soldiers fought
and served with all the courage and determination of their forebears,
the system itself floundered. Like so many others, Carter "was sur-

prised that so much was accomplished under a system so defective."
In words that echo Carter's conclusion, Russell Weigley offered a
pointed historical judgment: "The army stumbled to victory less because of its own prowess than because of the even greater disorganiza-
tion and demoralization of the enemy."[15]

In the war's aftermath, Carter, newly promoted to lieutenant colonel, saw grand opportunity for substantive change as Senator Grenville M. Dodge opened formal hearings to investigate the conflict's
disjointed efforts. "Incidents, trivial in themselves, sometimes are of
far-reaching effect," he later wrote. "Out of this postwar discord developed opportunities for army reforms which, probably, could never
have been carried out under normal, routine peace conditions." With
the army under intense scrutiny, the war provided an obvious argument for just the sort of reforms that Carter envisioned.[16]

To careful observers, the problems encountered in 1898 did not
result only from the Regular Army's numerical weakness, but from
failures in the basic relationships prescribed by American military
policy. Carter believed this situation would be self-evident to anyone
who cared to look beyond the surface:

> Our arms were uniformly successful on land and sea, yet
> while holding in contempt the sensational scandals pub-
> lished in some newspapers, the average American was shrewd
> and thoughtful enough to appreciate how very fortunate his
> country had been. Those who were closest to the sources of
> information, while not at all inclined to pessimism, recog-
> nized that we possessed an unlimited supply of men; beyond
> that point much was in doubt and confusion for want of pre-
> vious preparation.[17]

He was far from alone in this conclusion, but previous attempts to
find solutions, notably the prodigious work of the Burnside Committee in 1878, had met with little success—thwarted to large degree
by opponents' unwillingness to revise traditional mindsets. "Various
investigating boards and commissions had been convened," Carter
observed, "but under our peculiar system no useful effect was obtained . . . on the contrary, real reform was delayed."[18]

Although several postwar army bills contained interesting provisions, they were quickly lost amid partisan squabbling and gen-

eral disagreement. Confusion reigned in a hopelessly divided field of would-be reformers. In the War Department, it was Adj. Gen. Henry Corbin, Carter's own boss, who may have provided the greatest obstacle to reform in 1898. Corbin, a product of the status quo bureau system, wielded extraordinary influence over Secretary of War Alger, ensuring that any proposals emanating from the department maintained traditional staff-line relationships. As the target of postwar inquiry, Alger showed little ability to patch together a concerted effort, even had he been willing. His half-hearted attempt became known as the "Hull Bill," named for its sponsor, Rep. John A. T. Hull. The measure was conservative at best and promised very little in the way of real institutional progress. But alternative proposals scarcely offered more, although one put forth by Rep. George B. McClellan, Jr., son of the ambitious commander of the Union Army of the Potomac, would have combined the adjutant general's and inspector general's offices into a single general staff–like agency.[19]

In Congress, the Hull Bill and its competitors became mired in a political rhapsody that grew from partisan divergence on the issue of Philippine annexation. Democrats opposed steps to plan and execute long-term control of the islands, and viewed the army bill suspiciously as part of imperial efforts to subjugate the Filipino people. Conversely, Republicans argued for an enlarged Regular Army in terms of national expansion, and the two parties remained deeply separated on any related question. "The fact is that the increase of the standing army and the colonial policy of the Government are so closely interwoven, so intermixed," opened a Nebraska congressman, "that you can not well discuss one without discussing the other." Immediate postwar reforms were thus fettered from the start by their inextricable association with larger political debate, obscuring attempts to make an objective case for much-needed change.[20]

By this stage of his career, Carter fully grasped the dangers of allowing military legislation to become entangled in larger political and ideological issues. Since his earliest days at West Point, when the academy was embroiled in external social debate, he was constantly aware that the army was never far removed from partisan politics. Even questions seemingly devoid of contentiousness and defined solely in objective military terms somehow became catalysts for heated political discourse that skewed outcomes. As he saw it, current efforts were doomed to failure not because of any flawed argument but merely because they were not sufficiently removed from accompanying political baggage:

> Immediately following the war with Spain the question of reorganization was taken up by the War Department and a bill was submitted to Congress providing for an increase in every branch, but without any change in staff administration. It was supposed this would avoid any controversies, but defeat was encountered at the hands of Senators who opposed any permanent increase of the army. The result was a compromise measure of so unstable a character as to necessitate entirely new legislation after the Presidential campaign.[21]

Recognition that a much larger context surrounded military reform was a meaningful first step toward eventually framing and shepherding a bill through the Washington gauntlet.

Meanwhile, partisan debate on the Hull Bill ended in a compromise measure (under threat of Democratic filibuster) that temporarily increased the Regular Army's strength and authorized additional volunteers, but did virtually nothing to redefine the army's internal structure. The act passed the Senate on 27 February 1899 and was approved by the House three days later. In their initial disappointment, most regulars failed to recognize the measure as a symbolic victory that edged American military policy toward professionalist ideals. But Graham Cosmas accurately highlights it as a "long step toward one of the principal goals of Regular Army progressives: total federal control over the formation and administration of all military units." Carter, who along with Schwan helped draft the compromise, later maintained that "the Act was a temporary makeshift" that merely "tided over the emergency and gave time for the proper study of necessary army reforms." The entire process provided a painful education as he watched the measure suffer through several iterations before finally becoming law.[22]

With public pressure mounting in reaction to the fiasco in Cuba, Secretary Alger became the favored scapegoat. "Long-continued and violent criticism of conditions seemed to demand a sacrifice," remembered Carter, "and the Secretary of War surrendered his portfolio." On 1 August 1899, McKinley appointed civilian attorney Elihu Root to replace Alger, an act that bode well for Carter's personal career

as well as his progressive agenda. The president's choice was somewhat enigmatic. Root had excellent credentials in the legal field but
was wholly unacquainted with military issues when he accepted
McKinley's nomination. As he later told the story, his initial response
to the offer was less than enthusiastic: "Thank the President for me,
but say that it is quite absurd, I know nothing about war, I know
nothing about the army." Despite misgivings, Root proved a quick
learner and almost immediately became an active agent for military
reform.[23]

Root's experiences as a prominent New York corporate attorney
had paired him with the nation's industrial plutocracy, an association
that detracted from an otherwise impeccable reputation he enjoyed
as a man of no-nonsense integrity and ethics. According to one biographer, he had developed a rather "inured" attitude toward contemporary social issues, making him a less-than-likely candidate to lead
public reform of any type. But McKinley hoped that Root's brand of
pragmatic leadership would overcome the hidebound culture that
hampered the War Department's inner workings. Root thus assumed
office with a broad, if ill-defined, mandate to "restore self-respect in
the War Department" and bring some semblance of modern efficiency to the nation's military administration.[24]

Carter believed that McKinley preferred an attorney to head the
War Department due to the army's contemporary involvement in
prickly legal questions of global acquisition. The recent direction of
U.S. foreign policy certainly pushed the nation's soldiers and sailors
onto the stage of imperial governance with a complete lack of preparation for the role. This factor may have influenced McKinley, but it
seems unlikely that Root's experience defending New York's industrial trusts would be of any particular benefit to him as the head of a
tightly stretched military system. It was more important that the
president find someone with a firm grasp of administrative detail
who could approach the job with few embedded notions of how an
army should be run. The new secretary certainly fit this description.
Root "entered the War Department without any special knowledge of
military affairs," Carter remembered, adding that "perhaps it was
best for the country that this condition existed, for it induced him to
apply his great mind to the study, not only of the details of military
affairs, but to all the higher questions of military administration."
The war in Cuba made it clear to even the uninitiated that the army

required modification if it was to remain the strong arm of a newly expansionist foreign policy.[25]

Whatever the motivation for McKinley's choice, Root's appointment and accompanying mandate was encouraging to Carter, whose own influence in the War Department had expanded beyond his rank by virtue of the war's immense burden. In only a few short months, his stake had grown from junior assistant adjutant to department insider who was entrusted with framing important legislation. Under the cloud of dissatisfaction that chased Alger from the cabinet, there was little doubt that the coming months would provide Carter with ample opportunity to advocate the Uptonian ideas that he had been nurturing for two decades. Root quite naturally looked beyond the tradition-bound bureau chiefs as he searched for more progressive input. Very few officers who understood the army's bureaucratic administration were not already encumbered by its narrow vision. From his desk at the War Department, it must have seemed to Carter that the professionalists' time was finally at hand.[26]

Only a few weeks after assuming office, Root's intentions were made very clear in his first annual report as secretary of war. Instead of mimicking past efforts that addressed problematic symptoms piecemeal, he would reach to the very foundations of military organization and policy. He followed this declaration by repeating Sherman's earlier assertion that the Regular Army's primary peacetime mission was to prepare for war—a purpose that necessitated the systematic study of warfare and the educated planning for "all contingencies of possible conflict." In this first report, laid before Congress and the public, Root implicitly threw the authority and influence of his new position behind the Uptonian quest for a more modern army.[27]

Essential to Carter's vision of a new army was an officer corps steeped in a graduated approach to professional study. If the Regular Army was to claim its place as a prestigious fortress of martial preparedness and expertise, then it had to exhibit the recognizable trappings of this role. By the turn of the twentieth century, higher education was already the requisite platform for such pretenses, as a growing number of civilian disciplines staked their claims to social autonomy and prestige via the halls of burgeoning graduate schools. In a similar manner, the army's formal study of the military art would act as a sort of cultural gate to enable and legitimize a larger process

of progressive change. Root very purposefully noted this relationship when he linked professional education to the "plans for action
under all contingencies," a statement which forecast his support for
the more general reforms that were already contemplated by many
within the officer corps.[28]

Establishing a capstone professional school or war college was
only the beginning of the many institutional reforms envisioned by
forward-thinking soldiers. Prompted by Upton's observations in *Armies of Asia and Europe*, professionalists looked to an American general staff as a remedy not only for the disjointed interests of the staff
and line, but also as the foundation for a redefined chain of command.
They hoped to clarify the vague relationships that existed between
the secretary of war, the commanding general, and the several staff
bureaus. Although such hopes were plainly self-interested—the line
would clearly benefit from staff reform—they were also founded on
years of frustrating experiences in the field. From Carter's perspective, establishing a system of officer education was only a logical first
step toward treating the more difficult issues of staff reform—the true
prize of military progress.[29]

Root quickly became aware that there were officers around him
who shared his interests in reforming the army. Carter already carried
a reputation as a professionally opinionated officer and his proximity
made him a likely resource as the new secretary familiarized himself
with the issues at hand. His first audience with Root was not long in
coming, and he seized the moment to shout the virtues of progressive
change:

> The Secretary asked me one day what the trouble was in the
> Army. I began to unfold the ideas which had been in the
> minds of many officers, especially those embodied by Gen.
> Emory Upton in his report on "The Armies of Europe and
> Asia." His interest was immediately aroused. . . . I made many
> notes and briefs for the Secretary, and had many conversa-
> tions with him on the subject of the introduction of a General
> Staff in our Army, but there was so little known in Congress
> about the necessity for such an organization we felt sure of
> opposition of a very decisive character."[30]

For his part, Root was very receptive and began to see Carter and his
reform-minded colleagues as potential allies in the development of

his own plans: "The army has many able, educated, and competent officers who have thought much upon the subject but who have been unable to secure a change.... It is not reorganization which is needed, but the grant of opportunities for development along lines which are well understood and appreciated by the Army itself."[31] The relationship that grew between Root and the reformers was thus one of shared interests—a collaboration of thought and resources in which each party offered something of seminal value to the greater whole.[32]

Carter attempted to guide Root's interest during these early months by giving him a copy of Upton's *Armies of Asia and Europe* and then discussing with him the various ideas promoted therein. The secretary quickly grasped the salient issues surrounding military policy and accurately estimated the very political nature of the task that lay ahead. He recognized Carter's able hand and began looking to him as an expert tutor in the army's cultural peculiarities. From this beginning, the two men formed a lasting partnership that would, in its aggregate strength, bring success where others had failed.[33]

Root's intellectual relationship with his military advisors has since become the subject of scholarly discussion. Russell Weigley once questioned whether the turn-of-the-century impetus for military progress emanated primarily from internal sources (individuals within the regular officer corps) or the external influence of civilian intellectual trends. While suggesting that Root's proclivity for reform grew from his own philosophical links to the contemporary Progressive movement, Weigley minimized the influence of professional soldiers, emphasizing instead the developing civilian affection for organizational efficiency. "It was the civilian reformers," he hypothesized, "their interest precipitated by the Spanish American War, but sustained by the same search for order that generally characterized the Progressive era, who mainly supplied the initiative for army reform." But Root readily acknowledged that the basic framework for his ideas already existed, as shown to him by Carter and others at the War Department. Progressive activism might have oriented the secretary but it was by no means the primary catalyst for institutional shifts that took place in the army under his watch.[34] The historian William Roberts supports this assertion, characterizing Root as a political enabler who maintained a "delicate balance between opposing forces" while serving "as a spokesman or an interpreter of the reform proposals of army officers."[35] As a noted contemporary later wrote to

Carter: "Elihu Root is rightly called the Father of the General Staff, [but] we all know that the *real* origin and stimulus and brains came from yourself, for which Mr. Root has been always generous in giving you credit."[36]

But this is not to imply that progress was carried out with little more than figurehead-style support from the civilian secretary. The Root-era reforms were a genuine product of cooperative effort, a melding of executive clout with military ideas. In addition to the enthusiasm exuded by Carter and other professionalists, substantive progress required politically astute leadership to translate abstract ideas into workable legislative and executive action—an alliance that was missing from Emory Upton's earlier efforts to achieve similar outcomes. Success came only after the soldier's institutional vision was united with Root's shrewd guidance through Washington's legislative maze.[37]

Despite the historian's natural interest in identifying very specific determinants for actions and ideas of the past, the Root Reforms, like the reformers themselves, were products of complex influences, each adding its unique incentive to the collective quest for progress. Root came to the War Department at an opportune time with few preconceived notions of the army's proper direction, gaining insights into both the staff and line perspectives from professional soldiers around him. He evaluated these ideas and accompanying biases in the context of his own experiences and beliefs (certainly influenced by Progressivism and the period's emphasis on organizational efficiency), shaping conclusions that eventually helped reconcile existing Uptonian ideals with American political and cultural realities.[38]

In his first annual report, Root articulated his concept of the army's professional purpose and then served public notice that he intended to take specific steps toward this end. The "real object of having an Army," he concluded, "is to provide for war," and therefore the Regular Army's peacetime role was quite simply to study, plan, and prepare for that contingency so that a larger citizen-soldiery could rally to its standard in time of crisis. Here Root was on hallowed Uptonian ground, echoing a genre that drew its lineage through John C. Calhoun's "expansible army" all the way back even to the ideas of George Washington and Alexander Hamilton.

Pursuant to this definition, he then outlined several "requisites"[39] to the proper preparation for war: first, that an army war college should be established and vested with duties and functions very similar to those of a general staff, a term that was then only vaguely defined in American military circles, although used often with almost iconic reverence; second, that officers participate in the formal study of their profession and that such participation should continue throughout an officer's career; third, that staff billets be filled by rotation from the line; fourth, that the officer promotion system be modified to ensure a greater element of professional merit; and finally, that individual efficiency records be kept for the purpose of helping to determine officer assignments and promotions. Root believed that collectively these changes would bring the army to a footing of true professional expertise, better able to stand as the bulwark of national defense in a new century.[40]

Initially, perhaps as a means of blunting expected opposition, Root did not intend to remake the army with broad sweeping strokes, but instead sought to act through a more evolutionary process: "I believe that without any revolutionary interference with the general scheme of organization . . . a great improvement can be made in the way of conforming the organization and training of the army to its true purpose." Except for the creation of a war college, his themes were aimed at modification, making the army operate more effectively in its existing mold. With Carter's prodding, the secretary would later abandon this course and look toward more transformational goals, but in 1899, his objectives remained comparatively cautious.[41]

Nonetheless, Root's first report must have stirred concern in many members of his audience even as it generated excitement in others. Despite imperial policies that demanded a more able Regular Army, the American public remained fixed to more traditional views of military service—far removed from the sort of professional fighting force envisioned by Carter. Looking back, it might now seem as though the army's march toward modernity was a foregone conclusion pressed forward by a wave of events, but reformers would find the status quo a formidable opponent. Even if ultimate success was still in doubt, Carter and his like-minded colleagues had gained a powerful ally in the struggle. Invoking the Progressive imagery of his times, Root described the American solder "as part of a great machine which we call military organization." This "machine," he asserted, "is defective; it needs improvement; it ought to be improved."[42]

9

EDUCATING A NEW ARMY

S oon after Root made known his reformer's intentions, he began by creating the first War College Board. In late February 1900, Root ordered Brig. Gen. William Ludlow to chair a board to "take preliminary measures towards the organization of a War College for the Army, including the formulation of a project and general regulations for its future conduct and guidance." Army Special Orders no. 42 appointed Col. Henry C. Hasbrouck and Lt. Col. Carter as additional members, with Joseph P. Sanger added as a fourth member later that spring. This committee, sometimes referred to as the "Ludlow Board," was charged with developing both a concept of operations and an organizational plan for the institution:

> The purpose of the Department in establishing this College is to further the higher instruction of the Army, to develop and organize in accordance with a coherent and unified system, the existing means of professional education and training, and to serve as a coordinating and authoritative agency through which all means of professional military information shall be, at any time, at the disposal of the War Department.[1]

Root made it clear that he expected the board to act without delay, realizing that the political window of opportunity might well be short-lived.[2]

When the board convened for the first time on 26 February, it determined that the task at hand required a preliminary investigation of the existing war and staff colleges of other nations, as well as the U.S. Naval War College, established in 1884. After discussions that lasted into the following day, it was decided that Carter would undertake a thorough study of professional military education as well as the organization and functions of general staffs. From this simple record of the board's first meeting, it is evident that, just as articulated by Root, the subject of professional education in the form of a war college was part and parcel related to the subject of a general staff. Many within the army viewed a war college not only as an educational course in military theory and the like but also as a functioning body that might assume many of the roles currently performed by the staff bureaus. This concept of a multi-functioning war college was by no means a new idea either to Americans or to their European counterparts.

The Prussian Kriegsakademie had existed since 1810 when German reformer Gerhard von Scharnhorst was instrumental in its institution. Like Fort Leavenworth's Infantry and Cavalry School some years later, this German "war academy" had gone through its own set of growing pains, attempting to find the proper combination of basic academics, military theory, and field application. After the Prussian chief of staff, Helmut von Moltke, won decisive victories over Austria in 1866 and France in 1870, the world's armies closely scrutinized the German system in search of a key to modern battlefield success. In rapid succession, other nations adopted elements of its unique practices. In the United States, Emory Upton brought attention the German model with glowing descriptions in his book *Armies of Asia and Europe,* dedicating almost five pages to the Kriegsakademie alone. He carefully pointed out that "at the outbreak of the Franco-German War, every general in the Prussian army was a graduate of the War Academy," and concluded that such a school was an indispensable feature of a truly modern army.[3]

Since Upton's publication first appeared, calls for an American war college had become commonplace in professionalist writing and were often married to more general discussions of military reform. In

"An American War College" (July 1889), Arthur Wagner declared that Fort Leavenworth's steady professional and academic progress would soon give it the "proud claim of being a war college in every sense of the term." A few years later, in an essay that won the Military Service Institution's annual writing award, Capt. James S. Pettit asserted that a war college was an "essential part" of a modern, flexible staff system, for which the U.S. Army was sorely wanting. Thus, when Root chartered the War College Board, he did so in answer to a decades-old plea from within the officer corps itself.[4]

When the board met again on 8 July 1900, Carter had given the subject a great deal of thought and presented a formal report of his conclusions. He suspected that preexisting concepts of a war college's function probably clouded the board's thinking, a condition that might also confuse subsequent efforts to establish an effective institution. "Some of the ideas embodied in the letter of instructions appear to have brought confusion into the minds of the members of the board as to whether or not the War College is to become an active administrative staff bureau of the Army," he wrote, again displaying the brash confidence that marked his earlier endeavors. Carter believed that any attempt to combine permanently the functions of a general staff with those of a war college would only dilute the effectiveness of each of these important roles. He also doubted that such a combination could be accomplished without "infringing to some extent upon the legal duties of the present Corps [staff bureaus]," possibly invoking a legal argument in an appeal to Root's own interests and professional background. He thus began a conscious campaign to align the board's opinion with his own.[5]

Instead of politically shying away from explicit disagreement with Root's original instructions to the board, Carter seized the opportunity to highlight contradictions between his own vision and that suggested by Corbin's letter:

> Some of the ideas embodied in the original scheme for the War College . . . do not properly belong to a staff school or war college, but rather to one of the active administrative corps of the Army. Whether these questions are to be solved or administered upon by the Adjutant General's Department or Inspector-General's Department, or a combination of them, or by a new corps to be designated the general staff, is some-

thing for consideration between now and the re-convening of Congress. In order to reap the best results, however, it is absolutely necessary not to confuse war college instruction with staff administration of the live affairs of the army.[6]

In the above argument, Carter shrewdly plays to the sensitivities of his audience, implying that the alternative course might threaten the staff bureaus' legally defined missions. In a War Department still stinging from recent scrutiny, board members were very aware that any moves to divest the staff's authority—whether real or imagined— would meet with swift and likely vengeful opposition.

However, Carter's resistance to a war college that functioned as a general staff–like planning body was certainly not motivated by mere legal concerns. Instead, his position grew from fears that leaving the existing staff system in place without permanently changing the army's fundamental relationships of command and staff would be an incomplete and short-lived solution. After three turbulent years in the AGO, his suspicions of the bureaus' pervasive influence were confirmed. Any reforms that stopped short of creating a true general staff would effectively be foiled by the inertia of tradition and self-interested bureaucracy: "It was improbable that any chief of bureau would ever recommend any serious modification of a system under which he was one of a powerful group." He rightly concluded that a war college must be established primarily as an instructional institution to prepare senior leaders and that staff functions were better vested in an entirely independent body with a more utilitarian role.[7]

That Root originally planned the war college to function as a de facto general staff has become a topic of discussion among historians. Some hold that Root misunderstood the true nature of a war college, failing to realize the army's need for an institution that would graduate leaders who could think and evaluate issues on a broader strategic level. These scholars have pointed to the war college's early struggle for definition as evidence of this failing. But, as others have pointed out, it was instead a pragmatic compromise with the realities of doing business in Washington's tangled political forest. Carter's narrative unequivocally supports this latter conclusion. Root's decision to proceed with plans for a war college that performed roles normally associated with a general staff was, in the end, only a clever expedient to circumvent expected opposition from both Congress and the bureaus themselves. Although at first uneasy with its implications, the War College Board, like Root, eventually understood this gambit as a necessary opening. Carter was at the time refining his own thoughts on the subject, and was beginning to see with clarity the distinction between a general staff and a true war college. He recommended that the Ludlow Board report on two very separate courses of action: "One to embody the formation of a War College with instruction carried on by the university extension scheme of education, and the other to contain a plan for the formation of a General Staff." The board agreed that this idea had merit and warranted further development prior to constructing a final report.[8]

When the board adjourned on 8 July, members were each given specific areas to study before their next meeting. Carter was asked to consider the army's professional schools and also—in committee with Sanger—to build a conceptual plan for a general staff corps. For his part, Ludlow announced plans to depart for Berlin to observe and report on German military institutions of similar purpose. When the board reconvened later that fall, it was prepared to report on the issues with which it had been charged.[9]

The act of separating a general staff from the proposed war college has created some confusion for later observers. Historian Eugene V. McAndrews believed that the notion originated with Ludlow: "It seemed apparent to Ludlow as he assigned his board members their duties that Root sought more than just the creation of a War College," wrote McAndrews. "He saw that it was the beginning of a staff. Ludlow assigned Carter the task of studying the existing service schools and the possible organization for a General Staff." While this narration is technically accurate—Ludlow likely shared Carter's conclusions and, as board president, assigned topics for further consideration—it also ignores the recommendations laid before the board in Carter's "Memorandum—War College" of 8 July. The prospect of establishing a separate general staff corps that would centralize army staff and planning efforts by no means originated solely or even primarily with Ludlow, as evidenced in close proximity by Carter's report on the topic. It is very likely that to some degree the entire board shared a conviction that the army required a true general staff as opposed to merely adding its proposed functions to the war college's mission. But it was Carter's memo that articulated these thoughts in coherent fashion and thus documented his increasingly strong feelings on the subject. That the idea gained strong support among fellow board members is evident inasmuch as they eventually offered parallel recommendations.[10]

During the months that followed the July meeting, Carter worked to prepare a report that would strengthen his position on the planned reforms. He studied each of the army service schools as part of a greater, more systemic approach to professional education, and also put together a proposed bill to create a separate general staff corps of the kind contemplated by Upton. He viewed each step of an officer's education as important for the type of corporate expertise required of a modern army. Carter believed that an increasingly activist foreign policy demanded a more professional soldiery than that which he had joined in Wyoming decades earlier: "Upon the three service schools and the lyceums will fall the work of preparing officers to give the instruction necessary in a new army, the bulk of which are men of short service or recruits. Nothing but unceasing application and painstaking care will insure creditable results."[11] Bombastic rhetoric and jingoistic newspaper editorials justified overseas adventures before the voting public, but the more difficult task of executing such ventures would fall to the army's cadre of regular officers.

With an Uptonian voice, Carter called for wholesale reorganization of the army schools, invoking America's history of martial illpreparedness to emphasize his call for change:

> The history of all wars in which America has been called upon to organize armies, teaches emphatically that the gravest question which has uniformly confronted the government was the scarcity of trained officers, both line and staff. . . . The present Administration could leave no more worthy recognition of our recent war experience than to nourish and build up at once the great central schools of instruction, where regulars and volunteers alike can fit themselves for the high duties of commanding men, thus enabling these war schools to attain their highest usefulness.[12]

At the same time, in a manner somewhat self-aggrandizing, he claimed accolades for a new generation of officers that developed under the influence of heightened professional awareness in the 1880s and 90s:

The success which has attended the efforts of our generals has been largely due to the excellent state of instruction which has obtained amongst the junior officers whose professional ability and courage have stood every test. The service schools, especially that at Fort Leavenworth, deserve high praise for fostering a spirit of comradeship, enterprise and high professional attainment which assured the success of our arms upon widely dispersed fields of action.[13]

Carter was almost giddy about the grand opportunities that now seemed within his grasp. Root's appointment was a propitious stroke that virtually guaranteed his ideas a receptive audience.

The efforts of Carter and the War College Board were not the only actions in the name of American military progress. The army's strides toward increased professionalism did not occur within a vacuum. In addition to the dramatic changes taking place in civilian institutions, the U.S. Navy was also undergoing its own professional development with halting but nonetheless substantive results. A Naval War College presaged the army's own institution by several years, and in 1900 a group of reform-minded sailors were pursuing their own steps toward staff reform. The progressive interests and motivations of naval officers were similar to those of their army counterparts, and so their efforts were often parallel. In fact, it was Sherman's pioneering thoughts on military education that sowed naval reform through his influence on Admiral Stephen B. Luce, an officer who had served on Sherman's wartime staff and later founded the Naval War College. Luce consciously patterned the navy's senior institution after the army's contemporary schools at Forts Monroe and Leavenworth. During its first two decades of existence, the Naval War College had functioned primarily as an educational experience, but students also fulfilled a pseudo-staff function as they developed many of the navy's strategic plans.[14]

During the month of June 1900, Carter visited the Naval War College in Newport, Rhode Island, to view its operations firsthand. He noted that the school suffered much of the same frustration that met Leavenworth during its own embryonic stages—"the detailing of officers who have neither inclination nor interest in the work."

Nevertheless, Carter, after attending classroom lectures and watching several practical exercises, concluded that the Naval War

College was a resounding success in its efforts to increase technical knowledge while also prompting thoughtful discussion on contemporary issues from a maritime perspective. He returned to Washington thoroughly impressed by what he saw in Newport, and was convinced more than ever that a similar course would be of infinite value to the army.[15]

That summer, Carter spent many hours with Root discussing proposed reforms. The two men often went on afternoon horseback rides to escape the War Department's bureaucratic maze and sort through the day's more interesting problems. Carter, whose frontier heroics must have intrigued the urban-bred Root, became an expert resource to the secretary as he sought the finer details of his new job. He provided Root with insights into the army culture as it framed the work ahead, adding color and texture to the professionalist vision of a new army and pointing out the challenges that had foiled previous such attempts. This friendly advisory relationship, combined with Carter's invaluable corporate knowledge of the department's inner workings, may have cost him the chance to fill a primary leadership role in the China Relief Expedition.[16]

After it was decided to send an armed force to relieve the American legation in China during the Boxer Rebellion, Carter pressed to join the staff of General Adna Chaffee, a longtime friend from the Sixth Cavalry. Chaffee had been given command of the expedition and Carter ached to play an active part, being still somewhat bitter that he spent the entire Spanish-American War pinned behind a desk on the Potomac. Root politely refused this request, but assured Carter that he would be released from his staff duties if the Chinese situation deteriorated into general warfare. "As a sop to my disappointment I was handed a copy of a cable message to General Chaffee, stating that, 'If campaign assumes proportions Carter will be sent to you as chief of staff.' " He was still the cavalryman at heart and longed to take the field despite the years spent amid Washington's oak officescapes and bureaucratic red tape.[17]

But work in the War Department continued undistracted by world events, and Root asked Carter, who was already serving on the War College Board, to prepare a more permanent plan for army reorganization. This topic had been addressed only temporarily by the stopgap measure of 2 March 1899 that followed in the wake of the failed Hull Bill. Carter had appeared before the Senate Military Committee during debate on the 1899 act, and thus possessed a strong basic knowledge from which to begin work on a new measure. Authorization for an enlarged army terminated in July 1901, and Root wanted to preempt a last-minute partisan struggle by proposing politically digestible legislation months in advance. On 24 July 1900, the secretary sent a letter to the army's senior officers requesting input on the topic. The replies he received, although sometimes insightful and even thought-provoking, were too conventional in their scope, primarily revising the existent organization and suggesting little in the manner of fundamental change. The reforms that Carter had in mind were more pervasive in their reach, and he was already hard at work crafting such a bill when the original War College Board came together for the last time.[18]

When the board met again on 9 October, Carter laid out the foundation for a more systematic approach to professional education, consistent with the hierarchical graduate studies then becoming characteristic of the civilian professions. In its summary response to the secretary, dated 31 October 1900, the Ludlow Board recommended that a proposed war college fulfill several functions: "supervision of military education and information; provision for higher and special training for the command and management of troops and the conduct of military operations; and the original consideration and report upon the various aspects of military administration in general."[19] Although here the board charged the college with roles normally associated with a general staff, they closed with an important caveat that reflected Carter's previously voiced concerns:

> The Board, therefore, while convinced that the War College, if established and consistently sustained, can be made to effect valuable results, specially urges that the necessary legislation provision for a General Staff, on thoroughly considered and effective lines, be recommended for incorporation in the military service of the United States at the earliest possible time as a permanent feature of the organization of the Army.[20]

Thus, after almost a year of deliberation and careful study, the War College Board followed Root's purposeful instructions—temporarily rolling both staff and educational functions into a single entity—but warned that the expediency should be discontinued at the soonest possible hour.

Attached to its summary report was a five-page "Memorandum as a Basis for an Executive Order Establishing an Army War College." The duties delineated in this document were alarmingly broad and included many singularly important arenas. The war college would attempt to fill a great void by coordinating the army's several staff activities while at the same time functioning as a capstone professional course, planning for operational contingencies, and administering the army's education and training at all levels of organization. This overwhelming mission statement seemingly tried to solve all of the army's problems with one fell swoop. Carter's fears that each of these functions would suffer in the attempt appear to be well founded. But Root astutely recognized that first establishing a war college under executive order would build momentum for the political brawl sure to follow any attempt to dismantle the staff bureaus outright. Once the war college safely existed in fact, regardless of its prescribed duties, the more difficult task of creating a true general staff might be undertaken with leverage. Translating this strategy into executive and legislative reality would be no small undertaking.[21]

Carter's work on the War College Board embroiled him in a somewhat embarrassing and very regrettable conflict with Ludlow's widow and other family members. Several months after Ludlow's return from Europe in the fall of 1900, he submitted a lengthy report of his observations to the secretary of war's office, presumedly through the adjutant general. This report addressed a wide range of military topics, and was written in the highly technical style that earmarked much of Ludlow's professional work. It was subsequently misplaced or inadvertently destroyed in its path through the War Department, and its whereabouts remained unknown despite several attempts to locate it.[22]

Carter later recalled that Ludlow had mentioned very little about his observations of the Prussian system during the War College Board's October meeting, and did not produce draft copies of any report for the other members. Carter subsequently asked both Ludlow's military aide and civilian clerk for any such materials so that they could be entered into the board's formal proceedings—a reasonable request since Ludlow had made the trip to Germany as part of his official duties as board president. Neither of these men had any knowledge of an existing report or memorandum, nor did they know of General Ludlow's intention to produce one. This seemingly inconsequential set of events only became complicated when Ludlow died prematurely in the Philippines on 30 August 1901, and was thus not around to narrate his own role as the Root Reforms took shape. Carter gave the matter no further thought until almost a year later, when Ludlow's brother, a retired navy admiral, inquired as to the report's disposition.

Admiral Nicoll Ludlow implied that his deceased brother's work was being used as a template for army reform without receiving due credit, a charge that indirectly attacked Carter's personal integrity and sense of fair play. Several months later, Ludlow's widow followed up her brother-in-law's inquiry with a similar complaint, to which Colonel Sanger, acting for Root in his absence, requested an explanation from Carter. Carter indignantly refuted any inference that Ludlow's report had been purposely suppressed or shelved by him or anyone else, and presented a very plausible account of the circumstances.[23]

Carter claimed that the first time he had seen General Ludlow's report was in late June 1902, when General Henry Corbin had discovered a carbon copy piled beneath other work on his own desk. Corbin recalled that over a year earlier Ludlow had given him this personal copy—which he had filed away without reading—and supposed that the original had been hand-carried to Root. Corbin ventured that Root might have lost the original when moving to a new residence about the same time. For his part, Carter steadfastly maintained he had not read the report with any thoroughness until Mrs. Ludlow's inquiry, even when Corbin handed him this carbon copy to file in the AGO records:

> The report formed no basis of action in regard to the General Staff Bill and was never read by [myself] until long after the passage of that bill. . . . The loss of this report appears to have been due to General Ludlow's desire to hand it personally to the Secretary for if it had been sent in the usual way to the Adjutant General it would have gone to the Mail and Record room to be there recorded and entered before being submitted to any official.[24]

In his own defense, Carter stated that although "thousands of recommendations and reports" surrounding army reform had been written and submitted in recent decades, they had not been translated into substantive action until the current efforts undertaken by Root and himself. Thus, he reasoned, credit for the American conceptualization of a general staff was shared by a great many with equal claim, but credit for the act itself was rightly claimed by only Carter, Root, and those few others who directly helped in the process. "I am sure that no one was more earnestly in favor of the establishment of a General Staff than General Ludlow, but . . . I know of no action taken by him towards the passage of necessary legislation." In conclusion, Carter offered to discuss the situation with any representative that the Ludlow family cared to appoint, and regretted that the apparently innocent situation had been twisted into such a negative light.[25]

Despite this reasonable reply, Ludlow's closest friends in the army still harbored some animosity toward Carter, believing that he had consciously denied Ludlow a personal legacy in connection with the General Staff Act—a serious allegation in an officer corps blessed with an absurdly exaggerated sense of personal honor. Years later, in an interview with U.S. Army historian Harold Cater, Maj. Gen. Frank R. McCoy, one of Ludlow's staunch supporters, recalled approaching Carter about the matter while both were onboard a ship heading to the Philippine Islands. During this conversation, Cater related, "Carter gave him such a plausible explanation . . . that he was convinced Carter was right." Without Ludlow's personal testimony, the historical record on this issue remains incomplete, but it seems apparent that this relatively minor sideshow grew from the very fact that many officers, Ludlow included, shared Carter's professionalist vision of a functioning general staff, both in concept and in many details. When the vision finally came to fruition, many participants quite rightfully felt that their thoughts and proposals, in whole or in part, had been given life. But it was Carter who wrested physical action from extant ideas, and thus quite deservedly received the lion's share of credit for its eventual institution. Although later protective of his own role in the Root Reforms, there is no evidence that he ever consciously deprived others of their rightful due.[26]

With the Ludlow Board now dissolved, Carter could focus his attention on the forthcoming army reorganization bill. His work on the measure had begun months earlier, and in February 1900 a preliminary version of the bill had even passed the Senate. However, after partisan disagreement in the House, the act was tabled due to Republican fears that contentious debate on any military issue might

create a Democratic soapbox for embarrassing anti-imperialist sentiment during a national election year. In the months since, Carter had
continued to refine the proposal and fervently pushed to add provisions for a general staff. But Root wisely declined to launch such an
attempt until the much-needed political support could be marshaled.
He instructed Carter only to "draft a bill which should contain the
necessary force to meet the immediate requirements of the service,"
and to wait for a more favorable moment to press for the creation of a
general staff. Carter dutifully acquiesced and assured the secretary
that "in going over the bills submitted last year and the year before, I
have endeavored to select carefully that which you desire to go into
the new bill." In December 1900, a new army bill was submitted to
Congress without a general staff proposal. This effort illustrates the
complementary relationship that grew between Carter and Root, a
vital foundation for their eventual success in the name of progress.[27]

Carter and Root's mutual interests had a synergistic effect toward
carving progress from a system that had resisted change for several
decades. Root recognized that Carter's thirty years of military service
had given him a keen understanding of the army's professional and
organizational needs. Carter understood as well as anyone in the
army the institutional fabric that now desperately needed alteration.
Yet he lacked Root's natural political instinct, so indispensable in the
Washington struggle for legislative solutions. Other participants—
such as Ludlow, Sanger, and later Tasker H. Bliss—most certainly
added other voices to this cooperative effort. But during the vital
period of 1900–1903, it was Carter and Root who kept the War Department moving forward. As Harold Cater surmised, each supplied
"ingredients which neither possessed by himself but which were absolutely essential in the recipe for the making of a General Staff."
Together the two men developed a working relationship that allied
Carter's subject-matter expertise and enthusiasm with Root's political acumen, a combination that finally overcame plaguing obstacles
of inertia, self-interest, and partisanship.[28]

Carter found the Washington environment a frustrating venue
for the work of a reformer. The political wrangling that accompanied
almost every public decision proved time and again the same conclusions he had drawn about the nature of military affairs while still
a young West Point cadet. He realized even then, with much consternation, that political and social concerns were an annoying but

ever-present backdrop for military issues. This truth was played out a hundred-fold as Root led reforms down a political path of least resistance:

> I had now been in Washington long enough to learn the ways of Congress, and the extent to which politics was carried even in measures involving the national defense. . . . If nothing but the public service had to be considered, it would be a simple matter to reorganize and improve the existing military establishment from time to time. The human element, with its exaggerated ideas of the rights of and deference due to long occupancy of office, plays an important part and must be reckoned with.[29]

Carter had learned that, at least in a republic, military decisions did not take place in an objective vacuum defined solely by experts who "knew best" for the national good. This unwelcome axiom had exasperated Upton and other reform-minded officers in the past, leaving them despondent about the possibilities of ultimate success. But Carter pragmatically reconciled himself to the unwelcome nature of the game at hand and hoped that the opportune position in which he now found himself might still bear professional fruit.[30]

In drafting the reorganization act, Carter applied skills that were learned only through keen observation of the legislative process. He had gained much from his earlier work with Schwan as well as from accompanying Root before various congressional committees. Carefully watching the Washington political system operate gave him ample opportunity to contemplate strategies for future use. He was by now painfully aware that a measure's ultimate success often hinged not so much on its substance as on its political trappings or outward appearance. Carter readily acknowledged that much of what was proposed during the Root era was not original in its content but only in the manner in which it was framed: "There was much of stable character and tradition around which to build. Most lawyers content themselves with efforts to interpret statutes, and I had learned that the essential thing in preparing a bill was to express the intention in such language that honest men would not disagree as to the meaning or intent of words."[31] The secretary's office had received numerous letters and memorandums with opinions on the projected army reorganization, but much of this material proved "practically useless" when applied to the realities of writing public policy. Carter looked for help elsewhere, turning to men who—though lacking high title— possessed the true expertise to help him write a successful bill.

Carter adopted a resourceful habit of asking senior War Department clerks to look over early drafts of his legislative projects. Their criticism was invaluable in helping him prepare for questions that were very likely to arise in committee. "I based the law on the previous laws in the archives of the Department," Carter wrote, "and got my advice from old and experienced clerks . . . who had long been the responsible parties for army administration." There are interesting parallels between this practice and the practical education he had sought years ago from frontiersmen in Wyoming and Apache scouts in Arizona. Although the classroom had certainly changed, the results were apparently very similar—with an open mind, he learned a great deal about the business at hand from those who knew it best.[32]

When finally completed, Carter's reorganization bill went to congressional committee, where it was subjected to excruciating debate and repeated examination. As the so-called Philippine Insurrection dragged on, Congress was preoccupied by intensely partisan discussion of the administration's imperialistic foreign policy. The Regular Army's numerical strength and organization could not be separated from this larger argument. Expiration of the temporary measure (March 1899) was quickly approaching, adding a clear sense of urgency to the War Department's lobby for further action. On 2 February 1901, the bill finally passed with the vote running almost along party lines in both houses. Sanger, Carter's former colleague on the Ludlow Board, enthusiastically described line officers as generally "delighted with the Army Bill," and added that "nothing comparable to it had passed in the [military] history of the Country during the forty years I have been in service, and this seems to be the general opinion." Line officers could look to the measure as an opening success in the battle to break the staff's crushing grip on army bureaucracy.[33]

Although its primary purpose was to provide a permanent increase in the army's strength, the measure also took minor steps to rein in the staff bureau's dominance. It stipulated rotation between officers of the line and staff and also directed that subsequent heads of the staff bureaus and departments would serve for only four years, a provision that unfortunately did not affect the permanent appointees already assigned. These actions would not only broaden officers' professional experience and knowledge but would also dilute the cultural dissension that heretofore divided line and staff. Carter proudly noted these hopeful outcomes as a boon to the officer corps' professional evolution: "The establishment of a detail system for the various staff bureaus has opened a wider field of training for line officers, because it is now possible for them to perfect themselves along various lines not directly connected with their own arm, with the expectation that they will be allowed to put their knowledge into practical application in some one of the various departments."[34] The concept of staff-line rotation was by no means new to the 1901 Reorganization Act. Upton had recommended this course in *Armies of Asia and Europe* and the idea had been well represented in professionalist circles ever since. In 1878, James A. Garfield, then a congressman, had called for an end to the practice of permanent staff assignments in an article specifically written to marshal support for army reform. However, it was only after Root had mustered the full weight of his considerable political influence that such ideas were finally translated to reality. On 6 February 1901, War Department General Orders no. 9 implemented the act. Although often overlooked among the Root era's more celebrated victories, it was a significant first step beyond the Old Army's traditional structure toward a more modern military organization.[35]

The bill's passage ended an effort that Carter later described as the "most comprehensive task" given him during his time at the War Department. Fortunately, his next venture gave him a short break from Washington's tedious existence. Perhaps the months of hard work were beginning to wear on his good humor, because Root graciously sent him to Puerto Rico for a short visit that might combine business with a few days of much-needed relaxation. A conflict had developed concerning claims on buildings used by the army there, and a representative from the War Department was needed to help mediate the issue. Feeling the strain of endless meetings and congressional hearings, he gratefully accepted the assignment as a chance to leave Washington's stale hallways behind, if only for a few days.[36]

The journey began as something less than a vacation when Carter became seasick during a storm shortly after departure. But once past this initial obstacle, the trip proved an enjoyable and rejuvenating distraction. After spending several uneventful days in Puerto Rico, followed by brief port calls in Cuba on the return, he arrived back in Washington with renewed enthusiasm for the struggle. With the Reorganization Act now in place, attention turned to the more pervasive changes that Root had in mind.

At the heart of Root's conception of the Regular Army as a sort of brain trust of American martial expertise, was the army's responsibility to engage in a "systematic study" of the military art and science. Among the activities that the secretary painstakingly listed as characteristic of a modern army was the "study of the larger problems of military science and the most complete information of the state of the art."[37] Here Root referred not merely to an undergraduate training but to a "thorough and broad" education of the type found at American graduate schools—an approach that would dignify the army's claims to professional status. He did not discount practical training and experience as important facets of a soldier's education, but asserted that "the officer who keeps his mind alert by intellectual exercise, and who systematically studies the reasons of action and the materials and conditions and difficulties with which he may have to deal, will be the stronger practical man and the better soldier."[38] Like Carter, Root was convinced that the days of the natural-born warrior were now inarguably of the past. The world had changed and so too had the nature of military leadership. A new army for the dawning twentieth century required educated leaders steeped in the various complexities of the modern military art.

To this end, as noted in his earlier instructions to the Ludlow Board, Root sought a formal war college that could develop, organize, and coordinate a larger, more comprehensive system of professional military education. Officers were to nurture and maintain an active intellectual interest in their profession and this Root described in terms of higher-level discourse: "The comparison of different views, the contribution of different minds, the correction and evolution of discussion, the long continued, laborious, and systematic application of a considerable number of minds of a high order."[39] In language suggestive of contemporary evolutions in civilian higher education, he advised a truly graduate approach to officer education, in which participants would foster not only their own professional growth but also that of the institution generally. A war college would become the vaunted crest of this system, where the individual parts of professional development and study would come together in a coherent whole.[40]

Several crude historical models for such an institution certainly existed in the United States' military establishment, although none approximated the level of development and influence envisioned by Root. Perhaps the earliest of these was the Board of Navy Commissioners that was active from 1815 until 1842. This body of three senior naval officers served as a very rudimentary advisory committee to the secretary of the navy. Later, the War Board instituted by Secretary of War Edwin M. Stanton during the American Civil War, the Naval War Board during the Spanish-American War, and the so-called Secretary's Cabinet formed by Secretary Alger during that conflict's aftermath, all exhibited elements of the intellectual and functional characteristics desired of an army war college. As historians Herman Hattaway and Archer Jones highlight in their discussion of Stanton's War Board, it was the informal coordination sparked by these entities that predicted the later purposes of a war college or general staff. But unlike each of these American predecessors, the proposed war college would serve primarily an educational role, functioning as both a learning institution unto itself and also as a forward-looking bellwether for an entire system of army schools.[41]

In the spring of 1901, after returning from his brief sojourn to Puerto Rico, Carter rejoined the subject of officer education when he was sent to report on the status of the army's several schools of application. These institutions had unceremoniously closed when the army was overwhelmed by its mobilization for the war with Spain. After three years of physical neglect, it would be no small task to reopen the schools on a footing commensurate with their roles in a greatly enlarged officer corps. "With the reorganization of the army and the appointment of about one thousand new officers," Carter noted, "the question of instruction and training became one of paramount importance." Thus, the 1901 Reorganization Act, Root's opening salvo in the name of military reform, underlined the pressing need for a more efficient, systematic approach to professional military instruction. At Root's request, Carter took up the task of developing this concept and crafting an executive order for its implementation.[42]

He began by preparing a lengthy memorandum explaining his position that officer education should undergo a thorough review,

with changes extending even to its most basic level. The post lyceums, instituted by Schofield in 1891, had degenerated into "a very
defective system . . . which in general depended upon the personal
[qualities] of the commanding officer and with but few exceptions
had fallen into disrepute." The lyceums' curricula and format varied
so widely among garrisons that the program was sometimes completely unrecognizable from one post to the next, and in some commands was most accurately described as nonexistent. Officers never
actually "progressed" in the program or completed the instruction
in any given area, "forever going over and over the same things in
a perfunctory and half-hearted way without hope of graduation."
Though in complete agreement with its concept, Carter decided that
the lyceum system required extensive revision if it was ever to become a useful pillar in the larger scheme of army education.[43]

Rather than simply a continuing activity that was largely unrelated to any coherent outcome, the lyceums would become an elementary floorboard for a greater system, ensuring that officers were
prepared to meet the professional expectations of their grade. Standardized instruction would develop company-grade officers who were
not only competent in their current duties but also prepared for the
next higher level of responsibility: "If the lyceum can be made an effective means for training the lieutenants primarily in all their duties
including [military] theory, they would enter the service schools better qualified to take up the course than would be the case under the
present system of lyceum instruction."[44] The need for standardization grew in part from frustrations with the number of company-grade
officers who in the past had reported to Leavenworth without the
proper theoretical knowledge or even practical skills. Despite General Schofield's best intentions, the lyceums' haphazard application
did little to build any uniform competence or baseline knowledge
among young soldiers. Carter hoped to correct this troubling fact by
rebuilding the army's postgraduate schools from the bottom upward.[45]

His solution was a more formalized system of "garrison schools"
that would complement a progressive approach to education. Really
just an evolution of the lyceums, this plan called for courses to be
conducted at each post but with a standardized curriculum to "cover
the duties required of all first and second lieutenants, including the
theoretical knowledge of the various service manuals [and] Army
administration." One of the salient features of Carter's proposed gar-

rison schools was that a record of each officer's work would be kept as an indicator of his professional performance. At the end of each term or "season," a local board of more senior officers would examine participants and award certificates for satisfactory completion of each subject. Those who failed to meet expectations would be required to repeat the course. If an officer did not pass a failed subject on subsequent attempts, he would meet a higher board and the case could even progress to eventual discharge. This element of rewards and punishments, although perhaps detracting from the program's more erudite claims, would allow the army to identify and rid itself of officers who refused to participate in their chosen profession. Conversely, distinguished performers would attend the higher service schools, creating a merit-based pyramid of graduate instruction.[46]

The army's several branch schools, such as the Cavalry and Field Artillery School at Fort Riley and the Artillery School at Fort Monroe, remained as places where officers would hone specialized skills with an emphasis on practical experience. Carter specifically earmarked Fort Riley to function as a very focused practicum, conducted as if it were a "well-ordered post" with students gaining experience in the various billets and functions of a normal garrison. At the same time, Fort Leavenworth would broaden its orientation, shedding its branch affiliation as an infantry and cavalry school. Selected officers of all branches would now attend Leavenworth to learn the theoretical and practical skills of administering, supporting, and leading large numbers of troops both in garrison and in the field—benefiting from exercises conducted with actual units assigned there. Student officers who excelled and demonstrated potential at this intermediate level would then progress to an even higher rung to study their profession on the level of strategy and policy.[47]

The proposed war college, to be established in Washington, D.C., would be the system's pinnacle with a two-fold purpose. The school would operate on similar lines "to those of the Naval War College, except that young officers, detailed as heretofore indicated, from the service schools should remain on duty continuing their studies as available candidates for the General Staff, while the regular class, to be composed of officers as high as the grade of colonel, should participate in the work of the college during a portion only of each year."[48]

The war college (or "staff college," in the event that Leavenworth was renamed "war college"—there was some confusion regarding the naming of each institution) would prepare some officers for assignment to a still nonexistent general staff, while offering a shorter course of instruction to others (Carter suggested four months for the latter program after observing the Naval War College). While most graduates would simply return to a line regiment, a select few would become part of the general staff, an instrument for infusing their ideas directly into the nation's military policy.

Carter conceptualized a general staff as an institutional mind or nucleus, a repository for the army's professional expertise. Rather than merely assuming the very specialized administrative functions performed by the contemporary staff bureaus, it would take on a broad array of duties that required the ability and resources to consider military problems as they existed on a higher level of national policy. In a memorandum to the adjutant general, which presumably ended up in Root's hands, Carter defined the general staff's duties in a manner that clearly outlined his ideas:

> The duties of a General Staff should be to take charge only of such records as concern the Military Information Division, and the duties of its officers should be to supervise the War College or staff school, to mature in peace all the possible plans the trained mind can devise for war in such probable fields of action as any complications with other nations could bring about; to serve with all the various branches of the Army; bringing together a knowledge of the armament, equipment, and instruction of all kinds in one central bureau, where measures could be devised for correcting defects and improving existing conditions.[49]

Of course, even the prospect of such an entity would spark strident opposition from those whose personal careers were built on the bureaucratic authority of the existing staff system. Creating a general staff would require no small victory over the significant obstacle posed by the War Department's institutional inertia—perhaps the single most difficult fight that Carter would encounter during his military career. Realizing the challenges that lay before them, Root and Carter built a strategy that in the end proved very effective.

Carter's memorandum received Root's blessing and he immediately began work on an executive order to implement these ideas. Taking executive action instead of pursuing a more permanent congressional act was a carefully considered decision that carried with it an element of risk. By choosing this course, Root and Carter sidestepped a potentially damaging confrontation with politically powerful traditionalists, but at the same time left the army's education system vulnerable to future executive whim. Subsequent administrations could just as easily reverse the order, thereby dismantling the army schools and undoing the work of progress with the quick stroke of a pen—a risk that under the circumstances was regrettable but nonetheless wholly preferable. Cognizant of this danger, Carter avoided adding provisions that dared usurp the existent staff organization, thus hoping to strengthen chances that the order would survive future administrations intact.[50]

In a second memorandum that served as a sort of abstract for his proposed order, Carter again voiced his opinion that any staff functions vested in the war college by executive action should be shifted to a permanent general staff corps at the earliest feasible opportunity. After "a great deal of time and research," he remained convinced that any effort "to imbue the War College with General Staff functions is doomed to failure."[51] Clearly, he felt confident that whatever personal relationship he enjoyed with Root allowed him the liberty of unequivocally speaking his mind. After five years in Washington working within the very bureaucracy that he despised, Carter eschewed normal proprieties in his aggressive dedication to army reform.

Accompanying this memo were two proposed acts. The first was a final draft of an order to establish a coordinated system of officer education for the army. The second, as might be expected, was a preliminary draft of a legislative bill to create an army general staff. In Carter's mind the two actions were now inextricably related. He believed that a truly professional officer corps required not only a graduate system of education but also a centralized mind specifically entrusted with institutionalizing the army's collective expertise. Secretary Root signed the education order with only a minor change in language that politely paid homage to Leavenworth's pioneering contributions, and on 27 November 1901, it became an executive act. Carter's second proposal, pertaining to a general staff, remained shelved for the time being as Root contemplated the next step toward a new army.[52]

General Orders no. 155 established the army's education system on a parallel plane with that of contemporary institutions of higher education. Its overall purpose was to build and maintain high standards of purposeful instruction and preparation within "a coherent plan by which the work may be made progressive." To this end, it instituted a multi-tiered educational experience that began at West Point and progressed through a pyramidal system to its capstone, the newly established Army War College.[53]

An officer would receive instruction in the skills of a company-level subaltern at the garrison schools and then attend one of the service schools for further study in his particular branch or technical skill. The most promising were then selected to attend the new "General Service and Staff College" at Fort Leavenworth, a course that developed competencies across a breadth of professional areas. Top Leavenworth graduates would then matriculate to the War College, to be located originally at Washington Barracks in the nation's capital. This system of postgraduate education was carefully designed so that each level of learning might address an officer's current and immediately forthcoming duties and responsibilities. The curriculum was intended to progress from a primarily tactical arena to subjects concerning staff and command functions, and finally, to a broader study of military strategy and policy.

Leavenworth's important new role as a more generalized staff college, with instruction in "all arms of the service," was thus intended as an intermediate step between the garrison schools and the War College. Officers who demonstrated potential at the post schools, as well as those who did likewise at the branch schools, would be considered for assignment to Leavenworth. The Staff College curriculum, reflecting the clear pedagogical ancestry of Carter's colleagues Wagner and Swift, would continue to combine theoretical instruction with practical exercises. At the end of each class period, those "student officers as have especially distinguished themselves" would be recommended to advance up another rung of the army's educational ladder to the War College—the epitome of professional military study and application.[54]

In creating the Army War College, Carter was forced to meld its more permanent educational intent with its temporary role as a de facto general staff. But still, as historian George Pappas points out, his "emphasis was on the educational character of the institution, not on its functioning as the General Staff nor as a part of such a staff."[55] Carter maintained that the college was never meant to pursue a traditional course of classroom instruction. Instead, he described the program as a truly graduate experience, placing it atop a pedestal as the army's highest institution of professional study. Accordingly, Carter believed that War College graduates should be assigned to positions where their skills could be most useful. Like the War College itself, they could serve as a braintrust for the army's institutional direction. The guiding force behind this new system, which would ensure its intended fruition, was a second War College Board—a committee whose function would, at least for the time being, closely approximate that of a general staff.[56]

The War College Board, chaired by the president of the War College, was given powers to "exercise general supervision and inspection of all the different schools," an intentionally broad description that allowed its duties to evolve as required. The board consisted of five permanent members, "detailed from the army at large," as well as four "ex-officio" members: the chief of engineers, the chief of artillery, the West Point superintendent, and the commanding officer of the General Service and Staff College. In addition to supervising the new educational scheme as explicitly ordered, this body was clearly meant as a convenient transition toward a true general staff. Whether the concept came solely from Carter or not, the provision for a War College Board reflected his conviction that the War College eventually must function as an educational institution, complementary to but wholly separated from the duties of an independent general staff.[57]

In case the order itself left any doubt, Root underlined the intended status of the War College Board in his 1901 Annual Report: "The creation of the War College Board, and the duties which will be imposed upon it, as indicated in my report for 1899, is probably as near an approach to the establishment of a General Staff as is practicable under existing law." Though creating the board as a sort of expedient, Root now shared Carter's belief that only a permanent general staff might successfully provide the coordination and foresight required of a modern army. "A body of competent military experts should be charged with these matters of the highest importance," continued Root, opening his next campaign in earnest, "and to that end I strongly urge the establishment by law of a General Staff, of which the War College Board shall form a part." Harold Cater mistakenly interpreted this statement as evidence of Root's shallow grasp of the general staff concept and its relationship to the War College. Cater argued that "Root's preoccupation with the War College Board in this passage, and his absurd suggestion that the Board might even approach the performance of General Staff work" were indicative "that he had not yet grasped the full import of the meaning conveyed by the term 'General Staff' to anyone connected with the army in Germany." But this charge seems to ignore Root's carefully nuanced purpose.[58]

By noting that the board "is probably as near an approach . . . as is practicable under existing law," Root merely prepared his audience for the more permanent general staff that he "strongly urges" in the next paragraph. The very fact that he chose to establish the embryonic semblance of such a body by General Orders no. 155 only underlines the difficult terrain on which he and Carter were forced to strategize reform. Mimicking the Prussian or any other conceptualization of the term "general staff" was much less a concern to these men than the hard reality of building such an institution within the American military-political system. As the last member of the Ludlow Board still assigned to the War Department, Root's personal confidant, and by now a veteran reformer, Carter was an obvious torchbearer for the uphill legislative battle that would surely follow.

Carter believed that recent American experiences in the Caribbean and Pacific were only precursors to further foreign entanglements that would grow from the nation's expanding interests. In language that forecast "military preparedness" themes heard a decade later, Carter wrote, "[I]t has been clearly recognized that the present status of our country before the world makes it absolutely necessary that preparation for war should be more general than ever." Many of his peers shared this conviction, worrying that the army was not physically organized or intellectually prepared for its modern role in a more activist foreign policy. In James Abrahamson's estimation, "military officers placed foremost among threatening developments the 'new imperialism' that dominated European international politics in the nineteenth century's last quarter." Carter's parallel conclusion framed his approach to further reform.[59]

Shortly after beginning work on Root's legislative effort for a general staff, Carter took public stock of the army's recent progress and at the same time stumped for more. In "The Training of Army Officers," published in 1902, he applauded both staff-line rotation and the more systematic approach to professional education. But while acknowledging the positive impact of these changes, he reminded his colleagues that much good work still remained. "Everything that could be done to perfect the organization of the line for the immediate future has been carried to a successful conclusion," he proudly noted, but added that "it is remarkable and incomprehensible that there has never been a body of officers in our country made responsible for our military policy, nor for the preparation of plans of campaign and for national defense." Without such a body, Carter argued, Americans were blind to their own defense while the world around them became a smaller and much more dangerous place.[60]

Although the Army Reorganization Act and General Orders no. 155 were both founded on extant ideas, it was clearly Carter who played a primary role in translating those ideas into action. Carter's professional thought was shaped by many influences—certainly the writings of Upton and his Leavenworth service alongside Wagner and Swift are most easily identifiable among them. Upton's general arguments for a more professional army and even details of his proposals can be found in both instruments, as can the ideas of other officers involved in the process. It would be absurd to argue that Carter's work was accomplished single-handedly or that his convictions grew solely from original thought. Nonetheless, it was *his* painstaking efforts that translated professionalist ideals into coherent executive and legislative acts, bringing progress where others had only pleaded and wrung their hands to no avail. Root's role was that of a guiding force, providing the political strategy and public voice that simultaneously encouraged Carter and ensured the bureaucratic access for eventual success.

As Carter anticipated the coming battle to create a general staff, he saw it as a worthy capstone for the army's transition to modernity. He believed that the Old Army could become something better—a more efficient organization led by men who were well prepared to plan and conduct military operations in an industrialized world. A general staff became a sort of defining objective, taking on an almost iconic cultural importance that transcended even its intended role. With the groundwork for a system of professional education now in place, Carter set about its creation, believing that "upon its work success must hinge if we are to operate the army in an economical and business-like way." For forward-looking officers, a new army was finally drawing near to the horizon.[61]

10

Creating a General Staff

As Carter attempted to craft a workable general staff bill, he began to see the task as much broader and more complex than merely creating a functioning department with the proper resources and skills. A general staff corps, as he conceived it, would change the very relationships of command and authority upon which the current system depended. If a general staff was established as a nerve center for planning, mobilization, and operations, then, instead of the nominal commanding general of old, the army required a chief of staff who would serve as its central authority and also as "advisor and executive" to the civilian secretary of war. Although Carter realized such a proposal would excite hostile resistance, the more he studied the issues that demanded a general staff, the more convinced he became that the army's command structure was an indelible part of the remedy.

It seemed to Carter that any informed observer could not reasonably deny the army's urgent need for a general staff. Instead, opposition would come from selfish concerns by those with a vested interest in maintaining the status quo—the bureau system was an undeniably rich depository of individual power and influence. "The General Staff idea has been the subject of many essays and much discussion for some years in this country," Carter wrote. "Almost every scheme heretofore drawn up has encountered a personal obstacle, because the formation of such a corps naturally interferes with the present business methods of the War Department." After much deliberation, it was clear that these "obstacles" could only be overcome by redefining those traditional "business methods" themselves.[1]

At first Carter approached the general staff issue as separate from the plaguing frustrations of the army command structure. Perhaps naively, he assumed that a general staff corps could fit neatly into the current establishment, without disturbing the office and role of the commanding general. But this office had existed in confusion ever since Jacob Brown, the army's first commanding general, had felt about blindly for the boundaries of his new office. Hamstrung by an ill-defined role, its relationship with executive authority and even the rest of the army had often been tumultuous. The usual result was severely strained relations between the commanding general, the civilian secretary of war, and the chiefs of the various staff bureaus—a situation that was painfully exacerbated by the headstrong and overbearingly ambitious men who most often inhabited each of these offices. Personal intrigue and vicious vendettas marred matters still further, mocking the military concepts of good order and unity of command.[2]

Gen. Winfield Scott's legendary (and highly entertaining) antebellum quarrels with Secretary of War Jefferson Davis are perhaps the most notorious example of these troubling circumstances, but even in more recent years, the relationship had rarely encouraged cooperation. As commanding general, William T. Sherman became so embittered toward the secretary's office that he, like Scott before him, sought refuge by moving his headquarters from Washington until coaxed back by a secretary more to his liking. Nelson Miles was only the latest occupant of the office to be at loggerheads with an administration, but his vehement opposition to military reform was a personal feud that grew from his particular background. Miles was a Civil War volunteer whose postwar rise was marked by aggressive self-promotion. Even as the army's senior officer, he remained outside professionalist circles and was highly suspicious of their agenda. As William Roberts notes, "The commanding general had always led the fight for staff reform in the past," but Miles saw such efforts as a biting indictment of his own record. After his suspect performance during the Spanish-American War, he "viewed in intensely personal terms the long-simmering disputes over command administration which the war had uncovered." Thus in 1901, the army's senior general was ironically cast as perhaps the largest obstacle to the progress of his own service.[3]

With Root in the secretary's office, military progressives finally gained momentum and were supported by an increasing number of regulars who saw opportunities for both personal and institutional reward in advancing professional issues. Miles's belligerence toward the War Department was now much less representative of the army generally than it was even in the recent past. To Carter, Miles's outlook appeared as an antiquated relic of those same problems that he hoped to solve. After a senator asked him if the prospective general staff bill would "eliminate any of the historic friction" in this regard, Carter began to contemplate seriously a much broader solution that reached beyond the mere creation of a staff corps.[4]

Like so many other facets of the Root-era reforms, the notion of replacing the position of commanding general with a chief of staff was not original. The idea was broached early on by Alexander Macomb and resurfaced later with both Sherman and Schofield. But once again, it was Carter by virtue of his unique position in Root's War Department who was now able to translate extant ideas into real institutional progress. By legally defining a chief of staff position and removing the commanding general, he believed that true unity of command could be established through the secretary of war's executive authority. This relationship had existed twice in the recent past—first when Maj. Gen. Henry Halleck was commanding general under Secretary of War Edwin Stanton during the Civil War, and again when Schofield held the office in the early 1890s. As commanding general, each of these men assumed a de facto role that is better described as that of a chief of staff. These shifts took place due to the expediency of events as well as the personalities and professional convictions of the men involved. But in each case, the effective transition was never formalized and thus was merely a short-lived experiment. The Spanish-American War highlighted the difficulties of traditional arrangements once again when Miles refused to cooperate with Secretary of War Alger. With this history in mind, it occurred to Carter that Miles's personal opposition to reform was only symptomatic of the deeper, more plaguing problem of American military command—a problem that had to be addressed to realize any sort of lasting progress.[5]

For his part, Miles made this transition much more attractive by continuing to oppose army reform of any type, especially the creation of a general staff. With the advent of Root's general staff bill, "Miles' long resentment toward all civilian War Secretaries now burst into the open." For Carter, who had observed Miles's embarrassing struggle with Alger from the War Department's front lines, it became increasingly clear that the issue of staff reform and the enduring problem of army command were inextricably related. Root—already irritated with Miles's minor acts of insubordination and one-upmanship—proved easily receptive to this observation. With a wry sense of metaphor, the secretary wrote to President McKinley that Miles's conduct "acts on the department very much like mixing Seidlitz powder." Quite clearly, it was time to reconsider the office of commanding general.[6]

Months before he and Carter began pressing general staff legislation in earnest, Root wisely prepared the political battlefield. As early as his first annual report, he served notice of his intention to create an organization that could study and plan for "all contingencies of possible conflict" with the "most information of the state of the art" at hand. Two years later, in the 1901 Annual Report, issued just as the finishing touches were applied to General Orders no. 155, he again underlined the grave need for "a body of competent military experts" and in more specific language, urged "the establishment by law of a general staff." If he previously held any doubts, Root now shared Carter's concern that the War College could not function effectively as both a senior educational institution and a general staff on a permanent basis. Once again, the two men acted as a complementary team, the lawyer setting a course for the soldier's subject-matter expertise.[7]

Following the education act, Carter found himself busier than ever. In addition to beginning active work on the proposed general staff bill and fulfilling his duties as a principal assistant to the adjutant general, he now played a pivotal role on the second War College Board (WCB) that he helped to establish. The board was formally detailed on July 1902, and convened its first meeting later that same month. Along with Carter, the appointees were Maj. Gen. Samuel

B. M. Young, Brig. Gen. Tasker H. Bliss, Maj. Henry A. Greene, and Maj. William D. Beach. By Root's own description, this board would function as a sort of interim general staff and also oversee implementation of General Orders no. 155. Carter's presence on the board was not only appropriate by virtue of his experience—he was the sole member of the first War College Board still on duty in Washington—but also advantageous in that he was able to observe and participate in the embryonic stages of the very concept he was then developing in concert with Root. This seemingly never-ending work in the name of military reform left little time for much else.[8]

Little is known of Carter's personal life during these pivotal months. Since the family was living together under the same roof in Washington, few private letters were left from this period that might offer insights into their daily lives. Neither do his diaries cover these years, likely owing to the fact that he was left with little time to indulge such efforts—a deficiency that Carter later regretted. But from what is known of his marriage to Ida and also his close relationship with his sons, there is no reason to believe that he did not somehow carve out time for them in the War Department's busy schedule. He also continued to take daily horseback rides whenever his duties permitted—a habit that was by this time his one remaining link to prior days spent among troops on the frontier. Even during the intense turmoil of Washington's legislative battles, his love for horses served as a kind of tonic, returning him for a few minutes each day to the carefree adventures of his boyhood in middle Tennessee. But such moments were short-lived. Long hours were the standard, often through a seven-day workweek that sometimes found him at Root's home to hash out details of forthcoming meetings and proposals. Building a modern army had become a pervasive part of his life, and although he remained dedicated to its completion, he was amazed and frustrated by the extraordinary obstacles that seemed to lie in his path at almost every turn.[9]

It soon became clear to Carter that writing an effective general staff bill and planning its implementation was not nearly so difficult a task as it would be to overcome influential opposition. In early September 1901, news of President McKinley's assassination fell like a dark blanket over the country. The tragedy came as a personal shock to Carter, who had enjoyed many dealings with the president and deeply respected his leadership. But if McKinley can be described as generally supportive of Root's plans for the army, then after Theodore Roosevelt's inauguration, the White House became a staunch ally in the battle for military reform. Roosevelt was a friend of Root and his personal enthusiasm for military affairs was already a well-known facet of his larger-than-life public persona. The celebrated Rough Rider had served as an assistant secretary of the navy prior to the War with Spain, and upon his return from Cuba, continued to follow defense and preparedness issues with great zeal. Although he sometimes disagreed with military reformers over the details, he was a kindred spirit in their vision of a new army. Despite the fact that his own service had been at the head of volunteer troops, Roosevelt admired the military profession and shared Carter and Root's interest in pressing forward on the general staff issue. He undoubtedly realized that only a strong army could function as the proverbial "big stick" in an aggressive foreign policy. The chief executive's timely support was warmly welcomed as the general staff bill began to make its way through a politically charged legislative process.[10]

On 3 December 1901, only a week after General Orders no. 155 was formally signed, Roosevelt threw the presidency's full weight behind the general staff issue when he underlined its importance in his first annual message. But as work progressed and Carter and Root began to probe Congress for potential support, they were increasingly convinced that even the new president's political clout might not garner the needed votes. In a lengthy memorandum written during his initial work on the bill, Carter noted that a public battle on the issue could not be avoided. Rather than bemoaning this cold reality as an insurmountable hurdle, he now believed that opposition could be directly confronted and overcome with a carefully reasoned campaign of information:

> No complete scheme for a General Staff has as yet been devised for the American Army, because nearly all of the authors have undertaken to create a new corps while avoiding the antagonism of those already organized and having much power to defeat new propositions. It must not be expected that any plan can be proposed which will receive the absolute unanimous approval of the whole Army, but it is believed that a scheme can be devised which will carry conviction to the average officer that . . . ought to succeed on its merits.[11]

For Carter and other progressive officers, the need for a general staff seemed self-evident. The problem was the "complacent attitude of men in power who have participated in success under former systems, be they ever so faulty." Simply put, it was a difficult undertaking to convince Congress that the nation required a new army when the Old Army's victories were still fresh in the popular memory— even if such victories had been won under an inefficient and costly military system that was incompatible with modern warfare. As the bill went to committee, the problem of overcoming a deeply embedded cultural inertia loomed larger than perhaps even Carter had imagined.[12]

On 14 February 1902, a general staff bill authored by Carter was submitted to the Republican chairmen of the respective military committees in both houses. The proposal established a general staff corps "whose duties shall be to consider the military policy of the country and prepare comprehensive plans for the national defense and for the mobilization of the military forces in time of war." A "Chief of General Staff" would supervise the corps, but this office would not necessarily be held by the army's senior general. Assignment of the senior ranking general was not legally bound to any particular office or command. At the serving president's discretion, either the chief of staff or any other general officer could fulfill the titular duties currently performed by the commanding general—an interesting compromise that held both advantages and pitfalls. The bill also attempted to dissolve the staff system's political clout and break down its myopia by consolidating the quartermaster, subsistence, and pay departments into a single "Department of Supply." Carter opposed this last provision, but Root pushed for its inclusion, apparently believing it would be widely approved by the army line.[13]

With a view to the bill's ultimate passage, Carter chose his battles carefully, leaving Miles relatively undisturbed in his current role by naming him the first chief of staff until he retired from active service. As historian Philip Semsch points out, this was an artful attempt to make the legislation "more palatable" to Miles, but "one that was nonetheless futile." With similar purpose, those already serving under permanent appointments in the staff bureaus could continue in their positions and be promoted under existing rules until retirement depleted their number. By this time, Carter had become an astute participant in the political maneuvering that necessarily accompanied his work. Unfortunately, his efforts did little to appease those who now clamored to defend the status quo.[14]

The bill was eyed suspiciously by many in Congress who shared Miles's narrow outlook, and it struggled in committee almost as soon as it was introduced. Opponents charged that the bill diluted the army's command structure, confused functions of command with those of administration, and placed too much power in the hands of a "corps of detailed officers of junior rank." In defending the measure before both committees, Root testified to the bill's seminal importance to America's future defense. Responding to a senator's offhand remark to the effect that great captains such as Napoleon and Washington had not relied on formalized strategic planning for their victories, Root curtly replied, "They are dead; dead as our present organization." Quite evidently, he shared Carter's conviction that the Old Army's time has passed. But perhaps neither man expected that this "dead" culture could still pose such a potent resistance to those who would see it buried.[15]

Appearing a few days later before the Senate Military Committee, Miles loudly defended the existing system in traditionalist terms, calling it the "fruit of the best thought of the most eminent patriots and ablest military men that this country has produced." He shrewdly played to his audience's fears by associating Carter's general staff plan with the contemporary Prussian example, "one that is more adapted to the monarchies of the Old World." Miles's testimony found receptive ears among congressmen who were not inclined to disturb a system that had survived decades with little change. Complacency was proving a more able opponent than even Carter had imagined.[16]

Shortly after Miles's appearance on stage, Senator Joseph Hawley, chairman of the Senate Military Committee and Root's personal friend, informed Carter that the bill could not possibly hope to see a floor vote during the current session—a bitter setback. But never one to wither before adversity, Carter immediately began to plan for a more successful attempt during the next legislative session. In the interim, it was apparent that a different strategy was required. The general staff issue had to become the focus of a very public fight if it was to gain the needed support. In a conversation with Root shortly after the bill's defeat, Carter advocated a preemptive "campaign of education" to presage a "new bill that would forever do away with the incessant opposition and wrangling of the Commanding General, whose office had never been imbued with powers and duties commensurate with the rank of the generals assigned to command." Root wholeheartedly agreed and the battle for a general staff was fully joined.[17]

Perhaps betraying his passion for courtroom maneuver, Root responded by immediately bringing his own "star witnesses" to the stand. At the secretary's request, Generals John M. Schofield and Wesley M. Merritt, both bona fide heroes of the Old Army and also firm supporters of military reform, appeared before committee in early April, accompanied by Carter for expert reference. Carter was pleased by the positive impression left by Schofield and Merritt, noting with obvious satisfaction that their answers were "based on knowledge of facts and conditions, and not at all on sentiment, as had been that of General Miles." With this testimony, as well as written support introduced from other prominent general officers, it was hoped that Miles's damage was at least weakened. Root and Carter wanted to cast Miles in the same light as the office he held. The commanding general—both in person and concept—was a relic of antiquated ideas, completely divorced from the progressive thought that now pervaded much of the officer corps.[18]

Roused by the proceedings and not satisfied to leave the argument to others, Carter eagerly picked up the banner with pen in hand. With Root's blessing, he prepared several related articles for publication, written with remarkable clarity and unmistakable purpose. The first of these efforts appeared in the May 1902 issue of the *North American Review* under the title "Will America Profit by Her Recent Military Lessons?" Taking his cue from Upton's own work in *Military Policy of the United States* (with which he was familiar in manuscript copy), Carter underlined in both fiscal and human terms the existent military establishment's historical inefficiency—a deplorable condition that he believed was largely responsible for a complacent lack of peacetime preparedness.[19]

American defense, Carter argued, suffered from a dearth of expert planning and strategic forethought. "The one crying need of the army during the past half century," he concluded, "has been the want of a General Staff Corps, or body of officers whose business it is to do the preliminary planning for the army and make of its various elements a more harmonious working machine." As expected, he then called for a "chief of staff" to replace the commanding general so that the general staff might reach its full potential: "There is no place under our Constitution for a 'Commander-in-Chief' and a 'Commanding General'; and when this is recognized by appropriate legislation, the unbusinesslike methods and constant friction will disappear, to the great benefit of the country and the army."[20]

In the wake of its war with Spain, the United States had entered an international arena where it could "no longer afford to neglect questions of such grave import to its future welfare." Carter thus took his case beyond the closed doors of congressional conference to a much more public forum.[21]

He followed up this article with two others published later that summer. In August, "Recent Army Reorganization" appeared in *The United Service,* and in October, just before the start of the next legislative session, "A General Staff for the Army" in *The North American Review.* The first of these essays explained the purpose of both the Reorganization Act and General Orders no. 155 before calling for the creation of a general staff corps and the associated abolition of the office of commanding general. Carter was careful to point out that the proposed staff was not "a panacea for all the ills and misfortunes which may overtake a county," but an agency "through which the military and political policies of the country may be absolutely harmonized, as becomes a republican government." Although the second essay shared many thoughts and even verbiage with the first, it was a more direct attempt to answer specific charges posed by the opposition. Carter was clearly growing anxious for the coming fight as Congress prepared to reconvene that December.[22]

He took the offensive and attempted to distance the American general staff from its Prussian counterpart, emphasizing its role as a surrogate military mind for the executive branch of government—a relationship wholly congruent with republican political ideals. Miles's charges that a general staff would only "Germanize" the traditional American civil-military relationship had clearly stung Carter's patriotic self-image. He countered that such barbs only rendered "intelligent discussion of the objects of the bill" impossible, exciting emotional opposition on ill-founded and reactive grounds. With indignation, Carter remarked that "it is not contended for a moment that the German General Staff system is applicable to the United States army." Instead, he noted, drawing on Schofield's testimony, that the American general staff would depart from its Prussian counterpart in that it would act only in an advisory capacity, remaining entirely separate from the operational chain of command during both peace and war. Painfully aware that Congress and the American people were still sensitive to long-standing republican suspicions of European-style armies, Carter hoped to effectively counter this phony charge before it could once again damage his purpose.[23]

A fourth article, "The Training of Army Officers," appeared in the October issue of *The United Service*. As its title suggests, he began by explaining the newly instituted systematic approach to the development of a professional soldiery. After noting that "the best work of armies depends upon systematic organization and methods," he artfully transitioned to yet another plea for the general staff. The United States had ascended to a position of international prominence, he wrote, "which cannot be shirked and which demands a clear conception from a military point of view of the duties which will be forced upon us by reason of the great and constant conflict over commercial supremacy." It was incomprehensible that deliberate measures had not been taken "to prepare properly for national defense as well as aggressive war." Only a professionally educated and trained general staff could fill this void. It would be the logical complement to the army's educational pyramid, effectively translating professional intellect to action.[24]

In each of these essays, as in the several memorandums written for Root, Carter presses his belief that staff reform was a reasonable and necessary step as the Old Army transitioned to a new era. Only an educated general staff could provide the necessary "harmony" between civilian policy and its military instrument:

> Through the agency of a General Staff, military and political policies may be harmonized as becomes our form of government; and all the bureau chiefs of the War Department, the proper performance of whose functions has more to do with the success of war than the average layman can possibly comprehend, would be brought into line and work more coherently and to a common purpose.[25]

The army's historic separation of administrative and command functions, a jealously guarded tradition, was now only a misguided canon that would fail miserably if tested by modern warfare.

The vaguely defined office of commanding general had been a misnomer since its inception—in actuality commanding very little while shackling effective coordination through constant discord with the staff and secretary of war. Carter asserted that this very damaging circumstance could only be addressed by centralizing senior planning authority while decentralizing execution to fielded leadership. In peacetime, the general staff would study, plan, and prepare for the national defense while keeping apace with the dynamics of modern military science. In war, the general staff, through the chief of staff, would ensure that the secretary and executive cabinet had expert advice and information, and provide the same expertise and support to commanders in the field. Although still mired in a frustrating political process, the general staff bill was the cornerstone of Carter's foundation for a truly new army that could ensure America's defense in the twentieth century.[26]

Carter's valuable work, and perhaps also his relationship with Root, was not without significant personal reward. That spring, on 15 April 1902, he was promoted to the rank of full colonel—no great surprise for an officer of his responsibility, and roughly "on time" after four years as a lieutenant colonel. But it surely raised eyebrows both in and out of the army when only three months later, on 15 July, he was made a brigadier general. In his memoirs, Carter claimed absolute surprise at the honor, stating that he went to the White House at once to express his gratitude to President Roosevelt. Roosevelt, he recalled, told him that the promotion was given not so much for his accomplishments, but for his potential to perform as a general officer. Carter was detailed shortly thereafter as acting adjutant general in Henry Corbin's extended absence from the War Department, and perhaps it was Root's desire for an uninterrupted voice to represent that office during ongoing fiscal negotiations that helped prompt his promotion. Whatever the actual motivation—cronyism, personal competence, practical need, or some combination thereof—Carter's rising star alongside Root could not have been missed by even the most casual Washington observers.[27]

That summer and fall, while working to marshal support for the staff bill's reintroduction during the December session, Carter maintained his position on the War College Board. The board met on an irregular basis and addressed a myriad of topics. Records of these meetings build sympathy for Carter's assertion that the War College would fail in its purpose if saddled with both an administrative and general staff role. During the first months of its existence, the WCB was kept so busy with the most mundane administrative issues that it was left with very little opportunity to study matters of the higher or strategic nature intended for a general staff.

In addition to overseeing Leavenworth's rebirth under the broader context of a staff college, the board undertook various lesser subjects that on the whole prevented it from fulfilling a higher role. Distractions ranged from a request for the purchase of Spanish-language texts for troops at Plattsburg Barracks to an offer of plaster relief maps of the Gettysburg battlefield for use at the War College. An examination of board minutes during the six-month period from July 1902 to January 1903 reveals that of the several dozen topics discussed and assigned to subcommittees for further action, the board seems to have considered really only a single issue that might be described as appropriate for the attention of a general staff.[28]

On 18 October, Root asked the board to report on the necessary logistics and support for a potential overseas expeditionary force. This confidential request was more than just an interesting exercise of the WCB's announced function. Ongoing disagreement with Canada over Alaska's southern boundary had become heated due to the discovery of gold in the region, and Roosevelt contemplated sending troops to assert American resolve on the issue. In addition, German and British financial interests in Venezuela had soured, and both governments threatened a naval blockade in an attempt to recoup their losses—a prospect that threatened American claims of primacy in the Caribbean. Beginning with their meeting of 5 November, the WCB discussed this topic on an ongoing basis during the next several months. When later testifying before the Senate Military Committee, Root pointed to the work as a prime example of a general staff's valuable role in a modern defense establishment.[29]

But aside from this single higher-level task, the WCB was left with little opportunity to assert itself as an institutional intellect for the army's strategic direction. Administering the service schools, standardizing curriculum at the new garrison schools, and regulating the several military programs conducted at land-grant colleges and universities accounted for the overwhelming majority of the board's time. This experience only hardened Carter's conviction that a general staff had to be kept entirely separate from the War College or else it would flounder under the sheer magnitude of the army's growing bureaucracy.

Just as Congress convened in second session, one final but very important effort was made to swing political support. Root's annual report for 1902 was delivered with an eloquent plea for the forthcoming act's passage. He opened with applause for the successes that he and Carter had already achieved in redefining the army according to professionalist concepts of modernity: "Since the report for 1899 was made, many of the important measures then recommended for the greater efficiency of the Army have been accomplished or are in course of accomplishment under authority conferred by legislation." Then, with a Progressive's sense of efficiency and good order, he deplored the singular lack of a coordinating body that could direct this new army "so that all parts of the machine shall work true together." The general staff was to be the final act in a slate of reforms that would bring the army into a new century.[30]

Almost as a sort of preamble to his forthcoming testimony before the committees, Root spent six more pages arguing the very points that he knew would soon be questioned in congressional conference. Like Carter, he adamantly rejected accusations that a general staff would bring an authoritarian European flavor to the American military system, insisting that "the common experience of mankind is that the things which those general staffs do, have to be done in every well-managed and well-directed army." Republican traditions of civil preeminence would in fact by strengthened by doing away with the office of commanding general and replacing it with a chief of staff who would act as an executive agent. This change was more than mere semantics. It would reinvigorate the very relationship between civil and military authority—a longtime source of friction and disjointed action even during national emergencies. While Carter had carefully written the briefs and prepared the public jury, Root was delivering a powerful opening statement before the court.[31]

As the general staff act was readied for its second introduction, late-hour revisions were made in the hopes of weakening expected opposition. The exigencies of the debate demanded that Carter temper professional enthusiasm with compromise, a common-sense approach that was largely missing from the efforts of previous military reformers such as Upton. To this end, he rewrote much of the bill to avoid any confusing details of a "complicated and extensive nature" that might be vulnerable to opposing argument. Several sections of the previous bill were shed so that the only issue taken before Congress was the specific creation of a general staff. In hopeful deference to Miles in particular, it was stipulated that the act, once passed, would not take effect until after the current commanding general's retirement in August of the following summer. On 2 December, the revised general staff bill, now written in "simplest possible character," was one again introduced in the House of Representatives and the struggle was rejoined.[32]

Appearing before the House Military Committee, Root reiterated the need for a single coordinating body that could overcome the historically "out of joint" efforts of army command and administration. He illustrated his arguments by applying the general staff concept to the recent mobilization for Cuba, explaining exactly how a body of experts might have guided planning and coordination at key steps of the process—direction that was glaringly absent in reality. Paralleling Carter's efforts to streamline the bill itself, Root's address was marked by straightforward simplicity. "Those are the two great duties of the general staff," he summarized, "first to acquire information and arrange it and fit it into all the possible plans of operation, so that an order can be intelligently made; and second, when the order has been made, to exercise constant supervision."[33]

The committee questioned Root at length on the bill's various provisions, but the general tenor of their response seemed supportive. Carter was very pleased with this first step, and four days later accompanied Root to a similar hearing before the Senate committee. He noted that the proceedings were "remarkable in that two members of the committee, Senators Proctor and Alger, had served as Secretaries of War, and all the other Senators participating had served in the Union or Confederate Armies during the Civil War." This circumstance was more than just an interesting footnote. It was at once both advantageous and dangerous to Carter's purpose. Committee members would approach the hearings with a working knowledge of military affairs and be aware of past frustrations with the existing system. But at the same time, they doubtlessly harbored preconceived notions of how an army should be run—notions that were colored by nostalgic memories of their own experiences.[34]

In questioning Root and Carter, the committee—likely owing to their own service in Civil War armies ruled by traditions of seniority and rank—focused primarily on the relationship between the proposed chief of staff and the army's other general officers. Root maintained that it was not a relationship of command but rather one of "supervision," a term that was expressly chosen for its inferred meaning.[35] The committee had a difficult time fathoming the premise that during both war and peace there would be no single "commanding general of the army," either in name or in practice, except the president. The chief of staff would exercise "supervisory" power, an authority that would exist in a different context from that of "command" or "control." Owing to the historic attention and prestige (if not authority in fact) given to the army's commanding generals, Carter must have felt at times as if he and Root were arguing their case against an entire room full of heroic ghosts.[36]

With Carter sitting at his side, Root continued to answer a slew of questions on this issue, and the testimony evolved into almost a general discussion. A chief of staff would act only on the constitutional authority of the president as commander in chief, not on any independent command authority vested in the position itself. This departure from tradition fascinated the committee even while it raised suspicions, and there was lengthy debate about how it might actually be effected. When Root and Carter finally departed the Senate chambers at the end of the day, it was with a mixture of satisfaction and consternation. Questions regarding the nature of the proposed chief of staff at times overshadowed the bill's larger purpose, but at the same time, it seemed to be gaining the committee's tentative support.[37]

Not willing to sit back and await further developments, Carter immediately set to work on a memorandum that would attempt to explain the important meaning of the term "supervision" as used to describe the chief of staff's role. He recommended that Root give very careful thought to the ramifications of Senator Foraker's demand that the word be changed to either "command" or "control" before making any rush to appeasement. The exact terminology's implications were of great consequence, and Carter understood that it might well affect the general staff's chances for eventual success:

> The word "supervision" was adopted because in the military sense it indicates the overseeing of affairs in the interest of superior authority. The word "command" implies directly the power of the officer holding such command to issue or-

ders. The word "control" operates practically in the same way.... A Chief of Staff with supervisory control only would be required always to use this form; that is, he would give an order only in the name of the Secretary of War or of his superior commander.[38]

Carter had purposely crafted this verbiage to eliminate potential friction between the chief of staff and the executive branch, such as had plagued relations between the latter and commanding generals of the past. His authorship of the general staff bill, like his work on the Reorganization Act and General Orders no. 155, was considered with great concern for the army's long-term good. Root took Carter's advice on this point and after further painstaking discussion in committee, the term "supervision" remained intact.[39]

Once again, as expected, specific provisions of the bill came under intense fire from parties who fretted that their personal kingdoms were threatened. The Inspector General's Department was abolished under the proposed act, its duties partially given to the general staff corps. Gen. Joseph Breckinridge, the current inspector general, was already at odds with Root, and so his opposition to the bill was a foregone conclusion. But Breckinridge, like many others on the staff, enjoyed the support of well-placed friends. While Root and Carter made their case before the Senate committee, Breckinridge was testifying before the House in hostile opposition.

Breckinridge spoke poetically while arguing the importance of an independent inspector general's office. The "conscience of the Army" resided in its inspectors whose actions fell "like the gentle dews of heaven, equally upon the just and unjust." He warned the committee that to take away the department's independence would be tantamount to blunting its strength and effectiveness. His rhetorical style, likely found amusing if not outright laughable by some, was apparently persuasive to others and he induced the committee to strike those portions of the bill that affected his department. Inspection was removed from the proposed general staff's functions, an action that both Root and Carter believed was highly ill-advised. "You never will have effective inspection and the curing of evils revealed by inspection," Root testified, "until you have the same body of men charge with following up the things they find out." But Breckinridge was well accustomed to the Washington game, and, at least in this instance, the emotional appeal of his arguments prevailed over Root's more logical courtroom style.[40]

Two other important changes took place in committee, both of which Carter believed weakened the measure's overall effectiveness. Provisions were modified so that the chief of staff's supervisory powers extended only to those duties and activities "not otherwise assigned by law." This seemingly reasonable and benign revision was actually a shrewd gambit to build a sort of loophole into the general staff law. From Carter's perspective, it "opened the door of opportunity for any bureau chief with influence enough to secure legislation assigning matters definitely to his control." But Carter and Root hoped that such an eventuality would become less likely as "permanent" staffers retired from the service and were replaced with line officers detailed to the departments for four-year tours. A second, more onerous modification set the stage for conflict that would plague the army for years to come.[41]

Under pressure from Brig. Gen. Fred C. Ainsworth, chief of the Record and Pension Office, the bill was rewritten in committee so that, instead of supervising the collectively defined "several administrative staff and supply departments," the general staff would only supervise those bureaus that were specifically listed by name. Of course, Ainsworth's own office was conveniently left off the list at his insistence. This astounding political coup was due largely to Ainsworth's influence with several members of the committee, including chairman John A. T. Hull. As a permanent appointee, Ainsworth remained on staff duty until, as adjutant general over a decade later, he came to loggerheads with Secretary of War Henry L. Stimson and the chief of staff, Gen. Leonard Wood. With Ainsworth and Breckinridge working hard to preserve the status quo, Carter found that compromise was a bitter but nonetheless necessary handmaiden to progress.[42]

Despite these setbacks, the amended bill left committee and entered debate in both houses, where it met relatively little resistance. "A friendly poll of the Senate," remembered Carter, "disclosed that a large majority favored the bill in its final shape." Although many lawmakers still viewed the general staff as an experiment with European-style military structures, the act was passed into law on 14 February 1903, one full year after the original general staff bill had been introduced. Carter's elation at the hard-fought victory was tempered by the sobering realization that years of difficult work still remained in building a truly workable system. The legislative battle was won, but now the legal instruction had to be translated into a bona fide living and breathing general staff.[43]

Carter and Root realized that efforts to institute army reforms were really a two-fold process. First, a system of graduate education was required to provide the professional awareness and technical knowledge on which a modern system of military leadership might be founded. Then, once a sort of professional pipeline was in place to prepare educated and trained experts, a general staff was needed to provide a nucleus or intellectual hub for the army. This institutional mind was charged with studying and planning for contingencies of military consequence during time of peace, and coordinating mobilization and offering advice to the executive as well as fielded leadership during time of national crisis. Carter also recognized that there were accompanying intangible benefits. The general staff, he wrote, "must prove not only of great value to the Government but will command the respect and confidence of the army and nation." The social prestige and authority bestowed on professional expertise by the larger middle-class society was a worthy prize for soldiers who had endured thankless years scattered across the frontier.[44]

For Carter, professional education and the creation of a general staff represented a distinct institutional transition from an antiquated army that was marked by disjointed effort and professional disinterest to a modern army that was led by formal coordination, intellectual foresight, and educated expertise. His salient role and tireless efforts were acknowledged by an invitation to be present as President Theodore Roosevelt signed the General Staff Act into law. As a memento of his labors, Carter was given the fountain pen that Roosevelt used to sign the bill, a token later presented to the U.S. Military Academy for preservation. But though a job well done certainly offered great personal satisfaction and was a significant step toward reform, the achievements would be short-lived if not followed by swift and authoritative action to give them physical substance. The Old Army had been written from the books, but in its place a New Army still had not taken shape.[45]

Carter, in his third-class year (1869). This portrait was taken while he was in New York on leave due to the illness of his sister Annie. Photo courtesy of Carter family.

Carter, photographed while on leave as a West Point cadet in 1871.

William H. Carter as a West Point cadet in 1872. Photo courtesy of Carter family.

Carter, thought to have been photographed during a chemistry course in the spring of 1872. Photo courtesy of Carter family.

Ida Dawley, photographed in San Francisco in 1880, the year of her marriage to William H. Carter. Photo courtesy of Carter family.

Lieutenant William H. Carter, taken during the summer of 1874 in San Francisco by Morse Photography while en route to Arizona with the Eighth Infantry. Photo courtesy of Carter family.

Posing with several Sioux at the Red Cloud Agency, 1874. French painter Jules Tavernier is seated on the ground, with Lt. William H. Carter of the Eighth Infantry at far right. He is clasping the hand of a Sioux warrior believed to be Red Dog, who Carter noted was a key player in the Fetterman massacre some eight years earlier. NARA.

A similar scene: Carter, the artist Tavernier, and several Sioux at the Red Cloud Agency in 1874. Carter is at left, standing by Red Leaf, a noted chief later prominent in the Sioux Wars of 1876, and Tavernier is on the ground. Seated with hat and mustache is a trader named Dear, and kneeling at right front is Lt. James Buchanan. This photograph was taken by Maj. Thomas Wilhem, Eighth Infantry. NARA.

Lt. William H. Carter, photographed in Tucson, Arizona Territory, shortly after his arrival from Wyoming. Photo courtesy of Carter family.

Troop E, 6th Cavalry, at Camp Verde, Arizona, 1875. 2nd Lt. Carter is in front of line, just forward of the trooper holding the guidon. The officer on the gray horse is 1st Lt. Sebree Smith. Courtesy National Archives and Records Administration.

A company of scouts from Camp Verde, Arizona Territory, under Carter's command while in the field in 1876. At far right is famed frontiersman Al Sieber. Photo courtesy of National Archives and Records Administration.

B Company, Apache Scouts, Arizona Territory, circa 1876. Mickey Free, a mixed-blood interpreter and army scout, is at center, top row. Courtesy National Archives and Records Administration.

Officers of the 6th Cavalry in camp near old Fort Fetterman, circa 1891, during the "Rustling War." Capt. William H. Carter is standing at left, near guidon; seated, left to right: 1st Lt. Robert Howze; 1st Lt. B. H. Cheever; officer at far right has not been identified. Courtesy National Archives and Records Administration.

Captain William H. Carter, wearing the Medal of Honor awarded him for service during the battle of Cibicu Creek in the Arizona Territory. This photograph is believed to have been taken while he was assigned to the U.S. Army Infantry and Cavalry School at Fort Leavenworth, Kansas, from 1893 to 1897. Photo courtesy of Carter family.

Colonel Eugene A. Carr with officers assigned and attached to the Sixth U.S. Cavalry at the Pine Ridge Agency, South Dakota, in January 1891. This photograph was taken shortly after the campaign that ended in tragedy at Wounded Knee. Captain William H. Carter is seated on the ground second from the right. The young officer standing seventh from the upper right is believed to be Lieutenant (later General of the Army) John J. "Blackjack" Pershing. Photo courtesy National Archives and Records Administration.

A portrait of Captain William H. Carter entitled "military seat," used as an illustration in his highly successful book *Horses, Saddles, and Bridles*. Photo courtesy of Carter family.

Brigadier General William H. Carter, seated with U.S. Senator James A. Hemenway (Indiana) and Vice President Charles W. Fairbanks (right) during a summer encampment at Camp Benjamin Harrison, Indiana, in August 1906. Photo courtesy of Carter family.

Brigadier General William H. Carter, commander of the Department of the Lakes, on favorite "Tom Bass" while attending summer maneuvers at Fort Benjamin Harrison, Indiana, in 1908. Photo courtesy of Carter family.

Major General William H. Carter as commander of the Maneuver Division at San Antonio, Texas, 1911. Photo courtesy of Carter family.

Major General William H. Carter and his staff in Texas City, Texas, in 1913 with the Second Division. This division's mobilization and deployment was in response to growing revolutionary violence in Mexico and the threat to American interests there. Photo courtesy of Carter family.

Major General William H. Carter as commander of the Second Division during the spring of 1913. Photo courtesy of Carter family.

William and Ida Carter, in retirement with grandson Billie Carter. The couple split their retirement years between their home in Washington D.C. and a retreat cottage known as Eagle Rock Lodge in Virginia's Blue Ridge Mountains. Photo courtesy of Carter family.

TRANSLATING REFORM TO REALITY

Once the General Staff Act was written into law, another, perhaps even more intimidating hurdle lay before Carter's new army: building the institutional framework that would allow the new organization to take root and mature into a viable, functioning asset to the national defense. Carter realized that the victories would become but fleeting memories if not given the institutional strength to overcome decades of cultural inertia. As evidenced by the calculated efforts of Ainsworth and Breckinridge, staffers cut from Old Army cloth were not eager to roll over and embrace progress without putting up a strong fight. A general staff and a hierarchical system of professional officer education now existed on paper—the one by legislative act and the other by executive order—but the actual realization of both as living, breathing cornerstones of a modern army remained merely visionary concepts. Carter himself would soon find that troops engaged in enforcing imperial policies an ocean away from the War Department's offices and hallways had little time to reflect on these new developments.

On 18 February 1903, General Orders no. 15 formally announced the General Staff Act to the army. As Carter considered the immediate future, he recognized that it would be a struggle to implement the

measure in a manner that fulfilled its true potential. "I felt the obligation of helping to steer the new craft on its great voyage of high endeavor," he wrote with dramatic flair. "I saw very clearly that there
was a long and rough road to be gone over before the new corps would
find itself loyally welcomed in the War Department." The greatest
threat to the embryonic General Staff grew from the fact that its very
presence would challenge the power and influence of entities already
firmly entrenched, one of the risks of such far-reaching reforms.[1]

Carter continued to exercise his significant influence with Root,
apparently confident that the secretary still greatly valued his insights. He wrote a lengthy memorandum reminding Root of the strong
resistance that could be expected in the coming months as the army
attempted to tear down the very organization that had spawned and
protected bureaucratic fiefdoms for many decades:

> It is very desirable, in fact essential, that those staff bureaus
> most intimately connected with the preparation of the army
> for war should be brought into intimate and harmonious re-
> lations with the General Staff Corps at the start. It is assumed
> that details for the General Staff will be made from these
> departments, but it is essential that the chiefs of bureaus
> themselves shall be induced to give honest adherence to the
> new system. If indifferent, they can retard development, and
> if antagonistic they can do infinite harm.[2]

With sober first-hand knowledge of the personalities involved, he
worried that opposition might inflict irreversible damage before the
reforms could even be implemented. Although the institution of
a war college was not a controversial issue, the General Staff Act
sparked resistance from some even as it drew enthusiastic support
from many others. For this reason, Carter believed that from the very
outset, the General Staff had to be set on an institutional plane high
above the injustices of petty careerist politics. Otherwise, it would
fail to gain acceptance among both line and staff, a definite requirement for its success.

The manner in which officers were initially detailed to the first
General Staff corps would thus serve as a very important harbinger of
its eventual character. Past appointments to the several staff bureaus
were often secured by personal influence and political intrigue, a demoralizing situation for many competent line officers who could

never hope to gain that sort of support. Carter was adamant that politicking should not corrupt the General Staff's higher professional purpose: "The General Staff Corps will eventually have such a wide and controlling influence on the welfare of the Army that the recruiting of its personnel can not be too carefully guarded." He fervently recommended that detail to the General Staff be based entirely on an officer's "efficiency and aptitude," with due weight given to both field service and performance at the garrison and service schools. Carter was uncompromising in his belief that the General Staff should stand as "the mecca toward which the roads of professional endeavor lead," and competitive assignment on merit, "without any suspicion of favoritism," was an important foundation for such high expectations. As the War Department now turned its attention toward implementing the recently won staff and education reforms, Carter was steadfastly determined to preserve their original intent.[3]

It was during this same period, in fact taking life almost a month prior to the General Staff Act's passage, that the nation's militia system also received significant revision. Since the Militia Act of 1792 had established a lasting precedent of state-controlled militia as America's primary reserve, regulars had long argued for increased federal influence over the system, hoping to lend it at least some minor degree of standardization and efficiency. The current system, professionalists charged, was wracked by local indifference to standards of training and equipage as well as by often very provincial interpretations of national purpose. This circumstance left preparedness woefully lacking, a shortcoming that Upton and others had blamed for various episodes of the nation's martial ineptitude—specifically pointing to the lack of a federal reserve system that might have effectively squelched Confederate rebellion before it became a bloody four-year nightmare. Civil and military leaders alike were divided over the militia's proper role in a viable system of national defense.[4]

The very term "militia" was itself the source of much popular misunderstanding in the debate. The differences between the "organized militia," composed of standing units that ostensibly met and trained during peacetime, and the "popular militia," a sort of theoretical force that existed on the fundamental premise of universal obligation (meaning every citizen would take up arms and defend the country in time of crisis), were largely blurred and only rarely dif-

ferentiated in public discourse. As Russell Weigley observes, variations of both terms were indiscriminately used in reference to the
"whole military manpower potential of the country." This semantic
ambiguity often confused the issue in the public sphere, and due to
the term's republican ideological undertones, made militia reform a
difficult and politically sensitive endeavor.[5]

Since Upton had all but dismissed the militia's usefulness when
he called for a federal reserve as the nation's second line of defense,
professionalists had echoed these sentiments in kind. Their arguments generally demanded that the militia be subordinated to federal
leadership and control, hoping to mold it into the Regular Army's
image and ostensibly make it a more effective reserve. Such calls met
with fierce political opposition that drew strength from the nation's
traditional celebration of the citizen-soldier. By the early twentieth
century, most states fashioned their organized militia as "National
Guard" in an attempt to claim a national role, even if in name only.
During the post–Civil War decades, the National Guard Association
(NGA) had emerged as a formidable lobby in a Congress filled with
veterans of the war's great volunteer armies. As Root attempted to
engage the issue in the name of progress, Carter entered the discussion with a decidedly professionalist perspective, and it was this attitude that colored his approach to the efforts that finally resulted in
the 1903 Militia Act.

Carter declared that he "had long held views in harmony with
those of General Upton as to the urgent need of a force of federal volunteers, under no obligations as to State lines." Root was of like mind,
believing that the current militia system was useless for anything
more than local defense or other such minor duties even under the
best of circumstances. Most regular officers wholeheartedly agreed,
seeing the states' haphazard attention to the militia as a very loud and
convincing argument for federal intervention. However, rather than
calling for its complete eradication, many regulars also acknowledged—perhaps with begrudging resignation—that the National Guard
remained useful as a defense force of last resort, and consequently
supported actions that might increase its state of readiness. But they
simultaneously insisted on the creation of an actual federal reserve,
effectively leaving the militia in a tertiary role. In Carter's first article,
"One View of the Army Question," written in 1889, he beseeched
readers not to forget Upton's "pigeon-holed" proposals in this regard,

and called for a better-trained National Guard that looked to the Regular Army as its model. Mention of a federal reserve was distinctly absent from his argument then, possibly signaling an unwillingness to enter a heated debate in his first published effort. But his later thoughts on the subject had apparently evolved as he witnessed the NGA's intense lobbying during the turbulent weeks preceding the Spanish-American War.[6]

As war in Cuba became a foregone conclusion, Secretary Alger's War Department, including Carter as an assistant adjutant general, looked for a means of rapidly reinforcing the inadequate Regular Army. At that date, the militia was "much improved, but . . . far from a ready reserve for war duty." Its federal role had suffered from ambiguity since the American Revolution, when George Washington had relied on provincials for much-needed support even while bitterly complaining of their haphazard performance and often-fleeting presence. By 1898, Americans still had not defined this vital relationship and national preparedness suffered for it. In March of that year, the Hull Bill was introduced, an act that would have created an expansible army to meet the impending crisis. This scheme quite clearly reflected professionalist influence, and in principle drew on the concepts proposed by John C. Calhoun in 1821. But expectedly, state officials and the NGA vehemently opposed the measure and combined with powerful effect to defeat it. These opposing positions vividly illustrated the wide chasm that defined the issue of an appropriate military establishment.[7]

According to historian Jerry Cooper, the Hull Bill "represented the efforts of Army reformers to rationalize and centralize wartime manpower policy and curtail the role of state military systems in the conduct of war." Cooper's assessment underlines the Uptonians' fundamental inability (or perhaps unwillingness) to reconcile professionally sound conclusions with American cultural realities. Reformers' insistence on a federal reserve that circumvented the still-popular National Guard was myopic and doomed to meet defeat in the public arena. When the Hull Bill was unsurprisingly defeated, the army was forced to accept a compromise that relied on state volunteers, bringing militia units into federal service as intact organizations. With no system in place to organize, equip, train, and supply the throngs of volunteers, Carter and the rest of the War Department were overwhelmed by the over-enthusiastic response.[8]

Carter watched this confusion with a professional's contempt for the dilettante, and his Uptonian views on the issue hardened. Regulars were especially galled by the appointment of so many amateur officers who sprang from all walks of life, implicitly assailing the professionals' claims of martial expertise. "Only those who had opportunity for actual observation at the War Department during this trying time can comprehend the annoyance and delays which were occasioned," Carter wrote with disgust. "The best interests of the country demand that Militia or National Guard organizations should conform to those of the Regular Army." In 1902, when Root began pressing for militia reform to avoid a recurrence of the problems occasioned four years earlier, Carter approached the discussion guardedly with no small degree of pessimism. The resulting legislation may not have appeased his professionalist sensibilities, but it certainly taught him a lesson in the art of legislative compromise.[9]

Carter watched the militia reform process from very close quarters, and, in addition to offering advice, helped draft the final proposal at a Sunday meeting that took place at Root's home. According to Carter, Root's personal views on the issue moderated the two extremes: "He was in favor of extending every possible help to the organized or active militia, but was in entire accord with the proposal for the creation of a force of National or Federal volunteers in each Congressional district." After working all day on a bill that would extend federal monies to the states in exchange for greater control over militia training and organization, Root invited representatives from the state adjutant generals' conference to his home to try to win their support for the forthcoming legislative battle. Discussion became heated when the Guardsmen remained adamantly opposed to the establishment of any sort of national reserve or increased federal control of the peacetime National Guard. Root countered with a threat to withhold War Department support from any militia legislation that failed to offer a legitimate compromise on these provisions. "There was a pretense of acceptance [by the state officers]," remembered Carter, "but with evident intent to defeat the proposition after it was introduced." Clearly, the issue was one that excited deep-seated feelings on both sides, and the eventual outcome delicately balanced these positions without completely satisfying anyone.[10]

The Militia Act of 21 January 1903 became commonly known as

the Dick Act for the active role taken by Congressman Charles Dick, an Ohio Republican who was himself a Guardsman. Dick became a sort of "principal liaison" between the NGA, the congressional military committees, and Root's War Department. In addition to implicitly reaffirming the principle of universal obligation, the bill increased federal aid by discontinuing charges for arms and equipment, thereby allowing states to use federal appropriations for other related expenditures. In return, Root secured a greater federal voice in National Guard affairs, ostensibly ensuring at least minimal standards of competency. In order to continue receiving federal monies, state units had to meet annual training requirements and participate in regional field exercises with regular troops. Regulars would be detailed to inspect and also instruct state organizations, while some Guard officers would attend the army's service schools—provisions that appeared certain to strengthen cooperation and improve peacetime readiness.[11]

When viewed as a whole, the Dick Act created only a marginally stronger military system. Admittedly, the act was at least a step forward in the struggle to build a viable militia policy—as one historian contends, "a significant improvement over its archaic predecessor." But in its compromising language, the Dick Act failed to legally obligate the states to any real reform and did little to end the age-old rivalry that had marred public cooperation between the state and federal soldiers for generations.[12]

Regulars were disappointed by the bill's failure to provide for a bona fide federal reserve, but were satisfied that the War Department gained at least limited control over the militia. From the opposing perspective, the states were pleased to maintain their role as the nation's primary reserve and saw the compromise as a small price to pay for the benefits of increased federal support. But if compromise finally helped define an uncertain relationship, it also left many legal questions unanswered—ambiguities that would spark future debate across the very same partisan lines. The Dick Act by no means marked the beginning of a cooperative alliance between regulars and their militia counterparts. Before leaving Washington the next fall, Carter was already pressing Root to consider reorganizing the militia in a manner that would amplify its federal role. He and other professionalists saw the bill as an acceptable—albeit in a very limited sense—short-term victory on which they would continue to build at a more propitious date. In the meantime, efforts would focus on placing the finishing touches on those reforms already in place.[13]

On 21 February, one week after the General Staff Act passed Congress, a cornerstone was laid at the site of the new War College building to be constructed at Washington Barracks in Washington, D.C. With a long line of military and civilian dignitaries looking on, President Roosevelt and Secretary Root gave speeches that paid homage to the institution's national purpose. Root emphasized the "progressive nature" of the new system of officer education, pointing out that the War College would provide a capstone experience for those officers who demonstrated merit at the army's other professional schools—a description that echoed Carter's own language in the executive order. Root then compared the War College to the "great universities and technical schools" of the nation," drawing a parallel that elevated the officer corps to a place of professional prestige. Carter was undoubtedly very pleased with Root's comments as he proudly reflected on his own role in the recent progress and looked forward to carrying it to fruition.[14]

Throughout the spring and early summer, the WCB consumed greater amounts of Carter's time as it began to prepare for the physical creation of a general staff. He led a subcommittee that studied parts of Root's tasking of the previous October—perhaps the sole instance in which the board up to that point had been used as a true general staff-type body. Root had asked the board to analyze and report on industrial, logistic, and transportation needs for expeditionary forces of various strengths—information that has since become such a critical part of modern contingency planning. This question had become an ongoing project in which the WCB accumulated a great amount of data from various branch chiefs and field commanders before formulating its answers. During previous testimony before the Senate Military Committee, Root referred to this undertaking as a prime example of a general staff's role in building a coherent military strategy for the nation's security needs. This and numerous lesser WCB taskings kept Carter very busy during the months that followed the General Staff Act's passage.[15]

On 18 February, Root instructed the WCB to consider the question of how to go about actually building the General Staff. Ideas on the subject were submitted to the board in rather lengthy memorandums that, as might be expected, were largely founded on vague images of the Prussian staff system. Contradictory interpretations were advanced concerning the General Staff's proposed relationship with the remaining staff bureaus and also the exact nature of the new chief of staff's authority. Most army officers held only very broad notions of just what it was that a general staff was supposed to do, and thus, it was left to the board's own careful consideration to decide the army's future course. The General Staff's success depended on the WCB's ability not only to decide on its most effective organization and function but also to foresee areas of potential friction in its daily operations and relationships with other authorities. After discussing the topic for just over two weeks, the board presented their thoughts in a summary report that was derived from the work of a subcommittee consisting of Carter, Bliss, and Maj. H. A. Greene.[16]

Several conclusions, recorded in a series of fourteen rhetorical "questions and answers" on the topic, framed the WCB's approach to the General Staff's initial organization and administration. From this deliberation, Carter was tasked along with Bliss to consider and report on the desired working relationship between the General Staff and the existing staff bureaus—a subject that was extremely sensitive, given the bureaus' resentment of any encroachment on their territory.[17]

On 10 March, Carter presented a final report on the proposed general staff organization. He defined the chief of staff's role as a supervisory conduit between the secretary of war and the army at large. In a very similar manner, the individual chiefs of staff who would serve with different field organizations (e.g. expeditionary forces, divisions, and departments) would act as "the medium of communication between the subordinate parts of the army and the common superior." Furthermore, the report directly answered any surviving questions surrounding the chief of staff's relationship with the staff bureaus, providing that "upon assignment of a Chief of Staff at the War Department, all chiefs of bureaus shall report to him as the representative of the Secretary of War." In addition, the Adjutant General's Military Information Division (MID), an organization that had acted in many ways as both an embryonic intelligence bureau and planning staff since its inception in 1885, was officially transferred to the General Staff Corps, leaving the AGO as solely an administrative body for communications, correspondence, and record-keeping. From the foregoing provisions, there is little doubt that

Carter and the WCB viewed the General Staff as the army's guiding intellect, giving it the authority to address almost any defense-related question not specifically detailed to another organization. The chief of staff was meant to hold rein over all other staff functions by executive authority—a clear acknowledgment of the line's ascendance over the staff.[18]

Thus, the General Staff was given broad reach to identify and pursue issues of real substance so it did not, as Carter had previously warned, get bogged down in administrative details that were more appropriately handled by the bureaus. Cognizant of the potential for resentment and opposition to any newly vested authority, the WCB stipulated that staff officers were entitled to "the loyal and earnest cooperation of all militarymen," a reminder that the chief of staff not only represented the secretary's authority but also, at least under Root, his very personal interest.[19] Carter summarized the General Staff's functions in very broad terms:

1. To work out all necessary plans for the national defense and for mobilization of the military forces.
2. To investigate and report upon all questions affecting the efficiency of the whole army, to the end that its true state of preparedness for war maybe known to superior authority at all times.
3. To obtain, arrange and compile information and maps, especially such as relate to probable theaters of war.
4. To draft all important orders, which, upon approval of the official by whose authority the order is to be made, are then issued by and distributed through the offices of the Adjutants General.
5. To harmonize and coordinate the action of all parts of the Army, reporting . . . any necessity for action to correct existing or imminent evils.
6. To assist in the preparation of reports of campaigns, battles, etc. from journals and other information secured during the progress of operations.
7. To consider all questions concerning the militia; to prepare detailed plans and systematize methods for utilizing it under the provisions of the Constitution.[20]

The report certainly reflected Carter's conceptualization of the General Staff as much more than merely a staff section or division that would collect, organize and disseminate technical material. As Root articulated in his 1903 Annual Report, it was meant to provide the army with a degree of coherency in operational matters, both present and future—a characteristic that was singularly lacking in the Old Army.[21]

In late March, in accordance with the board's suggestion, Root moved toward translating thought to action by convening a committee for the purpose of recommending officers for detail to the General Staff. As per Carter's earlier contention that assignments had to be awarded solely on merit from the very beginning, the selections were "governed by the probable aptitude and efficiency of officers as established by their records." Appropriately, Carter was appointed to this committee, as were fellow WCB members Maj. Gen. S. B. M. Young, Brig. Gen. Tasker Bliss, and Maj. Henry Greene. They were joined by Maj. Gen. Adna R. Chaffee, Maj. Gen. John C. Bates, and Brig. Gen. Wallace F. Randolph. These men became the senior members of the first General Staff, and those officers whom they recommended would complete the organization.[22]

The importance of exercising the utmost care in putting together this initial cadre was that it would presage the manner in which the General Staff would operate. If those chosen were men with superior reputations for professional achievement, then it would underscore the serious nature of the corps' vital new role. "The army watched with marked attention," Carter recalled, "the course of the board of general officers who made the selections under oath, to guard the interests of the service." Had politics marred these first assignments, the General Staff's initial credibility would have been tarnished and its supposed high purpose met with cynical humor. In April, Root acted on the board's recommendations and assigned forty-two officers below the rank of general to the first American General Staff by virtue of Army General Orders no. 57. As these soldiers trickled into Washington and reported for duty, they began acting as a temporary staff to smooth the transition toward the permanent body later that summer.[23]

While the General Staff edged closer to reality, Carter did his part to ensure that the army's progress did not go unnoticed by the American public. According to modern social science, a requisite facet of any group's professional identity is that its clientele acknowledge their claims to professional status. Thus it was perhaps only natural that Carter continued to write for publication, seeking acclaim for the army's rites of modernity as well as some recognition of his own efforts. Private ambition seems to have affected Carter positively, undoubtedly driving his professional efforts but never becoming a consuming passion that distorted his dedication to the army's greater good. By this time, personal goals were so deeply intertwined with his vision of a modern army that the line of demarcation between selfish pretense and institutional interest was badly blurred if not indiscernible.[24]

In an article written for *Scribner's* in May 1903, Carter again overviewed the Old Army's historic inability to function with any coherency, condemning the endurance of a "hydra-headed" staff system that frustrated peacetime progress and encumbered wartime operations. Past victories, he claimed, had "come at great cost . . . in spite of the system, and not because of it." While (quite politically) applauding the Old Army's well-earned laurels over the past century, he observed that the nation's military methods had not advanced "one iota" in the glaring face of wartime lessons. The current round of reforms thus marked the beginning of a new era for the army. Reflecting on the progressive measures secured under Root's leadership, Carter noted the General Staff Act as "a fitting capstone to the long series of definite and comprehensive improvements secured in the War Department and army methods by the Secretary." He quite plainly viewed the General Staff as the final block in a foundation for a new army, one that could meet the demands of a modern world.[25]

Carter framed his thoughts in terms that were very comforting to his middle-class society. Echoing the Progressives' emphasis on organizational solutions to problems of all types, he wrote that under the new scheme "all the business of the army will be brought under the advisory control of a selected and highly trained body of experts, who, working in harmony with all the bureau chiefs, should accomplish co-operation and achievement of the most satisfactory character."[26] Carter's essay appealed to the sensibilities of *Scribner's* reading audience and reflects an acute awareness of the parlance that contemporary society reserved for the professional's true expertise. As historian James Abrahamson has pointed out, during the Root years "the language and methods of progressivism had supplanted Social Darwinism as an intellectual justification for military reform." When Carter reminded the American public that the army was becoming a more "modern" and efficient organization, it is not surprising that he did so in a manner that was familiar to his middle-class civilian contemporaries.[27]

Although it is arguable as to whether military reformers (and perhaps even Elihu Root) collectively identified themselves with Progressivism in the manner of Henry Cabot Lodge or Theodore Roosevelt, it is undeniable that their values overlapped those associated with Progressive ideology. Progressives "were members of the 'new middle class,' primarily professional and managerial people.... [who] continued the long-term trend toward rationalization, bureaucratization, and centralization in an industrializing society." This characterization also accurately describes military reforms pressed forward by soldiers that we now alternately identify as "professionalist" or "Uptonian." But military men were motivated largely by institutional concerns. Soldiers and sailors who latched onto Progressive reform did so for their own reasons: the good of their service and thus also themselves. The fact that their endeavors were aligned intellectually with the urban middle class did not necessarily identify them (individually or together) with any particular social-political movement. Many officers were drawn from the same social segments that spawned Progressive ideals, and thus logically grasped similar solutions for their own sets of issues and problems. If the Old Army lacked efficiency, coherency, and professional purpose, then the reforms that addressed these qualities were "progressive" in nature, whether officers such as Carter ever consciously identified themselves with "Progressivism" or not.[28]

During this same period Carter wrote a biographical essay on Gen. Samuel B. M. Young, whom Root had announced as the army's first chief of staff. Interestingly, Carter did not enjoy any special friendship with Young, although the two men apparently worked together amiably. Carter may even have resented his subordination to a non–West Pointer. Nonetheless, he described Young as a consummate example of "the typical American soldier," a warrior who was also comfortable with his profession's intellectual underpinnings. In this flattering portrayal, it may very well be that Carter was simultaneously extolling his own soldierly qualities—certainly he possessed the same professional virtues with which he broadly painted Young. But his interest in producing the piece was just as likely for the good of the army, from which he drew personal glory as well. After all, if the public was convinced that General Young was the cloth from which Americans cut their heroes, then this description was equally true of Carter and dozens of others. There was little need for selfish egotism because, at this point in his career, Carter could feel quite satisfied in sharing applause with colleagues.[29]

As the date on which the General Staff Act became effective neared, Carter began giving some attention to his own future. He had not been among troops for over seven years, a period during which the army had been involved almost continuously in a series of foreign wars and engagements. Many of Carter's contemporaries had garnered battlefield accolades, and he feared that if he did not return to the field quickly he would forever be branded a "swivel chair soldier" of the type that he so despised as a young cavalryman. He had all but begged for a field command during the Spanish-American War and later for a place in the expedition to China, but his timing was poor in both instances and his corporate knowledge of the Washington bureaucracy made him too valuable to let go from the War Department. Now, as a brigadier general, he asked Root for a command in the Philippines. By this time, Leigh's chronic ear affliction had become more manageable, so Carter placed the soldierly obligations of his career (and perhaps also his own ambitions) over those of family. Root acquiesced, promising an overseas assignment, but asked that Carter remain in place until the secretary returned from a planned trip to Europe.[30]

At this point, Carter's dominant role in staff reform waned as he prepared to leave Washington and passed the torch to those who would remain as part of the first General Staff. With Young as the chief of staff and Bliss as president of the new Army War College, Carter must have felt as though his beloved creations were being given to the care of others. Bliss assumed the chair of a committee to develop a "provisional organization" for the General Staff, "including its subdivisions for the performance of the work assigned to it, the duties appropriate to the respective subdivisions, and the personnel thereof." Although Carter would serve until his departure on the newly created "General Council," a de facto board of directors to oversee the General Staff's first months of existence, it was clear that the sacred work of military reform would continue without his guiding hand at the helm. On 15 August, General Orders no. 2 dissolved the War College Board and its duties were officially passed to the General Staff.[31]

Carter tinkered with several projects during these last months in Washington; foremost among them was general review of the nation's deteriorated seacoast defenses—an issue that had plagued the army for several decades. After weeks spent poring over old committee minutes, construction records and the like, he delivered a lengthy report that was perhaps a fitting end to his time alongside Root. He pointed out that nine different legally constituted boards and committees had ongoing executive or congressional authority to delve into the matter in one way or another. The result was a variety of contradictory opinions and inconsistent actions that made the federal government appear fragmented and less than forthcoming.[32]

Carter pointed to the obvious inefficiency and waste of this disheveled approach, and not surprisingly, proposed that the General Staff take up the issue to consolidate current knowledge and effort into a single strategic voice. Previously, issues of this magnitude would have floundered for lack of coherent direction. But now, with a General Staff in place, there was a body of experts to whom such questions might be directed with at least some hope of productive result. Thus, Carter's report on coastal defenses was much more than a critical review with a few good ideas in the closing paragraphs, it was a harbinger of a better future for the army. With this in mind, Root had copies distributed to each member of the General Staff as a signal illustration of exactly the sort of professional activity that he demanded from a modern army.

When Root returned from London that fall, Carter began preparations to depart Washington. In a sort of farewell memorandum to the secretary, he outlined his thoughts on the General Staff's best opportunities for eventual prosperity. He warned that its ultimate success and "lasting foundation" would likely depend upon the manner in which the secretary himself conducted the department's daily business and enforced the intended supervisory relationship between the chief of staff and the several bureaus. "Carping criticism should be expected and silent animosity may vent itself in preparing stumbling blocks," he warned, "but no great reform ever had less of these to contend with." Carter firmly believed that once the new staff system was on its feet, the great majority of officers would recognize its advantages and quickly become enthusiastic supporters. Its first months of existence were thus critical to its long-term success.[33]

Carter had arrived in Washington almost eight years earlier as a newly promoted major at the age of forty-five. Now, having earned a reputation as a resourceful staff officer and a prominent leader in the fight for military reform, he left duly rewarded as a brigadier general. His time on the staff had been well spent—productive for his own

advancement as well as that of the army. But such hard-fought progress, at the expense of deeply ingrained tradition, was not achieved
without accumulating some ill feeling in its wake. As Carter matter-
of-factly put it, "No one could do any original work or secure the
adoption of any reforms without arousing antagonisms." Added to
this provocation was Carter's own rapid rise in rank and influence—
not easily overlooked by some of his more ambitious and understand-
ably envious brother officers.[34]

With good cause, as later events would tell, Carter became concerned that negative fallout from his work would follow him and
bring harm to his career. "I fully appreciated the difficulties of my
position," he later recalled, "and knew that in the reformation of War
Department business methods . . . I would incur the hostility natural
and unavoidable in those who were to be deprived of former power."
But these fears must have been at least temporarily allayed by Root's
lofty expression of gratitude in his report that fall.[35]

Carter helped gather material for the 1903 annual report, completing the work at Root's home on Thanksgiving evening. The secretary was already considering his own departure from the War Department, and may have intended the effort as a sort of tour de force that
would leave a written record of his recent successes.[36] In recounting
the creation of the General Staff, Root described it as "the important
military event of the year affecting the Regular Army," and specifically praised Carter in very generous terms:

> Special credit is due to Brig. Gen. William H. Carter for the
> exceptional ability and untiring industry which he has con-
> tributed to the work of devising, bringing about, and putting
> into operation the general staff law. He brought thorough and
> patient historical research and wide experience, both in the
> line and the staff, to the aid of long-continued, anxious, and
> concentrated thought upon the problem of improving mili-
> tary administration, and if the new system shall prove to
> be an improvement the gain to the country will have been
> largely due to him.[37]

If Carter had privately longed for public acclaim for his tireless work,
he certainly had his reward. Only very rarely was the secretary's published report used as a forum for explicit individual accolades, and it
must have given him great satisfaction to be thus singled out.

His professional alliance with Root had grown into a strong friendship and the admiration expressed by the secretary was mutually felt. In the final days before Carter left for his posting as commander of the Department of Visayas, the two men went on a final horseback ride together and discussed their success. "I had now been on duty of an intimate character with Secretary Root during four years," he wrote later, "and recognized the great value of the association in perfecting my knowledge of my own profession, and in acquiring a broad knowledge of governmental administration and legislative procedure." Both men were very aware of the seminal importance of the reforms they had effected, even as the resultant institutions struggled in the uphill transition from paper to reality.[38]

Root assured Carter that his service to the nation could not have been greater if he had won distinction in Cuba or served with Chaffee in Peking. Their joint legacy to the army was of a more permanent type than fleeting battlefield laurels. Reflecting on this consolation, Carter noted that

> there were many fine men retained in administrative work during the War with Spain against their inclination and expressed wishes. Military men live in prayerful hope of opportunity for fame, aptly described as the radiant mist of glory, yet in the vast majority of cases, the interests of the individual are hopelessly submerged in those of the nation. I had not been allowed to choose the field of my employment, but I had given the best that was in me to doing well my appointed tasks. Coming fresh from nearly a quarter of a century of duty with troops, I was enabled to point out their needs in a way to secure many needed reforms.[39]

These comments highlight an important requisite to understanding Carter's success as a reformer. After "nearly a quarter century of duty with troops," he was undeniably a participant in the Old Army culture and understood its shortfalls with sober clarity. He had suffered the disjointed efforts that separated staff from line, listened in quiet disbelief as traditionalists scoffed at the idea of professional study, and witnessed the sorry disarray that resulted from the lack of coordinated planning and strategic direction. He was a bona fide trooper of the Old Army, but had managed to temper his acculturation with a personal intellect that transcended its inertia. Now, after helping lay the groundwork for a more modern army, he returned to the field a little unsure of his own place in a very dynamic institution.

Carter's time in Washington was marked by great changes in the American army, not only in its organization but also in its professional expectations. Beginning with the Reorganization Act, the Root Reforms, at least on paper, built a New Army that was characterized by a more "modern" approach to its functions both in war and peace. National defense in an industrialized world required armies and navies that were well prepared to meet lethal foes across vast physical spaces drawn smaller by new modes of transportation and communication. To this end, military progressives attempted to tear down traditional line-staff animosities, educate a more professional officer corps to be knowledgeable in the conduct of modern warfare, create a true general staff capable of long-term planning and strategic direction, and ensure that the militia assumed at least reasonable standards of preparedness and competence. Taken as a whole, these related acts centralized authority in the hands of experts who would manage the nation's defense with a sense of vision while standing ready to offer advice to civil authorities on matters of military importance.[40]

Although a laudable first step, the Root Reforms were only a beginning in the transition between old and new. On the occasion of Root's retirement from the War Department, Carter extolled the secretary's accomplishments while underlining the hard work that remained: "Secretary Root has laid the foundation for a state of preparedness for war on the part of the United States which has hitherto been unknown; it will remain for his successors in office to continue the great work which he has so thoroughly inaugurated, and to build upon the foundation so wisely laid during the past few years of active field and administrative experiences."[41] Carter, of course, hailed his own achievements by association in this passage, but nonetheless accurately identified the very tenuous nature of recent progress. He departed for the Philippines very aware that the Old Army's transition to modernity still promised to be a long and frustrating process.

An Army of Uncertainty

In the Philippines, the army was embroiled in a situation that was strikingly familiar. Soldiers were given the unenviable and inconsistent task of simultaneously securing the islands' return to peace while maintaining tightly held imperial rule. Many different factors combined to "create an atmosphere reminiscent of the 'Wild West': a boom or bust economy, an ethnocentric conqueror's mentality, and the ever-present threat of uprising." Enemies were not only the physical type—those bandits and guerillas who roamed the island mountains and preyed on isolated villages and farms—but also the spiritual states of misery, destitution, and hopelessness that gripped the Filipino people. Just as in the American West, the military was again cast as the strong arm of an unpleasant federal policy that, in its most extreme implications, called for the fundamental alteration of an entire culture. Thus, in 1904, Carter's return to the field was met by leadership challenges that were in many ways similar to those faced by his own superiors decades earlier.[1]

After taking a detour through England and France to report on each nation's system of procuring cavalry remounts, Carter rendezvoused in Gibraltar with Ida and Leigh—now nineteen years old—while continuing the journey eastward. William Vaulx Carter was by then a cadet in the West Point class of 1904, and thus did not accompany the family. The remainder of the trip took them through Malta, Egypt, Aden, and Singapore, and the many curious sights illustrated the fact that industrialization had "modernized" only parts of the world. "The older nations strive for the welfare of their own people," Carter remarked, "[while] the pursuit of wealth was absorbing Americans, to the great exclusion of all else," a realization soon underlined by the discouraging circumstances that greeted him in the Visayas a few days later. But after arriving in the Philippines, his attention quickly turned from philosophical reflection to the problems of leading an expeditionary army.[2]

General Carter assumed command of the Department of Visayas on 23 February 1904, accepting the reins of a situation that was proving very difficult to control. The Philippine Insurrection, as American historians most often remember it, had turned the department into a political, administrative, and military quagmire, to say the least. Two years after President Roosevelt's premature proclamation of peace, brutal banditry still ravaged the islands and American imperialism was far from reconciled with local realities. An illusive enemy, rampant disease, unfamiliar tropical climate, and shifting Filipino allegiances combined to make "pacification" a hollow promise of political hyperbole and a demoralizing test of endurance for the U.S. Army.[3]

In Carter's department, the islands of Samar, Leyte, Cebu, and Negros had all experienced outbreaks of widespread violence—less the result of any organized rebellion than the localized expression of collective discontent. Insurrection boiled under the guise of ethnic, political, and religious identity, creating a crisis with very few clear answers. Though foundations for a New Army had only recently been mapped in Root's War Department, there was no sign of these efforts in the Visayas, where conditions gave soldiers little opportunity to consider distant issues of lofty professional reform. "There is no such thing as peace in the islands, as we understand the term at home," Carter wrote. "Brigands under various names . . . exist in all the islands and live off of those who work or accumulate worldly goods." Cultural misunderstanding and antipathies exacerbated the tension, clouded by the well-developed American proclivity for Anglo-centric philanthropy. Just as "do-gooders" attempted to acculturate American Indian tribes in their own image, so did imperialists try to impose a "progressive vision of order, homogeneity and scientific reform," dismissing opposition "as further evidence of their charges' superstition, childishness, and irresponsibility." In short, American governance applied American-style cures to Filipino problems, wholly missing the coarse realities at hand.[4]

Carter was by no means immune to this tendency, despite heartfelt sympathy for the Filipino plight. He saw the situation in terms of a simple economic equation: "It is the old, old story of a long strike—discord, arson, and murder. When prosperity returns to the Visayas, those who are willing to labor will find ample employment; and the strong army of the government may then be effectively employed to restore order and give protection to life and property."[5] The Visayas grew large amounts of sugar and hemp and in fact were able to export portions of both crops abroad. But production was inefficient, and, as Carter noted disgustedly, the market was greedily manipulated by imperial "shylocks" who had no regard for the laborers or even growers. European interests controlled local commerce, extracting any profit potential from the region and leaving it nearly destitute. In a perspective that had obvious parallels with General George Crook's administration of the Apaches years earlier (which Carter observed first-hand), he believed that the solution lay in building access to profitable markets for the general populace. Like many others, Carter was convinced that Filipinos deserved the American Dream, even if they simply did not yet realize it.[6]

Administration in the Department of Visayas, like everywhere in the Philippines, was fragmented between military and civilian authority. Personal and institutional animosities impaired cooperation, a relationship eerily reminiscent of the one that had existed between the Frontier Army and the Bureau of Indian Affairs. In this difficult environment, Carter attempted to reconcile his enthusiasm for a modern conventional army with harsh unconventional realities. When querilla-style insurrection again gripped the island of Samar, questions of higher policy and professional growth were quickly reduced to the daily denominator of company-sized tactical patrols in isolated mountain valleys. With few resources beyond overt physical force at their disposal, soldiers attempted to patch together a lasting peace of the sort already claimed by Roosevelt. Carter deplored the army's inability to respond effectively to continuing attacks by numerous bands of *ladrones*. When an American soldier was ambushed and killed on Samar in early 1904, Carter anguished over the fact that his hands were tied by a colonial policy that forbade military action except in direct self-defense. He vented his anger over this and similar episodes by calling for an expansion of the army's authority.[7]

Instead of turning to the Philippine Constabulary, a sort of paramilitary police force, Carter wanted to employ the Regular Army to chase down and physically punish the guerillas. This argument actually signaled his loud entry into an ongoing debate over the most effective use of Filipino volunteers. Carter's firmly held opinion on the subject, expressed in his annual report, quickly became a source of controversy.[8]

In the absence of an organized insular army or, for that matter, even a functioning native government, the Constabulary was created as an agency through which colonial law enforcement and public responsibility might be shared with the Filipino people. Originally intended to "occupy practically the place filled by United States marshals in the United States," the Constabulary's role gradually became more paramilitary as banditry spread. At the same time, the army maintained Philippine Scout companies that trained and operated alongside American regulars. The simultaneous existence of these two organizations might have effectively complemented one another, but once again, competing personalities and institutional interests clouded an already-difficult situation.[9]

Army captain Henry T. Allen, the Constabulary's chief, had begun waging a campaign to widen the organization's authority and mission. Although such action allowed the army to pull back from forward-based commitments in many outlying areas, Allen sparked opposition with his simultaneous attempts to incorporate the Filipino Scouts into the Constabulary. Many regulars on the scene saw this as a high-handed appropriation of much-needed troops from their own organizations, and furthermore, as an obstacle to the eventual formation of a Filipino colonial army that might permit a diminished American presence. By the time Carter arrived in the Visayas, Allen's gambit had successfully placed over half of the Scout companies under civil authority alongside his Constabulary.[10]

As conditions in the department deteriorated during the summer of 1904, Carter entered this discussion with his penchant for written argument. He recognized that the question of the Scouts' utility versus that of the Constabulary reached deeper to the more basic issue of colonial authority. In a letter to the adjutant general, he implicitly attacked civilian oversight of what he considered an entirely military situation, deploring the governor's attempt to combat open insurrection (by means of the engorged Constabulary) without calling for the army's assistance. His ill-concealed jab at Samar's civil governance reflected the strained relationship between civilian and military authorities throughout the Philippine Islands. With his Uptonian roots showing, Carter chafed at what he interpreted as direct interference in military affairs by persons who lacked any martial expertise. If not war itself, then circumstances in the Philippines closely approximated war, and he believed that it was thus the army's indisputable business to translate policy to operations—not the business of a colonial government with the help of a paramilitary police force.[11]

Furthermore, Carter viewed the Filipino Scouts as a product of his own labor, having played a role in their creation through his authorship of the 1901 Army Reorganization Act. The measure authorized the enlistment of up to twelve thousand Filipinos as troops under the command of regular officers, thus giving birth to those organizations that were currently being absorbed by Allen's ambitious plans for the Constabulary.[12] Carter reminded the secretary of the Scouts' intended purpose, which, he asserted, was weakened by their long-term detachment to the Constabulary:

> It was intended to identify this force with the regular army just as the Indian Scout organizations were in the United States. There was no intention or thought of mixing the scout companies with a constabulary or municipal police force but to keep them as distinct as are the Indian Scouts and Indian Reservation Police in the United States. . . . The present course is tending to defeat the intent of the act of February 2nd, 1901.[13]

If allowed to run its course, Carter argued, Allen's plan would eventually destroy the "value of the scouts," and leave no alternative but to increase the presence of regular troops. This warning grew from his belief that cheery civilian descriptions of the Visayan situation were far removed from the reality of escalating violence.

Carter vented his wrath at Allen's efforts as an extension of his disgust with colonial authority. As a soldier, it disturbed him to watch idly as the Constabulary conducted combat-style operations within his department. And so his comments on Allen's use of the Scouts were really an indirect attack on the more basic circumstance of American imperial governance in the Philippines. Carter argued that, owing to a continued "state of grave disorder" in his department, the Constabulary could not hope to maintain peace without the direct intervention of the army and the Filipino scouts. Attempting to do so by altering the Constabulary's domestic role was incongruent with its organization, ability, and purpose. "The most business like and economical plan for the Philippine Government," Carter asserted, "is to stop the growing tendency of the constabulary to convert itself into a regular army and hold this force strictly to duty as a provincial and government police force." Of course, this argument demanded that civil authorities call for the army's help in situations that grew beyond criminal activity—a tacit admission of failed insular policy.[14]

Perhaps reflecting his recent immersion in Washington's raucous political arena, Carter stooped to an exaggerated description of the possible dangers that might result from Allen's expansion of the Constabulary's role. He implied that in combination the Scouts and Constabulary constituted numbers of armed natives who, when "removed from the restraints of army discipline," might become a real danger to American security. This racially loaded comment was surely calculated to snare the War Department's attention, as was his simultaneous argument that the costs of maintaining an enlarged Constabulary would far exceed the fiscal capacities of the Philippine treasury. Carter then revealed his true purpose, demanding that civil government respect the boundaries of army authority:

> In America there has never been any doubt as to the wisdom of, or hesitation about employing the regular army against Indian marauders who correspond to the organized bands of ladrones, tulisanes, babylanes, pulihanes and outlaws, of whatever name, in these islands, but there is a disinclination here to use the regular troops, except scout companies *when placed under command of constabulary officers* [emphasis his].[15]

He made it clear that the only feasible course was to increase the number of Scout companies from their present strength. They could then continue to act as a short-term reserve for the Constabulary while still augmenting the Regular Army. Carter's contention that civil government was attempting to solve military problems for which they lacked the necessary resources and expertise was soon evidenced when an odd spiritualism in the Visayas erupted into open rebellion.

By midsummer of 1904, sporadic violence on Samar had grown into a full-scale armed insurrection. The island's poverty and hopelessness gave rise to a "religious movement that promised both salvation and revenge." Adherents were known as "Pulahanes," but as violence spread, the term was soon applied to almost any unsavory group or individual. Carter described the outbreaks as spontaneous, with no real direction, religious or otherwise: "Whatever may have been the original cause of the outbreak, it was soon lost sight of when success had drawn a large proportion of the people away from their homes and fields. The lawless bands simply degenerated into opposition to all control and carried on a reign of terror throughout a large portion of the island."[16]

Very little is known of the religious beliefs that may have spawned the movement, but it seems to have been a very peculiar blend of Christianity and shamanism. Aside from a loose identification with the Pulahane movement, no particular objective or ideological interest seemed to motivate those who claimed membership. Its goals were less military or political than they were simple plunder, fear, and panic.[17]

Despite some success by the Constabulary in early 1905, Carter complained that Allen's "consistently rosy reports" obscured truly dismal conditions. "The situation gradually got beyond control of the constabulary and scout services," and by the end of May, the governor-general was finally forced to request army intervention. Allen, stinging from implications of failure, grumbled that "Carter now has a free hand in East Samar; let us see the speed with which he captures leaders and guns. . . . He will now be given a fair chance to learn that capturing and running down criminal bands in Samar requires time and is more difficult than criticism." Finally given the unfettered authority that he coveted, Carter immediately put his "free hand" to good use.[18]

On 4 June, the army took the battle to the very heart of the insurrection's leadership, making a daring attack on the camp of Enrique

Daguhob, the Pulahanes' self-proclaimed high-priest and chieftain. This victory, won by a mixed detachment of American regulars and Scouts, set the stage for the ensuing campaign and did a great deal to break the rebellion's back. Comparing the Pulahanes to the ghost-dancing Sioux, Carter was elated with the success:

> Daguhob claimed supernatural powers identical with those claimed by the medicine men who brought about the ghost dancers' craze which affected nearly all the Indians of the plains in 1890–91. . . . The people of northern Samar appear to have believed all this implicitly until a couple of Krag bullets removed Daguhob from the field of action, when they began presenting themselves to the authorities by hundreds.[19]

In harrowing hand-to-hand fighting that lasted over thirty minutes, Daguhob himself was killed along with ninety-four of his followers. Although the rebellion continued for several more months, many guerrillas subsequently gave up and reconciled themselves to the colonial order of things on their island.

On Samar, the army readily embraced the more subtle aspects of fighting an insurrection. Perhaps owing in part to his experiences under Crook in Arizona, Carter moved to reestablish the government's legitimacy by providing food, supplies, and even land to indigenous refugees while attempting to stop the exploitation of laborers and farmers by the *"presidentes"*—heavies who controlled local markets. These efforts were rewarded ten-fold as many *insurrectos* were coaxed in from the jungles and mountains and even turned against their former comrades in support of the U.S.–sanctioned government. An important factor in this strategy's success was that many Pulahanes, even some of the movement's most notorious chieftains, professedly harbored no real grudge against the American presence and had taken to violence out of sheer desperation with their deteriorated conditions. Thus, they readily returned to a peaceful existence when the excitement of rebellion turned sour.[20]

Once engaged, the army achieved swift success. Within a year, the Pulahanes were all but completely defeated with very few remaining in defiance of government authority. Under Carter's leadership, the insurrection was met with decisive military force, but without the rampant brutality and inhumanity that tarnished other such campaigns in the Philippines. Although his aggressive claim to jurisdiction came at Allen's expense and was likely motivated partly by institutional self-interest as well as personal ambition (Allen's biographer claims that Carter's actions in this regard were vindictively motivated), his overall management of the operation was very effective in restoring peace. Carter rightfully felt vindicated as the Pulahanes were dealt defeat after defeat. By the summer of 1906, the island was once again largely "pacified" and under colonial control.[21]

But sterile terms such as "control" and "pacification" are not necessarily congruent with a truly contented populace. Despite the Pulahanes' defeat, continued unrest and sporadic violence throughout the Philippines reflected the native population's fundamental misgivings about the state of affairs in their islands. Carter recognized this not-altogether-subtle reality and saw its ultimate solution in terms reflecting his own middle-class ideals. American imperial impulses have been characterized as a "a strange amalgam of humanitarianism and cultural arrogance," and this description neatly fits Carter's personal perspective. Individual labor bore material rewards, and thus the Filipinos could be satisfied if only provided with ready markets for their products and services. He saw the idealized American experience as an obvious panacea for the human ills that he witnessed around him.[22]

Carter translated the pitiful conditions in his department to western-style capitalism, finding "no relief" for the poverty and misery in the Visayas except through the development of competitive markets. Exploitation by a small number of corrupt middlemen in the few coastal towns caused dissatisfaction and set the stage for instigators who manipulated the circumstances for their own selfish ends. "A criminal element is always in waiting to take advantage of isolated situations and lead on disorder," Carter grumbled, "just as walking delegates and strike leaders do in more civilized communities, and with the same species of cruelty to those who wish to continue work instead of joining the law breakers." In this juxtaposition with the conditions of American labor unrest, he clearly failed to consider the many cultural differences that might render material solutions inappropriate or at least less than successful. Like so many other Americans, Carter saw the Philippines through a sympathetic but nonetheless ethnocentric lens.[23]

But the more Carter saw of the Filipinos' suffering, the more indignant he became, questioning aloud whether it was truly in the

United States' interests to deprive its "Oriental wards" of "simple justice." Although careful to define these injustices in material terms, he
argued for their solution on both practical and moral grounds. The
"mad struggle for commercial and industrial supremacy" should not
cloud the nation's moral obligation to the Filipinos, who lacked influence and representation to argue for themselves. The Philippines deserved a helping hand, if only to ensure their loyalty, and he advocated
removing tariffs to encourage free enterprise on the islands—an act
that would "bind the great body of property-holders and their employees to the government by ties of common interest."[24]

In a report submitted to the War Department in late August 1904,
Carter pressed economic development as a foundation for lasting
peace in the Philippines. He believed that the army's arrival with its
extensive support infrastructure had discouraged native commerce.
Presenting his ideas in terms of the greater colonial good, he espoused
privatizing transportation and communication routes to stimulate
internal trade. He hoped that this would spur the development of
products and services that currently lacked viable markets without competitive means of private transportation. "That something
should be done in the immediate future to build up commerce and
make inter-island trade a safe and profitable business, admits of no
controversy," Carter continued, "if the people are to be made pros-
perous and contented. Discouragement reigns throughout all classes
and failure and poverty confront the community as a whole." The
memo was endorsed with little enthusiasm on its way through the
department's cold bureaucracy, and eventually ended up as a nice idea
that warranted no further action.[25]

Carter's convictions reflect a combination of Progressive ideals—
holding up material reward as the natural outcome of hard work, fair
play, and international justice—and genuine compassion for the sorry
conditions in his department. He had not arrived in the Visayas with
such views: "When General Carter came over here," wrote an acquaintance on the islands, "he was one of the most enthusiastic Oriental expansionists whom I have had the pleasure of meeting, but
actual contact with conditions out here soon opened his eyes, as you
may judge from his report."[26] Carter supported the American presence, never really questioning the rights of imperial expansion, but
demanded actions to relieve the Filipino's demoralized state:

Whether or not it be true, the Filipino people regard themselves as victims of American greed and that our altruistic professions do not accord with our practice. Will the people of this great country . . . deal generously and justly by the Filipinos and give them a chance to share in some of the world's prosperity, or shall the present short-sighted policy be adhered to, with a certainty of closing every avenue leading to loyalty, respect and affection for America and Americans?[27]

As he did during his years spent near the Indians, Carter felt an inner tension between his role as military administrator and his fervently held values. He made few friends in Washington by publicly declaring his reservations, but conscience apparently overcame any immediate worries for his career.

In early August of 1905, with conditions in the Visayas steadily returning to government control, Carter was notified of his imminent return to the United States. In Washington, Adna Chaffee argued for Carter's assignment to replace Bliss as assistant to the chief of staff, but after some dissension over the choice, President Roosevelt squelched this plan in favor of another officer. This turnabout sparked a heated confrontation between Chaffee and several members of the selection board, characterized by one stateside newspaper as the "liveliest squabble in the war department for a long time." Carter was subsequently given command of the Department of the Lakes—a lateral move that must have come as no small disappointment. He later attributed this minor controversy to jealous animosity left over from his days with Root.[28]

By this time, Carter was beginning to see himself as a sort of tragic hero in the "cause" of professional progress. According to his own narrative, he "had no desire whatever to return to the War Department at that time," but only acquiesced to Chaffee's overtures to fulfill a perceived higher responsibility to the work already begun under Root. Carter maintained that he was already receiving requests from senior friends at the War Department to prepare a history of the General Staff Act, and thus consented to the detail "purely in the interests of the service." This may be an accurate self-portrayal insofar as it described his initial reaction to the proposed assignment, but by the time it had unraveled in such a public manner, Carter's professional ego was left bruised and very much out of sorts. The trepidation he felt for his career as he left Washington just two years earlier seemed to have been justified.[29]

In April 1908, two years after his return from the Philippines, Carter addressed a letter to Root that vividly illustrates his defensive reaction to this perceived slight. He worried that others privately wondered if his performance in Visayas had somehow tainted his record, and he wanted the former secretary to know that his service there had given him "no course to be ashamed." His recommendations concerning the islands' colonial administration, and specifically the Constabulary's use, were the result of "honest observations of . . . administrative mistakes, costly in life and public funds." For these efforts, Carter believed, he had "reaped the reward of the reformer," which he apparently translated to mean undeserved censure by senior individuals in the current administration and perhaps even the White House.[30]

Carter was also concerned that his handling of the so-called Grafton Case had made him the target of certain officials who "took umbrage and seemed to think that their authority would be impugned if justice was done." Private Homer Grafton was an American soldier who shot and killed two Filipino natives who attacked him while he was standing guard. After Grafton was acquitted by a military court for reason of self-defense, it was Carter's decision as department commander not to support the soldier's subsequent conviction by a civil proceeding. The case became a flash point for fierce debate on the issue of civil-military jurisdiction in the Philippines, and in simplified terms, it pitted the army against the insular government. Carter believed the civil trial was tainted by perjury and local prejudice and filed an appeal that was eventually upheld by the U.S. Supreme Court. But even so, he worried that this controversy perhaps also brought him the unspoken hostility of some in the administration. "Our history is quite filled with injustice to officials arising from adverse opinions drawn from particular incidents," he wrote. "The verdict of my own conscience is self-approval and in any event I have too many resources to waste my time in nursing a grievance."[31]

In another letter, written shortly after he assumed command of the Department of the Lakes, Carter shed some interesting light on the intrigue that he believed surrounded his rescinded assignment back to the General Staff. Chaffee had told him that it was

Gen. John C. Bates, Chaffee's replacement as chief of staff, who led opposition to his appointment. Apparently, Bates argued that Carter had "made enemies of the chiefs of bureau and certain newspaper correspondents," leaving grave doubts as to his effectiveness if indeed he returned to the General Staff. Needless to say, Carter deeply resented Bates's interference and felt the slight was an unjustified act of vengeance by those who opposed his earlier reform efforts. "You know Mr. Secretary," he advised Root, "that I never tried to push myself except by work which would justify my advancement legitimately, and I do feel rather unkindly to think of General Bates and others for allowing me, for such alleged reasons, to be injured in the public service." Increasingly feeling and playing the part of a martyr, he then accused his antagonists of purposely sabotaging the army's institutional progress, complaining that "the General Staff measure has been hurt by those high in authority who have never yet properly studied or comprehended it. I will say to you privately, this includes both General Bates and General Wade." Carter's professional pride bristled as he reflected on efforts at his expense.[32]

Under this cloud of animosity, he viewed Root's continued friendship and high opinion as a redeeming shelter for his professional self-image. At the age of fifty-four, he was well aware that the potential for battlefield glory at the head of a large army was quickly passing into the realm of unrealized boyhood dreams. But despite professional frustrations and personal disappointments, Carter could look back on his service in the Visayas with a sense of great accomplishment. He had performed admirably while taking on what proved to be a difficult and thankless task. Although his experience in the Philippines gave him reservations about the direction of American foreign policy, he remained dedicated to the professional soldier's objective role in a republican society. His first assignment after several years in Washington was eye-opening. He had left the War Department with full knowledge that the struggle for reform did not end with a legislative act, but likely did not realize the full impact that America's new imperial interests would have on the army's obligations and, in turn, its institutional progress. As he had learned, professional reform was a painstaking process, and the army's far-flung deployment under miserable conditions only made its implementation more difficult, dampening hopes that a truly New Army might become a reality anytime soon.[33]

After Carter served for several weeks in temporary command of the Philippines Division in Manila, he and Ida returned to the United States by way of Hong Kong, China, Japan, and Hawaii. The round-about itinerary included a memorable leave spent sightseeing and collecting souvenirs for friends and family at home. They marveled at Asia's historic sights and found Japan an especially enjoyable place, noting that its people were "wise, temperate, industrious, hardy and self-respecting." While in Yokohama, the Carters celebrated their silver wedding anniversary, a milestone that, as Ida reminded the general, was made all the more remarkable when one considered the numerous privations that army life had subjected them to. In a side-note, Carter observed that Japan had abandoned centuries of isolationism in its war with Russia, and was in the process of entering the imperial race with spoils in Korea and China. "Applying similar tactics to private quarrels," he pondered, "we would have two neighbors entering the yard of a third person to fight over their quarrel, and then adjourn to the doorstep of the third party and agree upon terms for evicting him from his house and grounds in order that the quarreling neighbors might divide the property on which they had fought."[34] With this analogy in mind, he decided that "much of international action in the past has verged closely upon brigandage on a large scale. What is accepted as merely adroit and resourceful in statesmanship becomes intrigue and crime when applied to individuals"—an appropriate subscript for his first tour in the colonial Philippines.[35]

The Department of the Lakes, headquartered in Chicago, had existed under various names with shifting boundaries since before the War of 1812. During the Indian Wars, department commanders were quite active in the daily operations that took place under their authority. But by 1906, with so many units engaged overseas and the disappearance of a geographic frontier in the western United States, territorial commands had become administrative in nature with training their most common activity. The Department of the Lakes could boast only two full regiments of infantry, a battalion of field artillery, and an assortment of other smaller detachments. But, as Carter put it, "a nation cannot go to war or maintain large armies just to test its generals." In the absence of more pressing challenges, he turned again to his profession's theoretical side to occupy his energies and satisfy his ambitions.[36]

The department's few operations during this period included

summer exercises that were held jointly with the National Guard. These endeavors were in the spirit of the Dick Act's emphasis on federal-state cooperation, ostensibly ensuring that the militia remained a viable component of the nation's wartime forces. Although Carter still suspected that state organizations would never truly provide an adequate reserve, he embraced summer maneuvers as a welcome escape from the tedium of headquarters life. At Camp Benjamin Harrison, Indiana, he instituted changes that encouraged a hands-on learning environment, departing from the competitively charged atmosphere of previous years that had drawn complaints. He hoped to provide training while not demanding unrealistic technical proficiency from National Guard attendees.[37]

Carter noted with equal pride that regulars and Guardsmen alike seemed to benefit from the experience, with valuable learning taking place before his very eyes. Charles King, prolific novelist of the Old Army and Carter's friend, observed the maneuvers and applauded obvious improvements in the encampment's training regimen. Since receiving a medical retirement from regular service, King had served with various militia organizations, and thus his dual perspective was of great value. Comparing the 1906 exercises in the Department of the Lakes to similar encampments elsewhere, King found Carter's effort to be the epitome of a "proper blending of the professional and non-professional military elements," and was delighted that his own Wisconsin units were eager to attend the next summer's training.[38]

As both Carter and King noted, the real advantage of joint maneuvers was that Americans were training as they would fight if called to war—professionals and amateurs side-by-side. The complaints of disgruntled Uptonians and some Guardsmen to the contrary, any national military effort in the foreseeable future would have to reconcile both mindsets with the cold realities of modern conflict. In the absence of a true federal reserve, such training was vital to improving the National Guard's readiness. Carter measured the value of these summer encampments in terms of preparedness for large-scale conventional warfare:

> These camps and others taught the younger generation to think in terms of brigades and divisions, instead of companies and battalions, as was the case with the army between

the Civil War and the War with Spain. I found that long periods in camp, in command of divisions, gave me a better opportunity to acquire knowledge of my own duties than could ever be done by remaining at the headquarters in a city.[39]

His open attitude toward the Guard's participation demonstrated an ability to overcome personal bias to make the best of less-than-desirable situations. Carter's mind had not changed—his views on the issue of a national reserve remained decidedly Uptonian, but he was able to compromise these beliefs for the greater good of the army and the nation, commendable for a professional soldier serving a democratic society.

During this same period, Carter was increasingly dissatisfied with the direction of his career. Correspondence with Elihu Root indicates that he feared Bates and other hidden enemies had successfully scuttled his further advancement. In June 1906, only a few months after assuming department command, he asked Root to look into Secretary Taft's plans to replace Gen. Albert Mills, who would retire as West Point's superintendent later that summer. "If they want a general officer for the Academy," he beseeched his friend, "I am the senior graduate of the brigadiers after General Bell, and would esteem it a great honor to succeed Mills and carry forward the great work begun at West Point." This appeal was well within the appropriate standards of the day, but it seems somewhat disingenuous for an officer who had often deplored the evil results of patronage on the army's professional well-being. Perhaps doing so made him feel uncomfortable, because he added the caveat that Root should ignore his request if the matter of Mills's replacement was already settled or if broaching the subject would cause embarrassment.[40]

A year later, Carter again asked Root to intercede on his behalf. This time, as the occasion of Major General Wade's retirement approached, he demonstrated aggressive ambition that, in retrospect, seems somewhat less than admirable. Carter asked for Root's support in the event that the army's senior brigadier, Frederick Funston, was for some reason not promoted to fill Wade's two-star billet. Funston, Carter implied, would be promoted only as a reward for service rendered rather than for any demonstrated capacity to lead the General Staff. "The need of high officers familiar with administrative and General Staff problems was never greater in our army than now," he argued, reminding Root "that many grave questions . . . now confront the army . . . which require study and technical ability of no mean order." Clearly, he was not above imposing on Root's friendship for his own advancement. But rather than a damning indictment of his personal sense of professional fair play, his efforts merely reflect the atmosphere of self-promotion and institutional politics that marked the contemporary officer corps.[41]

Carter was outraged when Brig. Gen. McCaskey, his junior in grade, was promoted over both Funston and himself in order that McCaskey might retire at the higher rank. "The President has been pestered to appoint all the elderly gentlemen approaching retirement," Carter exploded, "yet of all those so appointed not one has taken a serious hand in army improvement in recent years, nor [is] it natural that any of them should." His previously polite requests for Root's help had become almost indignant pleas for what he considered professional justice. Carter's arguments, although perhaps well founded, sounded increasingly less than gracious. Gentlemanly deportment became less of a constraint as opportunities for further promotion seemed to slip out of reach.[42]

By August 1907, it had been intimated to Carter that, although Funston likely would not be promoted, neither would he—a bitter disappointment that prompted yet another appeal to Root. In a tone that betrayed a sense of frustrated urgency, he again defended his record and all but demanded reconsideration:

> I feel sure that Secretary Taft is a man of too much character to subject me to the mortification of being passed over without a fair examination of my record. . . . I owe my present position to you and President Roosevelt and if promoted in turn I feel sure I will exercise the functions of the higher grade in a way to assure you both that if a war comes I will not be found wanting.[43]

That the nature of Carter's friendship with Root allowed such uninhibited and even artless requests is apparent—the two continued to correspond and exhibit mutually warm admiration for many years afterward. But the near-desperation exuded in these letters reveals an ambition that is difficult to reconcile with the selflessness of earlier years.[44]

Carter's willingness to engage in political intrigue grew from genuine concerns that his career was faltering. Like most professional soldiers, he had dreamed of heroic command since his days as a young cadet, and the fact that he remained in Washington during both the War with Spain and later the China Expedition grated on his self-image as the modern-day cavalier. A sort of inner tension is apparent in his simultaneous disdain for army politics as a bane of true professionalism and his willful entry into this very practice. To a degree, this inconsistency grew from the dichotomous nature of his career. On the one hand, he was the archetype of the new military intellectual, an active voice in issues that defined not only the nation's defense but also the army's relationship with the society it served. On the other hand, in his heart he remained a cavalryman of the old school and longed for his place at the head of an army. Carter fretted that indulgence of the former by virtue of his long service near Root might in the end deprive him of his grittier ambitions as an officer of the line.

While battling for promotion and attempting to revitalize training in his department, Carter continued to be productive with the pen. In 1906, he published *Old Army Sketches*, a collection of short stories and anecdotes that were left over from his previous research for *From Yorktown to Santiago*. The little book gave readers quaint insights into the army's frontier culture—at least as the soldiers themselves remembered it with no small amount of fraternal nostalgia. He hoped that the book would help imbue the respect and recognition that he felt the army deserved. He worried that America's youth were no longer awed by tales of martial glory and national service, and that the army was becoming something less than a cross-section of society at large.[45]

After returning to the United States from abroad, he wondered why so many seemingly vigorous and patriotic young men showed no interest whatsoever in pursuing military service. Carter was concerned that America's families of means and education were not encouraging their sons to return their good fortune through service to country. In "The Army as a Career," published in the *North American Review*, he specifically addressed this observation, questioning what attraction the "idle life of the leisure set" could hold for "men of education and character." He could not understand why young men might shun service to their country to live off accumulated family wealth. Carter's thoughts were constructed around traditional concepts of universal service—the Uptonian foundation for a national reserve.[46]

He firmly believed that citizens who enjoyed property and other rights duly protected by government "should not only be ready to take . . . part in its defense in war, but should regard it as solemn obligation to fit [themselves] properly for this duty by service in peace, at least for a time, in the Army, the Navy or the National Guard." He bemoaned the perception (accepting it as factual) that so many of the "able-bodied, well-educated descendants of virile ancestors" were content to merely observe and criticize rather than accepting the obligation of service themselves. Carter's discussion was not a critique of material wealth itself—he remained deeply convinced of the capitalist system's overall moral good—but was a call for the educated and privileged classes to return to public leadership. He attributed much of this disturbing trend to the widening chasm between America's established elite—"old money" families—and the rest of society, due to the excessive cost of living in an industrialized economy.[47]

After artfully transitioning this point to an attack on the travesties of inadequate army pay and allowances, he concluded that "with all the advantages and all the drawbacks weighed in the balance, there remains a goodly margin in favor of the Army as a career for a man adapted to the profession of arms."[48] The middle and upper classes, he reasoned, were a reservoir of "able-bodied, well-educated" young men in whom the army would find strong officer material. The article highlights the importance that Carter placed on his profession's social prestige, acquired through expert service for the public good. The "polite society" in which he and Ida circulated by virtue of his position as department commander no doubt encouraged such ideas.

It was also during this time in Chicago that a tragedy befell their family. Leigh Carter, their youngest son, suffered a fatal accident while attending the University of Illinois. Leigh had become interested in agriculture and was hoping to buy a small farm, with his father's help, after finishing school. In late August 1907, while travelling on official duties, Carter detoured toward Virginia in order to look at several properties for Leigh. At a whistle stop in Philadelphia, he received a telegram bearing the unwelcome news that his son had been injured in an electrical accident while working at the university.[49]

Carter had visited Leigh at school only a few months before, and the two had talked about his son's plans for the future. The general had convinced him to look at farming in the Virginia countryside where he and Ida planned to retire so that the family could finally be together. Carter later claimed to have felt a strange sense of foreboding upon his departure from the university, and knew that tragedy had befallen Leigh the moment he was handed the grim telegram. When he arrived in Chicago with his son's casket, several veterans of the Sixth Cavalry waited at the train station to serve as pallbearers for the young man who was born among them on the frontier. The family was deeply touched by this gesture, and after burying Leigh in Arlington Cemetery, Carter noted that "no more sincere grief was ever shown at the grave, than that of those bronzed veterans of the Indian Wars for the son of their old commander." Needless to say, this unexpected loss was spiritually crushing, and came at a time when their older son was preparing to leave for duty in the Philippines.[50]

William Vaulx Carter had graduated from West Point in the Class of 1904. After earning his commission, "Will" continued to follow closely in his father's footsteps by joining the Sixth Cavalry. At the time of his younger brother's death, Lieutenant Carter was in San Francisco about to embark with his troop for the Philippines. The Carters were justifiably proud of their oldest son's accomplishments and fully realized the importance that he "stand on his own" professionally, but, devastated by the loss of one son, they couldn't bear to have the other depart so soon afterward for duty in the Pacific.

Carter telegraphed Army Headquarters asking that Will be detailed as an aide on his own staff at the Department of the Lakes. Both the chief of staff and secretary of war approved the request that same day, and Lieutenant Carter was ordered to proceed immediately to Chicago to report as his father's aide-de-camp. This tragic episode reflects the close family relationship that the Carters enjoyed despite long months spent separated by campaigns and tours in out-of-the-way places. With his remaining family now gathered closely around him, Carter fought bereavement by taking some leave and continuing work on several projects that he had kept waiting for some time.[51]

In the fall of 1908, Carter traveled through Virginia for several weeks doing research on his family lineage. From this effort came

Giles Carter of Virginia (1909), a detailed history on which he had
been working off-and-on as a hobby for several years. Like his other
endeavors, the study was meticulously prepared and is still a highly
useful resource for persons interested in researching the Carter sur-
name as it stretches back to the earliest days of colonial Virginia. This
short escape from career worries and other more serious matters was
a welcome respite, and helped to blunt his grief over Leigh.[52]

Upon his return to Chicago, Carter was reassigned to the Department of the Missouri, with its headquarters in Omaha, Nebraska.
Like the Department of the Lakes, this command had a storied history in the taming of the frontier. Carter had served within its boundaries when it was previously known as the Department of the Platte,
both as a lieutenant at Fort D. A. Russell and later during the Pine
Ridge Campaign. But, by 1908, it too had become little more than a
training command that oversaw the organization and reconstitution
of units coming and going from parts across the Pacific. On 12 December 1908, he assumed command in the growing city of Omaha,
yet another horizontal career move that did very little to change the
nature of his daily existence or add any sort of challenge to his professional responsibilities.[53]

For better or worse, Carter's direct exposure to the National
Guard during this period gave him reason to question its ability to
meet federal obligations. His outlook on the issue was not born entirely of Uptonian cynicism, although certainly framed to some degree by the professional's disdain for the amateur. On a practical
plane, Carter recognized that the "emasculated" 1903 Dick Act fell
woefully short of ensuring minimal standards of proficiency among
the literally hundreds of state units. He lost no time in taking this
concern before a public audience, and in an article appropriately titled "When Diplomacy Fails," published early in 1908, he attacked
the current military establishment as inadequate to meet the nation's
growing demands.

His conclusions were founded on the premise that warfare was an
almost inescapable outcome of human interaction. Although applauding contemporary efforts to establish tribunals for the purpose
of peacefully adjudicating international grievances, he warned that
these lofty institutions were not likely to end physical confrontation
in a competitive world of finite resources. "Altruistic conceptions of
public virtue are jarred unceremoniously by the frequent appearance

of weak links in the human chain," he wrote, "and potent and unalterable principles remain to tease those who mistake all modern ideas for progress." Like Upton, he fretted that Americans had been lulled into a false feeling of security by previous victories, won by "pluck and luck" rather than any foresight or strategic readiness. The Dick Act was an unsatisfactory "jumble of compromises."[54]

Despite the act's intention to create greater uniformity and raise standards of militia performance, few states or organizations took constructive steps in this direction. Carter summarized this dismal state of affairs in terms that reflected corporate culture's growing popularity: "It is a wise business safeguard to take account of stock occasionally, and examine into current methods to determine if an establishment is on a proper basis as compared with competitors. These same principles apply forcefully to military preparation."[55] In 1908, Carter found that of 2,179 state units inspected by the Regular Army, only 1,437 were reported as ready to take the field. Given these numbers and considering also the War Department's prediction that only seventy-five percent of all Guardsmen would actually report when called for national duty, he concluded that the United States would have a difficult time fielding even two full corps in the event of a crisis. He now doubted the Guard's capacity to ever function as a viable reserve. It was not the underlying concept of an organized militia that he faulted, but rather the states' continued inability or unwillingness to meet collective standards. The nation's present military system was not so much "a broken reed" as it was "no reed at all."[56]

His article appeared in print during the same month that the War Department established the Division of Militia Affairs (DMA), an agency charged with centralizing federal administration and control over the Guard in a rather unashamed Uptonian spirit. The DMA was "headed by Army officers committed to rationalizing military policy and bringing the state soldiery more firmly under War Department control." Unsurprisingly, after 1908, federal efforts regarding the organized militia were "couched in paternalistic tones of professional wisdom," a description that is just as accurately applied to Carter's own distinctly professionalist themes. The DMA charged that despite the Dick Act's attempt to infuse federal standards at the end of an appropriations-laced carrot, state organizations still "fell short in almost every category."[57]

Carter's prescribed remedy was to expand the Regular Army and support it with a militia system that benefited from the concept of universal obligation. He proposed that every able-bodied male be required to serve one year in the National Guard, "in organizations in which the officers and non-commissioned officers are appointed and not elected"—a caveat intended to define the Guard's leadership according to professional standards. Under such a system, Carter believed, "rich and poor alike would learn that the Organized Militia knows no class and no creed," and it would therefore strengthen patriotic ideals and infuse a sense of citizenship into the population at large—perhaps a naïve premise when gauged by modern cynics.[58]

Carter closed with a warning for the NGA and its political supporters: "The handwriting on the wall is clear to those who pause to read; and, if the existing system does not produce more practical results, then it will be clearly the duty of Congress to provide for the organization of a National Volunteer Reserve, of generous proportions, entirely distinct from the Organized or Reserve Militia."[59] In Root's War Department, he had been confronted with the militia's cultural significance and political power, but in the years since, had witnessed first-hand the Guard's very haphazard state of readiness. He now brushed aside traditional arguments and began with the simple truth that the militia's effectiveness as a federal reserve was extremely limited without quick and drastic improvements. Despite its best intentions, the Dick Act did very little to compel such changes. Reform was proving a difficult and complex process that could defy even the most visionary efforts.

13

TWILIGHT ON THE
TEXAS BORDER

Half a decade after completing his work with Root, Carter was still watching as his reform efforts struggled to gain an institutional foothold in the army. Of the initiatives that he helped push to maturity, only the new system of officer education seemed to be moving steadily toward the success for which he had hoped. The General Staff was still misunderstood by most officers, including many of those assigned to its own divisions, and was opposed by others who remained interested in maintaining a semblance of the previous bureau system. Militia reform, which promised greater federal control under the provisions of the Dick Act, seemed inadequate in the face of what many soldiers believed was the increasing threat of war with a major foreign power. But despite these frustrations, Carter continued to campaign for the issues that he believed defined military progress.

Carter had been in Omaha for only a few weeks when he got wind of plans to move him once again to an overseas assignment—back to the Philippines in command of the Department of Luzon. According to his account, this tour resulted from a somewhat shrewd manipulation of army regulations by a coterie of officers interested in maintaining a tight-knit hold on stateside command. Although Carter only vaguely identified the "scheme" that he suspected led to this move, it amounted to a purposefully broadened definition of an officer's "foreign service," so that he appeared to be the general officer who was due to rotate overseas. "The man to be saved was in Washington," he remembered bitterly, "and there was reputed connection between his family and the one then about to occupy the White House." Regardless of whether this conspiracy actually existed, the upshot was that the Carters were left repacking their household goods in the same shipping crates in which they had only recently been delivered. With some disgust, Carter gritted his teeth and departed for Manila on 6 March 1909.[1]

The trip to the Philippines was long and wearisome, although it became a little more interesting when his ship, the *Logan,* ran aground on a reef in Honolulu harbor. But aside from this interruption, the voyage was painfully mundane, and Carter noted that "If there is any more lonesome part of the earth's surface than that between Honolulu and Guam, I have not discovered it." The seemingly endless miles of rolling ocean convinced him that a sailor's life was not his calling, and he passed the time by reading stories of the Old West—"where sometimes one encounters a bunch of cattle, or sees a coyote slowly loping away." Upon reaching Manila on 6 April, he took command of the Department of Luzon and also temporarily relieved Gen. Tasker Bliss, in command of the Philippines Division. Only a week later, as Carter reacquainted himself with Manila, he received news that must have seemed a just reward in light of recent disappointments.[2]

President William Howard Taft announced that Carter would be promoted to fill the army's next available major general's position. With ill-hidden satisfaction, Carter noted that "sometimes ambitious men over-reach their efforts to gain their goal by sidetracking presumed rivals." Whether the promotion came at least partly due to Root's intervention on his behalf is not known, but his friendship with the former secretary, who remained a powerful figure in the Republican Party, certainly could not have hurt.[3]

By the time Carter returned in 1909, the Philippines had become somewhat reconciled, at least outwardly, to America's imperial rule, and thus his second stay there was defined primarily by the ordinary work of department administration. Instead of the widespread banditry and insurrection that he battled in the Visayas, the only real excitement came from sporadic rumors of planned native demonstrations and public worry over a perceived Japanese threat—which Carter personally believed existed only in the minds of idle gossips and instigators. But the relative inactivity also gave rise to a familiar controversy in which he quite willingly became a repeat actor.[4]

Since Carter had left the Philippines some four years earlier, conditions had clearly changed for the better. The improving situation provoked further discussion over the appropriate roles for the Filipino Scouts and the Philippine Constabulary. Without an active insurrection to keep them occupied, the Scouts now seemed superfluous, and the Constabulary was able to enforce the peace without reinforcement. Thus, as the Scouts remained increasingly idle, it seemed to many observers that their former usefulness had reached its logical end. Still intertwined with the larger civil-military debate over colonial administration, the issue filled not only Fil-American newspapers but also professional military organs, such as the *Infantry Journal*, and the *Army and Navy Journal*. In their 1909 annual reports, both Carter and Gen. W. P. Duvall, the Philippine Division's commanding officer and Carter's superior, entered this discussion with strongly held—and very opposite—opinions, creating some discomfort for both officers.[5]

Although five years earlier Carter had championed the Scouts as a linchpin of the pacification effort, he now concluded that the situation had shifted in favor of the Constabulary, and saw no need to continue "two distinct bodies of native troops for the same purpose in these islands."[6] Perhaps Carter hoped that the Regular Army's authorized strength would be increased to replace the Scouts, or even more simply, Henry Allen's departure from the scene may have made the Constabulary less of an irritant. Whatever the motivation, he made his thoughts very clear in his annual report. Unfortunately, so did Duvall, who came out in strong support of the Scouts' continued existence and lashed out at those who called for their dissolution. He was, of course, shocked to learn that Carter, one of his subordinates, publicly contradicted him. Anxious to avoid having his command appear fragmented, Duvall immediately requested that the adjutant general strike portions of the reports which were "not germane" to actual department administration.[7]

In the end, after much consternation and several indignant letters between Manila and Washington, there was no real fallout from this episode, except that once again, Carter had become a centerpiece of internal controversy. Beyond Duvall's personal embarrassment, Secretary of War Jacob M. Dickinson did not see any real harm in publishing the opposing viewpoints and the matter died without official censure. Fortunately, the rest of Carter's time on Luzon passed without further incident for either him or his department, and shortly thereafter, when Secretary Dickinson called him back to the General Staff—as an assistant to the chief of staff—he enthusiastically accepted.[8]

Dickinson's telegram noted that the administration intended to introduce important military legislation during the coming term and thus Carter departed Manila with high hopes for the future, expecting to once again play a seminal role in the army's institutional development. Taft had named Gen. Leonard Wood as the chief of staff to replace J. Franklin Bell. Although Carter had not served alongside Wood for any length of time, he believed him an able choice to bring on a new round of reform.[9]

Upon arriving back in the United States, Carter was told that the secretary desired him to take a leave of absence until Wood, who was currently finishing detached service in Argentina, could return stateside and assume his position. The Carters happily acquiesced, and spent the time in Virginia, allowing the general to return to his genealogical research while enjoying a brief break from the army. This leave was unexpectedly cut short when it was learned that Wood likely would be detained in Buenos Aires much longer than expected, and Carter was ordered to assume the role of acting chief of staff.

The secretary's original wish for the two men to begin their new duties at the same time grew from fears that Wood would prove to be a difficult match for his new office and for anyone working around him—especially with strong-willed Gen. Fred C. Ainsworth nearby as the army's adjutant general. If this was Dickinson's reasoning, it certainly proved altogether too accurate, as Carter would soon attest.[10]

When he returned for his second tour on the General Staff—an institution very much of his own creation—Carter found that it had not developed as he and Root had intended. Although Taft (as secretary of war) and others had pointed to it as a trophy of the American military's march toward modernity, the General Staff seemed to be somewhat confused as to the nature of its true function. Its reports were voluminous in detail but difficult to translate into any sort of action that could be of real benefit to the army. Rather than being the "strategic brain," as Carter had hoped, the early General Staff completely abdicated any claims to providing the army with meaningful direction.

The first men to serve as chief of staff—S. B. M. Young, Adna Chaffee, John C. Bates, and J. Franklin Bell—searched for the limits of their position while trying to avoid the temptation to delve into the administrative duties of the bureaus. But these officers failed to recognize that real authority lay with daily decision-makers, those bureau chiefs who acted very much as gatekeepers between the War Department and the line army. They completely missed the purpose of that "supervisory" role which Carter painstakingly laid out for the chief of staff, in order to provide a check on just this sort of informal authority. Instead, as Jack Lane observes, "The general staff concerned itself with a theoretical rather than a practical American army and an abstract rather than a real military policy." With no experience or tradition as guide, the new General Staff seemed almost to shutter itself away in a soldierly marble tower, producing much in volume, yet very little of substance that addressed the army's pressing need for strategic leadership.[11]

According to John McCauley Palmer, a member of the early General Staff, the problem stemmed from a basic lack of understanding of a general staff's true nature and purpose. "I am perfectly satisfied that one of the principal causes for the confusion of thought in regard to a General Staff is that very few people know what a General Staff is," Palmer testified before a Senate subcommittee in 1919. In part, he blamed the inaccurate English translation of the German word *generalstab* for this failure. A more correct translation would be "general's staff" or "generalship staff," both terms that in their direct application would narrow the scope of such a body's function. In Palmer's opinion, by 1910 the American General Staff already had delved too far into matters that did not concern its primary role as a coordinating agency. Palmer faulted not only this mistaken conceptualization of purpose but also a general lack of professional preparation among early members for their new duties as staff officers.[12]

Palmer's critique is probably accurate. Despite Leavenworth's best efforts, the army still had only a relative handful of trained staff officers from whom to choose. Carter foresaw this predicament when he authored the act. Shortly after its passage, he underlined the importance of assigning to the General Staff those few soldiers who had already benefited from the embryonic system of professional education:

> The recognized requirements for successful performance of General Staff duties in the field are better understood by the graduates of the service schools than by the older generation. These schools and the post schools for officers will continue to supply ample material for the lowest grade in the new corps. It will require considerable examination and investigation to find just the right men for the higher grades at the start, but there should be no insurmountable difficulty.[13]

If the early General Staff suffered for lack of preparation, it was in large part due to the fact that educational reform and staff reform came only fifteen months apart. Without a history of specialized training in general-staff type competencies, a difficult developmental period was inescapable as the army caught up to its own progress.[14]

Others faulted the relative youth of early General Staff members as a factor in the institution's growing pains. James Parker, a forward-looking soldier who retired as a general officer, recalled that early members were younger than most of the permanent appointees who remained in the staff bureaus. Parker believed that this resulted in a sort of "generation gap," deepening the already-inherent tension between the General Staff and the extant bureaus and becoming a barrier to cooperation. The strength of this frictional relationship should not be understated. General Frank McCoy, another original participant, remembered that "opposition to the new GS [General Staff] was immediate, especially from the new TAG [the adjutant general, Ainsworth]. . . . Bureau chiefs hedged in the GS steadily right up to time of Wood [Leonard Wood]. They wanted the GS to plan only & they ignored its coordinating duties." All of these critiques likely have some foundation in fact. Several factors—lack of experience, an ill-defined charter, collective youth, and institutional inertia—contributed to the General Staff's early inability to act as intended. But in time, as more officers came to understand and appreciate its potential, these circumstances would improve and the General Staff would mature into its role.[15]

When Carter settled down to the work at hand in 1910, he recognized that matters were not right. Just as he had warned then, tension between the chief of staff and the separate bureaus had indeed become an unbearable nuisance. Open antagonism soured cooperation, leaving a situation not unlike that which had formerly plagued the bureaus and the commanding general. Partly to blame, Carter believed, was the fact that the secretary of war was now overburdened by his responsibilities under the weight of America's expanding foreign interests. This left a void of executive oversight, allowing army administration to devolve into a competitive tournament for personal and institutional power. Under Secretary Taft, the bureau chiefs and specifically Ainsworth had successfully reclaimed much of their former independence, placing them at loggerheads with the chief of staff.[16] Carter quite accurately analyzed the source of this trouble:

> Those who had previously held office as Chief of Staff had not experienced any great desire on the part of the Adjutant General to aid in the full development of the General Staff. As Acting Chief, I expected nothing but annoyance from him, and was not disappointed. . . . The Adjutant General was beset with the idea that the business of the War Department must be done his way or not at all. This spirit had grown upon him until his manners and methods were intolerable to the many modest and industrious officers engaged in carrying on the business of the army. . . . As he was a permanent bureau chief, installed through the strongest political influence I have ever known in the army, he succeeded in imposing his will for a long time on the officers of the General Staff Corps.[17]

Although he wrote this indictment several years after the fact with full knowledge of later events, he was certainly in agreement with many of his contemporaries. When Wood, an equally dominant personality, described as "mostly full of himself," finally arrived to become chief of staff, it heralded a classic fight to the finish.[18]

Wood and Ainsworth were both former army surgeons who had pushed their way to the top by combining noteworthy competence with extreme ambition. Wood had moved to the army line by a colonel's commission in Theodore Roosevelt's own volunteer "Rough Riders" during the Spanish-American War. His friendship with Roosevelt obviously did no harm to his subsequent career. Wood was unashamedly political and later became a primary figure among Replace, and according to Butt, rather proudly claimed a sort of sophomoric moral victory over his competitor:

> As soon as I took office I had an interview with Carter which he will not forget in some time. I told him frankly that the first time I found him interfering with legislation in any way or going over my head to the secretary I should demand his removal or leave the office myself. I also told him that I did not want him as an assistant, but that since the secretary had seen fit to place him over my protest he had to be governed by my orders.[24]

A keen observer of Washington's political carnival, Butt added his own insight that "[Secretary] Dickinson is as suspicious of Wood as Wood is of Carter." Competition between the two would in time prove an insurmountable obstacle to progress, but for now at least, their interaction for the most part remained strained but courteous, and their mutually held contempt was kept private.[25]

This amazing web of personal animosities and private agendas certainly created an unlikely environment for a repeat of Carter's earlier contributions to army reform. It appears that he and Wood never considered putting aside their egos for any cooperative effort in the name of greater institutional good. Perhaps by design, Carter spent much of the fall and winter of 1910 away from Washington, traveling to various posts to observe training encampments and inspect army remount stations. The next spring, while serving as chief of the General Staff's newly established Mobile Army Division, he found himself thrust into an unexpected role that took him many hundreds of miles from Wood and the War Department's intrigue.[26]

The worsening power struggle in Mexico threatened American interests when revolutionaries moved to topple the Díaz government, and intervention crept closer to a realistic consideration. Ambassador Henry Lane Wilson reported that forty thousand American citizens and over a billion dollars in investments would be in danger if open violence erupted, a situation that promised to become a political nightmare for the Taft administration if not met with immediate resolve. In early March, while the worsening relationship between Wood and Ainsworth simmered at the War Department, Carter left Washington to assume command of the Maneuver Division, a force

publican Progressives. Ainsworth's own ascendance was perhaps
so colorful but nonetheless impressive. After first serving in
Army Medical Bureau, he became an invaluable member of the AC
due to his keen knack for orderly and efficient administration. B
such talent can become pernicious when wielded as an instrument
personal power. For his part, Ainsworth succumbed to ambition an
his career quickly translated into an overriding quest for empire.[19]

These two titans were at first friendly. After Wood arrived ii
Washington as chief of staff, they spent many hours discussing thei
ideas and desires for the New Army. But this friendship soon dissolved as Wood increasingly disregarded Ainsworth's self-serving advice. Wood recognized that the adjutant general was a direct challenge to his own office, and thus would be no ally in effecting his grip
on the army. Both men were equally and utterly ambitious and each
was stubbornly convinced of his righteousness. Their proximity in
the War Department amounted to placing two young bulls in the proverbial china shop, and a shattering confrontation was inevitable.[20]

In 1910, the army's march toward modernity was still very much
an ongoing battle that was by no means a foregone conclusion.[21]
Henry Stimson, appointed to replace Dickinson as secretary of war in
1911, wrote that the service "was going through the pangs of a long-
delayed modernization, and in almost every issue . . . there was a
sharp distinction between men who preferred the old way—the way
of traditional powers and privileges—and men whose eyes were fixed
on the ideal of a modernized and flexible force."[22] As it turned out,
Carter's work on the General Staff this second time around proved
less rewarding than he hoped. Like Carter, Wood saw himself as a
torchbearer for further military reform, but instead of being kindred
spirits, the two men eyed each other as competitors. Wood was never
an "insider" among the army's professionalists, who may have seen
him as a sort of loud pretender due to his nonprofessional background. Carter's relationship with Wood started out with formal cor-
diality, but this only masked a growing tension. Perhaps this was only
natural when it is remembered that Carter's name had been publicly
considered for the chief of staff position as well, an office that he
surely coveted.[23]

In early August, Archie Butt, a White House military aide, recorded that Wood and Carter were already at odds. Wood seethed that
he had not wanted Carter as an assistant chief of staff in the first

ostensibly created for training purposes but in actuality deployed for possible action south of the border.

The provisional Maneuver Division concentrated near San Antonio, Texas, and rapidly grew to include three brigades of infantry, one brigade of field artillery, and an assortment of smaller supporting units, accounting for almost one-fifth of the Regular Army's total strength. Although at the time military intervention was unlikely, the circumstances dictated sober preparation and the War Department saw an opportunity to employ a modern army in an operational environment.[27]

The "dual" purpose of this move quickly generated public excitement, with speculation over the division's real mission and its contemplated timetable attracting international attention. "No one believed that we had assembled merely for maneuvers," mused Carter, but "I went right along, trying to execute the President's instructions to make the mobilization a first class training for the army." Taft's plan was to use the situation as a practical test of the institution as well as its men and matériel. The deployment was an excellent test of the army's ability to concentrate, operate, and sustain a large body of troops in the field. Far-flung (and often understrength) units were hard-pressed to meet the mobilization schedule and many new techniques and equipment were taken to the field for the first time. Carter's vision of military modernity was played out before his eyes as the division took shape, and the giant task ahead likely gave him pause to consider the evolving complexities of warfare.[28]

As soon as orders were issued to commence movement, Carter and several of his chosen staff departed by train for San Antonio. While en route, the decision was made to administer a still-experimental typhoid vaccine to the entire division, including the commanding general himself. In springtime southern Texas, health and sanitation became one of Carter's prime considerations as he hoped to avoid the tragic epidemics that had befallen other such expeditions. The second general order issued after arriving and setting up headquarters dealt explicitly with this subject, instructing subordinates to correct without question any sanitation defects noted by the camp inspector. With the nation watching, Carter was determined not to repeat mistakes of the past.[29]

The national press jumped on the deployment as perhaps the liveliest story since the Philippine Insurrection. Sensational accounts whipped up a frenzy of expectation and Carter was the center of attention: "Twenty Thousand American Troops Rushed to Mexican Border," "Whole Border From Gulf to California to Bristle With Arms Before Week Ends," and "Major General Carter, Who Directs Big Army on Mexican Frontier," were just a few of the headlines that graced newspapers across the country. One story claimed that Carter's life had been spared at Cibicu "by a bugler who leaped and knocked him flat to the ground just as a body of hostiles fired into the camp" (a very liberal translation of events at best), while another, perhaps more accurately, asserted that "there is no officer of higher professional attainment in the army." Of writers' occasional departure from the facts, Carter only smiled and commented that "they want the truth but a little splurge in the realm of fiction and personalities seems to go a long ways." The Maneuver Division and its commander were newsworthy items for several weeks, and Carter clearly relished the moment.[30]

Although the Maneuver Division's unspoken purpose as a warning to Mexican revolutionaries was clear to anyone who read the news, the army steadfastly maintained the division's overt training mission. In his first interview after arriving in Texas, Carter explained that "the movement was simply pursuant to a desire on the part of the General Staff . . . to test the new field service regulation." This "cover story" became increasingly accurate as the weeks wore on and a preemptive incursion into Mexico became less likely. For the time being, simply completing the initial movement and disposition of troops was a major undertaking. Of this, Carter wrote that "the experience of value comes at first from organization, etc.; the rest is just sitting around." Perhaps as expected, the primary enemy in Texas proved to be the weather, followed closely by boredom and the more "dangerous" attraction posed by nearby San Antonio. In addition, the daily administration of some twelve thousand restless soldiers in a static situation proved to be an enormous challenge, met successfully by good staff work.[31]

When Carter left for Texas, he was given maps, plans, and notes that had been prepared through the combined efforts of the General Staff and War College. "War Plan No. 1-A" detailed the mobilization, order of battle, and plan of operations for an American thrust into Mexico from the northern border. Although the plan was never really implemented, the army's posture at San Antonio mimicked the script on a somewhat smaller scale. This deliberate planning, a precursor to the elaborate planning processes of today's armed forces, was a product of the New Army, a direct result of the reforms championed by Carter and his colleagues. The fact that such materials even existed and were made available was a significant advance from the confusion that had reigned in the spring of 1898.[32]

By the time Carter arrived in Texas, one regiment was already on site, and the work of setting up a cantonment for nearly a full division began in earnest. The monsoonlike weather proved uncooperative, and the camp soon became a "sea of mud" for men and animals alike. Carter shared in his troops' misery, living in a tent rather than accepting quarters in nearby San Antonio. Despite the incessant rain and cold north winds, the work progressed and the division grew to over eleven thousand men in less than a month. Training began almost as soon as troops could be spared from the struggle to erect a camp. By 24 April, when Carter submitted his first formal report, each of three brigades had marched to nearby Leon Springs (twenty-three miles away), where they undertook simulated battle exercises. A progressive training plan was established that combined maneuvers of all three branches (infantry, cavalry, and artillery) at the division level—an ambitious effort under the circumstances.[33]

Impressed by the spirit of his troops, Carter gained confidence in his own ability to lead a fielded army. He bragged to Ida that he believed himself "as well equipped to organize [an army] as any one in the service. None of our generals has had the opportunity to fight a real army and I would not hesitate to undertake any thing which may fall to the log of this force. I have the greatest confidence in officers and men for there was never a more perfect fighting unit brought together in our service."[34] By early May, as conditions across the border improved and support for intervention waned, it became clear that the Maneuver Division would not likely venture beyond its training camps any time soon. Although expecting his command to be dispersed almost any day, Carter continued to prepare as if combat operations were imminent.

The army began sending many innovative gadgets and ideas to San Antonio, hoping to test their worth in a large-scale operation. This sometimes proved an annoying distraction, and Carter complained that "we are deviled with all sorts of things that people want tried out—forage, incinerators, soups, etc.—any and everything but *'soldiering.'* A whole lot of lieutenants want to be aviators *if* they are excused from other duties." Two airplanes, a Curtis and a Wright, joined the division in San Antonio, and the contingent operated with regularity from a field very near Carter's own tent. The airplane's obvious potential, even in its embryonic state, must have made him wonder what the future held for his beloved cavalry. He was amazed when one of the machines delivered orders to troops fifty miles away, completing the job "in a trifle more than an hour"—an eye-opening accomplishment to a soldier who had started his career on horseback during the Civil War.[35]

When aircraft participated in a formal review before General Carter's watchful eye at the end of April, it was a historic event for the U.S. Army and a vivid testament to the changing times. After observing the aero detachment for several weeks, Carter reported that aircraft were valid reconnaissance assets, but noted that the Curtis model, "a single propeller machine of very high speed . . . is not, in my opinion, so safe and valuable for observation of armies as the Wright model used here." After a mishap claimed the life of Lt. George Kelly, a young officer under his command, Carter immediately ceased flying operations, but still believed military aviation to be a worthwhile pursuit.[36]

Even in San Antonio, the War Department's rumor-mill proved an annoyance. When word circulated that Carter would soon be recalled to Washington, he tried to shrug it off with an air of practical indifference: "I am sure that I have all the benefit to be obtained through the mobilization," he wrote to Ida, "and if anybody wants to come here and *camp* they are welcome to do so." He dismissed such talk as the product of Wood's jealousy, and believed—with some foundation—that the chief of staff saw him as a potential rival. Carter also realized that armed intervention was now unlikely, and that rotating commanders was of obvious benefit to the army. Though no such change occurred, Carter remained convinced that Wood had indeed contemplated the move out of sheer vindictiveness. For now, with circumstances in Mexico stabilized for the moment, he concentrated on keeping his division occupied with something other than unhealthful visits to nearby San Antonio.[37]

Carter was pleased with the division's overall condition despite shortages of potable water, transportation, draft animals, and even

blank ammunition. Training was kept up on a scale previously unseen and, in both May and June, the entire division marched to Leon
Springs, where it conducted a series of field exercises.[38] Convinced
that the deployment was a triumphant demonstration of expeditionary might, Carter boasted:

> The progressive work of the division has been successful to a
> degree that has made the command well fitted for field service
> of the most arduous character. . . . This mobilization will be of
> far-reaching value to the army. From the Commanding Gen-
> eral to the junior second lieutenant, all have grown familiar
> with a daily contact with administration and command hith-
> erto known only in theory. . . . All will hereafter have a confi-
> dence in themselves born of actual practice gained in the pro-
> cess of mobilization.[39]

But while Carter had reason to be proud of the division, some in the
War Department and even among his staff were less than impressed.
One viewed the training as ineffective at best and pure "absurdity" at
worst. Even if the mobilization was groundbreaking in its attempt to
combine theory with application, there were those who apparently
sought more than training marches and sham battles as the measure
of a truly new army. Naysayers and critics pressed aside, Carter worried that the summer heat and continual work would begin to sap
morale, and started to encourage recreation and sporting activities as
a diversion. The fact that he even advised headquarters of his decision to slow training for the sake of the men rather than maintain a
"rough-and-ready" posture reflects an admirable brand of empathetic
leadership—of the type lacking in many of his martinet colleagues.
His ambitions, though well developed, were never pursued at the
expense of subordinates.[40]

The division didn't have to wait long for relief from the Texas
summer. By the time Ambassador Wilson visited the division in late
July accompanied by James Brown Potter, a wealthy American busi-
nessman with financial interests in Mexico, most observers were already convinced that the situation no longer dictated the army's continued presence on the border. After Potter spoke of keeping the
division in place to insure American investments, Carter wryly noted
that "men sell their own souls for money and are quite willing to give
away other people's souls and lives if they but interfere with busi-

ness." Soon after, he began making arrangements for the division's dispersal, and as expected, the Maneuver Division ceased to exist in early August 1911. While the various organizations broke camp and headed home, Carter himself returned to Ida and Washington with little enthusiasm for another round with Wood and the War Department's constant wrangling.[41]

The work in Texas had been successful in many respects but once again exposed the nation's military deficiencies. Mobilization brought together an army of twelve thousand troops and accomplished a great deal of excellent training and instruction. But Taft's orders had called for twenty thousand, and in the unsuccessful attempt to field these numbers, the army was forced to fill many participating regiments with raw recruits—acceptable under the circumstances, but a precursor to tragedy had the division been ordered into immediate combat. Wood latched onto this and other shortcomings as glaring evidence to support his plans to reorganize the army's department structure, and more generally, the policy ideas that he eventually championed under the term "preparedness."[42]

Carter's own conclusions about the recent border episode were pragmatic. He saw the operation as an important proving ground for theories taught at the army's service schools as well as a test of many innovative changes in organization and equipment. But he also recognized the same inadequacies that he highlighted a year earlier in "Military Preparedness," an article that espoused themes similar to those later parlayed by Wood in his own preparedness campaign. In strongly professionalist tones, Carter expressed doubt as to whether any sort of standing reserve could have responded with the desired speed. He called for an increase in the Regular Army that would allow an overseas military presence (as dictated by contemporary foreign policy) while maintaining domestic garrisons at or near wartime strength for unexpected crises. He observed that if Congress did nothing to improve the current state, "attention should be called to the necessity for a reduction in the foreign garrisons to such an extent as will enable a proper ratio of foreign and home service to prevail." In short, he was subtly telling the Washington politicos that they were asking too much of an overstretched army they refused to adequately fund and resource—an argument that was politically inexpedient but nonetheless sagely accurate.[43]

In an interview with the *New York Times*, Carter lamented the army's continued dispersal among relatively small garrisons, a practice that may have met the needs of yesterday's expanding frontier but not those of a modern imperial power. He wanted to concentrate brigades and even divisions in garrisons nearer the coasts and major rail terminals where they might respond more quickly and with greater economy to mobilization orders. Concentration would also allow units to train together on a larger scale to the great advantage of officers and men alike. These ideas were shared by Wood and many other contemporaries, but convincing a Congress that was beholden to local constituents with a vested interest in the status quo was no easy task, and as Wood was to find out later, the effort was an uphill struggle.[44]

While Carter and the Maneuver Division alternately battled the mud and dust in Texas, a volatile national campaign was brewing at home. In deference to the political liabilities of his Republican boss during an election year, Jacob Dickinson, a Democrat, had resigned as secretary of war and been replaced by Henry L. Stimson, a Republican with strong Progressive credentials. Carter believed that Stimson, a former law partner of Root's, was an honest man of great intellectual capacity, but nonetheless regretted the loss of Dickinson's personal friendship in the War Department. Wood and Stimson almost immediately formed a professional alliance in much the same manner as had Carter and Root, with Wood's reform-minded energies focused by Stimson's political acumen. But though Stimson was intellectually able, he lacked Root's keen knack for compromise. When this shortcoming was coupled to Wood's overbearing personality, it soon created an acrid environment that overshadowed many otherwise useful ideas. The resulting tumult eventually pushed Carter out of Washington and turned the War Department into something of a sideshow.[45]

When Carter returned to work on the General Staff, he found it very difficult to accomplish even daily tasks without becoming exasperated by Wood's methods. He believed that Wood was "bent on chasing butterflies . . . stirring everything up at the wrong time," and in the process spoiling the opportunity for more constructive effort. Tension between the two men grew despite their basic agreement on so many issues. There is little doubt that Carter still smarted from rumors of his removal in Texas, and was also sensitive to perceived slights to the leadership he demonstrated there. During the fall and winter of 1911, Wood supported his "preparedness" arguments by repeatedly pointing to the army's failure to meet expectations during the recent mobilization. Coming from Wood, these arguments seemed unfair to Carter, painting the entire operation as a failure and assailing his own abilities by implication. But at the root of the problem lay a simple clash of two very strong personalities.[46]

Wood's proclivity for bombast and competitive staging irritated Carter, and he later remarked, "As soon as General Wood was appointed to Chief of Staff, a coterie of able and ambitious officers attached themselves to his interests. I had never found it necessary or desirable to join any coterie or clique in the army, and I saw that difficulties would soon arise for me in the execution of my ordinary duties."[47] Whether merely perceived or real, it was an unhealthy atmosphere for any renewed struggle toward further reform. Personal differences smoldered beneath almost every interaction between the two, turning minor disagreements into immovable obstacles.[48]

Carter's interests did not include battling for institutional supremacy with a politically connected chief of staff, especially in a War Department that was already brimming with tense hatred between Wood and Ainsworth. During the remaining months of 1911, he began asking for assignment elsewhere, but Stimson still desired his presence and convinced him to remain in Washington for the time being. The secretary placed a premium on Carter's services in what he still hoped would be a new era of Root-like reforms. But the situation only worsened and it soon became painfully obvious that Wood had little need for an able assistant with independent ideas.[49]

On 7 February 1912, Carter's relationship with Wood descended into an embarrassing dispute over Carter's role in helping the Senate Military Committee prepare forthcoming legislation. Apparently, Wood had asked him to represent the War Department's interests regarding a proposed militia bill that was then before the committee. But when Carter conferred directly with Stimson on this issue at the secretary's own request, Wood became enraged and blustered loudly about "too many people interfering" with the department's legislative business. Shocked, Carter reminded Wood that he had specifically directed him to become involved in the committee's deliberations. The chief of staff denied all knowledge of any such instructions, and then, when Stimson left the room for a few minutes, snidely remarked that he had been "informed" of Carter's "gumshoe methods" of going directly to the secretary—a stab at Carter's previous relationship with Root.[50]

According to Carter's narrative of events, Stimson then returned and informed Wood that he in fact had asked Carter to his office to discuss the measure, and that he would continue to seek advice from officers as he saw fit. This should have ended the scene, but Carter's sensitivities were already severely ruffled, and with his usual air of self-righteousness, he sought redress by penning his resignation from the General Staff. Seeing the makings of a very ugly and politically hurtful story in the works, Wood went to Carter's home that night and extended the olive branch, admitting his error and asking that the resignation be withdrawn. Carter caustically recorded that "General Wood's mind is evidently overcrowded and many of his troubles come from undertaking so much of other peoples' affairs that he forgets even to whom he entrusts business."[51]

The next morning, Carter went to his old friend Root, now a United States senator, to seek advice and likely some solace for his bruised ego as well. Root, who was on good terms with both Wood and Stimson, advised him to dismiss thoughts of resignation but to demand that Wood explain the truth of the situation to the secretary. Carter followed this suggestion and supposedly secured Wood's assurance that he would let the secretary know of his error in accusing Carter of politically motivated mischief. This negotiated peace ostensibly ended the quarrel, but as he later noted, "such incidents strike too deep for men to forget." During the rest of his career, Carter would blame subsequent disappointments on this episode, believing that Wood had in fact turned many of his faithful headquarters "coterie" against him.[52]

The entire affair is insignificant if not downright trivial, but the manner in which it occurred tells a great deal about the personalities involved and the contentious nature of life in the period's War Department. The proximate success of such ambitious men made them obvious competitors in an arena that was largely defined by political relationships and public reputations. That Carter believed he acted on a higher moral plane is evident and grew naturally from his evolving self-image as the consummate professional who risked personal career for the greater institutional good. Since his service under Root, he had increasingly come to view himself as a tragic, selfless hero to whom rightfully belonged the army's torch of progress. When played opposite Wood's more crass political ambitions, this persona fit rather neatly, but it also contributed very little to any attempt at cooperative progress.

The confrontation was overshadowed within a few days by Wood's simultaneous engagement of Ainsworth, his prime enemy. After months of posturing, during which each man sought to define and expand his own authority, Ainsworth finally committed a gross error of conduct that gave Wood the opening he needed for an official assault. The specific circumstances seemed manipulated for effect, and as Jack Lane concluded, "it is difficult to escape the conclusion that Wood was consciously baiting Ainsworth." The clash emanated from a simple idea to consolidate several types of personnel records—a seemingly benign topic that reflected the period's preoccupation with corporate efficiency. But Wood knew that such an action also would infringe on the adjutant general's administrative empire and shrewdly pressed for its further study by the General Staff. At the same time, he prodded Ainsworth by restricting the list of officers from which recruiting assignments could be made—traditional plums wielded by the AGO as a prime source of patronage. If Wood hoped to embroil Ainsworth in damaging debate on the bureaus' subordinate role, his stratagem paid off royally when the adjutant general, thus provoked, finally replied in a strongly worded and singularly insubordinate message. When the resultant censure grew into a threatened court-martial, Ainsworth wisely retired, leaving the chief of staff's authority unchallenged—a wholesale but temporary victory for both Wood and the army line.[53]

Carter watched these proceedings with no small amount of disbelief, but like most line officers, was nonetheless pleased with the outcome. He recorded that there was "suppressed excitement" at the prospect of Ainsworth's public court-martial, and admitted that his downfall was a great relief to many of those officers and clerks who had worked near the adjutant general on a daily basis. The affair kept the War Department's rapt attention for several days, creating "a general air of 'what's next' " that preoccupied both the General Staff and the bureaus. For Carter, the whole proceeding, played out amid the clearing smoke of his own recent skirmish with Wood, underscored the dangerous climate of his current assignment. As he wrote in his diary with poetic simplicity, "Service in Dep't no longer agreeable."[54]

Carter remained in Washington as assistant chief of staff through the summer of 1912, performing yeoman work as he attempted to shepherd new army bills through both congressional military committees. But his enthusiasm for the job was blunted and he now believed that substantive progress was nearly impossible due to the turmoil that inevitably followed Wood to every endeavor. "He is so jealous," Carter noted, "he does not wish anyone to speak to a senator—great mistake for all the staff are trying to work with him." Although still in fundamental agreement with Wood on most professional issues, he was astonished at the manner in which they were pursued. "If he had started out with deliberate intention to create obstacles," Carter complained, "he could not have succeeded better along that line than he did."[55]

After the fiery exchange in Stimson's office, Carter's personal relationship with Wood once again became guardedly "courteous and considerate," but this formal façade hid a repulsion that was undoubtedly mutual. The two men often found themselves at odds on various questions—much less over substance than over the finest details that might have been hammered out through compromise, thereby building a concerted platform for the army's interests. But neither officer demonstrated an ability to rise above the conflict, and the friction between them only festered as time passed.

Years later, Carter claimed vindication in that he had requested to be relieved from further service under Wood long before their relationship became mired in personal animosity. Though true, this claim does little to excuse the tit-for-tat quibbling to which he became an active party. His actions were seemingly above-board and concerned with the army's progress and well-being, but an inability to transcend private quarrels for the greater good indicates that his own ego was a challenge to which, regrettably, he was at times unequal. Although never entertaining the thoughts of high grandeur nurtured by Wood, Carter's own aspirations to become chief of staff may well have affected his professional demeanor and personal judgment. This conclusion is unavoidable even in a narrative drawn largely from Carter's own words. Yet, in the War Department's tightly constrained arena of so many successful and ambitious men, perhaps the wonder is not that individual differences were unyielding but rather that they did not completely undo all that had gone before.

Carter increasingly felt that the army lacked any real representation in a Washington court that had become so bureaucratically complex and politically demanding that it distracted the secretary of war and his assistants from giving full attention to operational issues. Of Stimson's efforts as secretary, he wrote that "he is too busy to really attend to army matters," an indictment not intended so much for the secretary himself as for the political system in which he functioned. Under these circumstances, Congress continued to dominate decision-making on most military questions of any importance, wielding its "power of the pursestrings" with great authority. "Everything gives way to politics," Carter lamented. "Even the President is led to give orders based almost wholly on political backers."[56]

Amid this dissension and intrigue, the General Staff continued to confront problems that had challenged army leaders for decades. The relationship between the federal government and the militia still confounded those who worried over defense matters, and professional soldiers fretted that there was little in the way of a viable national reserve. Carter's work to update plans for military intervention in Mexico highlighted the existing militia system's fallacies. As he looked for manpower to wage an extended campaign, he concluded that the only solution was to deploy National Guardsmen beyond national borders—a contentious issue since the War of 1812, when American militia had balked at crossing into Canada. Although the Dick Act was revised by another militia bill in 1908 that supposedly addressed questions of geographic limits for the Guard, its legal ramifications were still suspect and posed an interesting dilemma for army planners.

Stimson submitted the question for formal review to Gen. Enoch Crowder, the army judge advocate general, and George W. Wickersham, the U.S. attorney general. Both issued opinions that the president lacked constitutional authority to order state organizations outside the United States proper, an interpretation that gave professionalists further reason to doubt the militia's utility as a national force. As Jerry Cooper summarized: "The ruling destroyed the Guard's value as a reserve," shaking the very foundations of the traditional "dual-army" policy and leading Stimson to withdraw support for a pending militia pay bill.[57] Irate Guardsmen suspected that the War Department had merely used the issue to fuel new arguments for a federal reserve. Carter's own words certainly add credence to these suspicions: "Mexican plans of invasion turned over to me. I made use of militia beyond our border. Judge Advocate General and Attorney General both of opinion that militia cannot be ordered out of U.S. It may prove a failure for all the millions expended but it might be well to have the question solved once [and] for all."[58] By 1912, the Mexican border had become an inescapable litmus test for the age-old militia question. But it would be years before it was "solved once and for all."

Carter was frustrated by life in the New Army as he attempted to reconcile personal ambitions with unrealized expectations, both for himself and the institution. Although working in a system partly of his own making, he had not foreseen the tremendous pressures that now appeared in determined opposition to the progress that he and Root had envisioned. Individual personalities and bureaucratic traditions acted in concert to keep the new command and staff system from materializing as originally intended by the 1903 General Staff Act. Against this disappointing backdrop, Carter considered his few remaining years in the army and longed to be rid of the turmoil that marked his time near Leonard Wood.

THE AMERICAN ARMY: WRITING A LEGACY

Discouraged by the tension surrounding Wood, as well as the constant distraction of department politics, Carter pressed for reassignment elsewhere while still tirelessly representing the army's interests before Congress. His final months on the General Staff only deepened a conviction that army headquarters was dominated by Wood's "coterie," who thought more of their own ambitions than the greater good of the service. Although still in fundamental agreement with Secretary Stimson and Wood on most issues of reform, he absolutely abhorred the crass manner in which Wood pursued his own interests. His preemptory demeanor and heavy-handed tactics, Carter believed, were detrimental to the army's ultimate well-being and defeated any hope for real progress under the current administration. By the summer of 1912, he resignedly concluded that little more could be accomplished, and looked forward to finding a more serene life beyond Washington's dreary conference rooms.

As early as July, rumors had surfaced that Wood, with Stimson's acquiescence, was pushing for changes among the army's general officers. The *Army and Navy Journal* reported that Carter would be heading to the Central Division, a new organization that was part of a general realignment meant to put the army on a more effective wartime footing. Stimson had decided to develop the Central Division as one of three stateside elements, creating, at least on paper, divisions that could act as coherent tactical units in time of emergency. When the secretary finally approached Carter with this idea, letting him know that his support for the move was fully expected, it seemed that the entire plan—including the displacement of several senior officers—had already been worked out in secret between Stimson and Wood. The implication was clear—Carter's presence was an impediment to Wood's consolidation of personal authority, and the Central Division was as good an escape as any other.[1]

On 31 August, Carter spent his last day at work as the assistant chief of chief, and cleaned out his office in preparation for a much-deserved three-month leave of absence before reporting to his new assignment. Disgusted with the War Department's "maze of controversies and intrigues," and disappointed by his own failure to accomplish more in the way of further reforms, he left with Ida for White Sulpher Springs, Virginia. "I have done much good but it has been constantly resented, at least not appreciated," Carter wrote. "It was a duty I owed *to the army* which has been unwisely abused in the house of its friends." In Virginia, the couple spent almost three weeks with little else to do but socialize with old friends, walk in the surrounding forests, and do a little fishing. The respite gave Carter a chance to reflect and consider the likelihood of further advancement in the army. Only three years from retirement age after having served his country for almost fifty years, he must have looked toward the immediate future with some apprehension.[2]

Perhaps due in part to this sense of passing time and also to grave concerns that Wood had ruined his chances to ever become chief of staff, Carter set about writing a book-length critique of the nation's military system. Under the circumstances, the endeavor must have been somewhat therapeutic. "Am working on a book and while it may never be printed," he admitted in his diary, "it will interest me to work it out along professional lines." His approach closely followed Emory Upton's methodology, with which he was thoroughly familiar. Like Upton, he founded ideas on historical discussion and then translated them into proposals for action. More than merely a forum for his thoughts on military affairs, the book shows Carter's desire to leave a solid legacy of his time with Root—a legacy that might transcend his less-than-triumphant stint as Wood's assistant. He later observed that "the only work of man which survives is that of written or printed record," and it was this notion that now urged him onward.[3]

Carter's study progressed quickly. Even while on leave, he sometimes spent hours at a time poring over notes, engrossed in his work. Much of it grew from ideas that were already present in many of his published articles. He thoroughly enjoyed the change of pace from his tiresome staff duties, and was very pleased with the outcome. Chapters were organized topically, with each addressing a specific arena of professional concern. Discussion was wrapped in a historical framework that built support for his editorialized opinions on the status and future of American military policy.

His constant thread was an underlying realism that accepted without question the need for professional armies to fight wars against great external powers. This somewhat pessimistic outlook reflected what Samuel Huntington later referred to as the "military mind." The professional soldier, wrote Huntington, "presupposes conflicting human interests and the use of violence to further those interests. . . . The military view of man is thus decidedly pessimistic."[4] In this vein, Carter asserted that warfare, however immoral, would continue its inevitable presence among competing nations: "In the face of accumulated and presumptuous wrong, affecting the commercial or political rights of a nation, all fine-spun and academic arguments against war are swept away in the rising tide of public opinion, against which parties and governments are as chaff before the wind."[5] With these "unalterable facts" as a starting point, he argued that it was incumbent on a nation to build a military policy congruent with the peculiarities of its culture, geography, economy, and form of government.

For the United States, Carter contended, republican government had precluded a consistent approach to national defense. Thus, Americans had historically approached military matters as "questions of expediency," without regard to a coherently developed strategic policy. "Nevertheless," he continued (perhaps more hopeful than certain), "there is a steadily increasing sentiment that a reasonable preparation for probable contingencies is the surest guarantee of peace." It was this sentiment that he believed dictated a strong military profession as the focal point of a broader policy to ensure rapid and efficient mobilization in time of crisis. Carter closed his introduction by conceding that strictly military solutions to questions of national defense were not always congruent with the popular will. Reconciling the two perspectives, he granted, "is for those in authority to determine." But, quoting Upton, he reminded readers that this did not absolve the professional soldier of an obligation to "frame and bequeath to succeeding generations a military system suggested by our past experience."[6]

Carter examined the traditional military policy through a template of several basic inadequacies first identified by Upton and bemoaned since by like-minded professionalists:

> First: The employment of militia and undisciplined troops commanded by amateurs.
>
> Second: Short enlistment terms for periods less than three years or a conflict's duration.
>
> Third: Reliance on wholly voluntary enlistments without complementary provision for some form of conscription.
>
> Fourth: The intrusion of the states in military affairs and a resulting approach to warfare more appropriate for a confederacy than a nation.
>
> Fifth: Confusing volunteers with militia and consequently surrendering to the states the right to commission volunteer officers as if they were officers of militia.
>
> Sixth: The bounty—a natural consequence of voluntary enlistments.
>
> Seventh: The failure to appreciate military education, and to distribute trained officers at higher command levels among volunteer organizations.
>
> Eighth: The want of territorial recruitment and regimental depots.[7]

Owing to contemporary debate over the creation of a federal reserve to supersede the militia, Carter centered a large portion of his discussion on "providing a proper scheme of expansion . . . from a peace footing to a war basis."[8] This question largely defined all other issues of national defense during what might be termed the "preparedness years" preceding the First World War.

Despite the Dick Act's attempt to improve the existing system, the subject of militia reform was still very much alive in 1912. The 1908 Militia Act had temporarily answered concerns that state troops could not be ordered beyond U.S. borders, but Stimson and Wood reopened this political hornet's nest when they sought higher interpretation of the pertinent statutes. The NGA was prepared to vigorously oppose attempts to deprive the Guard of its traditional place as America's reserve, but regulars were just as determined to correct a system they saw as inadequate for modern contingencies. Unlike many who spoke out on the topic, Carter based his own views less on ideological dogma or selfish institutional concerns than on conclusions drawn from very relevant experiences and observations. In the past, Carter, though skeptical, had made sincere attempts to pull the Guard up to a level of efficiency commensurate with its federal role.

As early as 1903, when the Dick Act was passed as a compromise measure to raise the National Guard's standards of performance, Carter had engaged the issue with a doubtful but nonetheless moderate voice. While begrudgingly acknowledging the citizen-soldiery's claim as a primary reserve, he warned that its future legitimacy was in grave doubt without immediate strides toward greater competence. "The time has arrived," he wrote, "when the national guard will have a fair opportunity to establish itself on an efficient basis." He tolerated the fact that state-appointed officers would continue to lead state troops, but demanded that these officers undergo the necessary training and education to ensure their effectiveness in time of war. Especially important, he advised, was earnest preparation in the staff and support areas, involving duties that required familiarity with national systems in order to realize immediate operational effectiveness once mobilized. The nature of warfare was changing, and so too were the competencies expected of the nation's citizen-soldiers.[9]

Within the professionalist ranks, there existed two schools of contemporary skepticism on the militia issue. The first was adamantly Uptonian, outright rejecting any further role for state troops in the national military establishment. The second genre was less opposed to the Guard's continued utility as a primary reserve, but cautioned that greater regulation was required to align the amateur tradition with modern realities. Carter's own views seem to have evolved over a period of years until he was more closely aligned with the former group than the latter—an important shift that was only reached after much consideration and eye-opening first-hand observation of the extant military system at work.[10]

Unlike many of his colleagues, Carter was at first not opposed to the Organized Militia as a functioning reserve, but believed that Americans could no longer allow its neglect. Each state should take immediate steps to mimic the federal military establishment in both organization and system, imparting standards that would improve joint training and operations. The Dick Act, he bemoaned, was a diluted measure that foolishly depended on local indulgence to give it any substance: "Much individual and combined effort is necessary to put the national guard on a proper military basis. The mere passage of an Act of Congress and the granting of money and stores will not accomplish it." In the absence of legislation that compelled action, he wondered, what could possibly ensure that the Guard would become an effective fighting force?[11]

By the time he wrote *The American Army*, Carter's use for the militia in its current role was sorely tried by events. Although he was impressed by some organizations' enthusiasm at the joint summer camps and was inclined to encourage the Guard's further development as a domestic auxiliary, he was increasingly convinced that its dual state and federal roles could never be reconciled with modern needs. While considering contingent strategies for the Mexican border, he recognized that state troops could not be relied upon for any sort of extended action beyond the nation's boundaries. Carter wrote that it was essential for a reserve to "possess a national character," and added that *"the militia, which, in the nature of things embraces all state troops, can not be invested with this national character until it has been called into the service and then only for a limited use within our borders* [emphasis his]." Despite the NGA's best efforts to promote the Guard as a national reserve, he pointed to recent legal interpretations to conclude that it could not be used for any purposes but those stipulated by the Constitution. Thus, with the Guard's inability to meet federal needs as a point of departure, Carter outlined his case for an alternative military policy.[12]

Like many of his contemporaries, Carter worried that the army would be stretched beyond its breaking point if called to defend American interests for any length of time without almost immediate reinforcement. An aggressive foreign policy had spread the Regular Army very thin, leaving it woefully inadequate to respond to any single point of crisis. After arguing that the army was in fact unable to meet its current obligations, Carter asserted that the nation's military policy was a failure:

> It should be apparent to any novice that our newly acquired liabilities leave us in a far worse plight, as regards our army within the continental limits of the United States, than before the war with Spain. Without any opening for criticism of advocating 'militarism,' it may be stated in the plainest manner, that we are allowing our insurance to dwindle below a reasonable guarantee of home protection.[13]

The solution, he believed, was a bona fide national reserve—capable of quickly and decisively answering an executive call to service. "I feel more and more convinced that General Upton's plan for a volunteer reserve is our only safe and wise system," he wrote, "and surely the only scheme under which each and every section of the country will share in the preparation for defense." In short, Carter was certain that America's needs had simply outgrown the state militia.[14]

In past conflicts—such as the Mexican War and the American Civil War—the nation had called on volunteers to fill federal military rolls. The volunteers eventually had served well and faithfully as these conflicts unfolded, but in the future, the luxury of time would likely disappear. In true Uptonian fashion, Carter abhorred reliance on untrained troops, clearly a liability in an industrialized world. Modern warfare, as evidenced by the recent Russo-Japanese War (1904–5), could erupt quickly with devastating results as nations competed for commercial supremacy with increasingly lethal arsenals. A country that took little interest in military preparedness was tempting fate by surrendering its interests and prerogatives. In *The American Army*, Carter held up a national reserve as a much-needed pillar for America's defense. It would incorporate the republican virtues of a traditional citizen-soldiery without the ruinous effects of state authority.[15]

The disparate positions taken on this subject were a source of high friction in Stimson's War Department. Wood attempted to disassociate himself from Uptonian professionalists in his campaign to institute the principle of universal training in a reserve system that was akin to a "nation in arms." Professionalists were dissatisfied and shocked by such proposals. In a chapter expressly addressing the nature of a federal reserve, Carter rose in opposition to one of the prime tenets of Wood's "preparedness" doctrine. Wood advocated legislation that would give enlistees an opportunity to serve on active duty for a three- or four-year term and then return to civilian life as reservists for the remainder of a seven- or eight-year enlistment, ostensibly creating a strong, well-trained federal reserve. However, this scheme implied an important reconceptualization of the army's purpose— from that of an expert cadre to that of an elaborate "training school," a shift that professionalists saw as a dangerous by-product of Wood's entire plan. In language that hardly concealed his disgust, Carter argued against such a course.[16]

During the Roosevelt years, the army had done a great deal to develop its enlisted ranks as a more "professional body of soldiers" through the introduction of special inducements, education, and pay. An important tenet of this endeavor was that the army proper, not just its commissioned leadership, was viewed as a skilled national asset. Carter considered "permanency of personnel" as a basic element of such a policy, and thus regarded Wood's interpretation as fundamentally flawed. Unlike Upton before him, he could not support a "skeletal" Regular Army—one that existed as merely a template for a much larger wartime force. Instead, the Regular Army should stand in peace as it would during war, and discharged regulars would become a source of trained expertise to bolster volunteer or militia organizations during national emergencies.[17]

Predictably, Wood labeled those who opposed his ideas as static and unprogressive, and just as predictably, it was this characterization that spurred Carter to the defense. "It is wholly unfair to question the motives of military men because they do not change their views with every new suggestion," he responded, denouncing Wood's ideas as "diametrically opposed" to his own. "All human institutions are subject to the laws of progress," he agreed, but reminded readers that "care is necessary to the end that mere change be not mistaken for reform." He found Wood's plan for universal training wildly impractical and laid out his own as the best workable solution.[18]

Perhaps fishing for political support, he also resurrected Upton's plan to organize a federal reserve according to congressional districts, thereby building on already existent local identities. The reserve would differ from the militia not only in its national disposition but also because it could not be called into state service, such as for the purpose of quelling civil disorder or quieting labor unrest. The Guard's popularity with wage-earning classes had suffered in recent decades due to several bitter skirmishes with striking workers, and thus Carter contended that a federal reserve would be seen as a more attractive alternative. It would excite patriotic interest without the stained reputation that came with a state constabulary. This argument conveniently ignores the similarly unpopular role played by the national government (including the Regular Army) in controlling labor disturbances. But however flawed, Carter's perspective reflects his vaunted image of national institutions.[19]

Rather than being simply a manpower pool, the reserves, once called for federal service, would remain separately constituted units. To recruit and fill regular and reserve organizations during both war and peace, Carter drew on a European concept highlighted for American soldiers by Emory Upton in *Armies of Asia and Europe*. Regional recruiting and training depots would give regiments a community flavor and provide a strong sense of continuity that was otherwise lost to a unit merely backfilled from a mass of volunteers or conscripts. Regimental depots, he maintained, were "absolutely essential to an economical and efficient conduct of war," not only for regular organizations but also reserve and volunteer units once called forth for national service.[20]

In addition to addressing issues of force structure, Carter detailed other troubling aspects of military policy that, in 1912, were still the subject of debate. His often-moralistic arguments generally echoed those of the professionalist genre, applauding the Regular Army as a bulwark of selfless, patriotic service while deploring the nation's lack of a coherent system that might render its sacrifices more fruitful.

In a chapter entitled "Command of the Army," he delivered a scathing sermon to the "coterie" he had only recently left behind in Washington. Carter recounted the historical evolution of the office of commanding general and, as might be expected, transitioned to discussion of the recently created office of chief of staff. He emphasized that the chief of staff was never meant merely to replace the historically weak commanding general. Instead, he was intended as a coordinator endowed only with administrative authority exercised in the name of the secretary of war: "It will be observed that while the Chief of Staff is entrusted with practically all the power denied in former years to the Commanding General of the Army, it is required that he shall not set up any claim of authority except in representation of the Secretary of War."[21] After establishing the chief of staff as a position of inherently greater strength than realized by commanding generals of the past, he warned that individual "lust for power" in the office might easily "create dissension," thereby undermining the public interest. This barb was undoubtedly aimed directly at Wood. When "those responsible for the administration and command of the army" acted with respect for their office and obligations, he lectured on, "controversies should cease and the Chief of Staff and all heads of bureaus move forward in harmonious action." If writing was an out-let for his private frustrations, then Carter was surely making the most of his therapy.[22]

He addressed other major topics in much the same manner, fol-lowing historical preamble with highly editorialized analysis. Chap-ters included discussions of the "The General Staff Corps," "The Corps of Officers," "Army Schools," and "The Organized Militia." The importance of contemporary advances in health and sanitation were expounded in "The Triumph of Medical Science," a chapter in which the Maneuver Division's recent success was trumpeted as a shining example of modern preventative medicine. Unsurprisingly, the Regular Army emerges heroic throughout the work and criticism is harshest for the very political nature of military decision-making.

The American Army was thus a combination of applause for re-cent progress and a forum for Carter's own well-developed opinions on the state of U.S. military policy. Although a significant historical work in the genre of Upton's *Military Policy,* the book's real value was as a coherent—even if somewhat hyperrhetorical—articulation of a professional soldier's view of contemporary defense issues. Written for a nation still coming to terms with its entry into the international arena, Carter's book helped explain the need for the New Army's continued transformation. Major themes of modernity—graduate ed-ucation, bureaucratic efficiency, and centralized command—are fea-tured prominently, placing the army on equal footing with the day's celebrated civilian professions.[23]

When the book was completed, Carter sought critique (as well as validation) from several likely places, including Elihu Root and even Secretary Stimson. Suggested revisions likely made the work more palatable and perhaps also blunted an otherwise biting indictment of Wood and the current War Department. Carter worried that its grow-ing length might prevent its publication for a popular audience, and felt it necessary to "limit the book to the size of a novel, in order to secure attention." Nonetheless, he continued to add material in revi-sion even as he pared down other parts. As it turned out, although the first manuscript copy was sent to Scribner's Sons in October 1912, *The American Army* did not reach print until March 1915, when it was released by Bobbs-Merrill. By then, the opening of the First World War in Europe had rendered Carter's topic timely indeed, and his comments on the need for a thoroughly prepared military system certainly proved prophetic.[24]

The American Army was positively received within military circles, but as Carter feared, did not sell well in the popular market. Maybe as Root noted in encouragement, the public was simply more interested in newspaper headlines. But for military progressives, the book captured many of the ideas for which they continued to struggle. James Harrison Wilson, retired hero of the Old Army and longtime supporter of military reform, wrote to Carter that his work was "well reasoned" and the proposals therein were "sounder and more practicable" than any he had previously seen or heard. Wilson was especially enthusiastic about the plan to establish regimental depots, claiming that he himself had suggested a similar scheme in a personal letter to Tasker H. Bliss a short time before. He urged Carter to draw up a bill based on the plan and believed that support would be assured by placing a depot in each congressional district— underscoring again the degree to which politics drove military policy.[25]

Although it never attracted popular acclaim and seems to be all but forgotten by modern scholarship, *The American Army* was a success when judged by its purpose. Carter never meant to write an exhaustive account of the nation's great military campaigns, nor did he offer highly detailed plans for legislative remedies. Instead, his intention was to highlight the great overarching issues that he believed defined and moved American military policy. He hoped to bring these topics to the forefront of public discussion, letting his own opinions and proposals guide readers toward what he believed were inarguable conclusions. Despite the fact that he sometimes descended into self-indulgent (and ill-concealed) attacks on Wood's own ideas and doctrine, Carter's book was not merely a soapbox for private disputes. He addressed areas that he believed wanting and tried to chart a path for their future solution. As he eloquently stated in the book's introduction, "The dignity of the service . . . dictates that the problems of the army should be clearly set forth, relying upon the merits of the case to secure consideration and leaving untrammeled the responsibility for action where the nation has placed it."[26]

A reviewer for *The Nation* recognized the book's appeal, explaining that Carter's contribution "is far broader than a narrow definition of his title would imply. . . . Gen. Carter has given the country a calm and philosophic discussion of the military question as it presents itself to the contemplation of serious inquirers after the truth." This description quite accurately summarizes Carter's intentions, both for the book and for his own role in army reform.[27]

About the time that a first draft of *The American Army* was completed, Carter's preparations to leave Washington with Ida were interrupted by another family crisis. Their only living son, Will, had been plagued by abdominal pain for months, and finally underwent surgery to relieve chronic appendicitis in early November—no minor operation in that day. Will's health greatly worried his parents, and they put all other activities on hold for several days while they anxiously awaited the outcome. After finally satisfying himself that the procedure was successful and his son was out of danger, Carter left for his new assignment while Ida remained in Washington for a few more weeks to close up their house and nurse Will back to strength. On 5 December, he assumed command of the Central Division, headquartered in Chicago, Illinois. The Carters had loved Chicago's active social scene and plentiful culture during their first stay in the city, and its lively calendar promised to once again provide an enjoyable distraction from more serious obligations.[28]

But after only two weeks in Chicago, Carter was summoned back to Washington for a high-level conference on the army's planned reorganization. Reflecting Stimson's desire to effect tactical divisions within the continental United States, Carter's Central Division thereafter ceased to exist and he assumed command of the newly established Central Department, which for purposes of mobilization would comprise the Second Division. This scheme grew in large degree from the War Department's experiences in putting together the hodgepodge Maneuver Division two years earlier. The plan would not have long to wait for its first test in the field. In what must have seemed like an encore performance, Carter soon found himself back in Texas, once more preparing an army with a close eye on events south of the border.[29]

Shortly after returning to Chicago, Carter was notified that President Taft was ordering the Second Division to Texas for exercises and possible intervention in Mexico if circumstances should warrant. Sometime during the night of 22 February, Mexican President Francisco Madero and Vice President José Pino Suárez were both assassinated in the capital city when Gen. Victoriano Huerta attempted to wrest power in a coup attempt. Carter decried the act as a "cold blooded deed" that was motivated only by Huerta's own despicable ambitions—a conclusion shared by many Americans. The situation quickly deteriorated into a dangerous power struggle between rival factions with little legitimate claim to governance. Carter did not expect orders, logically thinking that Taft would wait until President-elect Woodrow Wilson took office and appraised the situation for himself. But Taft refused to play the lame duck during his last days as chief executive, and Carter arrived in Texas City with instructions to establish the Second Division's base with a view to readying it for possible immediate operations in Mexico.[30]

Troops were rushed from points across the United States, traveling from as far away as San Francisco, California, and College Park, Maryland. When the Second Division began disembarking in Texas City in late February, it found a veritable swampland created by seasonal rains. As soon as the proper equipage arrived, the troops set about draining the inland areas and constructing a semi-permanent cantonment in anticipation of another extended game of "hurry-up-and-wait." Just as before, the national press clamored for an insider's perspective and printed stories of Carter's former exploits on the frontier. But even during these early weeks, Carter was less than convinced that the division would ever march triumphantly into Mexico. Realizing how public opinion could quickly shift with the political winds, he observed quite simply that the "bottom seems to have dropped out of the Mexican intervention." His earlier experience with the Maneuver Division proved a valuable lesson for the sake of his new command.[31]

In Texas, the Second Division was at first beset with confusion as officers and enlisted men worked to build a suitable encampment from a quagmire that one historian referred to as "a nightmare of bad drainage and mosquitoes."[32] After several days of torrential rain, the initial site (chosen previously by a staff officer) was rendered an unusable mud pit and the entire command was forced to move to another location nearby before it could even unpack. The excitement of an expeditionary campaign soon gave way to the monotony of camp life.

Carter's philosophical outlook on this transition highlights the complexities of modern military leadership: "It looks like a simple thing to command a division and so it is so far as the soldier part is concerned, but it is a different matter entirely when it comes to supply and administration generally." Like so many soldiers both before and after, Carter was finding that generalship required a very large degree of management skill. Unforeseen problems quickly cropped up that required the division staff's immediate attention—from horses arriving from Kansas City with influenza to the delivery of incomplete mess kits and tentage. Numerous such issues plagued the command and diverted its attention from, as Carter put it, "the soldier part." Despite these difficulties, once the division's three brigades and supporting units had established camp and seen to their initial housekeeping, a progressive training schedule was organized that, under the austere conditions, was ambitious.[33]

The deployment to Texas City in 1913 played out very much as did that of the Maneuver Division to San Antonio in 1911. The Mexican situation became an exercise in diplomatic frustration as President Wilson attempted to impose high-handed morality on the remnants of Taft's foreign policy. Meanwhile, division and brigade staffs attempted to keep the command in a high state of readiness while battling the weather, monotony, irritating oversight from Washington, and to some degree, even the press. This time, the months stretched even longer, and as the summer gave way to fall and winter, Carter's enthusiasm began to wane along with that of his troops.

Relying on his previous experiences, Carter believed that morale would suffer if incessant training continued with no particular "real-world" objective in sight: "Brief maneuver campaigns possess a marked advantage for training purposes over so-called maneuver camps of long duration, for in the latter it is difficult to keep up a sustained interest sufficient to prevent the command from growing stale."[34] As it became increasingly apparent that the division would remain in-place for the near term, Carter was convinced that training could relax without risk. As before, he shifted the regimen toward a pace that was more amenable to both men and animals: "Maneuvers should always be treated as the last and highest card in the training," he wrote, and "when concluded, complete rest and change are necessary for the men." This principle was not shared by all, and even some of his subordinate commanders were dissatisfied when hours of sporting activities, such as baseball, swimming, and polo, were added to the daily itinerary.[35]

Because of this move, and perhaps also due to his increasing age and growing reputation as a sort of intellectual warrior, some observers—both in Washington and in Texas—questioned whether Carter's drive or energy was up to the challenge. Although curbing the division's training tempo was seen by many as very realistic and wise under the circumstances, others, including the highly ambitious Robert Bullard, saw the action as showing weak leadership that only encouraged apathy. Later that summer, when it became known that Wilson intended to keep the Second Division in Texas for the foreseeable future, Carter began treating the command as he would have any other peacetime organization, seeing no reason to prepare feverishly for war when there was no war in sight. Ida came to Texas City, as did many other officers' wives, and the atmosphere largely turned into that of a typical, albeit temporary, continental garrison. To his detractors, likely led by Wood (who by this time was thinking of higher political office), Carter lacked the necessary vigor, and by December 1913, Secretary of War Lindley Garrison decided it was time for a change.[36]

For several weeks, Carter listened to rumors of his imminent removal, but received no official notice of reassignment or of the administration's displeasure. Perhaps with some degree of good cause colored by a touch of paranoia, he attributed such talk to the petty vindictiveness that he believed had followed him for the last several years. "I had received ample warning from friends that in event of intervention in Mexico it was not intended that I should have the privilege of going in command of the Division I had been training for nearly a year," he remembered bitterly. Thus, it came as no real shock when on 7 December, without formal notification from the War Department, stories appeared on the national newswires announcing his reassignment to command the Department of Hawaii. Adding salt to the wound, a few months later the Second Division was sent to occupy Vera Cruz in the wake of perceived provocation by Mexican authorities. Carter was certain that Wood's jealousy had brought about his removal at this crucial juncture. He would chuckle with satisfaction years later when Wood himself was relieved of a command just as it prepared to move overseas during the First World War. Then he wryly observed, while enjoying Wood's protests, that it sure "makes a heap of difference whose ox is being gored." Despite the many harbingers of professional progress, the army's senior command had by no means risen above the personal rivalries and pettiness that had so often tarnished previous generations.[37]

As events developed, General Funston and his brigade were bottled up in Vera Cruz for several months, gaining very little in the way of martial glory and probably suffering a great deal for their efforts. But for Carter, this last adventure was the curtain call for his long career as a soldier. On the last day of January 1914, the day before he departed Texas City, he rode in an automobile as Troop A of the Sixth Cavalry escorted him to a special assembly and elaborate outdoor reception in his honor—a fitting and somewhat metaphoric end to an old cavalryman's last field command. Hawaii promised an enjoyable two years and undoubtedly held its own challenges, but for the gray-haired "hero of Cibicu," the future promised little more than a comfortable retirement. He and Ida were very aware that this assignment would be their last, and it was with melancholy resignation that they left the Texas border behind.[38]

Before Carter left Chicago to catch a Pacific transport, an essay he had written for the *North American Review* appeared in print, causing some embarrassment in Washington. In the article, he took an unexpected position on the question of American intervention. His thoughts not only drew notice from the magazine's wide readership, but also, as likely intended, irritated Garrison and Wood to no small degree. Sounding almost pacifistic, he charged that "when destiny coincides with material interests, conscience is all but smothered, and in the multiplicity of arguments truth is relegated to oblivion."[39] Carter worried that as Mexican upheaval escalated out of control, regional emotion might easily trigger events that would push aside a more moderate and calmly reasoned policy. "With the *Maine* disaster and its consequences on public opinion," he cautioned, "we know full well the possibility of the nation being carried away by the excitement following some unexpected and unpreventable incident."[40]

After witnessing the effects of so-called "yellow journalism" several times during his career, Carter knew all too well that public sentiment was easily manipulated. He warned leaders not to let financial interests in Mexico or anywhere else dictate foreign policy. Perhaps these concerns grew from wariness of the manner in which corporate-industrial interests were beginning to dominate government at the expense of traditional republican virtues. "Our people seem willing to stand anything humiliating," he later quipped, "so long as dollars multiply."[41] The Mexican people, Carter advised, were quite capable of providing their own heroes and solving their own in-

ternal disputes without American help. He then concluded with obligatory applause for the Regular Army while reminding his audience that
grave danger still lurked in the nation's lack of a credible reserve.

Carter encouraged moderation when many contemporary pieces
shouted for military action with little thought given to its morality or
the risk of becoming embroiled in a foreign civil war. The *Army and
Navy Journal* gave the article a positive review and supported his position. But, as Carter expected, "Intervention" attracted a somewhat
less than salutatory response from friends at the War Department.[42]

Soon after the article's publication, Secretary Garrison wrote to
Carter expressing disapproval and reminded him in no uncertain
terms that the administration's intentions on the Mexican border
were not appropriate subject matter for a senior officer's public discussion. Garrison was of course correct—as recent commander of the
Second Division, Carter's insights on the issue were inappropriate—
but it is interesting that the secretary admitted outright that he had
not even read the essay when he condemned it. In itself, the matter
was unimportant—Carter's views were basically in agreement with
Wilson's efforts at diplomacy—except that once again, it demonstrated Carter's continued self-image as a martyr of professional conscience: the American public deserved the benefit of his opinions and
he made every effort to share them.[43]

For his part, Carter responded to Garrison's slap on the wrist
with a genuinely respectful and conciliatory letter, claiming that he
"would not knowingly embarrass the administration in any matter,"
particularly since he sympathized with the president's stated policy.
Opinionated or not, Carter recognized that he may have crossed the
appropriate boundaries of an officer's duty-bound obligation to objective service. Even so, he must have smiled inwardly at the obvious
annoyance that he had caused Garrison and Wood so soon after they
had sent him packing from Texas City.[44]

Curiously, Carter continued to indulge hopes that he might yet
reach the pinnacle of his profession—the chief of staff position that he
clearly coveted. A year earlier, he had written to Root about this
desire, but with Wood firmly entrenched in the position, was discouraged in the attempt. Although he must have known that such
thoughts were now highly improbable, he continued to feel out his
opportunities in case Wilson decided not to retain Wood. Carter even
took the brash step of forwarding a five-page letter to Garrison that

recounted his military record and attempted to establish a legitimate claim to the office. Although in hindsight these efforts seem incredible and even desperate, they were fanned by public speculation that Wood would not last much longer as chief of staff due to his well-known ties to the Republican Party. But despite his earnest pleas and Root's continued support, Wilson retained Wood as chief of staff and Carter's orders to Honolulu stood firm. After losing the Second Division and now realizing that he would never become chief of staff, Carter had good reason to feel disappointed as he began his journey to the Pacific coast.[45]

Moving to yet another department command was little consolation, but Carter's hurt pride quickly recovered and he faced his last assignment with enthusiasm. He and Ida reached Honolulu on 12 March, and after a year of enduring temporary quarters in Texas, were glad to enjoy the comforts of a good hotel while they looked for a more permanent home. After so many years of hard service, the couple's stay in Hawaii seemed like an extended vacation given them by a grateful nation. They found a vibrant if small American community whose "kindness and hospitality made one forget that the ocean rolled between us and the mainland." For recreation, Carter was pleasantly surprised to learn that Hawaii's active cattle industry supported numerous horse-related activities and events. He had brought his two favorite mounts with him, and spent a great deal of time in the saddle exploring the island.[46]

As commander of the new department, which in addition to Hawaii included regional dependencies such as Midway Island, Carter set about establishing livable working conditions for the several thousand troops already located there, and planning and managing the construction of a more permanent base. This effort consumed most of his daily attention as the army attempted to build a small piece of the continental United States on Oahu. The only reminders of the outside world's more violent endeavors were the occasional visits by foreign naval contingents.[47]

Although warships of many flags often called at Honolulu's neutral port, the intensifying struggle between Germany and other world powers gave Carter and his troops some pause for concern. At one point, they were treated to an altogether disturbing view of German and Japanese warships playing maritime cat-and-mouse just beyond Pearl Harbor's entrance, bringing forth American demands to observe the port's strict neutrality. Carter began to have real concerns for the islands' future defense if beset by a naval power. He specifically doubted his ability to defend Pearl Harbor, describing the prospect as "quite impossible as far as protection of property is concerned"—a chillingly prophetic observation in light of Japan's infamous attack on the U.S. Pacific Fleet at that place some twenty-six years later. Carter had little idea just how real his fears would become with the advent of new weapons and the changes they brought to military operations.[48]

Carter's two years on Oahu, during which he quietly celebrated his fiftieth anniversary of military service, sped by quickly and rather uneventfully. Beyond the appearance of foreign belligerents seeking safe harbor, the only excitement came one evening when he single-handedly captured an unlucky burglar who entered the couple's home through a downstairs window while they slept. After being awakened by Ida, who heard the breaking glass, the sixty-four-year-old cavalry-man surprised the hapless intruder and held him at gunpoint while waiting for the local police to arrive. Other than this unwelcome adventure, life in Hawaii was rather peaceful when compared to past assignments and came with few pressing obligations. "We have been content to remain quietly here," Carter wrote, "studying, reading, writing and enjoying the wonderful climate." After years of hard service through very tumultuous times, life on the island made for a smooth transition to the slower pace of retirement.[49]

In March 1915, Carter and other general officers were asked for their "views and recommendations" on issues relevant to creating a policy statement that might guide future military decision-making and legislative efforts. It would address many of those very themes that Carter and other professionalists had been preaching for several years. These included not only the strength and organization of the Regular Army and National Guard but also the question of a national reserve force and a plan for the organization of wartime volunteers. Such concerns had provided fodder for generations of debate, but in the spirit of professionalization and efficiency, Garrison was now encouraging the General Staff to build a set of generally acceptable guiding principles.[50]

Although doubtful that his efforts would find receptive ears in a War Department still under Wood's influence, Carter worked hard to summarize those views he had developed over a fifty-year career in both line and staff. His reply repeated much of what he had already asserted in publication: the militia was a failure for national purposes; some sort of federal reserve was an inarguable requirement; land forces should be based on a territorial scheme designed to encourage state and local support; and the entire system should be kept in a state of relative preparedness at all times. These ideas were by now familiar, even worn-out refrains, but importantly, in his tired pleading tone, Carter had begun to evince an outlook that Russell Weigley termed "Uptonian pessimism."[51]

He spoke to the frustrations that professional soldiers had felt for decades—perhaps even more so since American troops had been spread around the globe in support of an imperial foreign policy. Selfish and parochial concerns seemed to invade every aspect of public decision-making, and Carter's patience with the process had grown thin:

> Should public opinion and congress not sustain a reasonable increase of the army it should then be presented concisely and clearly that the army as now established cannot furnish garrisons for all the places requiring them and that it will be necessary to withdraw some of the troops. . . . In other words, ask congress to share the responsibility in fixing and executing a policy rather than action on isolated and fragmentary appropriation items.[52]

Just as he had years earlier as a West Point cadet, Carter blamed partisan politics as an evil detriment to the national defense—feelings shared by many of his contemporaries. Framing issues from a nationalist perspective, soldiers were galled by public leaders' inclination to approach questions of national importance according to the interests of narrow constituencies. Carter charged that such actions lacked a highly desirable characteristic that he broadly termed "statesmanship." He dutifully sent his response to Garrison, but had little confidence that any good would come of it. Exposure to the give-and-take of republican governance had indeed given him a tinge of pessimism, and he wondered if a truly coherent military policy would forever be an impossibility.[53]

On 6 November 1915, with his sixty-fourth birthday less than two weeks away, General Carter stepped down as commander of the Department of Hawaii. A squadron of cavalry escorted the Carters to the harbor where they boarded a transport to begin the long journey home. The formal "guard of honor" that assembled to bid them farewell stretched along the streets from their hotel all the way to the ship itself. For Carter, the trip home meant the end of a long and successful career in the service of his country.[54]

Upon returning to the couple's Washington home as a retired officer, he found many letters of congratulations and best wishes from friends, colleagues, and a wide assortment of government and civic leaders. Elihu Root quite aptly noted that Carter's retirement seemed to mark the ending of an era of great military progress:

> I look forward with great regret and a good deal of sadness to your retirement from the active list of the army. It seems to mark with great distinctness the passing away of a period during which we worked so hard together in taking advantage of the public interest and feeling following immediately after the War with Spain to put our army on a better footing.[55]

But though Carter's active-duty career was finally at its end, his participation in the military profession was far from over.

While in Hawaii, Carter had found a great deal of time to indulge his enthusiasm for writing. During the last months of his career and throughout his retired years, publication remained his link to the army's future, and increasingly his sole avenue to exercise any further influence on the institution that he had worked so hard to reform. In 1914, he published "The Human Element in War," an essay that not only won the Military Service Institution's prestigious Reeve Memorial Award but also seems to have provided a restorative outlet for his personal grievances and disappointments. He narrated the often-bitter human interactions that accompanied American military command throughout its history, deploring the "desire for power, jealousy of prerogatives, restiveness under control, [and] offended dignity . . . which involved the welfare of the nation at the most critical periods." Using historical examples that stretched from Washington's Continental Army to the Army of the Potomac, Carter condemned the vain pettiness to which many senior soldiers had fallen victim. He demanded that promotion and advancement in the modern army be governed strictly by merit, leaving behind "the haphazard method incident to personal and political friendships" which had marred the Old Army.[56]

That same year, Carter touted the growing strength of the army's education system in "The Greater Leavenworth." In this essay, he outlined Fort Leavenworth's evolution as part of the larger attempt to institute a progressive approach to officer education. Unsurprisingly, General Orders no. 155 was heralded as the army's crowning achievement. As its proud architect, Carter boasted that "the scheme of instruction beginning with the garrison schools and continuing through the War College affords opportunities for the present generation undreamed of by their forebears." Written so closely on the heels of personal disappointments, it is not surprising that Carter chose to highlight an act that was perhaps his greatest success. Unlike the embattled General Staff and inadequately reformed militia system, the War College found relative prosperity during the decade following its inception, charting an American military tradition in which a system of graduate education became an institutional standard. With ill-concealed pride, Carter could justifiably point to it as a trophy of his own professional vision.[57]

These articles added to a growing literary resumé which by 1915 included not only several books but also dozens of articles, reviews, and editorials that addressed a wide array of topics. They included equine subjects, such as "The Charger" (1912), and eclectic historical pieces, such as "West Point in Literature" (1908) and "The Master of Belle Meade" (1912). By the time he retired, his by-line had appeared over some eighteen feature-length articles and countless shorter pieces, making a prolific contribution to American literature. His work has a lasting value for the meaningful insight it offers into the period's professional culture. Even if unable to press his ideas to fruition through legislative act, he certainly kept them alive and before the public with a very active pen.[58]

Carter's final years on active duty were marred by his ongoing conflict with Leonard Wood. Service as Wood's assistant on the General Staff had at first held great promise, but animosity between the two dashed any hopes for a cooperative effort and further progressive reform. Carter grumbled that he had enjoyed more authority as a lieutenant colonel during his time with Root than he had as a general officer serving with Wood. Thoughts of repeating the successes of ten years earlier were grievously disappointed.[59]

Although embittered by his second term in the War Department,

Carter could nonetheless look back on the last years of his career with pride and a sense of accomplishment. As commander of the Maneuver Division and later the Second Division, he helped to establish a modern benchmark for the army's ability to mobilize and operate as an expeditionary force. Though he never led either organization south of the border, both deployments proved valuable learning experiences in the years preceding the United States' entry into the First World War. Despite personal disappointments, Carter's passion for his profession remained strong, and he continued to satisfy this ardor as a critical observer of national defense. Even in retirement, he refused to relinquish his rightful place on the field of reform.

15

THE JOURNEY'S END

Carter had no intentions of sitting around a warm fireplace at the veterans' club and whittling away retirement with shared tales of past glories. Instead, convinced that the army suffered a dearth of progressive leadership, he was motivated more than ever to remain an active voice in the public discourse concerning defense matters. Although he now lacked whatever formal influence he formerly enjoyed as a general officer, in retirement he shed the institutional reins of active duty and thus could increase the volume of his arguments for a more viable military policy. One of the most visible military writers of his day, Carter perhaps sought to achieve in print the recognition that he never attained on the battlefield.

The return from Hawaii brought personal changes in addition to those associated with retirement. The Carters took on a sadly unexpected responsibility when they began caring for their daughter-in-law and two-month-old grandson. While in Hawaii, they received the devastating news that Helen Carter had developed tuberculosis while accompanying their son on assignment to the Philippines. Her failing health was complicated by pregnancy and, at first, there were real fears that neither mother nor child would live. But fortunately, the Carters' first grandchild—the general's namesake, William Harding

Carter II—was born on 23 September 1915 without difficulty. Now, as they made the return trip across the United States, they stopped in El Paso, Texas, to take Helen and the baby back to Washington with them. Helen's health had improved in the arid Southwest, but she needed help caring for the child, and Will was still obligated to the army in Manila. The recently retired grandparents were only too happy to oblige—Carter took a special interest in the little boy as he was then the sole heir to the family name. Helping Helen and the baby was certainly no burden, but as her battle with the disease progressed, it increasingly defined the household's daily activities and the situation proved an emotional drain on the entire family.[1]

Soon after arriving at their Washington home, Carter took stock of his circumstances and set about organizing plans for the immediate future. As he unboxed and examined his accumulated papers, he recognized the historical importance of the events in which he had played an active role. He was justifiably proud of his contributions and this poignant realization gave him great personal satisfaction: "I am sure when we get the house all settled we will greatly enjoy it and soon be glad our roaming days are over. One who has kept active and at the front of things, in my opinion, is not so apt to suffer regret as one who has merely wandered through a routine existence."[2] Carter looked forward to the opportunity to assemble his thoughts and reflect on the many changes he had witnessed during his lifetime. "Should I live for a few years after my retirement," he mused, "I shall endeavor to arrange and annotate my papers so as to make them useful to some student of the future generation." Now, as he surveyed the immense amount of correspondence, reports, manuscripts, and other materials produced by fifty years of service, it must have been starkly evident that his army career had in many ways spanned two very different military epochs. With typical energy, he wasted no time taking up the effort to leave a record of his thoughts and observations on a variety of subjects.[3]

But before Carter could knock the dust from his desk and settle into retirement, Mrs. Adna Chaffee visited to discuss the possibility of his writing a biography of her deceased husband. He readily welcomed the project as a "labor of love" and promised to begin research for the book as soon as possible. There is little doubt that he relished the opportunity to eulogize not only an old friend but also the

Old Army while extolling the virtues of the New. At the same time, Carter became even more aware that with progress had come still more problems. While paying occasional visits to his former haunts at the War Department, he gained disturbing insights into the changes increasingly manifested in the New Army's culture.[4]

Carter felt that he no longer belonged among the officers who now inhabited the department's offices with a distinctly different outlook and manner. The changes he saw there were not for the better and certainly not as intended by men such as Elihu Root and Emory Upton. His concerns went beyond simple nostalgia for the past. With clarity now unencumbered by participation, Carter was horrified that the army's command and staff system was developing into an unmanageable bureaucratic maze—of the very type he had and Root had hoped to shatter with professional reform. Individual officers were becoming "merely cogs of a drive wheel with no opportunity for distinction," adding that "if one becomes of importance he immediately becomes an object of envy and jealousy and not infrequently of downright malice." Such observations were undoubtedly driven in part by lingering personal frustrations and regret that he was no longer an active part of the "wheel" himself, but they confirm an important historical perspective.[5]

William Roberts contends that the New Army slipped toward a more bureaucratic culture during the early twentieth century, encumbering the professional environment sought by progressives. Roberts faults the General Staff Act as an important even if wholly unintentional catalyst for this evolution—ironic in that Carter and Root meant to professionalize the army in part by dismantling the existing staff system's stultifying bureaucracy. Discouraged, Carter still hoped that he might play some role in setting the army's future course.[6]

In December 1915, military legislation was introduced in both congressional houses. Carter met with Senator George E. Chamberlain, Republican chairman of the Senate Military Committee, to offer his assistance. Garrison sponsored one of the bills, and the so-called Garrison Plan followed the same basic themes that Carter himself had embraced in *The American Army*. In fact, some of Garrison's arguments before committee were so familiar that Carter claimed "he gave almost the exact words of my book in hearing before Congress." He worried that attempts to move a preparedness bill through Congress would be summarily defeated unless strongly championed, and he believed that the secretary lacked the capacity to make such a case. If the work that he and Root had begun over a decade earlier had started the army down a path of reform, it was now going through its first complete iteration, and Carter burned for an active role as its shepherd.[7]

In the early weeks of 1916, the bills entered committee, and Carter was thankfully called back to public service as an official War Department advisor to the Senate Military Committee. He readily shelved work on the Chaffee biography and other projects and took up the job in earnest, making almost daily trips to one proceeding or another as the bills wound their way through various legislative hoops. Carter was intrigued by the different personalities that came together under the guise of public leadership. He detested the domineering James Hay, Democratic chairman of the House Military Committee, whom he considered pompous, combative, and highly partisan, but thought highly of Chamberlain, finding in him the desirable characteristic of broad-minded "statesmanship" that he believed wholly lacking in so many other politicians of both parties. He failed to understand how anyone could not share his own nationalist interpretation of issues he considered too important for parochial compromise.[8]

Hearings moved slowly and Carter doubted whether anyone in Congress was sincerely interested in substantive progress:

> I see no aggressive, forceful work to form or execute any policy and it makes one think the President [is] not very sincere about preparedness or else his party not close behind him. I think it very improbable that any serious legislation will be accomplished. The influential staff [bureaus] may get some plums but the outlook for advanced military policy not good.[9]

He was kept so busy testifying or advising at various conferences that retirement must have seemed like something that happened only to other men. Wood was also active in the proceedings, and quite predictably, Carter described his testimony as less than noteworthy. The former chief of staff was merely seizing the opportunity to hold "center stage," Carter noted disgustedly, perhaps suspicious that Wood was already jockeying for a future political career. For his part, the hearings offered the chance to advocate in person those ideas that he had been propounding in print for several years.

During these early weeks of 1916, Carter suffered from a deep cough that he described as "bronchial." The affliction had begun as a minor virus in Hawaii, but continued to nag him for several months. This condition, coupled with the long hours he dedicated to committee work, wore him down physically while worry about Helen and the baby wrung him out emotionally. But Carter despised soldiers who retired merely to "go quietly along to Arlington, seemingly content with their bridge, cigars and newspapers," and doggedly refused to slow his pace. As the defense bill struggled in conference, he continued to work closely with Chamberlain in an effort to find a workable solution that would meet his approval.[10]

Carter believed that his own thoughts on preparedness, as laid out in *The American Army* and other publications, were wholly "American" in their foundation and aligned with the concepts evinced by Grant, Sherman, and most of all, Upton. He fretted that renewed congressional enthusiasm over the Swiss system of popular service would derail interest in establishing a trained federal reserve of the type he advocated. Americans' continued preoccupation with European military systems, now fueled by the First World War, was a distraction from the nation's own peculiar needs. "My federal volunteer system is American entirely, and that may defeat it," he worried. "We adopted the French forage cap and after 1870 adopted the German helmet—what now?" Wood's own ideas only inflamed such notions as they relied on a broad concept of a trained citizenry under universal obligation. With the Hay Bill, Chamberlain Bill, and Garrison Bill competing for support, Carter feared that absolutely nothing would be accomplished.[11]

When Carter testified before the joint committee on 20 January, it was as if he had brought along Emory Upton's ghost as a supporting witness. He opened with an introductory account of how Upton's thoughts were ignored by Congress, although widely applauded by the professional military establishment. Upton's demand for an effective national reserve was rendered even more propitious by the shifts in global relationships that had since developed. "The trend of modern practice indicates an abbreviation of the period formerly available for preparations," noted Carter, thus predicating his case for a thoroughly trained reserve. "In an age when ruptures of diplomatic relations come so suddenly as to preclude the possibility of remedying grave defects, there should be no reliance upon any system concerning which there is a shadow of doubt."[12]

He then moved to a lengthy explanation of his plan to reorganize the Regular Army and establish a territorial depot system. Carter supported Garrison's bill inasmuch as it provided for a federal reserve, but emphasized the importance of physically defining and organizing such a force—disagreeing with vague conceptualizations of a trained populace that lacked any real structure as a standing reserve. Although he acknowledged compulsory service was likely the most effective way to ensure military readiness, he objected to its immediate institution as too drastic a step, wishing instead to give a volunteer reserve the opportunity to succeed or fail. Although Carter still relegated the National Guard to a domestic role as an "unsatisfactory element of any wartime force," he opposed Wood's assertion that the Guard should be denied federal monies unless it submitted to further federal controls—noting with biting implication that, unlike Wood, he "wished to build up, not destroy." His own proposal to incorporate a volunteer reserve into a territorial scheme was a renewed attempt to reconcile professionalist ideals with popular sensitivities, a lesson wisely learned from his years with Root.[13]

After Carter, other prominent soldiers testified, including Generals Hugh Scott and Tasker Bliss, as well as Nelson Miles. But as the legislative battle wore on, expertise again faded into a mere backdrop for political issues that appealed to narrow but nonetheless influential interests. Carter helped revise several versions of the bill, wincing as each draft departed further and further from his own plans. He blamed the militia lobby as a stumbling block to efforts to build any kind of effective consensus. "I fear our people will never get real military policy," he wrote with obvious exasperation, "for politics plays a far more important part than business principles." Perhaps the most intriguing gambit of this kind was the opportunity taken by General Ainsworth, the General Staff's now-retired nemesis, to shrewdly manipulate the situation for his private satisfaction.[14]

Acting through his friendship with Hay, Ainsworth successfully worked behind the scenes to add a provision limiting the number of General Staff officers who could be assigned to Washington at any given time. This legislative "rider" severely hampered the chief of staff's ability to function as intended by the 1903 General Staff Act, with the injurious effect of shifting a great amount of informal authority back to the staff bureaus. In addition, it confined the General Staff to war-planning functions and precluded it from infringing on the bureau's traditional claims to administration and supervision. Thus, acting through Hay, Ainsworth struck a major counterblow for the staff that reversed many of the earlier advances won at their expense.

Carter grumbled that Ainsworth's actions were merely a continuance of the same self-serving conduct he had revealed while on active duty, divorced from any sincere concerns for the army's greater good. He described the former adjutant general as a "clever, cold, revengeful, conceited, scornful man, determined to use his influence to prevent any development of the General Staff in our army." The net result of the Hay-Ainsworth proviso was a temporary return to the independence enjoyed by the bureaus prior to the Root era—a distasteful setback for Carter after so many years of struggle.[15]

Finally, in early May, a compromise grew from months of frustration, and the National Defense Act of 1916 was voted into law. The bill's final version drew only grudging acceptance from most parties and was received with very little real applause from anyone at all. From Carter's perspective, the resulting statute generally addressed some important issues of army organization, but otherwise suffered for many specific provisions that he typified as an offensive "combination of personal interests." This analysis is very well put in light of his predisposed professional bias—many regulars, especially dyed-in-the-wool preparedness advocates, condemned the bill as an outright travesty with little to redeem it as a step forward. But as Carter astutely recognized, the measure, at least on a fundamental level, also contained positive elements, although well hidden by its more disappointing particulars.[16]

While maintaining the National Guard as the nation's primary reserve, the act gave the federal government a much stronger hand in militia affairs, even requiring Guardsmen to henceforth take a national oath. Among other provisions, it guaranteed federal authority to prescribe standards for commissioned officers and dictate the number of annual training periods. The bill also established a sort of veterans' federal reserve, albeit one that largely existed on paper only. When viewed in its entirety, the act's legislative path accurately de-

scribed its patchwork content. Despite William Ganoe's characterization of it as "one of the greatest advances over all previous military
legislation," the 1916 National Defense Act was every bit a compromise of disparate views that left little common ground for real
solutions.[17]

History has taken little notice of Carter's role in the 1916 legislation, but his contributions were certainly not overlooked at the time.
While Senator Chamberlain offered up high praise for his untiring
work with the Senate committee, Carter was roundly criticized by
those who resented his efforts to create a federal reserve at the militia's expense. He basked in the approval and shrugged off opposition with the same self-assured conviction that he had demonstrated
countless times before: "There are always congressmen willing to
make capital by sneering at and abusing officers. . . . Representative
government has its very petty side." By this stage of his public career, Carter was accustomed to criticism as well as acclaim. The reformer's role very often stirred both responses for the very same
action.[18]

Exhausted by this foray into legislative work, Carter returned to
his research for the Chaffee biography, made time to do a little fishing
at his favorite spots outside the city, and again looked at homes for
sale in the Shenandoah Valley, where he and Ida hoped to eventually
escape for their last years together. He also purchased an automobile
and learned to drive—finding it now very dangerous to ride a saddle
horse on Washington's paved streets during the winter months. But
all of these activities were overshadowed by Helen's ongoing bout
with tuberculosis.

As her condition worsened, the Carters gradually assumed a
greater share of Willie's care and upbringing. In late April 1916, Helen
finally moved to her parents' home in Asheville, North Carolina,
leaving the grandchild in Washington. Retired and in their sixties, the
Carters once again took on full responsibility for raising a child—a
loving labor that at their age nonetheless proved physically and emotionally taxing. For Carter, the circumstances of his daughter-in-
law's deteriorating health eclipsed all other matters and added a very
sobering perspective to his own busy life: "It is all very sad," he wrote,
"everything must give way to saving Helen and the baby."[19]

A large amount of Carter's time was now spent amusing little
Willie, or "Billie," as he was most often called. After having spent so

much time away from his own children, Carter marveled at the baby's reaction to simple things and loved the chance to play "grandpa" on an everyday basis. Everything took a backseat to Billie as he took him for rides in the country and to the park in his new automobile. As this surrogate responsibility assumed primary importance in his daily schedule, professional endeavors had to compete for his remaining time and thus progressed very slowly toward completion.

While preparing his personal papers for a possible memoir, Carter saw the potential for yet another book-length study, a historical narrative of the 1903 General Staff Act. The work would stand as a tribute to the Root Reforms as well as offer a forum for his own vision of the army's future command and staff system. Carter felt that many officers still did not grasp the General Staff's fundamental purpose, a shortcoming that deprived the army of its full benefit. He addressed this very point in a 1916 essay appropriately titled "Can the General Staff Corps Fulfil its Mission?" Although pleased that the General Staff had made strides in its first decade and a half of existence, he reminded readers that its development was a process and not a panacea. As it evolved to meet the "more complex and difficult" demands of an industrialized world, there remained "fields of endeavor in which reform and progress must contend with inertia and indifference rather than studied opposition." Carter hoped that once the General Staff's true purpose was better understood within the army, it would garner the support and prestige that he and Root had originally intended. Writing the story of its creation became one of the many projects that kept him from settling into the sedentary lifestyle he so despised.[20]

Much of Carter's writing during retirement reiterated well-developed themes, arguing that current American military policy was inconsistent with contemporary realities. Shortly after the National Defense Act was passed, Carter published "Public Opinion and Defense" and "National Advantage Dependent Upon National Policies." In both of these essays, he deplored the political face of obtaining military reform, and criticized the woeful lack of objective discussion on defense issues. The American system, he wrote, was "hopelessly irreconcilable with military efficiency."[21] In a democracy, the powerful influence of parochial concerns seemed to cloud even appeals made on grounds of higher purpose: "There is a fellowship and a freemasonry in politics difficult for the layman to understand, but directly traceable to pressure of constituents in behalf of local interests. Many worthy causes are sacrificed as hostages to political expediencies even when great principles are at stake."[22] Such "expediencies" sometimes failed the nation as a whole, but Carter maintained a Jeffersonian-like conviction that an educated citizenry would, in the end, prevail over the folly of selfish interests and naïveté: "If any part of the machinery being provided at such greater expense for the nation's defense fails to respond in due time, an educated public opinion will demand its excision." It was not the democratic process that failed, but the singular lack of larger vision by its elected representatives—that desirable but apparently ephemeral characteristic he often referred to as "statesmanship."[23]

In both "Public Opinion and Defense" and "National Advantage," Carter once again articulated a decidedly nationalist stance that was a common thread in much of his work. His recent attempts to help mold a new defense bill only strengthened this larger viewpoint, and compelled him to present it yet again for the public's consideration. He believed that the nation wanted for real leadership, men of moral conviction who were willing to define issues from a national perspective without being swayed by lobbyists' more transient and selfish interests. He described the political "pork" heaped onto military bills as but "personal legislation," carefully disguised by the rhetoric of broader purpose, and he deplored the tremendous inefficiency of legislative haggling. Of course, Carter saw the Regular Army's needs as wholly congruent with the national good—a somewhat problematic starting point in that it was perhaps just as institutionally narrow as many of those views exhibited by the very "lobbyists" he so despised.[24]

Carter watched with growing alarm as the nation edged closer to entering the terrible war that was destroying Europe. Although he had supported Republican political candidates in the past, seeing in them the most pragmatic approach to defense issues, he now found very little reason to be enthusiastic about either party. His thoughts on the day's events grew increasingly cynical, and he was offended by the prevalence of crass economic concerns in foreign policy—interests with seemingly little regard for any greater moral justice. Wood's personal version of national "preparedness" was gaining a popular following, and the term became an oft-heard campaign slogan during the 1916 election. Carter wondered how many public leaders truly understood the significance of a more coherent policy that would translate peacetime strength into wartime security. He scoffed at contemporary political catchphrases such as "Peace-Preparedness-Prosperity," believing they were merely metaphors for the same old narrow interests of those who enjoyed power with little sincere regard for the nation. But despite such ill-hidden contempt, he still maintained the voice of an "elder statesman" on American defense issues.[25]

As the situation in Mexico once again boiled toward violence, Senator Chamberlain sought Carter's input and called him to a private conference with Secretary of War Newton Baker. Baker asked for Carter's opinions on a variety of subjects, and with the prospect of enlarging the military presence on the border, specifically discussed the president's authority to assign a junior officer to command a field army. When news subsequently broke that two companies of the U.S. Tenth Cavalry were attacked without provocation by a larger force of Mexican troops, Carter worried that more Americans would be committed to harm's way for mere political satisfaction without a well-defined purpose. "Looks as if Congress will have to determine whether we shall have war," he solemnly noted. "[T]roops should not be sent in unless to go at the business systematically." With an expeditionary force already patrolling both sides of the border with little effect, the entire situation seemed to illustrate the chasm that separated foreign policy from military realities.[26]

Carter privately criticized Wilson's handling of the Mexican situation, believing that the nation was merely reactively drifting from one emergency to another with no predetermined policy, strategy, or direction. He lamented those killed on the border as "victims" of the administration's "wishy-washy" or vacillating public stance. Like many regulars, he also found much wanting in the National Guard's mobilization for border service, seeing it as yet another example of why the nation desperately needed a federal reserve. But he was by now inured to the Guard's political clout and was pessimistic that this experience or any such episode would ever become a catalyst for positive change. His own experiences with the Maneuver Division in 1911 and the Second Division two years later had convinced him that little good could come of intervention in Mexico, and this opinion only strengthened as he watched Wilson's current efforts from Washington.

Dissatisfied with the government's handling of both military and foreign affairs and never content merely to grumble privately, Carter returned to his desk with a flurry of activity. He finally completed work on Adna Chaffee's biography in the spring of 1917 and it appeared in print later that year. The book is best described as a hagiographic tribute to an old friend, the first Regular Army private to advance through the ranks to hold the service's highest office. Holding him up as proof that the army was indeed a meritocracy without peer, Carter described Chaffee's professional ascendance in reverent terms: "His rise from the lowest to the highest rank in the American Army was due to no extraneous influence, but came as a just reward for meritorious achievements in competition with an exceptional body of men."[27]

The two had developed a close friendship while serving in Arizona, and Carter considered the former chief of staff a shining example of the American Dream. In this manner, *Chaffee* offers important insight into Carter's view of the institutional army. Though highly critical of specific facets of the American military system, he still believed that the army remained perhaps the purest model of republican ideals in a society that was increasingly marked by disparate interests with dubious values. Problems resulted from the effects of external politics rather than any shortcomings of the institution itself. Carter addressed this suggestion in two related essays that significantly revised his earlier opinions on the concept of universal obligation.

In "Our Defective Military System," published in the spring of 1917, he pleaded for public reconsideration of those gross errors that he believed the National Defense Act simply perpetuated. The best hope, Carter now argued, was the advent of some form of compulsory service for a newly created national reserve. The National Guard, he recommended, must finally be relegated to its more appropriate domestic role: "The whole scheme of attempting to create a proper military force by transposing the National Guard back and forth from State to national service, and the reverse, is wrong in principle and defective in practice." He proposed a joint congressional committee to frame a solution that included provisions for a viable reserve. Anything less only invited disaster in the face of international conflict.[28]

Carter followed this article six months later with a complementary one, "Universal Service in War and the Taxation to Support It," in which he attempted to explain how the public coffers might actually afford the costs of training, equipping, and maintaining an enlarged military structure. He admitted that the policy he now suggested flew in the face of American military traditions, but asserted that the time for such traditions had long since passed. "That which is objectionable in one situation is peculiarly appropriate in another," he argued. "That which is not to be thought of in one generation may be tolerated by the next and become a necessity to the third." While acknowledging that a volunteer force likely produced the most "intelligent class of soldiers," he lamented both the theoretical and practical outcomes of such a policy. Not only did a volunteer force prevent "a just and equitable distribution of the duties of citizenship"—an ideological underpinning of the American republic—but in practice failed to provide a reserve component adequate to meet the growing European threat.[29]

The Dick Act, Carter charged, had not brought any substantial improvement in the National Guard's collective ability to meet its federal obligation: "Thirteen years of experimentation has been had since the act of 1903 prescribed a reorganization of the militia system. While individual organizations have improved, the total strength of the organized militia has not materially changed." Traditional reliance on volunteers, he concluded, was an abject failure. Responding to critics who questioned the fiscal affordability of military "preparedness," he posited compulsory military service and taxation as related and intimate elements of a strong national defense. After discussing several types of taxation, he suggested that only a "universal" income tax would be an appropriate levy as it would distribute the burden across the entire population. Carter thus extended the concept of universal service from the muster roll straight to the citizenry's pocketbooks.[30]

Although clumsy in its presentation, "Universal Service" reveals the rationale that now convinced Carter to come out in support of universal obligation. He was convinced that the age-old militia system, founded on volunteerism, had fallen well short of national requirements. Under the growing cloud of world war, there was little doubt in his mind that circumstances did not permit further vacillation and debate. Compulsory service was now the only workable solution at hand, and a tax to support its application was the unavoidable cost of providing for the common defense. Despite traditional aversions to such measures, Americans simply would have to confront the dangerous times in which they lived.

In arriving at this conclusion, Carter fundamentally shifted his views in a manner that betrayed his growing consternation with the public process. His earlier opinions were founded on an Upton-style volunteer reserve that relied on territorial recruitment for its manpower. Although he previously had admitted that compulsory service was indeed more efficient than sole reliance on volunteers, he believed it was likely unattainable within American cultural realities, and thus should be viewed only as a last resort to restore the national security. But now, frustrated by government's deaf ear to the airtight reasoning of professional expertise, he abandoned previous misgivings and came out in full support of universal obligation:

> Experienced army men have been slowly but surely reaching the conclusion that our overseas garrisons should be maintained under the existing system of volunteer enlistments and that the organizations within the United States may well be divided into two classes, the one with organizations on a basis of readiness for immediate call, and the other to comprise skeleton organizations for use as schools of instruction under a system of universal training of young men for prescribed periods . . . [committing them] to remain available for active service in war.[31]

Carter now proposed a military system that was in many ways a compromise with Wood's favored plans for compulsory military training. Some regular units would be maintained at skeletal strength during peacetime with a primary purpose of training the citizenry for obligatory service in a national reserve.

This leap in thought was reached only after very deliberate consideration. His diaries demonstrate deep reflection on the topic as he looked to bridge the growing chasm that he believed separated American defense from the army's capabilities. He had grown so frustrated with the powerful National Guard lobby and other political influences that he now saw no alternative but to completely rebuild the military system along lines that fundamentally departed from its celebrated volunteer traditions.[32]

Like many of his generation, Carter harbored misgivings as he struggled to accommodate the trappings of modernity. Just a few years earlier he had seen Root, Roosevelt, and other public leaders make a very definite impact on large issues of national importance. Now it seemed to him that government and industry had melded into a giant awkward animal that responded slowly if at all to the prodding of individual leadership or reasoned argument. Although still hopeful for the nation's future, he doubted that his own efforts for further military reform would have any profitable effect. In the face of this realization, Carter turned increasingly toward his family, giving full attention to Billie's care and worrying constantly about Helen's failing health. In July of 1917, she died, leaving the child with the Carters for the foreseeable future while his bereaved father remained on active duty.

While Carter was drawn away from public affairs by this family sorrow, the nation itself seemed to rush through a dizzying script toward its own tragedy. Events drew him back to active service when it became clear that the United States would finally enter the First World War. He was not content to remain on the sidelines as an onlooker, and although too old for a field command, sought responsibilities commensurate with his vast experience. In early April 1917, he wrote to Secretary Baker, offering to serve in any capacity that the secretary found appropriate in the event of an American declaration of war. A few months later, as the United States frantically prepared to go to war, his offer was gratefully accepted. Carter was recalled to active duty and ordered to take command of the Central Department.[33]

Carter assumed his new position on 26 August, establishing headquarters in Chicago, where he had held command twice before during his long career. The Central Department was primarily a training organization that was also charged with securing the production and movement of war materials within its boundaries. He was responsible for roughly 150,000 troops, most of whom were federalized Guardsmen—a singular irony for a professional soldier who had spent several years arguing for the militia's demise as a national resource. But previous battles were all but forgotten in the grave emergency. As Carter aptly put it, "It was the time for team play, and criticism—unless constructive—was out of place." In a direct turn-about from peacetime political bickering, public officials now cooperated on military matters as young Americans prepared to leave for blood-soaked European battlefields.[34]

Carter's personal role in the enormous undertaking was almost wholly administrative and relatively short-lived. By the next spring, the services of a sixty-six-year-old general officer were no longer needed, and on 3 June 1918, he retired from the Regular Army without regret, for the second and final time. But his contributions did not end with his return home. The war brought to the forefront many of those ideas for which Carter had struggled most of his adult life, and the New Army was finally asked to break with its past and perform on the terrible stage of modern warfare. When he surveyed the army's transition to a wartime footing, it was with satisfaction that he noted the overwhelming success of many of those institutional instruments he had worked so hard to create:

> The creation of the Army War College in 1901 and the enactment of the provision for a General Staff in 1903, were the foundation stones on which we now rely for all the plans of organization and campaign with which we are about to enter the European conflict. The marked difference between our conduct of the present war and those which have occurred in the past is the business like way in which we are now proceeding to organize our armies upon a modern basis.[35]

These self-congratulatory claims were well supported by events and echoed by many to whom fell the burden of preparing an army for world war.

Faced with mobilization on a previously unseen scale, Congress, in one of its first acts after declaring war on Germany, passed an emergency measure that expanded the General Staff to almost one hundred officers. During the war, its responsibilities evolved from planning to supervision, and finally, to operations. By the time an armistice was signed, over one thousand officers were assigned to the General Staff's Washington divisions alone. The concept of a "directing brain" that could coordinate the activities of the army's many different parts had become of great importance to a modern war effort. As Carter had long predicted, once freed of the traditional reins that prevented its maturity, the General Staff would act as a "harmonizing agency" that would help focus the nation's military effort. The tragedy was that this cultural transition had not come years earlier, before dictated by the throes of a terrible crisis.[36]

The General Staff was by no means the only one of the Root

Reforms that was vindicated under fire. General John J. "Blackjack" Pershing, commander of the American Expeditionary Force (AEF), paid army education a significant tribute when he later wrote that "our most highly trained officers as a rule came from the Staff College at Fort Leavenworth and from the Army War College."[37] In *The Leavenworth Schools,* Timothy Nenninger notes the impressive contributions made by school graduates in almost every phase of AEF operations and support, both at home and "over there." Although, as Nenninger points out, no combination of practical and theoretical study could ever have prepared soldiers for the horrors of trench warfare, officers spoke of school experiences with high regard both during and after the war. Joseph T. Dickman, who as a young captain was assigned to the first General Staff and later served as a corps commander in France, wrote to Carter with high praise for the army's school system:

> There are many individuals and organizations who advance claims towards winning of the war but I have always assigned the first and largest credit to you and your great chief, Elihu Root.... Without the graduates of our war college and service schools the training of an efficient modern staff at Langres would have been a question of years instead of weeks. Without such staff we could not have functioned in the higher units.[38]

General Orders no. 155 had laid the cornerstone, and thus, as Dickman generously observed, Carter's efforts of a decade earlier proved vital to enabling American success in such places as St. Mihiel and the Argonne Forest.[39]

After the war, Carter viewed the inevitable soul-searching and fact-finding as grand opportunities for further military progress, and continued to offer his own insights for public consideration. While in Chicago, he had written yet another preparedness article, "Advancing on Difficulties," which interestingly applauded the newly enacted draft system not only for its great strides toward universal service but also for its tendency toward social integration—a characteristic that his middle-class sensibilities found previously lacking in an army inundated by recent immigrants in its enlisted ranks. Now, as the United States sought respite from its immersion in Europe's bloody nightmare, he produced several more essays that laid out a professionalist critique of the American war effort while, quite expectedly, also memorializing the Root era's contributions.[40]

"Advancing on Difficulties" was representative of Carter's efforts to draw further progress from the army's wartime experience. "The keystone of the arch of the modern army," he contended, "is found in the General Staff, upon whose studies combinations essential to the execution of the war policies of the nation are based." Any difficulties or confusion during the war's first months were attributable to years of neglect that left the nation with a military policy quite out of step with its broadened obligations. He challenged public leaders not to ignore such lessons in the coming months as the army demobilized and yet again underwent peacetime reorganization. But these pleadings fell on deaf ears as they so often had in the past, and Carter and his kind were left fairly disappointed when battlefield victories brought no lasting war chest for a peacetime army.

Postwar legislation largely returned the army to its prewar strength and did very little to capitalize on innovative wartime reorganization in both the staff and line. It seemed that the war's military progress was but a fleeting measure to ensure momentary success, and by the early 1920s, Carter was once again despondent over the state of national defense: "It is quite certain that the legislation placed upon the statute books since the close of the World War gives no assurance of entering the next conflict under conditions materially different from past experiences." Evincing a pessimism characteristic of Huntington's "military mind," he implored the country to heed the call for substantive change. "The lessons of the past are the only safeguards for the future so long as humanity remains the same—It is childish not to recognize that the most pacific policy on the part of the nation will not preserve it from being engaged in war at uncertain levels." But in repeating the same tired arguments in the name of soldierly expertise, Carter was losing influence. By the time he wrote "Our Military Policy in Eclipse" (1922), and "Tinkering with the Army" (1923)—articles that repeated calls for peacetime preparedness—he was rapidly becoming a relic of a past generation.[41]

Although Carter continued work on his memoirs, he now doubted that they would attract popular attention even if published. Just a few years earlier, he had written with some melancholy of his impending obsolescence as the army's voice: "After the war my work will not be wanted. It will be the men from France who will fill the libraries and

papers then." Regrettably, this prediction proved entirely too accurate
and provides a commentary on the army's own transition. Carter and
his peers, commissioned during the immediate post–Civil War decades, were culturally left somewhere between the celebrated generation that defeated Southern rebellion and that which later saved the
world from the German Kaiser. Identified primarily by their youthful
association with the Indian Wars—an undertaking already remembered by many as a stain on the national conscience—they were a
transitional influence that led the Old Army from the nineteenth-
century frontier toward twentieth-century modernity. But despite
professional success and promotion through the ranks, they never
seemed to emerge from this transition as a part of the New Army they
helped to create. As generals only a few years younger marched to
France and eventual immortality, their own battles and campaigns—
including those fought amid Washington's legislative halls—were
obscured by memories of Gettysburg and Belleau Wood.

Feeling that his earlier contributions were becoming but a faded
memory, Carter started work on a long-contemplated history of the
enormous efforts that resulted in the 1903 General Staff Act. As the
General Staff underwent reorganization in the years following its institution, other names, such as Franklin Bell, Leonard Wood, and
Tasker Bliss had become closely associated with it in the public eye—
with gradually less acknowledgement given to Carter as its true cre-
ator. He hoped that a history of the struggle to create the General Staff
would, like *The American Army,* become a part of his own professional legacy. He was justifiably proud of his accomplishments during the Root years at the War Department, and jealously protected
this record whenever he felt his role there was slighted. A few years
earlier, when it was made increasingly clear that he would never
ascend to the office of chief of staff, he penned the following thoughts
on the nature of military leadership: "For each acknowledged leader
there have always been accomplished subordinates, whose work has
counted for much in the achievement of comprehensive results. The
existence of such men, whether formally recognized or not, is essential to the success of all great enterprises."[42] Almost certainly,
this line was a subtle eulogy for his own career, a wistful plea for
the important work that he had carried on without the public fanfare reserved for soldiers who won great victories at the head of
large armies.

In July 1918, when an editorial in *The Military Surgeon* misidentified Gen. William Crozier as the author of a memorandum that planted the general staff concept in Root's mind, Carter immediately leapt to correct the error. In reply to Carter's inquiry, Crozier stated that he personally had made no such claims and, to the contrary, offered the following testimony: "I strongly favored the creation of the 'General Staff,' and so expressed myself, but I cannot claim any credit with regard to its organic act. I always understood that you had more to do with the drafting of this act than any other of the Secretary's advisors."[43] The story was later retracted as "false in fact and misleading in intentions," and the associate editor who was responsible eventually retired over the gaffe. Though unimportant in itself, the episode certainly illustrates Carter's sensitive pride of authorship. In this sense, *Creation of the American General Staff*, the outcome of his efforts to leave a permanent history of the measure's birth, can also be interpreted as a sort of stylized autobiography. For Carter, the Root Reforms were his crowning achievement and the army would forever bear his stamp.[44]

Creation of the American General Staff stands as the most detailed account of the cumulative efforts, events, and proceedings that enabled the 1903 act's passage and eventual institution of a general staff. Carter's monograph, appropriately subtitled "Personal Narrative of the General Staff System of the American Army," is an important historical record of this very important piece of legislation. Although clearly told from his own perspective with all of its expected biases, the sixty-five-page study reproduces a large number of primary materials that collaborate his assertions. After reading a final draft of the work, Root himself conceded he could make no corrections or suggestions, adding, "I find myself astonished that we were able to overcome the combined forces of selfishness and selfseeking . . . to get the new organization adopted, with nothing in its favor but the public interest." Carter's story of the General Staff is really one of cooperative human struggle to overcome the many obstacles posed by an embedded institutional culture.[45]

When finally published as Senate Document no. 119 in May 1924, reaction to Carter's narrative was extremely favorable. Contemporary readers, many of whom were active participants in the Root War Department themselves, recognized that it would preserve and memorialize a defining act in the army's transition to modernity.

Gen. Charles H. Martin, assistant chief of staff, notified Carter that a copy of his work would be given to each officer currently assigned to the General Staff: "It would be well for them to realize, even at this late day, what they owe to your industry, ability and foresight." Another officer observed that the work made a logical companion to Upton's *Military Policy*, updating his account of American military shortcomings with the story of subsequent actions to secure their solution. Root, now retired from the senate, sent Carter warm congratulations and noted that their combined efforts had paid the nation great dividends during the recent war. Such glowing accolades were certainly welcome, and all conceded that it was Carter's own tireless dedication which in the end meant the tenuous difference between the General Staff Act's success and failure.[46]

He and Ida purchased a retirement home in Virginia's Blue Ridge Mountains, as they had planned to do for so long. Although they still maintained the house in Washington, it was there, at "Eagle Rock Lodge," that Carter spent much of his remaining years. The couple rebuilt portions of the home, planted gardens, and spent the summers welcoming many old friends who came to reminisce and enjoy the mountain air. Even after Will remarried, Billie remained with his grandparents much of the time, sometimes joined by Woodbury, his new brother. Perhaps the children's youthful energy kept their grandfather from growing old at heart. Carter did not slow the pace of his professional and literary activity until almost the very end, churning out works that kept his now-familiar byline within easy reach of American readers. But at the same time, it was becoming more difficult to interest publishers in his material. In a nation that was awed by scientific harbingers of a brighter future, his discussions of military policy and army history appealed to a steadily dwindling audience.

In the fall of 1924, Carter became ill and developed a nagging case of bronchitis. The condition plagued him into the winter months and his overall health seemed to deteriorate further with the onset of cold weather. He soon found it difficult to leave the house, and only did so with the help of others. As 1925 approached, Carter told Idea that he would not need another journal in which to keep a diary, noting with resigned melancholy that his daily activities now consisted only of the mundane and warranted no written record. "I am sure my daily life is no longer of sufficient interest to continue entries in a diary," he lamented. "My views of current events are merely personal and not valuable. I know now . . . that my life must be a restricted one in every way." Accustomed to being in the very thick of national leadership, he found it hard to accept that old age was taking its physical toll. Still, he could look back with great satisfaction on the tremendous progress in which he played such a pivotal role.[47]

Fittingly, on New Year's Eve, 1924, the day of his last diary entry, Carter was visited by a man who had served with him as a young soldier during the Pine Ridge Campaign of 1890–91. They talked for hours and once again shared the bitter campaign that signaled the Frontier Army's symbolic end. The vivid memories that came pouring back added an air of poignancy as the year drew to an end.

On 24 May 1925, after a prolonged battle with respiratory problems likely stemming from heart disease, General Carter quietly succumbed at the age of seventy-three. Ida was near him at their home in Washington, D.C., just as she had been since their days at Fort Apache. During a military career that spanned over fifty years, Carter had lived exactly as he had wished when, as a wide-eyed young boy, he watched Union soldiers throng about his childhood home. From the time he donned the gray wool of a West Point cadet until the days when he commanded an expeditionary division on the Mexican border, he had truly been, in every sense of the term, a professional soldier. He had loyally served the Old Army but dedicated his career to building something new, something better than that which he found wanting as a professional institution. Although the glories of battlefield command eluded him, Carter died with the sincere respect of his brother officers and left behind him an important legacy that helped guide the American Army into a new century.

Carter's story is a clear reflection of the larger changes that moved the nation and its army during the so-called Gilded Age and the first years of the twentieth century. He began life in a rural southern community defined by slave labor and genteel plantation society and died three-quarters of a century later after having witnessed America evolve into an industrialized, largely urbanized nation with a markedly more global outlook. The army that he entered as a young lieutenant was still representative of generations-old traditions that had undergone very little distinct change since the nation's beginning. By contrast, the army from which he retired in 1918 had, for better or worse, transitioned to a new military culture, one that contemporaries and historians alike refer to as more "modern." But such changes did not occur naturally as the result of some evolution that was moved along almost imperceptibly by irresistible events. Instead, it came only from a long and difficult process, led by insightful men who recognized the dynamics of the world around them and realized that the army too would have to change if it was to remain a viable guarantor of the public security.

When he reported to Fort D. A. Russell in the fall of 1873, Carter found an army that was still defined by relative antiquity. Most veterans of the period looked upon successful military leadership as the product of innate genius that was honed only by hard-fought experience in the field. Collectively, the officer corps' rank and file had little use for study, discourse, or reflection on the more erudite aspects of military service. Individual officers who exhibited an interest in such activities were often scoffed at by their amused peers, their thoughts ignored except by the few others of like mind and kindred interests. Although the American army's professional process had begun decades earlier, its simmering presence was still exhibited in only the subtlest fashion.

Decades later, after Carter had retired from the army for the second and final time, an institutional shift toward modernity was evident to observers and participants alike. Deliberate planning, a system of graduate professional education, modern managerial processes, and competitive promotions all helped delineate the army as an organization clearly abreast of its times, attuned to the society around it. Carter played a seminal role in this process, and from his tireless efforts grew a legacy of progress.[48]

But perhaps more than his actions, Carter's clear and articulate voice stands as his most important contribution. During a period in which many Americans looked on the Regular Army as an antiquated reminder of a savage bygone era, he helped bring its issues and perspectives to the pages of public journals and periodicals with an articulate flourish. Like Upton, Wagner, and even Wood, Carter saw himself as a torchbearer for the army's progress, and believed that the American people as well as his colleagues deserved the advantage of his thoughts. To some degree, it was not so much the substance of what he wrote as it was the simple fact that he put it into print. Carter's active participation in a public forum mirrored the activities of his counterparts in the emergent civilian professions—in the process claiming a place for the army officer corps among the nation's social and professional elite. His ideas and actions reflected a sharp awareness of society's changing tastes and he was thoroughly a product of the times in which he lived.

This study also helps explain what has heretofore been a largely misunderstood aspect of the military reforms enacted during Elihu Root's term as secretary of war. The various executive and legislative measures that finally pressed the army toward a more professional footing were not, as some have claimed, "mostly the work of civilians." Instead, soldiers figured prominently in this institutional transition; first, through the foundational influence of Sherman and Upton, and later through the labors of Carter and others who took Root by the arm and helped guide him toward their own professionalist point of view. The importance of Carter's personal role is deeply documented by numerous memorandums, letters, and testimonies, in addition to his own narrative, which stood uncontested and even acknowledged when set before an audience of primary participants. But this is not to imply that military reforms took place in a social vacuum, without substantial influence from the larger world that moved outside the army.

Jack C. Lane rightly observed that a close relationship existed between civilian and military reformist impulses of the period. Concurrent social and intellectual trends in the civilian world most certainly built a strong framework for professionalist thought, providing an attractive model toward which officers collectively and individually aspired. Despite Samuel Huntington's best arguments to the contrary, American soldiers were inarguably part and parcel of the larger society and, to varying degrees, shared its ideals and cultural norms. Translating these ideas to the military subculture and its peculiar organization—the actual yeoman's work of reform—was undertaken largely by a handful of progressive soldiers whose ultimate success was enabled by their timely alliance with civilian leadership and contemporary social currents.[49]

In Carter's story, too, are seen the pitfalls of a reformer's extreme passion for his own vision. Like many of fervent conviction, he believed that he alone could light the army's way toward a better future marked by educated expertise and organizational efficiency. This tendency to self-righteousness irritated some of those around him, doing damage to his own interests and possibly also those of his beloved institution. Where the army's future was concerned, Carter participated in compromise only with the greatest reluctance. From this altogether human shortcoming fell missed opportunities—as prominently played out during his tumultuous service alongside the irascible Leonard Wood. Regrettably, he was unable to overcome his own ego in order to tame Wood's for the greater good. But Carter's personal imperfections and human frailties pale beside his many admirable traits and public leadership that resulted in an impressive number of enduring accomplishments.

Carter was a transitional leader, stepping forward to speak and write for the military profession at a time when events and personalities combined to prompt elemental change. He was unquestionably a bona fide hero of the Old Army, linked to its legends and tragedies by hard years of frontier service, yet he refused to remain mired in a celebrated past. Instead, he looked forward to building the foundation for a New Army. His personal career was a very accurate metaphoric reflection of the army's own passage to modernity. If the success he achieved in concert with Root did not provide immediate institutional transformation, it certainly marked a clear path for the army's future. Despite their incremental nature, the Root Reforms set "the Army on a different course and provide the base upon which others successfully built the armies for two world wars." Criticism that the era's military reforms did not rapidly provide the country with a modern military fails to recognize the deeply embedded cultural, political, and personal obstacles that Carter and Root struggled so hard to overcome.[50]

Carter's personal frustrations during the last years of his career only underline the fact that substantive organizational change is a difficult process that seldom reaches fruition according to the timely promise of legislative or executive act. The reforms put into motion during the twentieth century's opening decade were not simply a gateway through which the army could just march into the future, but rather charted a new course that would have to be carefully maintained and revised by subsequent generations. Carter played a significant role in setting this new course, but like the army from which he retired, found himself caught somewhere between the Old and the New.

ledstein, *Culture of Professionalism*, 30–31; Reardon, *Soldiers*
rs, 2.

eardon, *Soldiers and Scholars*, 19.

luntington proposed that a process of military professionalization
the army's supposed post–Civil War isolation. See *Soldier and the*
ton has since supplanted this theory in *American Profession of*
n "Samuel P. Huntington," 325–38. Skelton points to early strides
onal education, publication, and organization as evidence of an
a beginning. These divergent conclusions have largely defined
holarship that addresses the U.S. Army's institutional develop-
ers have also refuted Huntington's premise—see especially Coff-
g Shadow of the Soldier and the State," 69–82; Gates, "Alleged
f U.S. Army Officers," 33–37; Cooper, *Army and Civil Disorder*,
y and Industrial Workers," 136–52; Abrahamson, *America Arms*
Century; and Karsten, "Armed Progressives," 197–232. Each of
ies relates the army's cultural sensibilities to those embodied by
ary middle-class America.

Grandstaff analyzes demographic changes in the post–Civil War
ps in "Habits and Usages of War," 521–46. On military "anti-
lism," see Reardon, *Soldiers and Scholars*, 12–26; and Brereton,
ester and the Case against Army Reform" (paper presented at the
Robinson History Conference, Fort Robinson, Nebr., April 2004).
resistance during the antebellum period, see Coffman, *Old Army*,
. Skelton, *Profession of Arms*, xx.

Grandstaff, "Habits and Usages of War," 529; quotation from Weig-
ds an American Army, 126. Zais discusses contributing factors to
War military reform in "Struggle for a Twentieth-century Army,"
Cooper relates the army's postwar missions to its eventual profes-
on process in "Army's Search for a Mission," 173–95.

wo biographies of Emory Upton exist: Ambrose, *Upton and the*
more recently, Fitzpatrick, "Emory Upton." Ambrose portrays
he prophet of a military subculture that was out of touch with the
es of contemporary American society. Fitzpatrick disagrees, con-
at Upton understood the army's relationship with the nation's
opolitical realities. Russell Weigley uses the term "Uptonian"
a generation of post–Civil War professionalists who loosely es-
ton's principles as a panacea for American military policy. *To-*
American Army, 137–61. On Wagner, see Brereton's recent study,
the U.S. Army; and on Bliss, see Palmer's outdated but thorough
emaker. Swift lacks a complete biography, but is the subject of a
hesis that overviews his career. See Janes, "Selected Writings of
." Nenninger's study of the early Leavenworth schools is a valu-
on the subject. See *Leavenworth Schools and the Old Army*.

Veigley, "Elihu Root Reforms," 11–27, 25n10; Hill, *Minute Man in*
War, 180, 204; Jessup, *Elihu Root*, vol. 1, 226. Carter's *Creation of*
can General Staff reproduces a vast array of primary correspon-
nternal memorandums on the subject. Although certainly reflect-
's bias as a report of his own work, it must be remembered that

grew
State.
Arms
in pro
anteb
mode
ment.
man,
Isolat
and "*
for a
these
conter

officer
intelle
"James
Fifth F
On sin
98–99;

ley, *Tor*
post-C
11–32;
sionaliz

1(
Army,
Upton a
sensibil
cluding
larger s
to descr
poused
wards a
Educati
Bliss, Pe
graduate
Eben Sw
able stap

11
Peace ar
the Ame
dence an
ing Carte

Note

CHAPTER 1: A TIME I

1. Coffman, *Old Army.* Weigley use
chapter-length discussion of the period 18
313–41.

2. Carter, *Old Army Sketches,* 7. T
parture from an agrarian, rural, isolated,
twentieth-century one that is industriali
This author accepts Calhoun's assertion tl
fact of American life" during the last part
first years of the twentieth. See *Gilded Ag*

3. Linderman concludes that locali
United States at the time of the Spanish
along with concurrent scientific and tech
way Americans lived and communicated
see his *Mirror of War.* Curti describes ii
tionalism in *Growth of American Though*

4. Trachtenberg relates free-labor
rationale for competitive stratification i
see Wiebe's *Search for Order,* which rema
the topical essays in Calhoun's *Gilded*
the professions' historical development.
stein, *Culture of Professionalism;* Elliott
son, *Rise of Professionalism;* Pavalko, *So*
sky, "Professionalization of Everyone?" 1

when *General Staff* was written and published many of the primary actors were still publicly active. Thus, it is unlikely that he would have made self-aggrandizing claims that strayed too far from factual events. McAndrews later inferred that Carter claimed an undue share of credit for army reform. See his dissertation "William Ludlow," 223–27. But McAndrews' implication is not supported by extant evidence. Elihu Root testified to Carter's general accuracy after reviewing a pre-publication draft of *General Staff:* "I return the manuscript of your monograph on the creation of the General Staff. I have read it through with very great interest and have no corrections or suggestions to make." See Root to Carter, 9 June 1923, in Carter Family Papers. Harold D. Cater is perhaps the only historian to have formally investigated the working relationship that developed between Root and Carter. See Cater, "Evolution of the American General Staff," n.d., Harold D. Cater Papers, CMH. (Cater's research notes accompany this incomplete manuscript, hereafter cited as "Evolution of General Staff.") But Cater's unfinished work has only rarely been cited or even accessed by subsequent scholars. Cater, working in the 1930s and 40s, gathered much evidence interviewing primary sources and concluded that Carter's role was likely much larger than that for which he is given credit. Yet, this laudatory premise was for the most part unsubstantiated and Cater himself admitted that much research still remained. Roberts is perhaps the only historian to use Cater's work extensively, and his conclusions on the U.S. Army General Staff's early development (in his dissertation "Loyalty and Expertise") largely support Cater's and my own.

12. Carter, *American Army.*
13. Root to Carter, 10 Aug. 1915, Carter Family Papers.

CHAPTER 2: GROWING UP AMONG SOLDIERS

1. Carter's formally given name was William Giles Harding Carter, although he was almost invariably known more simply as William Harding Carter, even in government personnel records. His full name is only rarely seen in contemporary documents, and thus herein he will be referred to as William Harding Carter—this is also the manner in which he signed his name throughout life. Carter located his family's home at "about three miles from Nashville, Tenna., diary entry, 19 Nov. 1867, Carter Family Papers (copies in possession of the author). Hereafter cited as "Carter Diary," accompanied by date of entry and any other identification. Two of William's siblings died in infancy and two others died while William was still a young boy. Samuel Jefferson Carter also fathered three children with his first wife, Eliza Staggs, two of whom died prior to William's birth. Carter, *Giles Carter,* 111.

2. The scant information available on Carter's early childhood is taken from his unpublished memoirs. Manuscript and typescript copies are in the Carter Family Papers; a copy of the typescript is also in possession of the author. (Carter typescript hereafter cited as *Memoirs.*) Information about Carter's grammar school activities is gleaned from several extant report cards for the year 1858, in Carter Family Papers.

3. Maslowski, *Treason,* 1–6.

4. Carter, *Memoirs*, 5, 19–20. Carter's early life is also briefly overviewed in an obituary written by Eben Swift that appeared in the U.S. Military Academy's *Annual Report*, June 11, 1926, 123–27. Carter's fascination with Belle Meade and its owner remained strong throughout life. After retirement, he wrote "The Master of Belle Meade," published in *The Outlook*. His tale of a utopian-like southern plantation was certainly distorted by nearly sixty years of nostalgia, but his description of the plantation itself largely parallels that of Wills's recent book, *Belle Meade*.

5. Tillman, typescript of untitled memoirs, Samuel E. Tillman Papers, USMASC, Chap. II, 2. Tillman, who grew up outside of Shelbyville, later graduated from West Point (Class of 1869) and after duty as an engineer returned to the academy, where he spent the rest of his career as a chemistry professor. Carter befriended Tillman while both were cadets, and their families were apparently acquainted in antebellum Tennessee.

6. Wills, *Belle Meade*, 85. On middle Tennessee's swift change of heart on the secession issue, see Maslowski, *Treason*, 7–11. Maslowski concludes that Tennesseans were generally "conditional Unionists" in that they supported the North *only* if it acted with respect for southern political and social rights without introducing coercive measures. The phrase "storehouse of the western Confederacy" appears in Maslowski, 12.

7. Maslowski, *Treason*, 12; Carter, *Memoirs*, 8. Samuel J. Carter's neighbor, William Giles Harding, was a leading member of the Davidson County Committee of Vigilance and Safety, which met and "assisted authorities in locating and removing subversive elements from the community." Wills, *Belle Meade*, 85. Whether Carter's relationship with Harding saved him from the grief that met other Unionists is not known.

8. Maslowski, *Treason*, 12. Durham's *Nashville* narrates the extreme confusion and anxiety that accompanied Nashville's surrender, 22–42. Several report cards and tuition receipts from Nashville schools are preserved from short periods of 1862, 1863, and 1864. Though schooling during the war was likely haphazard at best, these documents are evidence that at least during the Union army's occupation, William received some instruction. See report cards from Hume School, Nashville, March–June 1862; University School, Nashville, 25 April 1864; and various tuition receipts from "R. Dorman, Dr." for January and February 1864, all in Carter Family Papers.

9. Durham, *Nashville*, 43.

10. Carter, *Memoirs*, 12; Durham, *Nashville*, 46–47, 55.

11. Carter, *Memoirs*, 13. Eliza S. Carter was born to Samuel J. Carter and Eliza Staggs on 3 May 1831; Laura O. Carter was born to Samuel J. and Anne Vaulx on 22 August 1843—see Carter, *Giles Carter*, 111. Interestingly, earlier in the war, soon after the Union army moved into Nashville, Laura was "arrested" and brought before Governor Andrew Johnson for allegedly spitting on Federal officers from the porch of her father's St. Cloud Hotel. Johnson, aware of Samuel's Unionist politics, supposedly laughed at the matter and immediately let her go. Obviously, Laura's politics, like William's, were at first confused by the very nature of civil war, but the entrance of one Captain J. B. Holloway, U.S. Army, soon made up her mind. This anecdote is related in Durham, *Nashville*, 89.

12. Two of the wounded men brought to the Carter home were John Haskell King and John Franklin Miller—both would become general officers before the war was over. See Carter, *Memoirs*, 18; and also Warner, *Generals in Blue*, 268–69, and 324–25. After the war, Miller served as U.S. senator from California.

13. Carter, *Memoirs*, 18.

14. Carter, *Memoirs*, 19–20; General R. W. Johnson to the Adjutant General of the Army, 30 Oct. 1896, in RG 94, ACP File 1873, NARA; Military Record of Captain William H. Carter, Sixth Cavalry, U.S. Army, in Ibid.

15. Van Duzer to Eckert, 30 Nov. 1864, *War of the Rebellion*, XLV, Pt. 1, 1168. For analysis of the Nashville campaign in a context of the war's larger strategy, see Hattaway and Jones, *How the North Won*.

16. Carter, *Memoirs*, 23. The Carter family living on Carter Creek near Franklin, Tennessee, was closely related to Samuel J. Carter. The battle was fought on and around the Carter property there—the house itself became a field hospital for wounded. Another of William H. Carter's cousins, Captain Theodrick "Tod" Carter, was a Confederate officer on the staff of Brig. Gen. Thomas Benton Smith. During the fighting, Theodrick was wounded and died near the rear doorstep to his own home, being found there the next morning by his family. Carter later corresponded with Moscow Branch Carter, an older brother of Theodrick, who also served in the Confederate army at Franklin—see M. B. Carter, Sr., to William H. Carter, 1 Feb. 1907, in Carter Family Papers. Also see Cox, *Sherman's March*, 81–98, as well as the detailed narrative of Stone, "Repelling Hood's Invasion," 440–64.

17. Carter, *Memoirs*, 26.

18. Ibid., 27.

19. Carter Diary, 25 Apr. 1869. This entry is made as a sort of foreword to a copybook that contains numerous lyrics and poems associated with the contemporary army and West Point. On postwar Nashville's initial reconstruction, see Maslowski, *Treason*, 146–51.

20. Carter Diary, 25 Apr. 1869; Carter, *Memoirs*, 28; and William H. Carter to Mrs. Samuel J. Carter, 19 Mar. 1871 in Carter Family Papers.

21. Carter Diary, 1 Jan. 1868. (This diary entry is incorrectly dated 1 Jan. 1867, but the entry was actually written on the first day of 1868, a natural error.) Maslowski summarizes Andrew Johnson's wartime service as Tennessee's military governor in *Treason* (see especially pages 22–26 for analysis of Johnson's personal qualifications for this challenging position). On Carter's experience under Hunter's tutelage, see Carter Diary, 7 Jan. 1868; and Carter, *Memoirs*, 28. Carter's only extensive diary entry regarding Hunter seems to describe classroom recitation, a popular contemporary method that often utilized math problems to exercise the mind's analytical abilities. Recitation was a cornerstone of West Point's classrooms until well into the twentieth century, and the practice was closely related to the school's reliance on the pedagogical theory of "mental discipline." On recitation at nineteenth-century West Point, see Tillman, "Academic History," 359–63, and also the dissertation by Dillard, "Military Academy," 66.

22. Carter Diary, 1 Jan. 1868.

23. Carter describes visits to the places mentioned as well as others in

Carter Diary, 19 and 26 Jan. 1868, 13 Feb. 1868, 15 Apr. 1868, and (in his last diary entry prior to arriving at West Point) 8 May 1868.

24. Carter Diary, 15 Apr. 1868; Carter, *Memoirs*, 28–29. The circular that caused Carter so much worry is preserved with his original letter of appointment in the Carter Family Papers. By a congressional act of 1 Mar. 1843, the president had the authority to appoint ten cadets "at-large" as well as one from the District of Columbia. See Boynton, *History of West Point*, 244. Carter read Boynton's *History* before reporting later that spring. See Carter Diary, 8 May 1868.

25. Carter Diary, 3 June 1868. Pappas imparts a strong feeling for West Point's nineteenth-century cadet culture in *To the Point*. Also see Schaff's contemporary reminiscence, *Spirit of Old West Point*. Schaff's nostalgic book reflects the high regard that many graduates of the period held for their alma mater and classmates. Dillard's "Military Academy" is a more critical account of the era's academic and faculty culture, placing West Point's development in a context of larger political and social issues. Ambrose's *Duty, Honor, Country* is less balanced than Dillard's study and does not reflect the primary research that marks Dillard's as a seminal resource. On the Thayer era, see dissertations by Denton ("Formative Years") and Molloy ("Technical Education"). Morrison addresses Thayer's continued influence on the antebellum academy in "Military Academy." For a contemporary explanation of West Point's professional mission, see Michie, "Education," 154–79.

26. On wartime bitterness and the postwar uncertainty that marked West Point's institutional outlook, see Dillard, "Military Academy," 102–29; and Morrison, "Progress and Turmoil," 240–52; as well as Morrison's "Struggle between Sectionalism and Nationalism," 138–48. Specific to Radical Republicans' assault on the USMA are Williams, "Attack upon West Point," 491–504; and Lisowski, "Future of West Point," 5–21. Also see Aimone, "Much to Sadden," 12. On West Point's governance from an insider's perspective, read Michie, *Life and Letters*, 246–51.

27. Two classic histories of American higher education summarize the period's pioneering educational development: Rudolph's *American College and University* and Veysey's *Emergence of American University*. More recent is Cohen's *Shaping of American Higher Education*. Descriptions of West Point as "stagnant" and "self-satisfied" during the era are found in Ambrose, *Duty, Honor, Country*, 191–218, passim, but refuted by Machoian's paper "Michie and West Point."

28. On the practice of hazing in the postwar period, see Pappas, *To the Point*, 355–59. In his memoirs, Hugh L. Scott (USMA Class of 1876) noted that "Far rougher things were done in those days in civilian colleges as a matter of course, and no notice was taken of them." *Some Memories*, 17. Scott's assertion seems reasonable in light of Rudolph's and Veysey's descriptions (*American College and University*, 144–55; *American University*, 268–94).

CHAPTER 3: A SOLDIER'S EDUCATION

1. Carter's earlier fears for his physical condition appear to have been well-founded—he returned to the post hospital three times for further exam-

ination before finally being cleared to enter training. A description of "plebe camp" is found in Carter Diary, 23 and 28 June 1868, and 19 July 1868. Examples of books that Carter read during the little personal time he enjoyed are *Lights and Shadows of Army Life* (author unknown), and Kip's *Army Life on the Pacific* and *Army Life on the Border.*

2. Carter Diary, 8 Jan. 1869. Carter was ranked forty-three in mathematics and thirty-three in French. This first semiannual examination of his cadet career is also described in two letters written to his mother, Mrs. Samuel J. Carter, dated 5 and 10 Jan. 1869.

3. Carter Diary, 13 Mar. 1869.

4. Ibid. Carter ranked forty-six in mathematics, thirty-six in French, and forty-four overall in his class after completing year-end examinations— see Carter Diary, 15 July 1869. Carter unashamedly related that when punishment tours were ordered to be marched inside the barracks' hallways one Saturday afternoon due to a snowstorm, "you may be certain that we did not stay there long, for each of us went into some room, and read all the afternoon," Carter to Mrs. Samuel J. Carter, 3 Apr. 1869.

5. Carter, *Memoirs,* 42–43. Carter mentions problems with geometry in diary entries of 27 Sept. and 30 Oct. 1869.

6. Carter Diary, 15 Jan. 1870.

7. Carter Diary, 18 Feb. 1870. "Furlough Blue" refers to the blue uniforms that cadets wore while away from the academy for purposes other than an organized cadet event, such as the rare personal leave of absence.

8. Carter, *Memoirs,* 43. Although never identifying him by name, Carter's summary description of the Negro cadet whom he thought "unworthy" identifies him as James Webster Smith. Carter Diary, 10 Nov. 1870 and 14 Jan. 1871. Later diary references to Smith's court proceedings, appeals, and punishments provide ample evidence of this conclusion. Smith remained at the academy for four years (repeating his plebe year) before being dismissed in 1874 on academic grounds. See Dillard, "Military Academy," 197–202. For further reading, see Flipper, *Colored Cadet.* Flipper was the first African-American man to graduate from West Point (class of 1877), and Taylor's introduction to the 1991 edition is a very valuable supplement.

9. See Foner, *History of Reconstruction.* On the army's role in the postwar South, see Dawson, *Army Generals and Reconstruction.* More recently, Simpson in *Reconstruction Presidents* highlights the importance of understanding Reconstruction as an administrative battle that tried the limits of federal authority. These three works provide a starting point for further reading. On the culture of prejudice that developed racial barriers in the post–Civil War United States, see Fishel, "African-American Experience," 137–61, and also Franklin and Moss, *From Slavery to Freedom.* Particular to higher education, Dillard compares the USMA circumstance with that of civilian colleges in "Military Academy," 191–92. Also of interest is Wagoner, "American Compromise."

10. Quoted in Pappas, *To the Point,* 374. For discussion of the larger issues surrounding the admission of African-Americans to the academy, see Taylor's introduction to *Colored Cadet,* xvi–xvii.

11. Carter Diary, 10 Nov. 1870. Pappas notes (without citation) that

the cadets requested a change of messing tables in *To the Point*, 374. Carter makes no mention of such a request in his diary, memoirs, or letters written home. Emory Upton, the commandant of cadets at the time, was a vehement abolitionist who had attended the racially liberal Oberlin College prior to his own admission to West Point (Class of 1861). See Fitzpatrick, "Misunderstood Reformer," 16–19, 46–47; and Ambrose, *Upton*, 12–13. Fitzpatrick devotes only brief attention to the Smith case, but his conclusions underline the very political nature of the events, 200–3. In *Upton*, Ambrose fails to mention the attempt to racially integrate West Point during Upton's tenure as commandant.

12. Grant quoted in Dillard, "Military Academy," 197. On the embryonic honor code, see ibid., 78–88; Fitzpatrick, "Misunderstood Reformer," 199–200; and also Pappas, *To the Point*, 379–81.

13. Carter Diary, 3 Feb. 1871.

14. Ibid. After Grant and Secretary Belknap issued their judgment, Carter editorialized in his diary, "Justice where art thou?" and added,"but then where is the abolitionist who does not believe the negro [*sic*] is gone back on?" Carter Diary, 16 June 1871.

15. Carter to Mrs. Samuel J. Carter, 12 Feb. 1871. Carter's end-of-the-year academic standing was number twenty-nine in mathematics, number thirty-three in French, number twenty-six in Spanish, and number seven in drawing, with a general (overall) class standing of number twenty-five—after semiannual examinations in January, he had stood number twenty-eight. See Carter to Mrs. Samuel J. Carter, 24 June 1871.

16. Carter to Mrs. Samuel J. Carter, 8 Oct. 1871. After semiannual examinations during his second class year, Carter stood number thirty-eight in natural philosophy, thirty-four in chemistry, and number four in drawing—a course that included mechanical and topographical drawing as well as more artistic material. Only a few weeks later, though, Carter was dropped to the lowest section of natural philosophy, a "misfortune" that prompted him to think of his alternative courses of action in case of later dismissal. Carter Diary, 11 Feb. 1872. At the end of this year he "passed a good, very good examination" and ranked number thirty-three overall in class standing. Ibid., 25 June 1872.

17. Carter to Laura Holloway, 17 Sept. 1871 in Carter Family Papers. Carter also wrote of Mahan's death in a letter to his mother, 24 Sept. 1871, and in his diary, 11 Nov. 1871. This entry was the first after Carter had lost his previous diary (in actuality, he *mistakenly* believed that he had lost the book—it is present in the Carter Family Papers). Thus, the 11 November entry summarizes some of the most important events of the preceding few months. On Mahan's life and influence on the academy, see the dissertation by Griess, "Dennis Hart Mahan."

18. Carter Diary, 3 Dec. 1871.

19. Carter Diary, 29 Sept. 1872.

20. Carter Diary, 2 Apr. 1873; ibid., 27 Apr. 1873. For references to Samuel J. Carter's earlier periods of illness, see ibid., 21 and 24 Nov. 1871 and 25 Dec. 1871.

21. Carter to Mrs. Samuel J. Carter, 8 Oct. 1871. Also see Carter, *Memoirs*, 48.

22. Coffman, *Old Army*, 281. The system of officer promotions was a prominent topic of debate among officers of the era. On this subject, see ibid., 230–34, 281; Weigley, *History of the Army*, 291; and Roberts, "Reform and Revitalization," 197–218.

23. Carter reflects on his class standing and the underlying causes for his academic problems in *Memoirs*, 46.

24. Carter, *Memoirs*, 48–49. Secretary Belknap was acquainted with Carter due to a recent event at the academy that required his personal attention. The secretary reviewed the assignments and assured Carter that when an unfilled vacancy became available his application would receive fair consideration.

CHAPTER 4: EXPERIENCING THE OLD ARMY

1. Carter describes his arrival at the Eighth Infantry in *Memoirs*, 50. The regiment's adjutant published the order assigning Carter to Company C, 8th Infantry on 28 Aug. 1873. This order also noted Carter as "having reported to these Hd. Qrs," but it is highly doubtful that this meant he had appeared in person as he only accepted the appointment to the 8th Infantry on 16 August from Brooklyn, New York. See Carter to Brig. Gen. E. Townsend, Adjutant General, USA, 16 Aug. 1873; extract of Regimental Orders No. 46, Hd. Qrtrs. 8th Infantry, Fort D. A. Russell, 28 Aug. 1873; both documents are filed with ACP File 3543, 1878, RG 94, NARA. It is more likely that Carter's acceptance of his appointment to the regiment was received by this earlier date, and thus, the order of 28 August was published.

2. Carter Diary, 19 Dec. 1873; Carter, *Memoirs*, 51. The Robinson to whom Carter refers is William W. Robinson, (USMA, Class of 1869). See *Centennial of the United States Military Academy*, vol. II, 425. In addition to Grandstaff's recent quantitative analysis, "Habits and Usages of War," several historians have cited a strong traditionalist outlook among older Civil War–experienced officers of the Frontier Army. A sort of "post psychology" developed among this stereotype and contributed to a strain of stagnant professional thought. See Nenninger, *Leavenworth Schools*, 16; Reardon, *Soldiers and Scholars*, 23–26; and Brereton, *Educating the Army*, xii–xiii.

3. Brereton, *Educating the Army*, xii–xiii. Coffman's discussion of the Civil War's impact on army culture imparts a deeper understanding of the difficult path undertaken by postwar military reformers. *Old Army*, 217–25, 230–34.

4. Coffman, *Old Army* 262; Carter Diary, 19 Dec. 1873. This monotony differed little for officers assigned to coastal forts and posts nearer to eastern population centers, except that their professional lives were more often interrupted by participation in the local social calendar. Many scholarly studies provide insights into different aspects of the frontier army, its missions and culture. Perhaps the best examples are Coffman's *Old Army*, Utley's *Frontier Regulars*, and Rickey's *Forty Miles*. Coffman and Rickey pro-

vide especially useful descriptions of soldiers' daily lives while in garrison. Foner's *United States Soldier* concentrates on the enlisted soldier during the postwar period. Peggy Dickey Kircus provides an excellent glimpse of contemporary military culture in "Fort David A. Russell," 161–92.

5. Carter, *Memoirs*, 52.

6. Ibid.

7. For discussion of contemporary America's conceptualization of "modernity," see Howe, *Victorian America*.

8. Ibid., 53–54.

9. Carter to Dr. W. H. Stennett, 12 Oct. 1911, in Carter Family Papers; Carter to Carter P. Johnson, 2 Sept. 1914, in Carter Family Papers; Carter, *Memoirs*, 57; Carter, *Sketch of Fort Robinson Nebraska*, author's manuscript copy, in Carter Family Papers, 1921. Note: Carter addressed the letter cited above to Maj. Carter T. Johnson, but this was apparently a typographical error, as it is clear from the content that it was written to Maj. Carter P. Johnson, a long-serving frontier officer who later ranched in the vicinity of Fort Robinson, Nebraska. Information gleaned from this author's telephone conversation with Tom Buecker, historian and curator of the Fort Robinson Museum, Fort Robinson State Park, Nebraska, on 17 August 2000, supports this conclusion. Johnson's interesting career is related in Beucker, "An Excellent Soldier," 12–17. In *Fort Robinson*, Carter identifies the two frontiersmen as Jack Hunton, a rancher on the Chugwater Creek, and Mr. Bullock, who was "an experienced trader among the Indians," 6. *Fort Robinson* was published as a pamphlet in very limited numbers by the Northwest Nebraska News, Crawford, Nebraska, in 1941 and 1942.

10. Carter, *Memoirs*, 57.

11. Leonard, "Red, White and the Army Blue," 176–90; Coffman, *Old Army*, 254–57; Smith, *Officers' Row*. More recently, Nobles studied America's westward expansion as a collision of disparate cultures. Like others, he concluded that, collectively, professional soldiers tempered their view of the Indian "problem" with a sense of moral justice—"many army officers realized that actual extermination was not a viable option, either militarily or morally." *American Frontiers*, 224.

12. Smith, *Officers' Row*, 107; Skelton, "Professionalization," 461. Written with similar purpose but with broader scope than Leonard's "Red, White, and the Army Blue," Smith's work is a groundbreaking look at the soldier's perspective of American efforts to conquer the West. In a related vein, Skelton examines the army's developing self-image as an objective servant of civil policy in *Profession of Arms*, 210; "Army Officers' Attitudes toward Indians," 113–24; and "Professionalization," 460–62. Robert Wooster supports Skelton's portrayal with his own conclusion that the army "saw itself as playing a noble role in the Western drama." *Military and United States Indian Policy*, 109. Tate's recent study of the army's diverse relationship with western society lends a deeper understanding of its self-image as public servants. See his *Frontier Army*. Also on this topic, see Cooper, *Army's Search for a Mission*.

13. Carter, *Memoirs*, 53.

14. Sherman quoted in Nobles, *American Frontiers*, 221; Smith, *Of-*

ficer's Row, 184. On postwar Indian policy, see Dippie, *Vanishing American,* 141–60; Nobles, *American Frontiers,* 220–21; and Utley, *Indian Frontier,* 129–34.

15. Andrist critiques white encroachment into the Powder River territory in *Long Death,* 240–44. On accelerating regional violence, see Utley, *Cavalier in Buckskin,* 115–23; and Gray, *Centennial Campaign,* 9–21. Carter considers the causes of the 1874 Sioux outbreak in *Fort Robinson,* 8. His narrrative is based on his own knowledge as well as the report of Mr. J. J. Seville, the assigned Indian agent at the Red Cloud Agency.

16. Carter, *Memoirs,* 59.

17. Ibid.

18. Carter to Stennett, 12 Oct. 1911.

19. Carter, *Memoirs,* 61.

20. Carter related this anecdote in *Memoirs,* 74, and *Fort Robinson,* 17.

21. Carter, *Old Army Sketches,* 10. Carter lists the dates and itinerary of his move to Arizona in his diary entry for 24 Mar. 1876.

22. Carter, *Memoirs,* 76.

23. While a cadet, Carter claimed an aversion to gambling in both his letters and diaries. For related examples, see Carter to Mrs. Samuel J. Carter: 9 Dec. 1871 and diary entries for 1 Jan. 1870 and 11 Feb. 1872. Although Carter's story of an evening spent near the famed Cody and Hickock cannot be directly corroborated, both men are known to have spent time in Cheyenne during the summer of 1874.

24. Carter, *Memoirs,* 78. Carter makes no specific mention of meeting Ida Dawley during this stay in San Francisco, but it is evident from the chronology of their ensuing courtship and eventual marriage that this is the only time he could possibly have met her, an assumption supported by family tradition. Carter's diary entry of 24 Mar. 1876 states that he arrived in Arizona on 26 Sept. 1874. Since it is known that the Eighth Infantry departed Wyoming on 29 July, it is reasonably assumed that he remained in San Francisco on detached duty for several weeks.

25. Carter, *Memoirs,* 79–80.

26. Carter, letter to the Adjutant General of the Army, 20 Oct. 1874, ACP File 1878, RG 94, NARA.

27. Carter to James Belknap, Secretary of War, 21 Oct. 1874, ACP File 1395, RG 94, NARA.

28. Special Orders no. 258, 28 Nov. 1874, Adjutant General's Office. Carter reported for duty with the 6th Cavalry by a letter to the regiment's headquarters at Fort Hays, Kansas, 21 Dec. 1874, ACP File 1395, RG 94, NARA.

29. Utley, *Indian Frontier,* 132. Utley's exhaustive bibliographic essay is an invaluable resource for research into associated topics.

30. Utley analyzes Grant's evolving Peace Policy in *Indian Frontier,* 129–55, and *Frontier Regulars,* 188–92, as does Dippie in *Vanishing American,* 144–54. For studies placing U.S. Indian policy in a larger context, see Dippie; Nobles, *American Frontiers;* Wooster, *U.S. Indian Policy;* and Gray's introduction to *Centennial Campaign,* 1–8. Also applicable is D'Elia, "Argument," 207–24.

31. Dippie, *Vanishing American*, 146; ibid., 132–33. Dippie conceptualizes the Indian issue as distinctly regional by its very nature on 132–38. Smith concludes that officers held diverse views on the "Indian question," defying monolithic generalization—a description that is also applicable to the larger American society. Individual outlooks were revised as soldiers reacted to particular events and experiences. *Officer's Row*, 182–84.

32. The Bascom Affair consisted of a young army lieutenant, George Bascom, carrying out orders to return a captured child and stolen oxen from Apache raiders. Cochise's band of Chiricahua Apaches were mistakenly accused, and Bascom's aggressive handling of his mission sparked retaliation by Cochise, beginning decades of regional violence. For more on this episode, see Utley, *Frontiersmen in Blue*, 161–63, and "Bascom Affair," 59–68; and also Roberts, *Once They Moved Like the Wind*, 21–29. Roberts describes the relationships that existed between the region's several Apache tribes, 34–35. An Apache account of the Bascom Affair is presented in Ball, *Indeh*, 25.

33. Efforts to negotiate peace with hostile bands were of only limited success, as shown by Wooster, *U.S. Indian Policy*, 148; and Utley, *Indian Frontier*, 139–40. For concise summaries of Crook's operations, see Utley's *Frontier Regulars* and Worcester's *Apaches*. Crook's own account is found in Schmitt, *General George Crook*. This book is an edited version of Crook's unfinished memoir, to which Schmitt added closing chapters. On Crook's innovative military career in the West, see Dunlay, "General Crook," 3–10; King, "George Crook," 333–48; and King's "Needed: A Re-Evaluation," 223–35. Also see Bourke, *On the Border*, a biased but nonetheless valuable reminiscence by one of Crook's staffers. Equally important is Porter's biographical study of Bourke, *Paper Medicine Man*, a history that adds depth to modern understanding of the army's efforts in the region.

34. Carter, *Memoirs*, 87.

35. Wooster discusses Crook's philosophy of "firm justice" in "A Difficult and Forlorn Country," 339–56. Also see King, "Indian Fighter," 344–45.

36. Carter Diary, 18 Jan. 1877. Also see Coffman's description of frontier garrison life in *Old Army*, 262–64.

37. Carter was formally assigned command of Company B, Apache Scouts, by Special Orders no. 162, Headquarters, Fort Verde, Arizona Territory, 23 Nov. 1875, copy in Carter Family Papers; and was ordered to the field in pursuit of the described hostiles by Special Order no. 173, 10 Dec. 1875, in Carter Family Papers. Carter described this particular patrol in *Memoirs*, 91–92, and in *From Yorktown to Santiago*, 182. On Sieber's legendary career, see Thrapp, *Al Sieber*.

38. Carter, *Yorktown to Santiago*, 181. Carter describes the scouts' brutal effectiveness when employed against members of their own tribe and even their immediate families on 180–81. For discussion of the use of native scouts as a little-understood clash of dissimilar cultures, see Smith, *Officer's Row*, 163–181. Also see Dunlay's excellent study, *Wolves for the Blue Soldiers*.

39. Carter, *Memoirs*, 93. Carter describes hunting forays with the Fifth Cavalry's greyhounds on 93–94.

40. Carter, *Memoirs*, 86.

CHAPTER 5: THE ARMY, THE MEDICINE MAN, AND CIBICU CREEK

1. Coffman examines the garrison community as a social system in "Young Officer in Old Army," 255–68. Huntington identifies a sense of "corporateness"—defined as a "shared sense of organic unity and consciousness of themselves as a group"—as one of several characteristics that marked the era's burgeoning professions, in *Soldier and the State,* 10. However, collective identity with the organization or institution did not necessarily imply internal harmony. As Skelton points out, a single harmonious voice was rarely heard from the officer corps. Instead, officers tended to occupy themselves with internal debate and bureaucratic competition in the name of regimental, branch, and departmental interests—see Skelton, "Army Officer," 61–70.

2. Maj. A. K. Arnold, U.S. 6th Cav., Report of the Acting Assistant Inspector General, Department of Arizona, 5 Aug. 1881, RG 95, M689, Roll 67, NARA; Carter, *Memoirs,* 87. For analysis of frontier officers' absence from their regiments, see Gates, "Alleged Isolation," 33; and also Coffman, "Young Officer in Old Army," 263.

3. Carter, *Memoirs,* 103. The loss of lieutenants J. A. "Tony" Rucker and Austin Henely is recounted in Carter's *Memoirs,* 102–3, and in his *Yorktown to Santiago,* 197–98. Carter had been with these officers only a few days before their deaths.

4. Carter, *Memoirs,* 97.

5. Ibid.

6. Lt. John B. Kerr, Adjutant, U.S. 6th Cavalry to Lt. William H. Carter, telegram, 20 Aug. 1878, in Carter Family Papers. For discussion of the officer promotion system and its effect on army culture, see Coffman's *Old Army.* Coffman's analysis places this subject in a context of professional reform. Also see Skelton, "Organization Man," in which he posits the seniority system of promotion as a source of dissension.

7. Col. E. D. Townsend, Adjutant General of the Army, to Commanding Officer, U.S. 6th Cavalry, 20 June 1879, in Carter Family Papers. Carter filled the quartermaster role while still formally assigned as an assistant until approved by Townsend's letter to date from 14 April 1879. See also Kerr to Carter, 20 Aug. 1878.

8. Carter to Adjutant General's Office, 16 Apr. 1879, in RG 94, ACP File 1878, William H. Carter, NARA; Oath of Office as first lieutenant, U.S. Army, sworn on 29 July 1879, in Carter Family Papers. Carter's promotion to grade was backdated to 14 April 1879, commensurate with his approval as regimental quartermaster. See Townsend to C.O., 6th Cavalry, 20 June 1879; Townsend to Lt. William H. Carter, U.S. 6th Cavalry, letter of transmittal, 26 June 1879, in Carter Family Papers; and General Orders no. 11.3, U.S. 6th Cavalry, 2 July 1879, official (signed) extract in Carter Family Papers.

9. Woodbury Carter, interview by telephone, 16 Oct. 2000. Family tradition holds that Carter met Ida during leave in San Francisco, and it was previously supposed that this leave was taken while assigned to the Sixth Cavalry in Arizona. Carter's memoirs make it clear that his wedding trip was in fact the first leave he enjoyed since commissioning. Thus, it is more likely

that the two met during the time he spent in San Francisco on the Eighth Infantry's journey westward from the Dakotas. This is supported by a letter Carter wrote to the Adjutant General's Office, 3 Aug. 1882, in which he stated, "I have been in Arizona since 1874, with the exception of one trip to San Francisco," RG 94, ACP File 1878, William H. Carter, NARA. This "exception" could only be his wedding trip, taken in the fall of 1880. The leave that he postponed to accept the quartermaster position was very likely a planned trip to San Francisco to see Ida. Kerr to Carter, 20 Aug. 1878. No other materials found by this author shed further light on this minor mystery.

10. Carter, *Memoirs*, 117. Cruse's account places Carr's strength at six regular companies plus three companies of Indian scouts, differing somewhat from Carter's own recollection. See *Apache Days*, 84. Whether U.S. Army operations significantly contributed to Victorio's defeat is questionable. In *Al Sieber*, Thrapp discounts the army's part in pushing Victorio toward Mexican troops, 219. But, in *Conquest of Apacheria*, Thrapp asserts that the American pursuit in fact pressed Victorio toward his end. Worcester reaches a similar conclusion in *The Apaches*, 230–231. On the Sixth Cavalry's role in hunting Victorio, see King, *War Eagle*, 192–95, and also Carter, *Yorktown to Santiago*, 199–208.

11. Ibid., 208. For excellent summaries of the Victorio campaign, see Thrapp, *Apacheria*, 170–210, and Worcester, *The Apaches*, 208–33.

12. In describing the peaceful "lull" that existed in the department during the summer of 1881, Maj. A. K. Arnold wrote that "up to the present time it has been as safe to travel in any part of Arizona, as in any of the more populated states." Report of the Acting Assistant Inspector General, Department of Arizona, 5 Aug. 1881, RG 94, M689, Roll 67, NARA.

13. The Cibicu Apaches were one of five subtribal groups of the Western Apaches in late nineteenth-century Arizona. Collins explains the complex organization of the Apache peoples in *Apache Nightmare*, 5–11. The names applied by this author to different Apache groups are primarily those that appear in contemporary army accounts—regrettably, such terms may be inappropriate when compared to an ethnologist's more knowledgeable application. Although Cibicu is often spelled "Cibecue" in modern sources, most contemporaries (including Carter) used the spelling "Cibicu."

14. Col. Eugene A. Carr to Assistant Adjutant General, Department of Arizona, report of interview with Apache subchiefs Santo and Not-chi-clish, 17 Aug. 1881, RG 94, M689, Roll 66, NARA. This report contains what Carr presented as a verbatim transcription of his interview with the two Indian elders. Not-chi-clish stated: "The Medicine Man has now over a hundred head of stock, given him to raise the dead. . . . I think for my part that it will be years before the Medicine Man accomplishes what he undertakes and that by that time the Medicine Man will have all they own." It should be noted that Charles Hurrle (also spelled Hurle) interpreted this and many of Carr's other conversations with Apaches. Suspicion was later cast on Hurrle's credibility and some even blamed him for purposedly contributing to the general misunderstandings that grew into violence. See Collins, *Apache Nightmare*, 227–30; Thrapp, *Apacheria*, 20–22; and Worcester, *The Apaches*, 249. Cruse, who as commander of the Apache scouts likely would have known otherwise,

accepted without reservation Hurrle's ability to speak the Apache language—see *Apache Days*, 100–101. However, Carr himself later noted that some of the Apaches seemed to have difficulty understanding portions of Hurrle's interpretation during Nockay-del-klinne's arrest—see Col. Eugene A. Carr, Report of Operations, to Headquarters, Department of Arizona, 2 Nov. 1881, RG 94, M689, Roll 37, NARA. Questions surrounding Hurrle's role will likely remain unanswered and open to historical interpretation. Details of Nockay-del-klinne's Ghost Dance are related in Mooney, *Ghost-Dance Religion*, 704–5.

15. Carter, *Yorktown to Santiago*, 209.

16. Collins, *Apache Nightmare*, 18; Carter, *Memoirs*, 121. The Apache explanation of Nockay-del-Klinne's Ghost Dance and its meaning is recounted by Asa Daklugie in *Indeh*, 52. For brief sketches of the medicine man and his particular brand of spiritualism, see Thrapp, *Apacheria*, 217–18; Worcester, *The Apaches*, 236–37; and Wharfield, *Cibicu Creek Fight*, 12–17. For Colonel Carr's estimate of the situation as it worsened, see Col. Eugene Carr, U.S. 6th Cav., to Adjutant General, Department of Arizona, 1 Aug. 1881, RG 94, M689, Roll 38, NARA. Note: This letter appears as "Appendix A" to Carr's Report of Operations, 2 Nov. 1881.

17. Carter, quoted in Collins, *Apache Nightmare*, 22. J. C. Tiffany, the San Carlos agent, is sometimes referred to as "Major Tiffany," in reference to his volunteer service during the Civil War. Although Tiffany's relationship with the army was cooperative, it was by no means one of mutual admiration. King asserts that Tiffany may have pressed for Nockay-del-klinne's arrest out of fear that his own corrupt activities might be exposed by renewed violence—see *War Eagle*, 198. Asa Daklugie related the Apaches' dissatisfaction with Tiffany to Eve Ball—see *Indeh*, 52–53.

18. Wharfield speculates that the distrustful relationship which existed between Carr and Willcox likely motivated Carr's curious attempts to shift responsibility. *Cibicu Creek*, 21–25. Carr's initial report, issued on 18 Sept. 1881, appears intended to dissuade blame for the events surrounding Nockay-del-klinne's arrest.

19. Carter, *Memoirs*, 122–23. The scouts, under command of Thomas Cruse, had shown signs of becoming obstinate and difficult to lead as they came under the Ghost Dance influence. In his memoir, Cruse details Carr's decision to take the scouts into the field—*Apache Days*, 99–103. Also see Worcester's analysis, *The Apaches*, 242, and Collins, *Apache Nightmare*, 32–33. On Carr's discussion with the scouts, see his Report of Operations to Headquarters, Department of Arizona, 18 Sept. 1881, RG 94, M689, Roll 36, NARA. This report was later revised and resubmitted as Report of Operations, 2 Nov. 1881. At the end of this meeting, Carr showed the scouts how to observe a comet through his field telescope, hoping to discredit Nockay-del-klinne's previous claim to have placed it in the night sky. Carter recounts his bout with a headache in *Memoirs*, 124. He suffered from severe headaches until about forty years of age; see also Carter to Ida Carter, 19 Mar. 1911, in Carter Family Papers.

20. Carter, *Memoirs*, 125.

21. Carr, Report of Operations, 18 Sept. 1881, 9. Carter's account of the

arrest generally agrees with those of Carr and Cruse, as does the Apache version related to Eve Ball in *Indeh*, 54. Another extant Apache account is that of Tom Friday, a member of the White Mountain (Coyotero) Apache subtribe. In 1938, he related an oral history of the Cibicu battle to a white missionary friend. Friday's version was based on traditions heard from tribal elders who, according to historian William B. Kessel, "presumably were directly involved in these events." Although Friday was the son of "Dead Shot," an Apache scout who was later tried and executed for his role at Cibicu Creek, he was likely too young to have heard much of the battle from his father. As might be expected, Friday's second-hand oral tradition differs in many details from accounts of white participants and even from Daklugie's. See Kessel, "Battle of Cibecue," 123–34. Provocative commentary on the difficulties of ascertaining empirical truths about frontier events is found in Monnett, *Massacre at Cheyenne Hole*. Monnett's discussion of the nature of both Anglo records and Native-American oral traditions provides an interesting foundation for similar historical examinations.

22. Cruse, *Apache Days*, 108; Collins, *Apache Nightmare*, 46–47; Worcester, *The Apaches*, 244–45.

23. Carr noted "a little after 3 P.M." as the approximate time when he sent Hentig to warn away the encroaching Apaches, while Collins's study places Nockay-del-klinne's arrest at three o'clock and thus the events at the campsite somewhat later. See Carr's Report, 18 Sept. 1881, 15; and Collins, *Apache Nightmare*, 43, 49.

24. Carter, *Memoirs*, 125; Carter, *Yorktown to Santiago*, 214–16; Collins, *Apache Nightmare*, 53–56.

25. Carter, *Memoirs*, 125. Cruse placed the attacking Apaches' initial strength at approximately three hundred warriors, and believed that this number was strengthened in short order by some two hundred more hostiles from surrounding villages. By nightfall, when the shooting began to subside, Cruse claimed that somewhere around eight hundred Apaches were in the immediate area. *Apache Days*, 118. These estimates hardly seem probable, but whatever the exact numbers, it is clear that Carr's command was badly outnumbered at Cibicu Creek. King estimated from his own research that "perhaps five hundred" Apache attackers were in the general area at nightfall, but does not elaborate on his sources for this number. *War Eagle*, 211. Carter placed the initial number of attackers at "more than a hundred" but made no attempt to guess the total number of warriors eventually involved. *Memoirs*, 126. The Apache scout named "Dead Shot" had befriended the Carters since Ida had provided condensed milk and other items for his newborn child. Carter firmly believed that Dead Shot ordered the other scouts to avoid shooting him during their first volley and thus saved his life. Carter remembered later looking over the field where he had taken aim at the scouts during the fight's initial moments, and commented that he had seen no bodies or even signs of striking his targets: "I have never bragged on my marksmanship with a pistol since that experience." *Memoirs*, 134. Cruse stated that Sergeant Mose was the only scout to remain loyal during the battle, and he helped guide Carr's column back to Fort Apache during the night. *Apache Days*, 116, 122.

26. Cruse, *Apache Days*, 114; Carr, Report of Operations, 18 Sept. 1881.

27. Carter did not mention this brave action in either *Memoirs* or *Yorktown to Santiago*—perhaps to avoid the crass appearance of self-congratulation. Collins's narrative of this episode disagrees on minor specifics with Cruse's primary account (which is relied on by this author). See Collins, *Apache Nightmare*, 57; and Cruse, *Apache Days*, 115. Carter and Richard Heartery met again in 1906 when Carter commanded the Department of the Lakes, where Heartery was employed as a civil servant.

28. Cruse, *Apache Days*, 120. Cruse recalled (117) that Carter said a quick prayer after the dead were buried.

29. Carter, *Memoirs*, 129; Carter, *Yorktown to Santiago*, 219; Collins, *Apache Nightmare*, 61, 242n40. Collins relies on Carter's narrative of Nockay-del-klinne's death, but notes that variations exist in other sources. Also see King, *War Eagle*, 211.

30. Cruse, *Apache Days*, 125; King, *War Eagle*, 212.

31. Carter, *Memoirs*, 131. Cruse states that after hearing rumors of another Custer-like disaster at Cibicu Creek, "Mrs. Carter had said that Carter would soon turn up," while Carr's wife "had asserted calmly that the Indian wasn't alive who could kill General Carr." *Apache Days*, 125. Coffman examines the lives of frontier soldiers' wives and children in *Old Army*, 104–35, and 287–327. And for a book-length treatment of this often-ignored subject, see Eales, *Army Wives*.

32. These headlines are taken from clippings of the *New York Tribune* (n.d.) and the *Brooklyn Eagle*, Sunday, 5 Sept. 1881, in Carter Family Papers. Numerous such clippings were apparently mailed to the Carters and carefully preserved in a scrapbook, most without publication information. Premature obituaries for Carter appeared in several newspapers, examples of which are also in the scrapbook. One of these, printed by the *Brooklyn Eagle* (n.d.) noted that he "was a brilliant and promising officer, possessing in an unusual degree not only the qualities which go to make up the gallant soldier, but also those which form the perfect gentleman and the manly, whole hearted friend and brother."

33. Gen. William T. Sherman, Commanding General of the Army, to Gen. Irving McDowell, Commanding General, Pacific Division, 15 Sept. 1881, RG 94, M689, Roll 66, NARA. This was a handwritten copy of a telegram sent from Sherman to McDowell that was furnished to General Willcox, at Headquarters, Department of Arizona. Also see Gen. R. C. Drum, Adjutant General, to Gen. Irving McDowell, Commanding General, Pacific Division, 12 Sept. 1881, RG 94, M689, Roll 66, NARA. On changes in operational command after Cibicu, see Worcester, *The Apaches*, 248, and King, *War Eagle*, 215–20. Letters written to the Carters by Mrs. Dawley during this period reveal the anxiety that frontier service sometimes caused a soldier's extended family and friends—see Mrs. Dawley to Ida Carter, 8 Oct. 1881, to W. H. Carter, 8 Oct. 1881, and to Ida Carter, 11 Oct. 1881—all in Carter Family Papers.

34. Troop movements in response to the Cibicu outbreak are described in a report by Gen. O. B. Willcox, Commanding General, Department of

Arizona, to the Asst. Adjutant General, Military Division of the Pacific, 12 Dec. 1881, RG94, M689, Roll 37, NARA. For a summary of these deployments, see Thrapp, *General Crook*, 32–37.

35. Thrapp presents a deeply researched account of the violence that followed Cibicu in *Crook*, while Odie B. Faulk focuses on the army's efforts to capture the now-legendary Geronimo in *Geronimo Campaign*. In addition, more generalized discussions such as Thrapp, *Apacheria*; Worcester, *The Apaches*; and Roberts, *Once They Moved Like the Wind* place these events in the context of the Apache's larger struggle against white and Mexican encroachment. Also, see the accounts of Cruse (*Apache Days*), Bourke (*On the Border with Crook*), Schmitt (*General George Crook*), and Davis (*Truth about Geronimo*). As early as General Willcox's Special Report, 12 Dec. 1881, it was clear that Carr's role would be formally scrutinized. Willcox's dislike of Carr, fully returned, as well as a desire to shift any potential blame from himself, certainly made Carr a likely target. See Willcox, Special Report, 12 Dec. 1881.

36. Captain Harry C. Egbert, U.S. Twelfth Infantry, Special Report to Asst. Adjutant General, Department of Arizona, 10 Dec. 1881, RG 94, M689, Roll 37, NARA. Worcester incorrectly names this officer as Benjamin Egbert in *The Apaches*, 249. Thrapp summarizes Egbert's conclusions in *Crook and the Sierra Madre*, 41–45.

37. Judge Advocate General of the Army to the Secretary of War, "Summary of the Charges and Specifications Preferred Against Col. Eugene Carr," 26 Jan. 1882, RG 94, M689, Roll 38, NARA; General Orders no. 125, Adjutant General's Office, 21 Oct. 1882, RG 94, M689, Roll 39, NARA; Carter, *Memoirs*, 139–40; Cruse, *Apache Days*, 115–16; and King, *War Eagle*, 223–26.

38. Quotation is excerpted from "How General Carter Won the Medal of Honor Fighting the Apache Indians," *New York Sunday Herald* (14 Apr. 1912). Carter and Private Richard Heartery were awarded the congressional Medal of Honor for their efforts to save Captain Hentig and Private Bird on 30 Aug. 1881 at Cibicu Creek. The citation is preserved in the Carter Family Papers and reads: "For distinguished bravery in action against hostile Apache Indians in rescuing with the voluntary assistance of two soldiers the wounded from under a heavy fire of hostile Indians at Cibicu Creek Arizona 30 Aug 1881, while serving as First Lieutenant and R.Q.M. and Acting Adjutant 6th Cavalry."

CHAPTER 6: COMING IN FROM THE FRONTIER

1. Bledstein's study, *Culture of Professionalism*, relates professional activity to concurrent social and economic shifts in American society. For further reading on this subject, see n. 13 of this chapter.

2. Gates, "Alleged Isolation," 42–43. The defining literature of the new professionalism was detailed in the introductory chapter of this book.

3. Carter, *Giles Carter*, 112.

4. For in-depth discussion of the line-staff relationship and its impact on the military profession, see Roberts, "Loyalty and Expertise," and Skelton, *Profession of Arms*, 221–37. For a concise history of the American staff system up to the time of the Civil War, see Hattaway and Jones, *How the North*

Won, 101–7. Roberts's study posits line-staff competition as a manifestation of deeper disparities between professional and bureaucratic cultures, downplaying the role of professional interests and emphasizing the political battle for institutional authority.

5. Carter, *Memoirs,* 142.

6. Ibid. According to Skelton, the tradition of "antagonism" between the army's staff and line stemmed from line officers' distrust of the staff bureaus' autonomy and political power. Animosity partially grew from the line's jealousy of perceived staff advantages in career progression as well as general quality of life. See *Profession of Arms,* 232–37. In addition, as Roberts notes, issues of "prestige, career advancement, and job security" all played roles in the staff-line dispute. "Reform and Revitalization," 199. Also see Cosmas, *An Army for Empire,* 24–25.

7. Carter to Commissary General of the Army, 8 Nov. 1883, reprinted in its entirety in *Memoirs,* 142–43.

8. Ibid., 144.

9. Carter, *Yorktown to Santiago,* 241–42; Carter, *Memoirs,* 145–46.

10. Carter, *Memoirs,* 147–48; Carter Diary, 18 Sept. 1815. Carter's specific duties and the various campaigns in which he took part are recorded in Special Orders no. 33, Headquarters U.S. 6th Cavalry, 4 Apr. 1887.

11. Carter, *Memoirs,* 153; Carter described the night of Leigh's birth in Diary, 30 May 1916. The Carters took a month-long leave of absence upon their arrival in Newark so that Leigh Carter could undergo a surgical procedure in New York City to correct the trauma his ear had sustained during a bout with scarlet fever. Carter to Adjutant General of the Army (through Asst. Adjutant General, Recruiting Service), 9 Aug. 1888, in RG 94, ACP 1878, William H. Carter, NARA. On Leigh's condition, also see an inscription by William Vaulx Carter in the frontispiece of a copy of Holloway, *White House* (hereafter cited as Carter inscription in Holloway, *White House*). The term "Gilded Age" is derived from the title of a popular satire written in 1873 by Mark Twain and Charles Dudley Warner. See Calhoun's introduction to *The Gilded Age,* xi–xii.

12. Carter, *Memoirs,* 153.

13. Carter to Adjutant General of the Army (through Commanding Officer, 6th Cavalry), 3 Aug. 1882, in ACP 1878, William H. Carter, RG 94, NARA. Carter notes in this letter that "I have never been east, nor have I seen any of my relatives since I was graduated in 1873." Also see Carter, *Memoirs,* 141–42. This leave of absence was cut short when Carter was ordered to return to his regiment. There is a wide body of literature addressing the various cultural shifts in American society during the Gilded Age. Excellent starting points are Calhoun, *Gilded Age;* Trachtenberg, *Incorporation of America;* Porter, *Rise of Big Business;* and Schlereth, *Victorian America.* The emergence of an observable middle class in American society has been the subject of scholarly debate. Wiebe casts some doubt that a truly definable middle class actually existed as a social entity until possibly very late in the period. *Search for Order,* 111–32. But although Wiebe argues that America's class system was actually highly dynamic, he admits that a social segment indeed coalesced around a set of sensibilities that have since been typically

attributed to the "middle class." More recently, Bledstein and Trachtenberg readily accept the advent of a middle-class culture in which large numbers of Americans overtly identified with an ideology marked by formal education, public participation, and socioeconomic mobility. On the related development of professions and their cultural importance, see Bledstein, *Culture of Professionalism.*

14. Carter, "One View," 573–78. The term "Uptonian" is used by Weigley to describe professionalist efforts to reform post–Civil War American military policy—see *Towards an American Army,* 144–61. Weigley includes Carter in this category.

15. Nenninger, *Leavenworth Schools,* 16; Reardon, *Soldiers and Scholars,* 16–17, 23–26; and Brereton, *Educating the Army,* xii–xiii. Military progressives' struggle to overcome an anti-intellectualist strain among their peers mirrored the frustrations encountered by civilian reformers. See Hofstadter, *Anti-intellectualism in American Life.*

16. As Grandstaff writes, " 'old army' officers like William T. Sherman" provided an undeniable link with antebellum professional ideas and efforts— see "Habits and Usages of War," 543–44, and 544n77. In varying degrees, Weigley (*History of the Army* and *Towards an American Army*), Cooper ("Army's Search for a Mission") and Nenninger (*Leavenworth Schools*) also emphasize Sherman's leadership as a catalyst for postwar reform. Fitzpatrick discusses Upton's view of the Regular Army as a peacetime repository of specialized skills in "Misunderstood Reformer," 295–96.

17. Weigley emphasizes Upton's lasting influence on a professionally active group of younger army officers in a chapter that is appropriately titled "The Disciples of Emory Upton," in *Towards an American Army,* 137–61.

18. Carter, "One View," 573–74.

19. Ibid., 575.

20. Ibid., 574.

21. Calhoun's report is the subject of Spiller's "Calhoun's Expansible Army," 189–203. The concept an "expansible army"—skeletal regular organizations that would grow to authorized strengths by the addition of citizen volunteers during wartime—existed as early as 1798 when both George Washington and Alexander Hamilton advanced plans for American defense essentially founded on this principle. The idea's subsequent life as a basis for U.S. military policy is the subject of modern discussion. In addition to Spiller, see Weigley, *Towards an American Army,* 35; Cress, *Citizens in Arms,* 176–77; Skelton, "Huntington," 329–30, and Skelton, *Profession of Arms,* 127–30. Upton's proposals for an expansible army appeared in *Armies of Asia and Europe,* 337–53, and later in *Military Policy of the United States,* xiv. That Upton based his concept on Calhoun's original "expansive organization" is evident from his analysis of the Reorganization Act of 1821—see *Military Policy of the United States,* 149–52.

22. Fitzpatrick, "Misunderstood Reformer," 300; Upton, *Military Policy of the United States,* XIV. Although Fitzpatrick convincingly rejects assertions that Upton's proposals were wholly removed from the realities of American culture (e.g., Ambrose, *Upton and the Army*; Weigley, *Towards an American Army*), the fact remains that he lacked an understanding of the

importance of local leadership in the volunteer or militia tradition. Upton assailed any suggestion that citizen-soldiers could adequately lead troops into battle, ignoring the fact that contemporary Americans still viewed military institutions from a localist perspective. As historian Linderman notes, even by the Spanish-American War the American citizenry still did not accept an active federal government in their daily lives. Thus, many Americans deeply resented regular officers who were placed in command of local sons who volunteered to fight a national war. Military leadership was seen as a community prerogative, not a right assumed by an outsider commissioned by the federal government—see Linderman, *Mirror of War*, 60-90. Cooper similarly concluded that many "reformers of the Uptonian persuasion" emphasized federal control over the entire American military system, rejecting any role for state or local leadership—see *Rise of the National Guard*, 92. Jack C. Lane observes that the American outlook slowly shifted from nineteenth-century localism to twentieth-century nationalism, a transition that naturally extended to their view of military policy—see Lane, "Commentary on 'Roots of American Military Policy,'" in *Soldiers and Civilians*, 44. In 1889, Carter, like Upton before him, largely misunderstood Americans' perceptions of public authority.

23. Carter expounded at length on the importance of trained, professional leadership to the successful execution of military operations in "One View," 574. Also see Upton's "Introduction" to *Military Policy of the United States*, XII-XIV.

24. Carter, "One View," 575-76. In acknowledging the National Guard, Carter diverged from Upton's outright dismissal of the state-organized militia for any but the most drastic crises. Although calling for professional leadership of state forces, Carter seems to have recognized the political inexpedience of discarding the Guard entirely—a view that certainly forecast his later work on the 1903 Militia Act. Cooper has delineated a "second group" of Army reformers who departed from a strict Uptonian rejection of the state militia. This group favored stronger national regulation so that the Guard could become a more effective reserve. See *Rise of the National Guard*, 92. Brereton maintains that Arthur Wagner, Carter's contemporary and fellow reformer, also viewed the militia as a less-than-efficient but nonetheless necessary part of the American system. Like Carter, Wagner proposed that regulars serve as a working model for the National Guard's improvement, and that Guard officers even participate in postgraduate education. See Brereton, *Educating the Army*, 8-10. For representative examples of contemporary articles relating to this topic, see the Military Service Institute's annual prize-winning essay for 1885, Capt. George F. Price, "The Necessity for Closer Relations between the Army and the People," 303-30; and Giddings, "How to Improve the National Guard," 61-75.

25. Bledstein, *Culture of Professionalism*, 121. On education as a legitimizing factor for the professions, see also Wiebe, *Search for Order*, 121. The acceleration of graduate education in the United States followed the transition of higher education toward a university model based loosely on the German-style research institution. On this development, see four classic studies that continue to influence the historiography of American higher

education: Rudolph, *American College and University*, 275–86, 334–43; Veysey, *American University*, 130–31; Hofstadter and Hardy, *Development and Scope of Higher Education*, 57–100; and Brubacher and Rudy, *Higher Education in Transition*, 175–223.

26. Report of the Commanding General, in Secretary's Annual Report, 1891, 58.

27. Abrahamson, *America Arms*, 34. On Leavenworth's early development and especially its role as a professionalizing influence, see Nenninger, *Leavenworth Schools*, and Brereton, *Educating the Army*.

28. Carter, "One View," 576.

29. Ibid., 575.

30. Carter, *Memoirs*, 154.

31. During the last year of his recruiting tour, Carter had applied for a staff billet in the Quartermaster's Bureau. But in May 1889, he formally withdrew this request—possibly after becoming aware of the opportunity to command a 6th Cavalry troop. See Carter to Adjutant General of the Army, 31 May 1889,in RG 94, ACP 1878, William H. Carter, NARA, and also, Asst. Adjutant General to William H. Carter, 4 June 1889, ibid. Material pertaining to Carter's activities between the time he departed Newark and the time he reported to Fort Lewis is drawn from *Memoirs*, 154–55; and also from Carter to Adjutant General of the Army (through Hdqrtrs., Army Recruiting Service), 2 Sept. 1889, in RG 94, ACP. 1878, William H. Carter, NARA. Carter was officially ordered to Fort Lewis by Sec. 7, Special Orders no. 271, Headquarters of the Army. These orders coincided with his commission as a captain in the Sixth Cavalry, dated 20 Nov. 1889, and transmitted to him on 7 Feb. 1890 by the Adjutant General's Office—in RG 94, ACP 1878, William H. Carter, NARA.

32. Carter, *Memoirs*, 151.

CHAPTER 7: GHOST DANCE OF THE OLD ARMY

1. Carter, *Memoirs*, 155. Carter received his commission as a captain on 7 Feb. 1890. See Adjutant General's Office to Capt. William H. Carter, 7 Feb. 1890, ACP 1878, William H. Carter, RG 94, NARA.

2. Carter, *Memoirs*, 155. Carter lodged an official protest in a letter to the Adjutant General's Office that outlined a brief argument on legal grounds, Carter to the Adjutant General of the Army, 6 Aug. 1890, ACP 1878, William H. Carter, RG 94, NARA. He later noted with some bitterness that subsequent legislation fixed "a minimum limit for each troop of cavalry and company of infantry, so that in [the] future it will not be legal to skeletonize any portion of the army." See "War Department," 669.

3. During the move overland from Fort Lewis to Fort Wingate, the Carters lost several trunks of personal baggage when one of their wagons overturned in a large mud hole near Sulpher Springs, New Mexico, while crossing the Navajo reservation. Much of the contents was ruined and Carter sought compensation for the amount of $190.10 under a federal act of 3 Mar. 1885. After two years of correspondence, the claim was denied because the personal items were only "damaged" and not wholly "lost or destroyed" as

worded in the applicable regulation. Carter disgustedly noted in his memoirs that "claims against the Treasury are like running for office—somebody is always disappointed." See Carter to Adjutant General of the Army, 2 Mar. 1891 (and attachments); Carter to Third Auditor, U.S. Treasury Dept., 28 Apr. 1891; and Third Auditor's Office to Carter, 8 July 1891—all in Carter Family Papers. Also see Carter, *Memoirs*, 157–58.

    4. Utley, *Frontier Regulars*, 402. This description of the "Messiah" theology is based on Utley's analysis in *Last Days*, 64–71. Utley's study stands as the best comprehensive history of the events that culminated in the Pine Ridge Campaign. In 1891, ethnologist James Mooney undertook an extensive investigation of the Ghost Dance religion under the auspices of the Bureau of American Ethnology and the Smithsonian Institution. His exhaustive report was published in 1896 as Part Two of the Bureau of Ethnology's "Report XIV," and is reprinted as *The Ghost Dance Religion and Wounded Knee*. Also see Utley, *Indian Frontier*, 253–54, and Coleman, *Voices*. The latter work is a recent synthesis of primary testimony that, in a manner very much like Ball's *Indeh*, illuminates the divergence between white and Indian interpretations of historical events. An interesting contemporary description is found in Scott, *Some Memories*, 146–55. Frederic Remington sketched the Ghost Dance as practiced by the Ogallala Sioux at the Pine Ridge Agency in *Harper's Weekly* (6 Dec. 1890): 960–61.

    5. Utley, *Frontier Regulars*, 403; Fletcher quoted in Coleman, *Voices*, 5. For discussion of the manner in which Wovoka's message was altered, see Utley, *Last Days*, 72–72; and Wooster, *Nelson A. Miles*, 178. Also see the translated text of a speech made by Short Bull at the Pine Ridge Agency on 31 Oct. 1890, in Mooney, *Ghost Dance Religion*, 788. Capt. W. E. Dougherty, U.S. First Infantry, wrote that the Ghost Dance only became problematic due to the militant connotation it assumed among the Sioux. "Recent Indian Craze," 576. Kicking Bear's particular prophecies are described in DeMontravel, "General Nelson A. Miles," 26–27. On the Indian Bureau's blatant mismanagement of the Sioux agencies during the years immediately preceding Wounded Knee, see DeMontravel, 26; Mooney, *Ghost Dance Religion*, 845; Coleman, *Voices*, 12–24; and Utley, *Last Days*, 38–9. The several acts and agreements that resulted in the fragmentation of the Great Sioux Reservation are detailed by Utley in ibid., 40–59. For a very moderate primary interpretation, see Richardson, "Some Observations," 512–31.

    6. Special Agent E. B. Reynolds to Commissioner of Indian Affairs (CIA), 2 Nov. 1890, copy in Nelson Miles Papers, MHI. On the situation's increasing scope, see Indian Agent D. F. Royer to CIA, 30 Oct. 1890, copy in Nelson Miles Papers, MHI; Acting Secretary of the Interior George Chandler to The President, 13 Nov. 1890, copy in Nelson Miles Papers, MHI; and Utley, *Last Days*, 99–112.

    7. Wooster, *Nelson A. Miles*, 180. Elmo Scott Watson examines the media's role in "Last Indian War," 205–19. President Benjamin Harrison authorized military intervention in a letter to Secretary of War Redfield Proctor, 13 Nov. 1890, copy in Nelson Miles Papers, MHI.

    8. Carter, *Memoirs*, 158. Orders for the Sixth Cavalry to proceed to South Dakota were received on 1 Dec. The regiment arrived in Rapid City

eight days later after traveling by a circuitous route that took them through Denver, Colorado, and Columbus, Nebraska. The Sixth Cavalry's movements during the Pine Ridge Campaign are detailed in a manuscript copy of "Report of Operations of the Sixth Cavalry between Nov 22, 1890 and Feb 9, 1891" (written in Carter's hand), Carter Family Papers. It is likely that this was a draft copy of Carr's formal report to department headquarters, possibly prepared by Carter due to his previous experience as regimental adjutant (hereafter cited as Sixth Cavalry Report of Operations.) The army's mobilization plan for the Pine Ridge Campaign is described in Utley, *Last Days*, 118–19.

9. Carter, *Memoirs*, 158–59. Parts of this paragraph also appear in *Yorktown to Santiago*, 258.

10. Carter to Ida Carter, 14 Dec. 1890, Carter Family Papers.

11. Ibid.

12. Sixth Cavalry Report of Operations, 4; King, *War Eagle*, 240. Utley describes the "Stronghold" in *Last Days*, 121–22 (see also the regional map, 170–71).

13. Quotation in Utley, *Last Days*, 133. Also see Wooster, *Nelson A. Miles*, 181.

14. Carter to Ida Carter, 13 Dec. 1890, Carter Family Papers.

15. Representative field orders for these patrols are found in Lt. F. G. Hodgson, Adjutant, Sixth Cavalry, to Capt. William H. Carter, Commanding Troop F, Sixth Cavalry, 21 Dec. 1890—copies in Carter Family Papers. Carter and his troop were ordered to scout a twenty-mile section to the east of the Sixth's position in search of "any Indians found off their reservations" who were to be "captured or destroyed." Interestingly, Carter was reminded to "not engage too deeply with any force superior to yours," perhaps indicative of the lasting influence of the Little Big Horn disaster on the army's approach to Indian fighting.

16. Utley, *Last Days*, 146–66; Coleman, *Voices*, 180–217.

17. Ida Carter to William H. Carter, 14 Dec. 1890, Carter Family Papers. In this letter, Ida also asks about the possibility of future assignment to either Fort Leavenworth or Fort Riley, both in Kansas. From her correspondence, it seems clear that the continued prospect of living at austere outposts and losing her husband to weeks of patrol was growing wearisome. Also see Ida Carter to William H. Carter, letters of 19, 30, and 31 Dec. 1890, 1 and 3 Jan 1891, Carter Family Papers. This collection of letters offers great insight into the haphazard manner in which information reached the homefront, tormenting a soldier's family with worry. In making the move to South Dakota, the Sixth Cavalry vacated their quarters at Fort Wingate. While some families went to Rapid City in trail of the regiment, others remained at posts farther south, such as Fort Leavenworth. See Col. Eugene Carr, quoted in Utley, *Last Days*, 188–89.

18. Carter to Ida Carter, 21 Dec. 1890, Carter Family Papers.

19. Carter to Ida Carter, 21 Dec. 1890; King, *War Eagle*, 240–41. Remington published several articles associated with the campaign, including one titled "Galloping Sixth"—see 57–58. Carter's later history of the Sixth Cavalry, *From Yorktown to Santiago* (1900), included several Remington

sketches, two of which were completed during the Pine Ridge Campaign. Representative of Remington's field coverage of the Ghost Dance "rebellion" are "Sioux Outbreak," 57, 61–62; "Lieutenant Casey's Last Scout," 85–87; "Art of War," 947; and "Chasing a Major General," 946–47.

20. Utley, *Last Days*, 179–86; King, *War Eagle*, 243; Coleman, *Voices*, 242–46.

21. Carter detailed his patrol of 22–23 December in a letter to Ida Carter, 23 Dec. 1890, in Carter Family Papers. He described a very precarious crossing of the Cheyenne River, and noted that "it was great good fortune that we got over without losing someone or an animal." In this same letter, he observed that even the Cheyenne River encampment seemed "real home-like" after enduring the Dakota winter.

22. Carter, *Memoirs*, 160. The courier who arrived in Carr's camp carried a message from Sumner regarding Big Foot's supposed course of march–Carter, *Yorktown to Santiago*, 259.

23. Sixth Cavalry Report of Operations, 7; King, *War Eagle*, 243.

24. Carter, *Yorktown to Santiago*, 260.

25. Sixth Cavalry Report of Operations, 7–8.

26. Gen. Nelson Miles to Gen. John R. Brooke, quoted in Utley, *Last Days*, 192. For Sioux accounts of Big Foot's surrender and the subsequent tragedy, see Collins, *Voices*, 261–78. Lt. John C. Gresham, an officer who was with Whitside's battalion, presented his own record of events in "Story of Wounded Knee," 106–7. Testimonies from both sides contain obvious bias, leaving modern historians to arbitrate conflicting accounts in an attempt to build an accurate narrative.

27. Utley, *Last Days*, 205–6. Notice that Utley's spelling of "Minniconjou" differs from this author's.

28. Quoted in Utley, *Last Days*, 212. Utley concludes on 211–13 that Big Foot's warriors fired first, an assertion that is validated by Mooney's extensive (and balanced) study. See also Mooney, *Ghost Dance Religion*, 870. Although Coleman does not draw a summary conclusion, his presentation, on 289–301, seems to credit Indian traditions that allege the soldiers shot first. (It should be noted that Mooney's investigation included numerous interviews with actual participants and witnesses on both sides of the affair.) In "The Story of Wounded Knee," 106, Gresham claimed that wounded Sioux captives told him that "it had been resolved in council the night before to attack the troops." Although this claim is unsubstantiated, it seems reasonable that at least some of the young men in Big Foot's band were determined to resist surrender in spite of Big Foot's intentions.

29. Utley presents these casualty numbers in *Last Days*, 227–28. Utley, whose deeply researched study is probably the most balanced modern account, makes it clear that the Seventh Cavalry attempted at several points to minimize casualties inflicted on women and children. In the confusion of a battle that neither side expected nor desired, noncombatant casualties were almost impossible to avoid. Also see the official conclusions of Maj. J. F. Kent and Capt. F. D. Baldwin, division inspector generals, 13 Jan. 1891 (with supplements), in Nelson Miles Papers, MHI. Although this report might be dismissed as sympathetic to the army, it must be remembered that Kent and

Baldwin undertook the investigation at the behest of Miles, who was actively (and publicly) interested in scapegoating Forsyth and the Seventh Cavalry. Thus, the two officers in fact had every reason to investigate the matter with a bias toward *faulting* the Seventh's conduct at Wounded Knee. Their report cleared the regiment of patent wrongdoing or disregard for noncombatant life, although they strongly questioned Forsyth's disposition of troops before the action. Kent and Baldwin note that the Sioux warriors acted with extreme "fanaticism" that morning, and, in a manner very uncharacteristic of Indian warfare, fought from among their own women and children rather than attempt to separate themselves. Also see the conclusions of Secretary of War Redfield Proctor, memorandum of 12 Feb. 1891, copy in Nelson Miles Papers, MHI. With a revisionist's enthusiasm, Elmo Watson summarily dismissed Kent and Baldwin's investigation as a "whitewash," although he never provides historical justification for this assertion. "Newspaper Jingoism," 217.

30. Sixth Cavalry Report of Operations, 9–10. The number of Sioux who reached Kicking Bear and Short Bull is drawn from Utley, *Last Days*, 252. Utley's estimate parallels that of Mooney in *Ghost Dance Religion*, 875.

31. Utley, *Last Days*, 254; Carter to Ida Carter, 31 Dec. 1890, in Carter Family Papers. Weigley notes that severe winter weather often proved a distinct tactical advantage for troops campaigning against the Indians. *History of the Army*, 269.

32. Carter, *Memoirs*, 162–63; Carter, *Yorktown to Santiago*, 261–62; Sixth Cavalry Report of Operations, 10–11; and Carter to Mr. P. S. Crawley, 28 May 1915, in Carter Family Papers. Interestingly, this last letter was to congratulate Mr. Crawley, a representative of Buffalo Bill Historical Picture Company, on his company's portrayal of the Pine Ridge Campaign in a film that Carter refers to as "The Indian Wars Refought." Carter wrote that the film, made "under the personally guiding hand of Buffalo Bill," presents "a very faithful picture of the occurrences in the Indian Wars of that period."

33. Col. Carr recommended Carter for the brevet rank of major for "bravery in action on White River near Grass Creek, South Dakota, January 1st, 1891." Carr to Asst. Adjutant General, Division of the Missouri, 2 Feb. 1891, ACP 1878, William H. Carter, RG 94, NARA. This recommendation was endorsed by General Brooke, commanding Department of the Platte, and General Miles, commanding Division of Missouri, but was later suspended by Gen. John M. Schofield, Commanding General of the Army, after first approving it. See Adjutant General's Office, Case no. 49 (summary), ACP 1878, William H. Carter, RG 94, NARA. Several documents maintained in Carter's ACP file trace the progress of this recommendation (and also Carr's recommendation of brevets for Carter's actions at Cibicu and Fort Apache) through formal army channels. No reason is given to the suspension in this case, but it appears that Schofield suspended further action on a large block of such recommendations during this time period. See letter to Col. William H. Carter dated 19 Nov. 1900 (unsigned) that delineates the disposition of several similar recommendations for brevets and awards during the Pine Ridge Campaign, in RG 94, ACP 1878, William H. Carter, NARA.

34. Carter, *Memoirs*, 163–64.

35. Carter voiced similar conclusions years later when he caustically

attacked "advancing civilization" as a wasteful endeavor marked by the "perpetration of wrongs," while noting the army's selfless service in "miserable" conditions at the behest of civil authority. "War Department," 668. He also described the army's role on the frontier as a difficult, "thankless sort of service," in "Next Head of the Army," 811. For a description of Miles's formal review at the Pine Ridge Agency, see DeMontravel, "Miles and Wounded Knee," 42–43; Utley, *Last Days*, 267–70; and King, *War Eagle*, 245–46. Utley also comments on the campaign's poignant symbolism in *Frontier Regulars*, 409–11.

36. Carter, "Army Question," 875. On the army's recognition of impending change in its role, see Abrahamson, *America Arms*, 5–6, 35–40; and Coffman, *Old Army*, 270. Turner articulated his famous thesis at a conference of the American Historical Association at the 1893 Chicago World's Fair. He framed his arguments with the assertion that America's western frontier had in fact ceased to exist. See Turner, *History, Frontier, and Section*, and also Faragher, *Rereading Frederick Jackson Turner*. On the cessation of Indian fighting, see Wooster, *U.S. Indian Policy*, 214. The Sixth Cavalry's regimental headquarters was assigned along with Troops A, F, G, E, and K to Fort Niobrara, Nebraska, following the Pine Ridge Campaign. See Carter, *Memoirs*, 164; Carter, *Yorktown to Santiago*, 264; and Sixth Cavalry Report of Operations, 13.

37. Carter, *Memoirs*, 166; Sixth Cavalry Report of Operations, 13–14.

38. As the officer-in-charge of purchasing remounts for the Sixth Cavalry during the months following Wounded Knee, Carter outfitted his own Troop F with matched steel-gray horses. Troop F was selected to lead the opening parade at the 1893 Chicago World's Fair, and their good impression on those in attendance may well have contributed to the troop's assignment to Leavenworth only a few months later. Carter, *Memoirs*, 172. When assigned to Leavenworth, the troop left their gray mounts at Fort Niobrara and received bay-colored horses upon arrival in Kansas.

39. Quotation in Carter, "War Department," 669. On the impact of consolidation, see Coffman, *Old Army*, 281–83; Coffman, "Long Shadow," 80–81; Cosmas, *An Army for Empire*, 9–10; and Weigley, *History of the Army*, 290. Hays observes that a prime motivator in the trend toward functional organization was the recognition that collective voices were of greater effect than individual protests. See "New Organizational Society," 7.

40. Bledstein underlines the importance of symbolism to the professional's search for social legitimacy. *Culture of Professionalism*, 98–99. Hays outlines the growing prevalence of functional organizations in late-nineteenth-century American society in "The New Organizational Society," 5–9. The growth of printed material as a source of broad-based communication during the Victorian period is related by Schlereth, *Victorian America*, 182–87, and Trachtenberg, *Incorporation of America*, 122–23.

41. Reardon, *Soldiers and Scholars*, 5; and Weigley, *History of the Army*, 274. In addition to these sources, see Abrahamson, *America Arms*, 35–36; and Coffman, *Old Army*, 278.

42. Nenninger, *Leavenworth Schools*, 35. Also see Coffman, *Old Army*, 276–77, and Reardon, *Soldiers and Scholars*, 15. During Fort Niobrara's

1891–92 lyceum season, Carter taught "Elements of Field Engineering," a required course for all lieutenants serving at the post. This class met once a month and was part of a curriculum that included eleven different courses. See "Officers Lyceum," by Lt. F. G. Hodgson, Adjutant and Secretary of the Lyceum, Sixth Cavalry, 9 Nov. 1891, in Carter Family Papers. Carter explained his ideas for the lyceum system's reform in several essays and memorandums; representative are Carter, *Memoirs*, 170; *General Staff*, 5; *American Army*, 246; and "Army Reformers," 553.

43. Carter, "Infantry and Cavalry School," 752. On the school's early development, see Wagner, "American War College," 287–304; Nenninger, *Leavenworth Schools*, 21–31; and Brereton, *Educating the Army*, 13–21.

44. Carter, *Memoirs*, 170. Carter was assigned as an assistant cavalry instructor by Special Orders no. 5, 25 Aug. 1893, U.S. Infantry and Cavalry School, Fort Leavenworth, Kansas, copy in Carter Family Papers. These orders assigned Lt. Thomas Cruse, the Carters' friend from Fort Apache days, to the same position. An example of the field exercises undertaken in support of the School of Application is found in Special Orders no. 203, 25 Oct. 1893, Fort Leavenworth, Kansas, copy in Carter Family Papers.

45. Quotation from Cruse, *Apache Days*, 246. *Horses, Saddles, and Bridles* was published in 1895 by the Lord Baltimore Press and went into three subsequent printings with minor revision (1902, 1906, 1918). See preface to the third edition (1906). As Cruse notes in *Apache Days*, 245–46, there was a scarcity of American textbooks in many military-related fields. During the post–Civil War years, many instructors at both Leavenworth and West Point produced textbooks for the army's use. Prominent examples are the works of Arthur Wagner, Carter's contemporary at Leavenworth, who wrote *The Service of Security and Information* (1893) and *Organization and Tactics* (1895). On officers' publication during the period, see Reardon, *Soldiers and Scholars*, 5; and on the dearth of available texts in military science, see Brereton, *Educating the Army*, 39–40. Bledstein names publication as one of the powerful "symbols of authority" wielded by Gilded Age professionals. *Culture of Professionalism*, 99.

46. Carter, *Horses*, iii.

47. On Wagner's and Swift's "applicatory method," see Nenninger, *Leavenworth Schools*, 45–48; Reardon, *Soldiers and Scholars*, 37–41, and Brereton, *Educating the Army*, 58–63. According to Nenninger, Wagner instituted the applicatory method and Swift "refined and adapted" it to the American army. *Levenworth Schools*, 39.

48. Carter, "Infantry and Cavalry School," 753.

49. Ibid., 754.

50. Ibid.

51. Carter's emphasis on the combination of "theory and practice" surfaced even in his more technical writing on the subject of hippology. As editor of the *Journal of the United States Cavalry Association*, he admonished readers that a "knowledge of horses acquired from books, and not firmly fixed by practical work and examinations, will prove of little value to the service or country"—a direct translation of his ideas on professional study in general.

See Carter, "Professional Notes," *Journal of the United States Cavalry Association* IX (Sept 1896): 264.

52. Carter, "Infantry and Cavalry School," 759.

53. Ibid.

54. Carter, *Memoirs,* 176, 181–82. While serving as editor of the *Journal of the United States Cavalry Association,* Carter penned short editorials that appeared in a section titled "Professional Notes." Topics varied, but examples include the training of remounts, the value of cavalry in the National Guard, and the professional value of young officers writing for publication. See *Journal of the United States Cavalry Association,* IX, nos. 32–34 (1896). Cruse notes that he spent much time "discussing technicalities with old friends such as Carter" while assigned to Leavenworth. *Apache Days and After,* 251.

55. Cosmas, *Army for Empire,* 16–18; Coffman, *Old Army,* 280.

56. See, for example, Lt. Col. Theodore Schwan to "Whom it May Concern," 5 Dec. 1896, in ACP 1878, William H. Carter, RG 94, NARA.

57. Carter attached seven current recommendation letters to his application, as well as excerpts from several earlier endorsements that he had kept from previous years. His most impressive support came from Senator Bate, who wrote a letter on his behalf to the secretary of war. See Bate to Secretary of War, 23 Oct. 1896, ACP 1878, William H. Carter, in RG 94, NARA. See Application of William H. Carter for assignment to the A.G.O., 27 Oct. 1896, ACP 1878, William H. Carter, in RG 94, NARA. In an informal memorandum to the Adjutant General's Office, Secretary of War Russell A. Alger advised that Carter was his first choice for the present opening in the AGO. Thus, whether solely by merit or perhaps due to Bate's influence, Carter gained the secretary's support—see Secretary of War Russell A. Alger to Adjutant General's Office, AGO Doc. File 49775, RG 94, NARA. On Carter's admiration for Bate, see Carter, *Memoirs,* 253–54. By comparison, T. R. Brereton found that Arthur Wagner's contemporary application to the Adjutant General Corps carried thirty-one different endorsements, *Educating the Army,* 67.

58. Carter, *Memoirs,* 174.

CHAPTER 8: A NEW SECRETARY AND AN ERA OF REFORM

1. Carter was relieved of his duties at Fort Leavenworth and ordered to Headquarters of the Army, Washington, D.C., by Special Orders no. 64, 19 Mar. 1897. This same order applied to Maj. Arthur Wagner, Carter's contemporary at the Infantry and Cavalry School.

2. Carter to Gen. George. D. Ruggles, Adjutant General of the Army, 4 Feb. 1897, in ACP 1878, William H. Carter, RG 94, NARA.

3. Carter, *Memoirs,* 186.

4. While at the War Department, Carter relied greatly on the services of Mr. Henry Brinkerhoff, an assistant clerk in the AGO, who "had a store of precedents and knowledge of administrate unequalled by any one of his generation." Carter Diary, 3 Jan. 1916. This entry was made after Carter had attended funeral services for Brinkerhoff.

5. Carter was formally assigned to "take charge of examination papers

and the subject of examination of officers" by authority of a memorandum issued by Gen. George D. Ruggles, Adjutant General of the Army, 29 Mar. 1897. Copy in Carter Family Papers. On the 1890 changes to officer promotions, see Weigley, *History of the Army*, 291; Coffman, *Old Army*, 233.

6. Carter's time in grade is derived from known dates of rank as noted in "Military Record of Lt. Col. William H. Carter, Asst. Adjutant General," in Carter Family Papers. On the contemporary officer promotion system, see Coffman, *Old Army*, 230–34; Skelton, "Army Officer as Organization Man," 65; and Roberts, "Reform and Revitalization," 201. Abrahamson concludes that dissatisfaction with the officer promotion system became an important motivator for the period's "military reform impulse." See *America Arms*, 48–54. On Upton's views on the promotion system, see Fitzpatrick, "Misunderstood Reformer," 297.

7. Carter, *Memoirs*, 188.

8. Ibid.

9. Carter, *Memoirs*, 194. Carter was listed as one of the regular officers who might be considered for appointment as brigadier general of volunteers in case the war lasted indefinitely. See Brig. Gen. Henry C. Corbin, Adjutant General of the Army, to Maj. Gen. Nelson A. Miles, Commanding General of the Army, 21 Apr. 1898, in Henry C. Corbin Papers, Container 1-A, Manuscript Division, LOC.

10. Carter, *Memoirs*, 198.

11. Linderman discusses the media's influence on public support for the Spanish-American War in *Mirror of War*, 28. In a related vein, he explains the cultural dynamics that developed contemporary newspapers into highly influential instruments in a chapter titled "The Popular Press and the War," 149–73. Carter himself believed that the press "had done much to hasten the war with Spain." *Memoirs*, 195.

12. Carter, *Memoirs*, 201–2.

13. Brig. Gen. Henry C. Corbin to Lt. Col. T. Schwan, Lt. Col. A. L. Wagner, and Maj. W. H. Carter, 13 Apr. 1898, copy in Carter Family Papers; Schwan, Wagner, and Carter, "Memorandum for the Commanding General," 14 Apr. 1898, Doc. File 147558, RG 94, NARA. Also see Carter, *American Army*, 206–11 (includes copies of the above documents); Cosmas, *Army for Empire*, 99; and Brereton, *Educating the Army*, 73–75.

14. For details of the debate surrounding legislation for an expeditionary army, see Cosmas, *Army for Empire*, 89–102; "From Order to Chaos," 105–21; and "Military Reform," 13. On the feelings of localism that influenced mobilization, see Linderman, *Mirror of War*, 60–75, 148–49; and Cooper, *National Guard*, 100–101.

15. Carter, *General Staff*, 1; Weigley, *Towards an American Army*, 148. On the war's woeful execution, see Cosmas, *Army for Empire*; Weigley, *History of the Army*, 300–306; and Millet and Maslowski, *Common Defense*, 301–3. Many specific incidents of staff failure during the Spanish-American War are related by Lt. John H. Parker in "Our Army Supply Departments," 686–95. Parker's article gives modern readers great insight into line officers' frustrations with the contemporary staff system.

16. Carter, *Memoirs*, 204. Carter had been promoted to lieutenant colo-

nel on 18 May 1898—see RG 94, ACP 1878, William H. Carter, NARA. On the Dodge Commission, see Weigley, *History of the Army*, 310–11.

17. Carter, "Army Reorganization," 113.

18. Ibid., 114. The Burnside Committee was an early attempt to review American military policy from the ground up. In 1878, this investigation, conducted by a joint committee chaired by former Union General Ambrose E. Burnside, received strong professionalist input, but the resulting seventy-page bill was an unwieldy compromise that was summarily defeated. Almost twenty-five years later, Carter and Root purposely sought to avoid pursuing such broad-based legislation, fearing that it would attract opposition on both political and ideological grounds. On the Burnside Committee, see Fitz-patrick, "Misunderstood Reformer," 356–77.

19. Graham Cosmas cites Corbin's influence over the War Department as an obstacle to any sort of far-reaching reform in "Military Reform," 13. On the McClellan bill and its proposal for combined staff functions, see 14.

20. Quoted in ibid., 15. My brief paragraph on this topic is a very simple description of what was in actuality a very complex political stage. For analysis of contemporary partisan struggles, see Hofstadter, *Age of Reform*, 85–93, 272–75.

21. Carter, "Army Reorganization," 113.

22. Cosmas, "Military Reform," 17; Carter, *Memoirs*, 239. Carter maintains that he and Schwan helped write the compromise bill of 2 Mar. 1899 in *General Staff*, 4. Also see *Memoirs*, 238–39, and "Memorandum for Col. Sanger, Acting Secretary of War," in Doc. File 311224, RG 94, NARA. (Although undated, this last document was clearly written during the latter part of summer 1903, as surmised from an attached handwritten memorandum and the circumstances of its purpose.)

23. Carter, *General Staff*, 1; Root quoted in Jessup, *Elihu Root*, vol. 1, 215.

24. Leopold describes Root's attitude toward social issues in *Elihu Root*, 20. For analysis of Root's unspoken mandate, see 24–26. Jessup's earlier biography draws similar conclusions concerning Root's appointment—see his *Elihu Root*, vol. 1, 215–22.

25. Carter, "Elihu Root," 110. Root claimed to have accepted the appointment only with McKinley's assurance that no military expertise was expected of him. Instead, the president was more interested in his legal mind and administrative talents—quoted in Jessup, *Elihu Root*, vol. 1, 215. Also see Leopold, *Elihu Root*, 24–25; Millis, *Arms and Men*, 173; and Cater, "Evolution of General Staff," Harold D. Cater Papers, CMH, 48–50.

26. Carter, *General Staff*, 1.

27. Secretary of War's Annual Report, 1899, 56th Congress, 1st sess., Doc. No. 2, Washington, D.C.: GPO, 1899, 46. Hereafter cited as Secretary's Annual Report with the year of publication.

28. Secretary's Annual Report, 1899, 45–46.

29. An example of growing support for staff reform among the army line is reflected in Bingham, "Prussian Great General Staff," 666–76. Several articles of like topic followed Bingham's, appearing not only in the *Journal of the Military Institution of the United States* (*JMSIUS*) but also in other military

journals of the day. For a summary of the developing idea of an American general staff within army circles, see Cater, "Evolution of General Staff," 36–42. Roberts asserts that the general staff idea was one which, although loosely based on the German model, had, by 1898, taken on a distinctly American form through evolution of Uptonian ideas. "Loyalty and Expertise," 214–17.

30. Carter, *General Staff*, 2.

31. Secretary's Annual Report, 1899, 46.

32. Grace I. Palmer, Carter's secretary during the reform period, said years later that Carter's "first meeting with Root may well have been due to the fact that Root had heard about him and took the initiative himself by coming to the TAG's [adjutant general's] office to see him. . . . Root knew nothing about the army and needed a man like Carter to help him." From a summary transcript of Harold D. Cater's "Telephone Conversation with Mrs. Grace I. Palmer," in Cater Papers, MHI. (Note: The date on this transcript is 3 Dec. 1917, but other material and the known circumstances of Cater's project demonstrate that this is undoubtedly a typographical error. The conversation more likely took place on 3 Dec. 1947, during the same period in which Cater conducted other such interviews. Only a single box of transcribed notes from Cater's interviews conducted in 1947–48 is maintained at the MHI; the balance of the Cater materials is deposited at the CMH.) Some insight into Root's public personality is given by Wellman, "Elihu Root," 35–44. Although Wellman's essay is overtly flattering to Root's leadership, his character sketch supports conclusions that Root synthesized the ideas of those around him into a coherent and more workable whole. Wellman also seconds the assumption that McKinley chose Root more for his personal attributes rather than any particular technical ability or knowledge. Harold Cater described Carter's relationship with Root as that of a "principal councilor [*sic*]" who planned and executed the secretary's more general ideas. "Evolution of General Staff," 62. This conclusion is supported by the comments of Mrs. Palmer, who told Cater that "Root depended upon Carter and seemed to have the utmost reliance in him." "Interview with Grace Palmer," Cater Papers, MHI.

33. Jessup portrays Carter as Root's able assistant and as a sort of expert alter-ego throughout the reform process, giving him credit for exposing the secretary to Upton's work and fulfilling "the roles of all the staff departments" during legislative efforts. *Elihu Root*, vol. 1, 242, 260. Carter was later instrumental in the publication of Upton's *Military Policy*—see Carter to Elihu Root, 20 Nov. 1903, Container C-32, Root Papers, LOC.

34. Weigley, "Root Reforms," 17. Robert Wiebe characterizes Root's personal variation of Progressivism as "a cautious reconstruction that paid as much attention to foundations as to improvements." *Search for Order*, 211. This description seems accurate in light of the methodical, incremental manner in which Root pursued military reform while secretary of war. Roberts questions whether Root was ever really a true subscriber to Progressive ideology at all, noting that he diverged from the movement's "mainstream" in his emphasis on the individual rather than the organization as an instrument of reform. "Loyalty and Expertise," 219–20. Weigley points out structural similarities between the Root Reforms and the Progressive's bureaucratic ap-

proach to public administration in "Root Reforms," 21–24. Like Weigley, Lane also emphasizes civilian influences in his biographical study, *Armed Progressive*—see especially pages 148–49.

35. Roberts, "Loyalty and Expertise," 220.

36. C. D. Rhodes to William H. Carter, 31 July 1923, in Carter Family Papers. Rhodes was assigned to the General Staff's Military Information Division during the Root years and was instrumental in revising Upton's *Military Policy* for publication.

37. On the relationship that existed between Root and his military subordinates, see also Roberts, "Reform and Revitalization," 207–8.

38. Barrie Zais emphasizes the cumulative effect of aggregate influences that defy any single interpretation—see especially his concluding chapter in "Twentieth-Century Army," 279–95. Zais's premise is supported by this author's study of Carter as an exemplar of the period's professionalist reformers. Carter's own motivations and influences were diverse, but the singular outcome was a career-long push for professional reform.

39. Secretary's Annual Report, 1899, 45.

40. Ibid., 49–51. Root related these proposals to his larger theme of peacetime preparedness. Although he did not use the term "general staff," his war college would be vested with many of the classic functions associated with a general staff (49). Writing a decade later, Carter observed that "there was very little definite knowledge of General Staff employment other than that of the German Army, which was adapted to a monarchical government but not entirely suited to ours." This was an accurate assertion, but it certainly did not stop contemporary army officers from exploring the possibilities of an American general staff. In 1900, the topic of the *JMSIUS* annual essay contest was "The Organization of a General Staff." It is perhaps telling that the society found none of the entries merited the award of "first prize," although three submissions were published. See the essays by Allen, Scherer, and Langdon, each entitled "The Organization of a Staff Best Adapted to the United States Army."

41. Root, Secretary's Annual Report, 1899, 46. William Roberts concludes that Root's original intentions for reform were somewhat less pervasive than the several acts that were eventually accomplished under his name. "Loyalty and Expertise," 218–21.

42. Root, *Military and Colonial Policy*, 3–4.

CHAPTER 9: EDUCATING A NEW ARMY

1. H. C. Corbin, Adjutant General of the Army, to Brig. Gen William Ludlow, 20 Feb. 1900, in Doc. File 311224, RG 94, NARA. In this memorandum, Corbin was relaying Root's conceptualization of the Board's purpose.

2. Ibid. The War College Board was formally detailed by Section 31, Army Special Orders no. 42, 19 Feb. 1900, copy in Carter Family Papers. Lt. Col. Joseph P. Sanger, a later participant, was not named to the original War College Board by Special Orders no. 42 and did not attend the meetings of 26–27 Feb. 1900. Sanger was added to the board by Section 11, Special Orders no. 145, 21 June 1900. Extract published in "Proceedings of a Board of Officers

Convened at War Department, Washington, D.C.," in Doc. File 311224, RG 94, NARA. Carter's narrative in *General Staff,* 3, supports this documentation. McAndrews inadvertently names Sanger as a member of the original board in "William Ludlow," 213. Clarification of this minor discrepancy explains Sanger's absence from the earlier February meetings. (Hereafter the War College Board Proceedings will be cited as WCB Proceedings, with date of entry.) Presumably to avoid confusion with the later "War College Board," several historians have referred to this body as the "Ludlow Board." See Weigley, *History of the Army,* 316–17; Pappas, *Prudens Futuri,* 15–20; and Ball, *Of Responsible Command,"* 61–65. Carter refers to it as the "War College Board" in "Memorandum for the Secretary of War," 14 Oct. 1901, in *General Staff,* 10.

     3. Upton, *Armies of Asia and Europe,* 219. Upton describes the "War Academy, Berlin" on 213–18, and delineates its desirable purpose on p. 319. Also see Fitzpatrick, "Misunderstood Reformer," 278; and Pappas, *Prudens Futuri,* 8–10.

     4. Wagner, "American War College," 288–89; Pettit, "Proper Military Instruction," 36. Also see Allen, "Proposed Reorganization," 26–30. The above works are merely representative of a genre of contemporary literature that refers to or discusses the American staff structure. Many of these writers addressed the need for far-reaching reforms in the manner of a general staff or a similarly functioning body. In addition to *JMSIUS, The United Service,* the *Army and Navy Journal,* and the *Army-Navy Register* are excellent primary resources for further research on the topic.

     5. William H. Carter, "Memorandum: Subject-War College," submitted to the War College Board, 8 July 1900, in Doc. File 311224, RG 94, NARA.

     6. Ibid.

     7. Carter, *Memoirs,* 225.

     8. Carter, "Memorandum—War College"; WCB Proceedings, 8 July 1900. On scholarly debate over Root's original concept of a war college, see Wainwright, "Root Versus Bliss," and also Pappas, *Prudens Futuri.* Wainwright specifically arbitrates this discussion, and accurately concludes that Root proposed a war college with general staff-like roles as merely a first iteration in the struggle for an independent general staff. He faults Tasker Bliss for redirecting the War College from Root's intended educational purpose during its early years, giving rise to institutional confusion in its first decade of life. For Harold Cater's analysis of Carter's conceptual evolution of the general staff problem, see "Evolution of the General Staff," Harold D. Cater Papers, CMH, 66–68.

     9. In addition to the subjects assigned to Carter for study, Hasbrouck was tasked with studying "the formation of a volunteer reserve" and the further training of National Guard organizations, and Sanger was to report on the status of military education at colleges, universities, and the several National Guard schools. "Proceedings," 8 July 1900. Ludlow left for Germany on 11 July on AGO orders dated 3 July 1900. In Doc. File 311224, RG 94, NARA (copied into the record of "Proceedings," 8 July 1900). Also see McAndrews, "William Ludlow," 215–16.

10. Ibid., 215.

11. William H. Carter, "Memorandum on Service Schools," no date, in Doc. File 507114, located in "Box 59, Room 30," RG 94, NARA.

12. Ibid.

13. Ibid.

14. The Naval War College was established on 6 Oct. 1884 by Secretary of the Navy William E. Chandler through Department of the Navy General Order no. 325. Copy in Doc. File 507114, in "Box 59, Room 30," RG 94, NARA. For a brief summary of the Naval War College's founding, see Millett and Maslowski, *Common Defense*, 274–74; and for an in-depth history of its institutional development as part of the emergent American naval profession, see Spector, *Professors of War*. See Luce, *Life and Letters*.

15. William H. Carter, "Report on Naval War College," submitted to War College Board as appendix to "Memorandum on Service Schools." Carter was sent to the Naval War College as a War Department representative in response to an invitation from Frank W. Hackett, assistant secretary of the navy, 7 May 1900—in Doc. File 507114, "Box 59, Room 30," RG 94, NARA. Attached to Hackett's invitation is a "Memorandum as to Course for 1900," which provides valuable insight into the Naval War College's early curriculum.

16. The friendship between Root and Carter is supported by correspondence between the two that lasted until near Carter's death. Carter refers to taking "customary" horseback rides with Root in *Memoirs*, 229, and also in a six-page note (30 Apr. 1903) that he attached to a letter sent to him by Gen. Adna Chaffee, 28 Apr. 1903. See Carter Family Papers. Philip Jessup seconds this characterization with his own description of Carter's role in the Root War Department. *Elihu Root*, vol. 1 225–26, 260.

17. Carter, *Memoirs*, 229.

18. Carter, *Memoirs*, 229, 238; Carter, *General Staff*, 4. The many responses to Root's 24 July 1900 request for input are maintained in Doc. File 335338, RG 94, NARA. Perhaps the best of these is the report written by Theodore Schwan, Carter's former colleague in the AGO. Schwan's thirty-eight-page reply covers a variety of topics and points out many possible pitfalls to reform ideas that were then currently popular within the army.

19. Brig. Gen. William Ludlow to Adjutant General of the Army, 31 Oct. 1900, in Doc. File 311224, RG 94, NARA.

20. Ibid.

21. Ibid. See attached "Memorandum as Basis for an Executive Order Establishing an Army War College."

22. Documentation of Ludlow's trip to Germany and the ensuing controversy over his formal report is maintained in Doc. File 311224, RG 94, NARA. In a letter written to the adjutant general from Berlin, Ludlow reported that he was scheduled to meet with the chief of the Prussian general staff on the next day, and made it clear that he intended to produce a record of his observations. Ludlow to Adjutant General of the Army, 29 July 1900.

23. See Admiral Nicoll Ludlow to Secretary of War Elihu Root, 1 June 1902, Doc. File 311224, RG 94, NARA. In this letter, Admiral Ludlow im-

plicitly questioned Carter's honor when he stated that "I very much fear that these reports are not regarded with particular favor by certain army officers— especially by those engaged on the present reorganization bill."

24. William H. Carter to Col. Joseph P. Sanger, Acting Secretary of War, 27 Aug. 1903, in Doc. File 311224, RG 94, NARA. Few copies of Ludlow's report still exist in the public domain. This author used what is maintained in the Harold Cater Papers, CMH.

25. Carter to Sanger, 27 Aug. 1903. When the "Corbin copy" of Ludlow's report was given to him, Carter (with Nicoll Ludlow's inquiry in mind) realized the need to address any appearance of impropriety and attached an explanatory memorandum. This memo is helpful in recreating the circumstances of the "Ludlow Report's" disposition. See William H. Carter, "Memorandum," 25 June 1902, Doc. File 311224, RG 94, NARA.

26. "Interview with Maj. Gen. Frank R. McCoy," 15 Oct. 1947, in Cater Papers, CMH. Harold Cater's summary of the episode largely parallels conclusions drawn by this author. Claims by Ludlow's friends and family were unfounded inasmuch as the conceptualization of a general staff was not intellectual property and Carter made no such pretenses. The original report was evidently misplaced, and it had no apparent influence on the 1903 General Staff Act beyond that which Ludlow himself exerted during the October 1900 meetings of the War College Board. With so many active participants (such as Lt. Halsteed Dorey, Ludlow's aide; a Mr. Baker, Ludlow's civilian clerk; and Henry C. Corbin) still living and able to refute his own version, it would have been self-defeating for Carter to concoct the story that he relayed to Sanger in his own defense. Also on this controversy, see Roberts, "Loyalty and Expertise," 233–34; and McAndrews, "William Ludlow," 221–24. McAndrews presents the Ludlow family's version of events, but fails to reconcile this portrayal with Carter's plausible explanation. Though it is true, as McAndrews claims, that Ludlow is due "some credit for the establishment of the General Staff," it is not because of any action on Carter's part that he did not receive such credit. McAndrews's comment that "the Ludlow family was to dispute Carter's claim-to-fame as sole author of the General Staff when Congress made it a reality" is sharply skewed in its implication. Carter readily admitted that the concept of an American general staff was well known within the army. To have claimed otherwise in the face of so much existing literature would have been, as Carter put it in his letter to Sanger (27 Aug. 1903), "the height of absurdity." In articles such as "General Staff Corps" and "General Staff for the Army," Carter applauded the popularity of the general staff concept among the Regular Army's line officers. If Carter has a "claim to fame," it is not as the idea's originator, but as its champion.

27. Carter, General Staff, 4; Carter to Elihu Root, 9 Nov. 1900, Elihu Root Papers, Container C-7, Manuscript Division, LOC. Roberts, "Loyalty and Expertise," 223–25.

28. Cater, "Evolution of General Staff," 80.

29. Carter, Memoirs, 239–38.

30. Carter, Memoirs, 240; Weigley, Towards an American Army, 125–26, 146–61. Weigley emphasizes that an air of pessimism pervaded the Uptonian outlook during the late-nineteenth and early-twentieth centuries.

31. Carter, *Memoirs*, 244.

32. William H. Carter to James H. Wilson, 19 May 1915, in James H. Wilson Papers, Manuscript Division, LOC. Also see Carter, *Memoirs*, 244–45. Carter appeared with Root before the House Committee on Military Affairs, 14 April 1900—see Hearing before the Committee on Military Affairs of the House of Representatives on Senate Bill 4300, transcript copy in Henry Corbin Papers, Container 8, Manuscript Division, LOC.

33. "An Act to Increase the Efficiency of the Permanent Military Establishment of the United States," 56th Congress, 2nd sess., 2 Feb. 1901, copy in Doc. File 335338, RG 94, NARA (hereafter cited as the 1901 Army Reorganization Act.) The bill increased the number of regular infantry regiments from twenty-five to thirty; the number of regular cavalry regiments from ten to fifteen; reorganized the regular artillery as a "corps" that consisted of thirty field artillery batteries and 126 coast artillery companies; and also provided for a regiment of Philippine Scouts and a Puerto Rican regiment. Other particulars of the measure clearly addressed the executive ability to support American foreign policy in the Philippine Islands. Quotation is taken from Col. Joseph P. Sanger to Elihu Root, 2 June 1901, Elihu Root Papers, Container C-22, Manuscript Division, LOC. Weigley summarizes the Reorganization Act in *History of the Army*, 317–18, and Roberts notes it as a minor victory of line over staff in "Loyalty and Expertise," 226.

34. Carter, "Training of Army Officers," 337–42.

35. Sections 26 and 27 of the 1901 Army Reorganization Act pertain to the rotation between staff and line. Upton suggested the rotation of staff and line in *Armies of Asia and Europe*, 324–25. In 1878, James A. Garfield, then a Republican congressman, was familiar with Upton's work and addressed the concept in the second installment of a two-part article, "Army of the United States." Garfield's proposals are analyzed by Fitzpatrick, "Misunderstood Reformer," 350–55. The idea of line-staff rotation was also present (as noted in Chap. 8 of this study) in post–Spanish-American War legislative proposals. For further discussion of the 1901 Army Reorganization Act, see Roberts, "Loyalty and Expertise," 222–26.

36. Carter, *Memoirs*, 244. Carter describes his trip to Puerto Rico on 249–50.

37. Secretary's Annual Report, 1899, 46–47.

38. Secretary's Annual Report, 1901, 21.

39. Secretary's Annual Report, 1899, 47. Concurrent developments in civilian higher education emphasized a similar trend toward a pyramidal structure of learning—see Rudolph, *American College and University*, 334–36; and Veysey, *American University*, 171–79.

40. Corbin to Ludlow, 20 Feb. 1900.

41. Roberts, "Loyalty and Expertise," 227–28. On the War Board, see Hattaway and Jones, *How the North Won*, 102, 123–24; and more specifically, Hattaway and Jones, "The War Board, the Basis of the United States' First General Staff," *Military Affairs* 46 (Feb. 1982). On the Naval War Board, see Shulimson, *Marine Corps' Search for a Mission*, 168–69; and on Secretary Alger's short-lived "Secretary's Cabinet," see Cosmas, *Army for Empire*, 305.

42. Carter, "Recent Army Reorganization," 116–17. Carter's trip to

forts Leavenworth and Riley was made as a member of a board convened by Special Orders no. 48, 27 Feb. 1900. This board was to recommend a plan for the reconstruction of service schools that had temporarily closed due to the war with Spain. See Carter, "Greater Leavenworth," 177.

43. Carter, "Greater Leavenworth," 184, and "Army Reorganization," 117. Carter had criticized the lyceum system as early as 1894 in "Infantry and Cavalry School," 752.

44. Carter, "Memorandum for The Adjutant General, 25 May 1901," in *General Staff*, 5.

45. Carter's memorandum of 25 May 1901 (ibid.) explained his views on the need for stronger education at the post or garrison level.

46. Quotation is taken from Carter, *General Staff*, 5. For specifics of the proposed garrison schools, see "Memorandum No. 1" on 6–7.

47. Ibid.

48. Ibid., 8.

49. Ibid.

50. Carter, *Memoirs*, 260; Carter, "Memorandum for the Secretary of War," 14 Oct. 1901, in *General Staff*, 10; and Semsch, "Elihu Root and the General Staff," 20.

51. Ibid.

52. General Orders no. 155, War Department, 27 Nov. 1901. Copies of this order appear in several contemporary documents; the most accessible are Carter's *General Staff* (11–14) and the Secretary of War's Annual Report for 1901 (Appendix A). In the Secretary of War's Annual Report for 1902, Root refers readers to the 1901 appendix as a valid copy of General Orders no. 155.

53. General Orders no. 155, in *General Staff*, 11.

54. Ibid. Nenninger maintains that the several branch schools—the Artillery School at Fort Monroe, the Cavalry and Light Artillery School at Fort Riley, the Engineer School of Application in Washington, D.C., and the School for Submarine Defense at Fort Totten, New York—existed on an organizational level wholly separate from the new General Service and Staff College. Although the branch schools' curricula sometimes overlapped that of Leavenworth, graduates could still be selected to attend the Staff College. This particular intention is not clear from Carter's language in General Orders no. 155, and the specific relationship between the branch schools and the Staff College lacks definition. See Nenninger, *Leavenworth Schools*, 58; and also Secretary's Annual Report, 1901, 23. It should be noted that grandiose plans for a progressive curriculum were stymied in the years immediately following General Orders no. 155 by the poor level of preparation among students. Instruction at Leavenworth devolved into little more than a tactical review instead of the staff and command subjects envisioned by Root and Carter.

55. Pappas, *Prudens Futuri*, 21.

56. Carter, "Training of Army Officers," 341–42.

57. General Orders no. 155.

58. Root, Secretary's Annual Report, 1901, 25; Carter, "Evolution of General Staff," 61.

59. Carter, "Training of Army Officers," 340; Abrahamson, *America Arms*, 42.

60. Carter, "Training of Army Officers," 339–40.

61. The quotation is a combination of excerpts from Carter, *Memoirs*, 260, and "Training of Army Officers," 342.

CHAPTER 10: CREATING A GENERAL STAFF

1. Carter, "Memorandum no. 1," in *General Staff*, 8.

2. See Skelton, "Commanding General and the Problem of Command," and also Weigley, *History of the Army*, 192–94, 284–90.

3. Roberts, "Loyalty and Expertise," 218. Winfield Scott twice established a sort of self-exiled headquarters in New York, and Sherman later moved his office to St. Louis—see Weigley, *History of the Army*, 193, 286–87. Carter was aware of the difficult history between the commanding general and the executive branch of government. For example, see Carter, *American Army*, 184–204, and "A General Staff," 558–65.

4. Carter, *Memoirs*, 261. Senator Cockrell brought up the possibility of restructuring the office of command general during initial conversations with Carter concerning the general staff bill—see 261–62.

5. Weigley, *History of the Army*, 289–90; Millett and Maslowski, *Common Defense*, 286–87; Bernardo and Bacon, *American Military Policy*, 285; Semsch, "Root and the General Staff," 21–22. Harold Carter points out that Carter did not originate the chief of staff idea, although in a memorandum written to Sanger (no date, presumed 1903) he made what seem to be exaggerated claims to this effect. "Evolution of General Staff," 66n2. Carter again makes this claim in his memoirs, stating that "no one had ever presumed before to suggest abolition of the high office, but I was cognizant of so many untoward incidents connected with it that I felt justified in undertaking the long uphill fight before us." *Memoirs*, 262. This author can only conclude that Carter truly did not realize, or at least did not remember, that the notion of replacing the commanding general with a chief of staff had been heard decades before his own attempt. To have maintained such a lofty pretense in the face of generally available evidence otherwise would have been foolish and clearly without reward on his part. This conclusion is borne out by Carter's otherwise sound predilection for avoiding bombastic claims in the voluminous amount of other public material that he left.

6. Semsch, "Root and the General Staff," 21; Root quoted in Jessup, *Elihu Root*, vol. 1, 244. On Miles's conception of the office of commanding general, see Cosmas, *Army for Empire*, 62, and on his running conflict with Secretary Alger, see 144–46, 284–94, 310, and Wooster, *Nelson A. Miles*, 214–31. Jessup chronicles Miles's difficulties with Root in *Elihu Root*, vol. 1, 244–51.

7. Root, Secretary's Annual Report, 1899, 46–47; and Root, Secretary's Annual Report, 1901, 25; Semsch, "Root and the General Staff," 19; and Carter, "Memorandum for the Secretary," 14 Oct. 1901.

8. General Orders no. 64, sec. 2, Adjutant General's Office, 1 July 1902.

The board was also joined by the four ex-officio members stipulated in General Orders No. 155, sec. 4. Although Carter was not promoted to brigadier general until 15 July 1902, (see note 27 of this chapter), the orders assumed his new rank. Carter had been listed as the "principal assistant adjutant general" in charge of the A.C.P Division, Returns Division, and Records Division in an AGO Memorandum of 5 Oct. 1901, W.C.D. 639–12, RG 165, NARA.

9. Carter, *Memoirs*, 258. Almost a decade later, after beginning to keep a diary for the first time since leaving West Point, Carter stated that he regretted not having done so earlier, "during the very busy days of my career since I left the cavalry and active line duty." Carter Diary, 1 Jan. 1913 (in "Memoranda" at back of 1912 Diary).

10. Carter, *Memoirs*, 268; Semsch, "Root and the General Staff," 20–21; Jessup, *Elihu Root*, vol. 1, 254. Leopold saw Root's relationship with Roosevelt as a seamless transition from the one he enjoyed with McKinley, even using the term "McKinley-Roosevelt-Root" to describe their defense policies. *Elihu Root*, 42–43.

11. Carter, undated memorandum, in *General Staff*, 17.

12. Ibid., 16.

13. On 14 Feb. 1902, the first general staff bill was introduced in both houses as HR 11350, 57th Congress, 1st sess.; and Senate 3917, 57th Congress, 1st sess., respectively. A copy of these identical bills is reprinted in Carter, *General Staff*, 22–25. On Root's support for the consolidation of the several departments into a Department of Supply, see Roberts, "Loyalty and Expertise," 241.

14. Quotation in Semsch, "Root and the General Staff," 21. Section Seven of the bill specifically addressed Miles's role in the reformed system. Carter, *General Staff*, 23–24.

15. Quoted in Cater, "Evolution of General Staff," Cater Papers, CMH, 74.

16. Quoted in Roberts, "Loyalty and Expertise," 244–45; Gen. Nelson Miles's testimony is excerpted in Carter, *General Staff*, 31–32.

17. Quotations in Carter, *Memoirs*, 262. Also see Carter, *General Staff*, 35, and Cater, "Evolution of General Staff," Cater Papers, CMH, 73.

18. Carter, *General Staff*, 36; Cater, "Evolution of General Staff," Cater Papers, CMH, 75–76. In a later interview with historian Harold Cater, Maj. Gen. Dennis Nolan, an early member of the general staff, maintained that it was Gen. Tasker H. Bliss, then Schofield's aide, who "persuaded Schofield to go before Congress and represent the most distinguished Army opinion at that time." See Cater's notes in "Interview with Maj. Gen. Dennis E. Nolan," 14 Nov. 1947, in Cater Papers, MHI. Root directed Carter to accompany Schofield before the committee—see Root to Sen. Joseph Hawley, Chairman of the Committee on Military Affairs, 9 Apr. 1902, in Carter, *General Staff*, 36. Letters of support were introduced from generals George W. Davis and Samuel B. M. Young, and are excerpted in *General Staff*, 36–43. Carter's analysis of efforts to dilute Miles's testimony, written with ill-concealed satisfaction, is found on 43.

19. Carter, "Memorandum for Col. Sanger," 27 Aug. 1903. In *Military Policy of the United States*, Upton presented a very biased interpretation of

America's military ineptitude as historical support for his policy proposals. Carter was familiar with Upton's work, and apparently was influenced by his methodology as well as content. See "Will America Profit by Her Recent Military Lessons?" 658–70. On the battle waged for public support in the day's media, see Semsch, "Root and the General Staff," 22–23.

20. Carter, "Recent Military Lessons," 671.

21. Ibid.

22. Carter, "Recent Army Reorganization," 120. Carter's "General Staff for the Army" was followed by a second, similar article that was clearly intended for the military reading audience. In "General Staff Corps," 677–81, he attempted to build support within the army just as the general staff act was approaching a floor vote. In crafting these essays, Carter demonstrated a keen appreciation for American cultural peculiarities. Each article was carefully nuanced to appeal to a very specific audience. He presented the *North American Review* essay in a context of progressive middle-class values—arguing the greater efficiency of a military system that benefits from a general staff. The second article relies on a more direct appeal to his military peers, couched in arguments befitting *The United Service*'s professional readership.

23. Carter, "General Staff for the Army," 561. Carter also directly refutes the opposition's charges of German mimicry in "General Staff Corps," 679.

24. Carter, "Training of Army Officers," 338, 340, 342.

25. Carter, "General Staff for the Army," 563.

26. This analysis is based on his discussion in the several memorandums found in *General Staff*, as well as the three articles he wrote during the spring and summer of 1902. See especially "General Staff for the Army."

27. See oaths of office and service summary, ACP 1878, William H. Carter, RG94, NARA. In this same file, see General Orders no. 84, 22 July 1902, and supporting Elihu Root memorandums appointing Carter as acting adjutant general from 22 July 1902 until 1 Nov. 1902. For Carter's own account of his promotion, see *Memoirs*, 269–270.

28. Minutes of the War College Board, 5 Nov. 1902, in RG 165, NARA; Minutes of the War College Board, 17 Nov. 1902, in RG 165, NARA. The board noted that "few post schools will voluntarily assume the study of Spanish," but recommended the books be purchased, anyway, providing that the officer in charge of the school report back on the success of the proposed instruction. The Gettysburg relief maps were not purchased, although the board assured the anxious solicitor that his handiwork was impressive. The WCB met on ten different occasions during its first six months of existence, July 1902–Dec. 1902, and then began meeting with greater regularity as work on the General Staff's implementation accelerated in early 1903. See Minutes of the War College Board, passim.

29. For Root's description of the WCB's consideration of expeditionary force requirements as exemplary of general staff work, see "Efficiency of the Army," Testimony before the Senate Committee on Military Affairs, 57th Cong., 2nd sess., in *Establishment of a General Staff Corps in the Army*, Washington, D.C., Government Printing Office, 1902, 53–54. (Here

after cited as *Establishment of a General Staff.*) Also on this topic, see Ball, *Of Responsible Command*, 73–74.

30. Secretary of War's Annual Report, 1902, 42–43.

31. Ibid., 44.

32. Carter, *General Staff*, 43, 50; Cater, "Evolution of General Staff," Cater Papers, CMH, 76. The bill contained a proviso that it "shall take effect on the 10th day of August, 1903." The second general staff bill, as it was submitted to committee during the second congressional session in December 1902, is printed in *Establishment of General Staff*, 31–32. The major change made to the second bill is that it did not address the consolidation of the several supply departments. Other sections that originally appeared in the bill of 14 Feb. 1902 were also left out of the second bill, but were not of issue to the proposed general staff. Such miscellaneous topics included examinations for noncommissioned officers, number of electrician sergeants in the army, public sale of surplus army goods, regulations regarding the disbursement of funds, number of surgeons on duty in the Philippine Islands, etc. See Senate Bill 3917 in Carter, *General Staff*, 22–25.

33. See "Statement of Hon. Elihu Root, Secretary of War," Testimony before the House Committee on Military Affairs, 57th Cong., 2nd sess., in *Establishment of General Staff*, 14.

34. Carter, *General Staff*, 43. Maj. Gen. Dennis E. Nolan, one of the early participants on the first American General Staff, noted in an interview with Cater that many of the current congressmen were former Civil War soldiers who had little but contempt for the new generation's intellectual approach to military affairs. According to Nolan, their traditionalist ideas about "soldiering" often hampered reform efforts in the postwar era. See Cater, "Interview with Maj. Gen. Dennis E. Nolan," 19 Mar. 1948, in Cater Papers, MHI. (This is the second of two interviews that Cater conducted with Nolan.)

35. Section 4 of "A Bill to Increase the Efficiency of the Army," in *Establishment of a General Staff*, 31.

36. On the chief of staff's "supervisory" relationship with subordinates, see Section 4 of "A Bill to Increase the Efficiency of the Army," in *Establishment of a General Staff*, 31. Lane implies that the use of the term "supervision" to describe the chief of staff's role grew from parallels with contemporary corporate structures whose executives ideally managed only through authority vested in others. See *Armed Progressive*, 148–49.

37. Carter interjected only once during Root's testimony, clarifying a minor point regarding the AGO's issuance of formal orders. *Establishment of a General Staff*, 45. For further characterization of Root's testimony, see Cater, "Evolution of General Staff," Cater Papers, CMH, 77.

38. Carter, "Memorandum for Secretary of War," 27 Dec. 1902, *General Staff*, 44.

39. Carter, *General Staff*, 43–44.

40. Quoted in Cater, "Evolution of General Staff," Cater Papers, CMH, 78; Root's "Testimony before the Senate Committee," in *Establishment of General Staff*, 39. Cater points out that Root later rid himself of Breckinridge by arranging for his promotion with the understanding that he apply for im-

mediate retirement—this ploy secured the desired result and thus removed a prime dissenter from Root's War Department. "Evolution of General Staff," Cater Papers, CMH, 79.

41. Carter, *General Staff*, 45. Carter compares the bill's language as it appeared before and after the various modifications on 45–46.

42. Carter, *General Staff*, 46; Cater, "Evolution of General Staff," Cater Papers, CMH, 79; Cater, "Interview with Maj. Gen. Dennis E. Nolan," 14 Nov. 1948, in Cater Papers, MHI. Further development of the Wood-Ainsworth controversy is found in Chap. 13 of this study.

43. Carter, *General Staff*, 49. Interestingly, on 25 January 1903, Root hosted a luncheon for forty-one distinguished Washington figures, including members of the congressional military committees. It cannot be ascertained at this point whether his intention was celebratory—anticipating success in the forthcoming floor vote—or whether this luncheon was a shrewd last-minute effort to solidify support and possibly even garner a further favorable vote or two. See "List of persons who have accepted invitation of the Secretary of War to luncheon at Country club, Sunday, Jan. 25th [1903]," in Root Papers, Container 32, LOC.

44. Carter, "General Staff," MS copy, 13.

45. Carter, *General Staff*, 50.

CHAPTER 11: TRANSLATING REFORM TO REALITY

1. General Orders no. 15, Headquarters of the Army, 18 Feb. 1903; Carter, *General Staff*, 51.

2. Carter, "Memorandum for the Secretary of War," n.d., in *General Staff*, 51.

3. Ibid., 52; Carter, "General Staff Corps," 679.

4. In *Military Policy*, Upton uses historical arguments to support his assertion that the nation required greater military preparedness under professional guidance. For example, he contends that "twenty thousand regular troops at Bull Run would have routed the insurgents, settled the question of military resistance, and relieved us from the pain and suspense of four years of war." See xv and, for similar passages, 225–33. Earlier, in *Armies of Asia and Europe*, Upton had crafted a more subtle plea along similar historical lines, 321–23. By 1903, Carter himself viewed the nation's dismal state of preparedness in 1861 as glaring evidence of the need for general staff reform and similarly criticized the extant militia and volunteer system. For representative arguments of this type, see Carter, "Recent Army Reorganization," 119, and "Infantry in War," 1–15. Carter's contemporaries addressed the topic of militia reform in a wide variety of journal articles. Of representative interest are Frazier, "National Guard National in Name Only," 518–23; and the prize-winning essays submitted by Col. Britton, Capt. Barry, and Maj. Taylor, to the *JMSIUS* in its annual (1900) writing contest, pertaining to the topic "In What Way Can the National Guard be Modified so as to Make it an Effective Reserve to the Regular Army in Both War and Peace?" Frazier's article is especially interesting in that he was the assistant adjutant general of the Illinois National Guard but took a professionalist perspective, arguing for

greater federal control and supervision over the militia in order to ensure standards of proficiency and organization.

5. Weigley, *History of the Army*, 321.

6. Carter, *Memoirs*, 258. Barrie Zais summarizes Root's views on the topic in "20th Century Army," 264; and for Carter's early thoughts on the militia, see "Army Question," 575–77.

7. Cosmas, *Army for Empire*, 11—on the Hull Bill, see 89–93. Cooper, *National Guard*, 97–99. For acerbic critique of the debate surrounding American mobilization for Cuba from a National Guard partisan, see Hill, *Minute Man*, 154–58. This Hull Bill should not be confused with a later "Hull Bill" that was introduced after the war in reaction to the U.S. military system's demonstrated shortcomings. A vast literature addresses the militia's relationship with both the regular military and American society. Excellent starting points in this broad area are Weigley, *Towards an American Army*, 1–29; Cress, *Citizens in Arms*; and Cunliffe, *Soldiers and Civilians*.

8. Cooper, *National Guard*, 98. Cooper discusses these events as a failure to compromise in a manner that served the national purpose, 97–101.

9. Carter, *Recent Military Lessons*, 662.

10. Carter, *Memoirs*, 258; Jessup, *Elihu Root*, vol. 1, 266. Carter and Root worked together on the draft at Root's home on 18–19 January 1902. Historians have accurately maintained that Root sympathized with the professionalist position but lacked the political clout to pass legislation without compromise. See Zais, "20th Century Army," 266–71; and Weigley, *History of the Army*, 320. Zais notes (272n1) a minor historiographical "debate" on the exact nature of Root's evolving views on the militia and reserve issue. Under mounting pressure from strong opposition, Root abandoned any ideas of forging a completely federal reserve force such as that envisioned by Carter and other Uptonians. As Cooper concludes, "Root could not have ignored the National Guard even had that been his inclination." *National Guard*, 108.

11. Weigley characterizes Dick as a "principal liaison" in *History of the Army*, 321. The states maintained authority to appoint Guard and militia officers, a practice that Uptonian-minded professionals found galling as an assault on their own expertise.

12. Zais, "20th Century Army," 272.

13. See Carter to Root, 30 Oct. 1903, in *General Staff*, 58. Carter specifically credited Upton's *Military Policy* (which he was then reading in manuscript form) for encouraging his ideas for further militia reorganization. Particulars of the Militia Act of 1903 are found in Cooper, *National Guard*, 108–12; and Weigley, *History of the Army*, 321–22.

14. Elihu Root, "Address at the Laying of the Corner Stone, Washington, D.C., February 21, 1903," in *Military and Colonial Policy*, 123. Also see Ball, *Of Responsible Command*, 79; and Pappas, *Prudens Futuri*, 28–30.

15. Root's tasking was delineated in a "Memorandum for the War College Board," 18 Oct. 1902. This memorandum was read into the Senate committee records and printed in *Establishment of a General Staff*, 53–54. Carter's work on the project continued throughout the spring of 1903—see "WCB Minutes," 55, 57. Lesser projects that fell specifically to Carter during this period included serving on subcommittees (sometimes consisting of only a

single member) that reviewed and approved textbook purchases for Leaven-worth's fledgling General Service and Staff School, revising General Orders no. 102 concerning the particulars of the garrison schools, and studying and revising planned construction at various posts. "WCB Minutes," passim. Harry P. Ball notes that Root's project forecast modern practices of deliberate planning, in *Of Responsible Command*, 74.

16. Elihu Root,"Memorandum for War College Board," 18 Feb. 1903, in "Report of the War College Board made pursuant to the following instruc-tions," 9 Mar. 1903, WCD 639, RG 165, NARA (hereafter cited as WCB Re-port–9 Mar 1903). Root's memorandum and this report are also reproduced in Carter, *General Staff*, 52–54. This letter and the drafts of two proposed gen-eral orders were read into the WCB's minutes a few days later on 12 March. "WCB Minutes," 82–95. The WCB discussed the general staff issue as an ongoing project; for example, see "WCB Minutes," 63–82, passim. Various suggestions and models for the general staff's organization were considered by the WCB. Some of these are maintained in AWC 521, E288, RG 165, NARA. Reference to these suggestions, which were reviewed by each mem-ber in turn, is found in "WCB Minutes," 65. Several reports and memoranda are present, but most are unsigned and otherwise gave little indication of their authorship. That Carter was the final report's primary author is self-evident from an existing draft copy of like verbiage that is partially handwrit-ten (in Carter's hand) and bears his signature. "Memorandum giving views of the War College Board," 24 Feb. 1903, AWC 521, E288, RG 165, NARA. This draft appeared in final copy as "WCB Report–9 Mar 1903."

17. "WCB Minutes," 68–70. The very specific nature of these fourteen guiding "conclusions" is represented in the following example: "Ques.—Shall the War College Board recommend the establishment of the various sections or divisions of work, and prescribe a council or General Staff board; if so, shall a sub-committee be appointed to draft [a] tentative proposition? Ans.—It is believed that the Chief of Staff and the General Staff should do it."

18. Proposed general orders, attached to "WCB Report–9 Mar 1903." Organization of the Military Information Division (MID) was begun in 1885, but it was not until April 1889 that a separate division of the AGO was established for this purpose. For detailed histories of the MID's early develop-ment, see Col. Thomas Vincent, "Memorandum for the Honorable Secretary of War Relating to the Division of Military Information," 13 Oct. 1896, WCD 639, RG 165, NARA; and Lt. Carl Reichmann, "Notes on the Military Infor-mation Division for the Honorable Secretary of War," 14 Sept. 1897, WCD 639, RG 165, NARA. Both histories were written by officers with a vested interest in the MID's mission. For discussion of the MID as a professional-izing influence on the contemporary army, see Coffman, *Old Army*, 280; and Roberts, "Loyalty and Expertise," 199. Roberts cites further secondary sources on this topic.

19. Proposed general orders, attached to "WCB Report–9 Mar 1903."

20. In proposed general orders, "WCB Report–9 Mar 1903." The above-quoted "functions" are paraphrased and complete only insofar as necessary to impart their meaning.

21. Secretary's Annual Report, 1902, 43–46.

22. General Orders no. 35, Headquarters of the Army, 29 Mar. 1903, copy in Carter Family Papers; Carter, *General Staff,* 54.

23. Carter, *Memoirs,* 273; General Orders no. 57, Headquarters of the Army, 17 April 1903. Junior members of this first general staff included Capt. John J. "Blackjack" Pershing and Capt. Peyton C. March, both of whom assumed senior leadership of the U.S. effort during the First World War. Those officers who reported to Washington before 15 August under instruction of General Orders no. 57 were tasked (along with the WCB) to design and report on a proper organization for the general staff and also to undertake "such other matters as shall be referred to them from time to time prior to the 15th of August, 1903." See General Orders no. 69, Headquarters of the Army, 9 May 1903, copy in AWC 521, E288, RG 165, NARA.

24. It is apparent that, much as any professional rationalizes his actions in terms of a client's needs, Carter had come to see himself—and especially his reform actions—as serving the nation and the army. Thus, what might seem as self-serving acts, consciously intended to garner public accolades for personal gain, were actually wrapped up in a professional self-imagery that refused to admit or acknowledge more selfish concerns. This "client orientation" is a common theme in the literature surrounding the development of professionalism. See Huntington, who discusses the professional-client relationship in *Soldier and the State,* 9. Also, Bledstein asserts that a professional's responsibility to clientele—normally society as a whole—transcends, at least outwardly, exclusive self-interest. *Culture of Professionalism,* 89. Notice that this characteristic is an important facet of a profession's *self-imagery*—the way that members *prefer* to view themselves rather than the manner in which the profession actually functions or is perceived by society.

25. Carter, "War Department," 664, 665, 673.

26. Carter, "War Department," 673. Carter used similar corporate-oriented language to argue the merits of a general staff in "General Staff Corps," 680.

27. Abrahamson, *American Arms,* 105–6.

28. Chambers, *Tyranny of Change,* 134. Although there is little modern consensus on the exact definition of Progressivism or its ideology, military reformers espoused values that have largely become associated with Progressive thought and action, even if they lacked the social awareness that often defined their civilian counterparts. Also see Karsten, "Armed Progressives," passim; Abrahamson, *America Arms,* 105–27; and Roberts, "Loyalty and Expertise," 219–20. Roberts observes that, although it was the army reformers' intention to overcome the bureaucratic "red-tape" which had grown as a by-product of the War Department's disjointed efforts, the reforms they instituted actually had the opposite and unintended effect of increasing army bureaucratization—see Roberts, 265–66.

29. Carter, "Next Head of the Army," 810–11.

30. Carter, *Memoirs,* 273. The language relieving Carter from the general staff stipulated that he would proceed to the Philippine Islands only "at such time as it shall seem advisable in the discretion of the Secretary of War." General Orders no. 88, Headquarters of the Army, 20 June 1903,

copy in AWC 521, E288, RG 165, NARA. Root traveled to England that summer as part of the Alaska Boundary Commission. See Jessup, *Elihu Root,* vol. 1, 392–401.

31. Untitled memorandum by Maj. Gen. S. B. M. Young appointing a committee to consider and report on the provisional organization of the General Staff, 13 May 1903, AWC 521, E288, RG 165, NARA. This committee was dissolved by General Orders no. 74, Headquarters of the Army, 16 May 1903, copy in AWC 521, E288, RG 165, NARA. The Bliss Committee organized the General Staff into three functional subdivisions.

32. Carter to Secretary of War Elihu Root, 3 Oct. 1903, Container C-32, Elihu Root Papers, LOC; Carter, *General Staff,* 55; General Orders no. 2, War Department, 15 Aug. 1903. Referring to the coastal defense review, Carter announced to Root that he was engaged in "what I shall make my last General Staff study before leaving for Manila and trust to have it in shape by the time you return so you may use it in your annual report if you so wish."

33. Carter to Secretary of War Elihu Root (Through the Chief of Staff), 30 Oct. 1903, in *General Staff,* 55, 59. Root returned to Washington in mid-November. William H. Carter, "Around the World," handwritten journal, 1903–4, in Carter Family Papers, 1.

34. Carter, *Memoirs,* 236.

35. Ibid., 273.

36. Ibid., 278–79; Carter, "Around the World," 2. Root in fact retired from the War Department two months later on 1 Feb. 1904. Jessup, *Elihu Root,* vol. 1, 412.

37. Secretary's Annual Report, 1903, 8.

38. Carter, *Memoirs,* 273; General Orders no. 88, 20 June 1903.

39. Carter, *Memoirs,* 276–77.

40. Linn summarizes the fundamental transformation of warfare in *Guardians of Empire,* 53.

41. Carter, "Elihu Root," 117.

CHAPTER 12: AN ARMY OF UNCERTAINTY

1. Linn, "Long Twilight," 149. Linn concludes that, although the armies of the American Frontier and the Philippines shared many characteristics, there is no evidence to suggest that "forces in the Philippines were consciously or subconsciously refighting the Indian Wars." Carter drew a similar comparison even while still in Washington. After reflecting on reports from the Philippines, he noted that "the conditions resemble those encountered at various times on the frontier when general war had to be proclaimed against all Indians off the reservations." Carter to Secretary of War Elihu Root, 21 Aug. 1902, Container C-25, Root Papers, LOC. On the Philippine Insurrection generally, see Linn, *U.S. Army and Counterinsurgency;* Gates, *Schoolbooks and Krags;* and Wolff, *Little Brown Brother.* More critical studies of U.S. involvement in the Philippines are Miller, *"Benevolent Assimilation";* and Schirmer, *Republic or Empire.* Flint places the army's involvement in the Pacific into a context of institutional modernization during the decades pre-

ceding the Second World War in "United States Army on the Pacific Frontier," 139–59.

2. Carter, *Memoirs*, 286.

3. On the violence and disorder that followed the "official" end of the Philippine Insurrection, see Linn, *Guardians of Empire*. President Theodore Roosevelt proclaimed peace in the Philippines by virtue of presidential proclamation on 4 July 1902.

4. Carter, "Around the World," 96; Linn, *Guardians of Empire*, 24. Iriye presents a provocative discussion of cultural misperceptions in "Western Perceptions and Asian Realities," 9–19.

5. Carter, "Economic Questions Affecting the Visayan Islands," 693.

6. Carter, "Economic Questions," 688–89, and "Around the World," 98–99.

7. Carter, "Report of the Department of the Visayas," 1 July 1904, in Annual Reports of the War Department for the Fiscal Year Ended June 30, 1904, 235–36. Also see Linn, *Guardians of Empire*, 26.

8. Linn notes that "the Constabulary's efforts to incorporate all Filipino forces within its ranks precluded any real possibility of forming a Fil-American colonial army, and thus became a major source of civil-military tension." *Guardians of Empire*, 19. A contemporary opinion is lodged by 1st Lt. Moseley in "Colonial Army," 242–52.

9. Endorsement of the Major General Commanding, 22 Aug. 1904, regarding letter of Henry T. Allen, Chief Philippine Constabulary, to Secretary of War, 18 Aug. 1904, Doc. File 931398, RG 94, NARA. On Henry T. Allen's role in developing the Constabulary, see Twichell, *Allen*. Specific studies of the Scouts and Constabulary are found in Woolard, "Philippine Scouts," and Coats, "Philippine Constabulary." Of related interest is Johnston, "Employment of Philippine Scouts," *JMSIUS* (Jan.–Feb. 1906): 67–77, and (Mar.–Apr. 1906): 389–98. Johnston, in command of a scout battalion, summarizes the organization's history and performance and then argues for its expansion.

10. See Linn, *Guardians of Empire*, 27–28; and Woolard, "Philippine Scouts."

11. Carter to the Military Secretary, U.S. Army, 7 Sept. 1904, Doc. File 931399 RG 94, NARA. Civil-military relations in the Department of Visayas were especially poor, boiling over during the tenure of Brig. Gen. Jacob H. Smith. See Linn, "Struggle for Samar," 173.

12. Section 36, 1901 Army Reorganization Act.

13. Carter, "Memorandum on the Organization and Employment of Philippine Scouts, U.S. Army and the Philippine Constabulary," 5 Oct 1904, Doc. File 931399, RG 94, NARA, 2–3. (Hereafter cited as "Organization of the Scouts and Constabulary.") William Johnston commented that the term "scout" had become a misnomer as companies were gradually employed in the same manner as any other infantry organization. "Philippine Scouts in War," 71.

14. Carter, "Organization of the Scouts and Constabulary," 4.

15. Ibid., 9.

16. Linn, *Guardians of Empire*, 30; Carter, "Report of the Department

of the Visayas," 1 July 1905, in Annual Reports of the War Department for the Fiscal Year Ended June 30, 1905, 286.

17. On the Pulahane movement, see Linn, *Guardians of Empire*, 30–31; and Twichell, *Allen*, 137. Although contemporaries often spelled the name "Pulajanes," the modern phonetic spelling "Pulahanes" will be used here for the purpose of consistency.

18. Carter, *Memoirs*, 319; Carter, "Report of the Department of the Visayas," 1 July 1905, 286–87; Allen quoted in Twichell, *Allen*, 140. Gen. Henry C. Corbin, commander of the Philippines Division, agreed with Carter's assessment of the Constabulary's inadequacy for the situation. See Corbin, "Report of the Philippines Division," 1 July 1905, in Annual Reports of the War Department for the Fiscal Year Ended June 30, 1905, 264. For details of Allen's unsuccessful campaign, see Twichell, *Allen*, 137–40; and Linn, *Guardians of Empire*, 31–32. Carter's "Organization of the Scouts and Constabulary" (see n. 13 above) was accompanied by a letter objecting to the Constabulary's conduct of the campaign. See Carter to the Military Secretary, 7 Sept. 1904, in Carter Family Papers.

19. Carter, "Report of the Department of the Visayas," 1 July 1905, 292. The battle in which Daguhob was killed is detailed on 288–89. Also see the 1906 "Report of the Department of Visayas," filed by Brig. Gen. James A. Buchanan, Carter's successor.

20. Carter's efforts to win back the Filipino's "hearts and minds" were by no means original or innovative. American soldiers recognized and practiced this strategy with varying results throughout the occupation of both Cuba and the Philippines. See Gates, *Schoolbooks and Krags*; Flint, "Pacific Frontier," 146; and Linn, *Guardians of Empire*, 33, 45. Linn notes (47–48) that such experiences were never translated into a coherent doctrine that might have guided a future generation of soldiers in Southeast Asia. On the suggestion that many Pulahanes held no real hatred for the Americans, see Carter, "Report of the Department of Visayas," 1 July 1905, 292; and Linn, *Guardians of Empire*, 31.

21. Carter touted his successful campaign against the Pulahanes in a letter written to Elihu Root, 21 Jan. 1908, in Carter Family Papers. Although Twichell claimed that Carter was motivated by a "personal vendetta" against Allen, this author found no evidence of such animosity. Instead, in his memoirs Carter observed that Allen was an "able, energetic officer" who was soon convinced that the Constabulary was inadequate for the campaign. See Twichell, *Allen*, 134; Carter, *Memoirs*, 319.

22. Millett and Maslowski, *Common Defense*, 318.

23. Carter, "Report of the Department of Visayas," 1 July 1905, 292.

24. Carter, "A Plea for the Filipinos," 383, 385.

25. Carter, "Memorandum on Conditions in the Visayas Islands," 30 Aug. 1904, Doc. File 935888, RG 94, NARA, 3; ibid., 5. (This memorandum was forwarded through War Department channels to the secretary of war.)

26. Grenville M. Dodge to Maj. Gen. Henry C. Corbin, 1 Mar. 1905, Container 1-A, Henry C. Corbin Papers, LOC. Dodge was quoting an unnamed friend who had written to him in opposition to the continued American presence in the Philippines. The correspondent apparently knew Carter in the

Visayas and counted him as a sort of kindred spirit in his anti-imperialist views. From the content of Dodge's letter, it seems that he mentioned the matter to Corbin with the intention of making trouble for Carter.

27. Carter, "Plea for the Filipinos," 388.

28. See Gen. Fred C. Ainsworth cablegram to Gen. Henry C. Corbin, 2 Aug. 1905, and Gen. Henry C. Corbin to the Military Secretary (Gen. Ainsworth), 4 Aug. 1905, copies of both in Carter Family Papers. Corbin reported in the second cable that Carter "has duty suppressing Pulajanes apparently well in hand and should be allowed time to complete it." The controversy surrounding Carter's reassignment to the United States is recounted in "Carter Causes Army Squabble," an unidentified newspaper clipping, 29 July 1905, in Carter Family Papers. Carter's own very important narrative of this unusual episode (oddly related in the third person) is found in "Memorandum," Chicago, 21 July 1908, in Carter Family Papers. Study of this three-page document makes it clear that Carter was very much concerned that he had been cast in a professionally negative light. It is also of interest that Chaffee wrote to Carter on 8 June 1905, and although he made no mention of Carter's prospective assignment to the General Staff, was concerned about the very "personal" nature of the selection process. See Gen. Adna Chaffee to William H. Carter, 8 June 1905, in Carter Family Papers.

29. Carter, "Memorandum," 21 July 1908.

30. Carter to Elihu Root, 28 Apr. 1908, Container C-54, Root Papers, LOC. An undated draft of this letter is maintained in the Carter Family Papers. Related content is also found in Carter to Elihu Root, 23 Mar. 1907, Container C-49, Root Papers, LOC.

31. Carter to Root, 28 Apr 1908; ibid. On the Grafton case, see Linn, *Guardians*, 27. Linn's narrative relies on the contemporary coverage given the case by the *Army and Navy Journal* during both its original proceeding and later after the conclusion of its appeal. For representative articles, see "Soldiers' Rights in the Philippines," *Army and Navy Journal* 42 (4 Feb. 1905); "The Equity of the Grafton Case," *Army and Navy Journal* 44 (23 Mar. 1907); "The Grafton Case," and "Hearing in the Grafton Case," both in ibid., and "Lessons of the Grafton Case," *Army and Navy Journal* 44 (18 June 1907).

32. Carter to Elihu Root, 5 Feb. 1906, Carter Family Papers. This letter was written shortly after Carter assumed command of the Department of the Lakes. Root's copy of this letter is found in Container C-44, Root Papers, LOC.

33. Carter to Root, 28 Apr. 1908.

34. Carter, *Memoirs*, 347.

35. Ibid. For Carter's appointment to temporary division command, see General Orders no. 70, 7 Oct. 1905, Headquarters, Philippines Division.

36. Carter, *Memoirs*, 351; Carter, "Report of the Department of the Lakes," 1 July 1906, in Annual Reports of the War Department for the fiscal Year Ended June 30, 1906, 89. When Carter assumed command, three infantry regiments were assigned to the department, but on 30 June 1906, the U.S. First Infantry was deployed to the Philippine Islands.

37. The summer camps' organization and instruction were outlined by General Orders no. 110, War Department, 18 June 1906. Exercises took place

at seven locations during the summer of 1906, each under the command of a regular general officer. Also see Carter, "National Camps of Instruction," in Comment and Criticism. On the summer exercises at Camp Benjamin Harrison, also see Carter, "Camps of Instruction," 115–21; and Carter, *Memoirs,* 354–56, 359–60.

38. King, "National Camps of Instruction," in Comment and Criticism, 367.

39. Carter, *Memoirs,* 356.

40. Carter to Elihu Root, 11 Jan. 1906, Container C-44, Root Papers, LOC.

41. Carter to Root, 23 Mar. 1907. Brian Linn found that one of the shared characteristics of the Old Army and its "new" counterpart during the twentieth century's early years was the "constant jostling for promotion, the open jealousy and factionalism, and the relentless drive for advancement"—see Linn, "Twilight of the Frontier Army," 145.

42. Carter to Elihu Root, 9 Apr. 1907, Container C-49, Root Papers, LOC.

43. Carter to Elihu Root, 1 July 1907, Container C-49, Root Papers, LOC.

44. Carter's correspondence with Root during this period makes it clear that the two remained friendly as they had during their service in the War Department. See letters cited above and also Carter to Root, 19 Aug. 1908, Container C-54, Root Papers, LOC.

45. *Old Army Sketches* contained a number of line drawings by artists such as Remington and Howard Chandler Christy. A thumbnail sketch of a mounted officer (circa 1900) on page 99 bears a remarkable resemblance to contemporary photographs of Carter. Also see the review of *Old Army Sketches* that appears in the *Army and Navy Journal,* 13 Oct. 1906.

46. Carter, "Army as a Career," 870.

47. Ibid., 870–71.

48. Ibid., 876.

49. Carter, *Memoirs,* 371–73.

50. Ibid., 373. In addition to pages 371–73 in Carter's memoirs, Leigh Hays Carter's death is recounted in several unidentified newspaper clippings maintained in the Carter Family Papers and also noted in an inscription on page 112 in the copy of *Giles Carter* in possession of the Carter family.

51. Carter to Adjutant General of the Army, 29 Aug. 1907, Doc. File 529936, RG 94, NARA; and Special Orders No. 203, 29 Aug. 1907, War Department, copy in Doc File 529936, RG 94, NARA. (Doc. File 529936 is William V. Carter's personnel file.)

52. Carter, *Giles Carter.*

53. Carter, *Memoirs,* 360–61; General Orders No. 121, Headquarters Department of the Missouri, 12 Dec. 1908; and also William H. Carter telegram to Adjutant General of the Army, 12 Dec. 1908, in Doc. File 1462478, RG 94, NARA. Lt. William V. Carter accompanied his parents to Omaha, still assigned as his father's aide, via Special Orders No. 2, Headquarters, Department of the Lakes, 5 Jan. 1909.

54. Carter, "When Diplomacy Fails," 23, 26.

55. Ibid., 25.

56. Ibid., 29–30. Statistics are taken from Carter's discussion on 31. No attempt was made by this author to determine their accuracy.

57. Cooper, *National Guard*, 112. Cooper makes it clear that, from 1908 on, regulars intended to enforce federal standards on the Guard or press forward an alternative policy in the form of a national reserve. See 112–27.

58. Carter, "When Diplomacy Fails," 32–33.

59. Ibid., 33.

CHAPTER 13: TWILIGHT ON THE TEXAS BORDER

1. Carter, *Memoirs*, 374. After assuming command of the Department of the Missouri on 12 Dec. 1908, Carter then relinquished it on 1 Feb. 1909, according to General Orders no. 10, Headquarters Department of the Missouri. Also see General Orders no. 14, War Department, 27 Jan. 1909, which formally assigned Carter to command the Department of Luzon, Philippine Islands.

2. Carter, *Memoirs*, 375; ibid., 376; General Orders no. 27, Headquarters, Department of Luzon, 6 Apr. 1909; General Orders no. 15, Headquarters, Philippines Division, 6 Apr. 1909; and Brig. Gen. Tasker H. Bliss to Adjutant General of the Army, 6 Apr. 1909. Carter held division command for two weeks until Gen. W. P. Duvall arrived to assume the position. See General Orders no. 21, Headquarters, Philippines Division, 23 Apr. 1909.

3. Adjutant General of the Army, telegram to William H. Carter, 17 Apr. 1909; and Maj. Gen. J. Franklin Bell to the Adjutant General of the Army, 16 Apr. 1909. Copies of both of these documents are maintained in the Carter Family Papers.

4. Carter, *Memoirs*, 377–79.

5. For discussion of the Scouts' deterioration as a useful native auxilliary and related implications, see Woolard, "The Philippine Scouts," 145–67.

6. Carter, "Report of the Department of Luzon," 1 July 1909, in Annual Reports of the War Department for the Fiscal Year Ended June 30, 1909, 186.

7. Maj. Gen. W. P. Duvall to the Adjutant General of the Army, 27 July 1909, Doc. File 1562346, RG 94, NARA.

8. Official correspondence on this issue is found in Maj. Gen. Fred C. Ainsworth (telegram) to Maj. Gen. W. P. Duvall, 15 Sept. 1909; Ainsworth (telegram) to Duvall, 18 Oct. 1909; and Duvall (telegram) to Ainsworth, 21 Oct. 1909. Copies of each of these telegrams are appended to Duvall's memorandum of 27 July 1909. The War Department's final response to Duvall's request is found in Doc. File 1586280, RG 94, NARA. This file consists of a summary "Memorandum for the Secretary of War," prepared by Brig. Gen. William W. Wotherspoon, Asst. to the Chief of Staff, 28 Oct. 1909 (endorsed by Maj. Gen. J. Franklin Bell, Chief of Staff, 1 Nov. 1909); and an attached memorandum dated 9 Nov. 1909 that explains the secretary's decision and directs the reports' publication as submitted. Carter was notified of assignment to the General Staff through Secretary of War J. M. Dickinson (encoded telegram) to William H. Carter, 17 Feb. 1910, in Carter Family Papers.

9. Dickinson (telegram) to Carter, 17 Feb. 1910. Dickinson's message

read: "Probability important legislation affecting U.S. Army will be presented for action of Congress during next year few." Carter's only regret in leaving Luzon was that he was forced by quarantine laws to sell "Tom Bass," a favorite gelding that he had specially selected from the army's school of equitation at Fort Riley, Kansas. He was later horrified to learn that Tom Bass had been relegated to use as a carriage horse in Manila. See Carter, *Memoirs*, 381.

10. Carter claimed later that he was aware at the time of Wood's irascible reputation. See *Memoirs*, 386–87. Carter was formally ordered to return to the United States for duty as assistant chief of staff by Special Orders no. 40, War Department, 17 Feb. 1910, and assumed the office under Special Orders no. 133, War Department, 8 June 1910.

11. Lane highlights the informal authority still wielded by the staff bureaus by virtue of their grasp on the army's daily operations in *Armed Progressive*, 156–57. For critique of the early chiefs of staff, see Powe, "Great Debate," 79–82; Weigley, *History of the Army*, 323; and Edward M. Coffman, "Sidelights on the War Department General Staff in its Early Years," commentary on Hewes, "The United States Army General Staff," 71–72. Major General Dennis E. Nolan, a contemporary observer, told Harold Cater that the General Staff's early impotence was possibly due to the fact that the first few chiefs of staff were older men who were largely appointed as an honor prior to retirement (Bates served in the capacity for only four months—January to April 1906). Nolan believed this circumstance greatly hampered the General Staff's early development. See Cater, interview with Nolan, 14 Nov. 1947, in Cater Papers, CMH.

12. Palmer's statements are quoted from "Reorganization of the Army," a transcript of testimony given before the Senate Subcommittee on Military Affairs, 10 Oct. 1919, in John McCauley Palmer Papers, Container 3, LOC. For Palmer's further opinions on military policy and his critique of Uptonian ideas, see his book *America in Arms*. Also see Weigley, *Towards an American Army*, 225–41.

13. Carter, undated "Memorandum for Secretary of War," in *General Staff*, 52.

14. Carter's own definition of the General Staff relied on the idea that it would often act as a *coordinating* medium for various other agencies and commands. For example, see Carter, *American Army*, 217, and "General Staff Corps," 678–79.

15. Parker is quoted in Zais, "Struggle for a 20th Century Army," 280n1; Cater, interview with Frank R. McCoy, 15 Oct. 1947, Cater Papers, CMH. Parker and Carter were friends and shared many views on professional issues. See Carter Diary, 11 Feb. 1912.

16. Carter to Elihu Root, 29 Aug. 1905, Container C-40, Root Papers, LOC. This letter reflects Carter's growing conviction that internal competition between the chief of staff and the bureau chiefs would undermine the General Staff's purpose. On the bureaus' reclamation of their former influence, see Hewes, *From Root to McNamara*, 13–14.

17. Carter, *Memoirs*, 387–88.

18. For Carter's conclusions about the General Staff's development (as well as some discussion of the subject between him and Root), see Root to

Carter, 19 Aug. 1904 in Carter Family Papers; Carter to Root, 5 Feb. 1906; Carter to Root, 11 June 1906; Carter to Root, 24 July 1907, Container C-49, Root Papers, LOC; and Carter to Root, 15 Dec. 1912, Container C-92, Root Papers, LOC. Lane describes Wood as "mostly full of himself" in *Armed Progressive*, xv.

19. Lane portrays Wood as a man who was "obsessed to succeed," with a keen knack for manipulating people and events for personal gain. For a full account of Wood's public career, see Lane, *Armed Progressive*, and also Hagedorn's earlier, less critical biography, *Leonard Wood*. On Ainsworth, see Deutrich, *Struggle for Supremacy*. Cater's characterization of Ainsworth's personal ambition is taken from "The War Department General Staff: What It Is and How It Developed," typescript draft (attached to interview with Gen. John McCauley Palmer) in Cater Papers, CMH. Palmer had apparently read and annotated comments on this essay for Cater.

20. Cater, "War Department General Staff," 4–5. Cater notes that Wood was even a guest in Ainsworth's home during the first few weeks after he arrived in Washington. Also see Deutrich, *Struggle for Supremacy.*

21. Carter recognized the glaring need for continued military reform and expressed his thoughts on the subject in "Military Preparedness," 636–43.

22. Secretary of War Henry L. Stimson, quoted in Lane, *Armed Progressive*, 158.

23. Carter and Wood corresponded amicably concerning operational topics during this period, even though Carter's letters to Ida betray a growing mistrust for Wood. In an earlier letter to Root (5 Feb. 1906), Carter noted that Wood was "alright," in reference to continued reform efforts, but this view soured when Wood was made chief of staff over Carter. Representative are William H. Carter to Ida Carter, 19 Mar. 1911, in Carter Family Papers; Leonard Wood to William H. Carter, 29 Apr. 1911, in Carter Family Papers; Wood to Carter, 6 May 1911, in Carter Family Papers; Carter to Ida Carter, 22 July 1911, in Carter Family Papers; Carter to Root, 23 Jan. 1914; Carter, *Memoirs*, 387–89, 396–409; and "Prospective Army Changes," unidentified newspaper clipping in Carter Family Papers. Carter later claimed that Secretary of War Dickinson had in fact recommended his own [Carter's] detail as chief of staff in 1909, but that President Taft derailed the appointment in favor of Wood—see Carter to Secretary of War Lindley M. Garrison, 26 Dec. 1913, in Carter Family Papers. Lane opposes the depiction of Wood as "an outsider" who was never accepted by the army's rank and file professionals. Instead, Lane asserts, Wood's ascendance to the position of chief of staff was initially applauded by such men as Bliss and Pershing. Lane analyzes Wood's very complex relationship with the army's professionalist genre in *Armed Progressive*, 148–55.

24. Quoted in Butt, *Taft and Roosevelt*, vol. 2, 465.

25. Ibid.

26. Carter was assigned to the Mobile Army Division by direction of General Staff Corps Memorandum, 26 Sept. 1910, WCD 639, RG 165, NARA. This organization was part of a new General Staff structure established by Wood shortly after he assumed office. See Lane, *Armed Progressive*, 168–69;

Weigley, *History of the Army*, 333; and Nenninger, "Army Enters the Twentieth Century," 224. Carter maintained that his selection as commander of the Mobile Army Division was due to Secretary Dickinson's personal support—see *Memoirs*, 396.

27. Special Orders no. 54, War Department, 7 Mar. 1911; General Orders no. 35, War Department, 13 Mar. 1911; President William Howard Taft to Gen. Leonard Wood, 12 Mar. 1911, in Carter Family Papers (Carter was sent a copy of this confidential letter at Taft's direction). In addition to the units formally organized as part of the Maneuver Division, the War Department created the "First Separate Brigade" at Galveston, Texas, under the command of Brig. Gen. Albert L. Mills, another "Separate Brigade" in Los Angeles, under Brig. Gen. Tasker H. Bliss, and the "Independent Cavalry Brigade," commanded by Brig. Gen. Walter S. Schuyler. All of these units were organized independently and were not responsible to any geographical command. Carter referred to the Maneuver Division as the "largest unit of regulars ever assembled in our army, up to that time." *Memoirs*, 391. The Reorganization Act of 1901 legally established the army's strength at 3,820 officers and 84,799 enlisted men (Weigley, *History of the Army*, 317–18). The Maneuver Division's strength fluctuated during its existence, but was maintained at about 12,000 enlisted troops (11 Apr.–11,167; 11 May–12,375; 11 June–12,586), giving Carter field command of roughly fifteen percent of the army's (legislated, not actual) strength at the time. *The New York Herald* (8 Mar. 1911) presented a very thorough overview of the mobilization, analyzing its purpose and also its larger international context.

28. Carter, *Memoirs*, 392; Taft to Wood, 12 Mar. 1911. Innovative organizations and technologies exercised and tested by the Maneuver Division are discussed in Carter, "The Border Patrol," 977. It is interesting that, only several months before, Carter had argued for the establishment of training cantonments to be used for division-level exercises for both regular and National Guard troops. These cantonments, he explained, could also be used as ready-made points of assembly for volunteers during times of crisis. See Carter, "Military Preparedness," 642–43.

29. General Orders no. 2, Headquarters–Maneuver Division, San Antonio, Texas, 11 Mar. 1911, reprinted in Carter, "Border Patrol," 974–75. The U.S. Army Surgeon General recommended that typhoid vaccinations be administered—see memorandum to the chief of staff, 8 Mar. 1911, Doc. File 1755376, RG 94, NARA. Carter's personal staff is named in Special Orders no. 54, 7 Mar. 1911.

30. *The New York Herald*, 8 Mar. 1911; other headlines are drawn from various unidentified newspaper clippings maintained in Carter Family Papers. For examples of short biographies of Carter that appeared in papers, see "The Commander of the Army in Texas," *New York Sun*, 16 Mar. 1911; and "Genius of the Maneuvers," *Washington Post*, 22 June 1911. Carter's comment is found in a letter written to Ida Carter, 27 Mar. 1911, in Carter Family Papers. He was concerned that the papers were printing "vile" photographs of him and made arrangements for a better photo (one more to his liking) to be distributed to interested parties—see his letter to Ida Carter, 19 Mar. 1911.

31. Quoted in "Gen. Carter Denies U.S. Has Ulterior Motives," 13 Mar. 1911, unidentified newspaper clipping in Carter Family Papers; and Carter to Ida Carter, 19 Mar. 1911.

32. See Gen. W. W. Wotherspoon to William H. Carter, 8 Mar. 1911, in Carter Family Papers; War Plan, no. 1-A, Mexico, Army War College, Doc. File 6474, Folder #2, WCD Series 296, RG 165, NARA; and War Plan no. 1, Strategic Study, Mexico, Army War College, Doc. File 6474, Folder #4, WCD Series 296, RG 165, NARA. The Maneuver Division began receiving recruits at its San Antonio encampment in order to bolster its regiments to fighting strength. For a schedule of the deployment and also related recruiting efforts, see various memoranda contained in Doc. File 1755376, RG 94, NARA.

33. Carter to Adjutant General of the Army, 24 Apr 1911, Doc. File 1755376, RG 94, NARA; Carter to Ida Carter, 8 May 1911, Carter Family Papers; Carter, "Border Patrol," 978.

34. Carter to Ida Carter, 27 Mar. 1911.

35. Carter to Ida Carter, 8 May 1911; Carter, "Border Patrol," 977–78. A newspaper reported that both the Wright and Curtis aircraft took part in a division review, following their marching counterparts as the parade's last participants. See "Aeroplanes Are Reviewed for the First Time," *San Antonio Express*, 23 Apr. 1911, clipping in Carter Family Papers. Earlier in the day, Frank T. Coffyn, a civilian, set a new rate-of-climb record in the Wright machine, ascending at three hundred feet-per-minute.

36. Carter to Adjutant General of the Army, 11 May 1911, Doc. File 1755376, RG 94, NARA. Lt. George E. M. Kelley [Kelly] died in a flying accident on 10 May 1911, one of the first American serviceman killed in powered flight. Kelly Air Force Base in San Antonio, Texas, is named for Lt. Kelly. Interestingly, two of Carter's grandsons, William H. Carter and Leigh Carter, both served as pilots in the Army Air Forces during the Second World War.

37. Carter to Ida Carter, 18 May 1911, in Carter Family Papers. Also see his letters to Ida Carter, 19 Mar. 1911 and 22 July 1911; and Taft to Wood, 12 Mar. 1911. The number of lost man–days due to illness and injuries were one-fifth of those lost to venereal disease—San Antonio apparently affected the division's health as well as its morale. See Carter to Adjutant General, 11 May 1911.

38. The article "Aeroplanes for the First Time" in the *San Antonio Express* (23 Apr. 1911) supports Carter's reports of shortages in transportation and equipment.

39. Carter to Adjutant General, 11 May 1911.

40. On the march to Leon Springs, as well as comments on the "progressive course of instruction" conducted thereon, see Carter to Adjutant General of the Army, 22 May 1911, Doc. File 1755376, RG 94, NARA; Carter to Adjutant General of the Army, 13 June 1911, Doc. File 1755376, RG 94, NARA; Carter (telegram) to Adjutant General of the Army, 9 June 1911, Doc. File 1755376, RG 94, NARA; and Carter, "Border Patrol," 978. For discussion disparaging the Maneuver division's attempts at tactical exercise, see Palmer, *America in Arms*, 152–54.

41. Carter to Ida Carter, 22 July 1911; Gen. Leonard Wood to Adjutant

General of the Army, 7 Aug. 1911, Doc. File 1755376, RG 94, NARA. Wood's memorandum directed that the Maneuver Division be notified that it was officially discontinued as an organization.

42. For Wood's perspective of the 1911 mobilization and its subsequent presence in his reform ideas, see Lane, *Armed Progressive*, 169–71.

43. William H. Carter, "Memorandum by General Carter," 16 July 1912, in Carter Family Papers. A notation on this memorandum (in Carter's handwriting) states, "copy handed to the secretary of war." One of his themes therein was that regimental depots should be established for any subsequent reserve system, making emergency mobilization more expeditious and creating a sense of coherency.

44. See "We Need an Army of 150,000 Says Gen. Carter," *New York Times*, 7 May 1911. On Wood's later efforts to concentrate the army at larger garrisons of strategic relevance, see Lane, *Armed Progressive*, 171–73.

45. On the Stimson-Wood relationship and the characteristics that each man brought to military reform, see Lane, *Armed Progressive*, 157–59; and Hewes, *From Root to McNamara*, 14–15.

46. Carter Diary, 31 Jan. 1912.

47. Carter, *Memoirs*, 396.

48. For example, see Carter, *Memoirs*, 396–403; Carter Diary, 5 Jan. 1912, 21 Feb. 1912, and 13 Mar. 1912. Some of these clashes were over relatively minor instances, e.g. when Wood added a favorite aide's name for assignment to the General Staff, circumventing the action of a board headed by Carter. Carter's irritated response to this transgression, based on a professed desire for consistency and fair play, was indicative of the much deeper animosities that existed between the two. *Memoirs*, 396–98; Carter Diary, 6–7 Mar. 1912; and 12 Mar. 1912.

49. Carter Diary, 3 Jan. 1912; Carter, *Memoirs*, 398.

50. This narrative is drawn from William H. Carter, untitled memorandum for self, 11 Feb. 1912, in Carter Family Papers; as well as his "Memorandum for the Secretary of War," 8 Feb. 1912, copy in Carter Family Papers; and *Memoirs*, 398–99. Carter recorded his version of the exchange, likely out of fear that he would soon need to recall the facts in defense of his good name.

51. Carter, memo for self, 11 Feb. 1912. In his own support, Carter was able to produce a copy of the proposed bill that Wood had given him with desired corrections annotated. In addition, he offered testimony from a subordinate staff officer, Maj. Johnson Hagood, who could support Carter's version of the affair. See Carter's 11 Feb. memo and also *Memoirs*, 399. Carter tendered his resignation in "Memorandum for the Secretary of War," 8 Feb. 1912.

52. Carter, *Memoirs*, 399. Carter attributed Wood's "forgetfulness" or evasiveness to conscious efforts to undermine would-be competitors—see Carter Diary, 13 Mar. 1912.

53. On the controversial episode that resulted in Ainsworth's premature retirement, see Lane, *Armed Progressive*, 161–65; Deutrich, *Struggle for Supremacy*, 111–32; and Hewes, *From Root to McNamara*, 17–19.

54. Carter Diary, 16 Feb. 1912, 19 Feb. 1912. Ainsworth's controversial fall and subsequent retirement is mentioned in each of Carter's diary entries

from 15 to 19 Feb. 1912. Seeing an opportunity for professional reconciliation with the bureaus, Carter advised line officers "not to gloat over his [Ainsworth's] downfall." Ibid., 17 Feb. 1912.

55. Carter Diary, 21 Feb. 1912; Carter, *Memoirs,* 401. It is interesting that, while Carter clearly detested Wood's conduct of army affairs, he and Mrs. Carter continued to exchange social formalities with General and Mrs. Wood, although clearly not on a basis that would imply any sort of personal friendship.

56. Carter Diary, 12 Mar. 1912, 4 Apr. 1912.

57. Cooper, *National Guard,* 114—on legal discussion of the Guard's national role, see 114–15; Weigley, *History of the Army,* 337–38; and also Millett and Maslowski, *Common Defense,* 330–31.

58. Carter Diary, 4 Mar. 1912.

CHAPTER 14: THE AMERICAN ARMY: WRITING A LEGACY

1. Carter Diary, 13 July 1912; *Army and Navy Journal* 49 (13 July 1912): 1435; and Secretary of War Henry L. Stimson to Maj. Gen. William H. Carter, 24 Aug. 1912, in Carter Family Papers. On the army's reorganization into four continental divisions, see Lane, *Armed Progressive,* 170; and also *Army and Navy Journal* 49 (13 July 1912): 1425–26 and 1443–44. This move was partly in reaction to the difficulties experienced in mobilizing the Maneuver Division in March 1911. On the plan's implications for the National Guard, see Cooper, *National Guard,* 115–16.

2. Carter, *Memoirs,* 409; Carter to Adjutant General of the Army, 26 Aug. 1912, ACP 1878, William H. Carter, RG 94, NARA; General Orders no. 28, War Department, 27 Aug. 1912; Special Orders no. 202, War Department, 27 Aug. 1912; Carter Diary, 31 Aug. 1912. The claim of "almost fifty years of service" at this point includes Carter's duty as an army messenger during the American Civil War.

3. Carter Diary, 6 Aug. 1912; Carter, "Diaries," 159.

4. Huntington, *Soldier and the State,* 62–63. Huntington's discussion of the "military mind" forms a basis for his later assumptions about an isolated military subculture. For complete explanation of this theoretical construct, see *Soldier and the State,* 59–79.

5. Carter, *American Army,* 7.

6. Carter, *American Army,* 8; ibid.; Emory Upton quoted in ibid., 13.

7. Carter drew this listing of Upton's American military "weaknesses" from *Military Policy,* XII–XIV. He left out Upton's ninth and tenth "weaknesses": the want of postgraduate schools and the assumption of command by the secretary of war. Clearly, he felt that these last two had since been corrected. Carter, *American Army,* 31.

8. Ibid., 75.

9. Carter, "Organized Militia," 792.

10. Cooper, *National Guard,* 91–92.

11. Carter, "Organized Militia," 794.

12. Carter, *American Army,* 133.

13. Ibid., 75.

14. Carter to Elihu Root, 15 Sept. 1914, Container 119, Root Papers, LOC.

15. For Carter's discussion of federal volunteers, see *American Army*, 75–76, 133–50.

16. On Wood's "preparedness" proposals for a citizen reserve and the resultant legislative authorization of 1912, see Lane, *Armed Progressive*, 177–78; Weigley, *History of the Army*, 340; and also a representative example of Wood's own version in Harmon, "Bolstering Up Our Army." Wood's scheme received only scant congressional support and was passed in a much-diluted version that failed to pay soldiers during their reserve status. Legislation created a seven-year enlistment with three years spent on active duty and four more in a vaguely defined reserve status. The plan was unsuccessful, resulting in only sixteen reservists in two years.

17. Carter acknowledged some minor value in Wood's preparedness scheme as it pertained to training reserves—but supported it only as a tertiary mission given to a limited number of active units constituted specifically for the purpose. *American Army*, 115.

18. Ibid., 104, 103.

19. On the Regular Army's experience in contemporary labor unrest, see Cooper, *Army and Civil Disorder*" and "Army and Industrial Workers"; and Weigley, *History of the Army*, 281–82. For specific discussion of the National Guard's role, see Cooper, *National Guard*, 49–57 and 148–52. Carter outlines the use of congressional districts as an organizational table in *American Army*, 111–12. He also expanded on this idea in a letter to Tasker H. Bliss, 15 Apr. 1915, in Carter Family Papers.

20. Carter, *American Army*, 117. The depot system was explained in Upton's *Armies of Asia and Europe*, 318. Carter was familiar with this summary and inculcated much of it into his own ideas, dedicating an entire chapter to its discussion, 117–31.

21. Carter, *American Army*, 201.

22. Ibid., 203–4.

23. Although Carter's *American Army* is highly opinionated, this may have been with a purpose. He recorded in his diary that he feared "to render it dull with detail" and thus relied on lively rhetorical argument to carry discussion. See Carter Diary, 10 Oct. 1912. For Weigley's brief critique of *The American Army*, see *Towards an American Army*, 272n47.

24. Carter to Capt. Powell Clayton, 7 July 1915, in Carter Family Papers; Elihu Root to William H. Carter, 29 Nov. 1913, in Carter Family Papers; and Carter, *Memoirs*, 437. Carter finished his first draft in October 1912, but continued revision for some months afterward. He sent a copy of the final manuscript to Henry Stimson with a letter asking that he and Asst. Sec. Breckinridge provide critical input. See Carter to Secretary of War Stimson, 3 May 1913, in Carter Family Papers. Scribner's Sons notified him that the manuscript would appeal only to a narrow audience (see Carter Diary, 4 Dec. 1912), and he subsequently sought publication with Harper's before reaching an agreement with the Bobbs-Merrill Company. Bobbs-Merrill released

prepublication advertisement for the book in February 1915, billing it as "a timely book of first interest to every patriotic American." See *Publisher's Weekly* (20 Feb. 1915): 532.

25. Elihu Root to William H. Carter, 27 Feb. 1917, in Carter Family Papers; James H. Wilson to William H. Carter, 1 May 1915, "Misc. Letters," Container 6, James H. Wilson Papers, LOC; and James H. Wilson to William H. Carter, 7 June 1915, in Carter Family Papers. Wilson noted that a distinct failure of Upton's *Military Policy of the United States* was not proposing the congressional district as the basic unit of American military organization. See Wilson to Carter, 1 May 1915.

26. Carter, *American Army*, 13.

27. Clipping from *The Nation*, 11 Nov. 1915, copy in Carter Family Papers. This particular review was a very in-depth consideration of both the book's purpose and content. Other representative reviews are found in *JMSUIS* 56 (May–June 1915), 486–87; and the *San Antonio Express*, 11 Apr. 1915.

28. Carter Diary, 6 Nov. 1912. Will had been plagued by abdominal pain for months, and Carter's diary entries chronicle his son's health problems. See, for example, Carter Diary, 8, 15, 29 Oct. and 2 Nov. 1912. On Carter's assumption of command of the Central Division, see Carter to Adjutant General of the Army, 5 Dec. 1912, ACP 1878, William H. Carter, RG 94, NARA; and Carter Diary, 5 Dec. 1912. In an interesting aside, after a few days among Chicago's "upper crust," Carter complained of "too much tobacco smoke everywhere I turn," and sometimes took long outdoor walks to try to get the odor to leave his hair and clothes. He noted that "smoking seems to be allowed everywhere and one who does not like it must submit or leave"—an observation that certainly seems to be ahead of its time by several decades—Carter Diary, 21 Dec. 1912.

29. Carter, *Memoirs*, 410; Weigley, *History of the Army*, 334–35. Carter established a headquarters for the new Central Department and assumed its command via telegram to the Adjutant General of the Army, 15 Feb. 1913, ACP 1878, William H. Carter, RG 94, NARA. Although created on paper, the army's reorganization had not yet seen any further action, such as physical consolidation. When ordered to Texas, the Second Division ws still geographically separated—a point that Carter emphasized in "Our Army in Texas." Undated typescript copy in Carter Family Papers.

30. Carter Diary, 22, 23 Feb. 1913. Movement of troops did not begin until 22 February, with Carter and his staff departing Chicago on 25 February. Russell Weigley mistakenly asserts that the 2nd Division was ordered to Texas City and Galveston, Texas, under the command of Brig. Gen. Frederick Funston. Funston was actually given a separate brigade at Galveston, while Carter led the much larger 2nd Division. See *History of the Army*, 335. Aided by Stimson's recent reorganization, Wood required just five written lines to mobilize the 2nd Division—only two years before, it had required dozens of complex orders to build the Maneuver Division for similar purpose. For an account of the assassinations of Madero and Suarez, see Hanrahan, *Blood below the Border*, 158–59.

31. Carter Diary, 1 Mar. 1913. Numerous newspaper articles concern-

ing the mobilization are maintained in the Carter Family Papers—many, as in 1911, referred to Carter as the "hero of Cibicu Creek." In an essay titled "Our Army in Texas" (MS in Carter Family Papers), Carter included a sketch of the 2nd Division's mobilization that depicted travel distances and the constituent units' various points of departure.

32. Millett, *Robert L. Bullard,* 253.

33. Carter Diary, 4 Mar. 1913. The last troops arrived in Texas City as part of the initial mobilization on 3 March. The 2nd Division began moving from their original campsites (as staked out by a staff officer from the Department of Texas) only three days later. This work continued throughout the month, and building an elaborate system of drainage ditches occupied the division's engineers—see Carter, "Report of the Second Division," 30 June 1913, in Annual Reports of the War Department for the Fiscal Year ending 30 June 1913, 113–14; Carter Diary, 6, 11, 12, 17 Mar. 1913. The combined effects of the rain and wind kept Carter's "aeroplane" squadron grounded much of the time at Texas City—a great personal disappointment after he had witnessed their good use in 1911. See Carter Diary, 17 and 21 Mar. 1913. The First Aero Squadron functioned as a training school while assigned to the Second Division, and by early June, most of its personnel had returned to their permanent station. Carter, "Report of the Second Division," 119.

34. Carter, "Our Army in Texas," 5–6.

35. Carter, *Memoirs,* 415. When storms rendered the Texas City encampment too muddy for field maneuvers, Carter sent units to Galveston where beaches could be used for recreation and bathing. See 420.

36. The Second Division's training schedule came under scrutiny at the War Department as early as June 1913. Wood directed the General Staff to draw up a plan for large-scale maneuvers appropriate to the division's purpose and conditions, and later submitted this plan to Carter under the secretary's authority. See the several memorandums contained in WCD File 7854, RG 165, NARA. Despite Millett's characterization of Bullard's opposition to such activity, Bullard later published an article that proclaimed the great importance of organized recreation for troops in garrison. He even pointed to the Second Division's efforts to relieve monotony as instrumental in maintaining soldierly morale and health. See Bullard, "Occupying United States Soldiers," 388–97.

37. Carter, *Memoirs,* 421–22. General Orders no. 80, 20 Dec. 1913, War Department; and Special Orders no. 14, 17 Jan. 1914, War Department. On Wood's removal from division command prior to its embarkation for overseas duty in France, see Lane, *Armed Progressive,* 224–25.

38. Carter Diary, 30 Jan. 1914; Carter, *Memoirs,* 424; "Farewell to General Carter," *Army and Navy Journal* 51 (7 Feb. 1914), 718. This article describes the farewell reception in great detail, including the decoration of the dancing pavilion and refreshment tents.

39. Carter, "Intervention," 193.

40. Ibid., 194. Carter's essay is consistent with Samuel Huntington's description of the "military mind." The professional soldier, he asserted, often "contributes a cautious, conservative, restraining voice to the formulation of state policy." See *Soldier and the State,* 69.

3⸀

41. Quotation in Carter Diary, 23 Apr. 1916.

42. "Gen. Carter on Mexican Intervention," *Army and Navy Journal* 51 (7 Feb 1914): 714.

43. Secretary of War Lindley Garrison to Maj. Gen. William H. Carter, 7 Feb. 1914, in ACP 1878, William H. Carter, RG 94, NARA.

44. Carter to Secretary of War Lindley Garrison, 13 Feb. 1914, in ACP 1878, William H. Carter, RG 94, NARA.

45. Carter to Elihu Root, 15 Dec. 1912, Container C-92, Root Papers, LOC; Elihu Root to William H. Carter, 20 Dec. 1912, Container C-92, Root Papers, LOC; Carter to Secretary of War Lindley Garrison, 26 Dec. 1913, in ACP 1878, William H. Carter, RG 94, NARA. Also see Carter to Elihu Root, 23 Jan. 1914, Container C-119, Root Papers, LOC. Wood's unbridled ambition and close ties to the Republican Party gave Wilson good reason to consider replacing him. See Lane, *Armed Progressive*, 178–79.

46. Carter, *Memoirs*, 432; William H. Carter, telegram to Adjutant General of the Army, 14 Mar. 1914, in ACP 1878, William H. Carter, RG 94, NARA. Carter later wrote that finding Hawaii's many horse and cattle ranches was the "biggest surprise of my life." *Memoirs*, 434.

47. For the bulk of routine reports and correspondence between Carter, his subordinates, and the War Department concerning the ongoing construction of a physical garrison on Oahu and its planned defense, see Doc. File 1383705, RG 94, NARA.

48. Carter Diary, 16 and 20 Oct. 1915; Carter, *Memoirs*, 437. Interestingly, Carter assumed the presence of friendly submarines in his discussion of Hawaii's coastal defenses. *Memoirs*, 444–45.

49. Carter Diary, 30 Sept. 1915. On the burglar episode, see Carter, *Memoirs*, 442; Carter Diary, 17 July 1915; and unidentified newspaper clippings, 18 July 1915, in Carter Family Papers. Carter's fifty years of military service at this point is calculated when one begins with his brief volunteer duty during the American Civil War. This "anniversary" was noted with a short tribute in the *Army and Navy Journal* 51 (20 June 1914).

50. Memorandum Regarding the Strength and Organization of Armed Land Forces, Adjutant General's Office, 22 Mar. 1915, Doc File 2269569, RG 94, NARA. A suspense date for replies to this memo was originally set for 1 Aug. 1915 but seems to subsequently have been changed to 1 May 1915.

51. Carter to Adjutant General of the Army, "Study Regarding Strength and Organization of Armed Land Forces," 22 Apr. 1915, Doc. File 2269569, RG 94, NARA. Carter expressed doubts about the likelihood that his or any other reply would be considered with any objectivity—see Carter Diary, 15 Apr. 1915. Unlike other respondents, he attached a sample piece of legislation to his reply, "An Act to Increase the efficiency of the army and military establishment of the United States," enclosure to Carter's "Study Regarding . . . Armed Land Forces," 22 Apr. 1915. (In addition to the incomplete copy of this memorandum in the cited NARA file, there is a complete copy maintained in the Carter Family Papers.) On so-called Uptonian pessimism, see Weigley, *Towards an American Army*, 156–61. Weigley concluded that Upton himself blamed the "basic folly of civilian control of the military for all

the various follies of American military policy," a belief shared by many professionalists of the following officer generation.

52. Carter, "Study Regarding . . . Armed Land Forces," 22 Apr. 1915.

53. Carter's own perspective departs somewhat from Weigley's "Uptonian pessimism." He fundamentally believed that civilian control of the military was a proper and much-needed foundation for a democratic society—thus his emphasis on the role of the chief of staff as an advisor to the executive branch of government. But he regretted that so many public leaders allowed parochial politics to cloud larger issues of national importance. On matters of military policy, he became increasingly despondent due to slow progress.

54. Carter, *Memoirs*, 445–46; Carter Diary, 6 Nov. 1915; Brig. Gen. John P. Wisser, telegram to Adjutant General of the Army, 6 Nov. 1915, in ACP 1878, William H. Carter, RG 94, NARA; Special Orders No. 270, 19 Nov. 1915, War Department.

55. Elihu Root to William H. Carter, 10 Aug. 1915, in Carter Family Papers.

56. Carter, "Human Element in War," 179, 191. In addition to the professional laurels that accompanied the Reeve Memorial Award, recipients received a cash prize of one hundred dollars.

57. Carter, "The Greater Leavenworth," 189.

58. Carter's "West Point in Literature," originally published in *JMSIUS*, was reprinted a year later in pamphlet form by Lord Baltimore Press.

59. Carter Diary, 4 Dec. 1915.

CHAPTER 15: THE JOURNEY'S END

1. The sad saga of Helen Hunter Carter's battle with tuberculosis is detailed in Carter's diaries of 1915 and 1916, as well as in *Memoirs*, 440. In April 1915, after visiting the Carters in Hawaii, Helen traveled to Fort Bayard, New Mexico, to convalesce in the hospital that Carter had helped to construct in 1884–85. Beyond the natural attachment to a first grandchild, Carter's interest in "Little Willie" as a namesake was very apparent. He prominently mentioned this point in diary entries of 9 Apr. 1915 and 12 Dec. 1915.

2. Carter Diary, 29 Nov. 1915.

3. Carter Diary, 25 Apr. 1915. As one of the first points of business after returning home, Carter went through his personal papers. He had collected almost anything that he thought might be of future interest, and now wished to pare down his load of boxes and folders. He destroyed many materials, keeping only what was "useful and desirable," and planned to begin writing a personal memoir as soon as his papers were sufficiently organized. See Carter Diary, 2 and 24 Dec. 1915.

4. Carter notes Mrs. Chaffee's visit in his diary entry for 3 Dec. 1915.

5. Ibid., 19 Dec. 1915.

6. Roberts suggests that despite the professionalists' best intentions, an eventual result of the hierarchical command arrangement that grew from the 1903 General Staff Act was a more bureaucratized army culture. See "Loyalty and Expertise," 265–66.

7. Carter Diary, 7 and 8 Jan. 1916, 14 Feb. 1916.

8. For Carter's remarks on Hay and Chamberlain, see Diary, 31 Dec. 1915. Carter's diaries during the early months of 1916 contain numerous descriptive references to both men. He viewed Chamberlain as a reasonable ally of the professional army while he saw Hay in an opposition role—see especially remarks in diary entry for 29 Apr. 1916.

9. Ibid., 20 Jan. 1916.

10. Ibid., 30 Jan. 1916.

11. Ibid., 26 Jan. 1916. During the first session of the 64th Congress, several military bills came under simultaneous consideration. In addition to those listed in the text, measures also specifically addressed militia pay and universal military training.

12. The quote is combined from pages 106 and 109 of "Statement of Maj. Gen. William H. Carter, United States Army, Retired," Preparedness for National Defense, Hearings Before the Committee on Military Affairs United States Senate, 64th Cong., 1st sess., pt. 3., Washington, D.C.: GPO. (Cited hereafter as National Defense).

13. Carter opposed Wood's denial of funds to the National Guard in National Defense, 135; and voiced support for the Garrison bill in principle on 138. For Wood's remarks on the Guard's continued existence, see "Statement of Maj. Gen. Leonard Wood, United States Army, Commanding the Department of the East," in National Defense, 68–69.

14. Carter Diary, 22 Feb. 1916. Scott and Bliss both testified before the Senate Committee on 21 Jan.—see National Defense, 141–86.

15. Carter Diary, 30 Apr. 1916. For the Hay amendment's ramifications, see Hewes, From Root to McNamara, 19–20. On Ainsworth's specific manipulation of the bill, see also Nenninger, "Twentieth Century," 226; Weigley, History of the Army, 348–50; and Hewes, "Army General Staff," 70.

16. Carter, Memoirs, 451–52.

17. Ganoe, United States Army, 456–57. Ganoe concentrates on the bill's reorganizational aspects with no mention of its more subtle outcomes, such as the shift of power from the chief of staff back to the bureaus.

18. The quotation is a combination of remarks entered in Carter Diary, 15 and 16 Apr. 1916. For Chamberlain's expression of thanks for "patriotic service," see Senator George E. Chamberlain to William H. Carter, 2 June 1916, in ACP 1878, William H. Carter, RG 94, NARA. Sen. James A. Reed of Missouri accused Carter of acting solely in the interests of the cavalry branch without regard for the army's larger good—a charge Carter refuted in a letter subsequently read into the Congressional Record. See Carter, Memoirs, 451–52; and Carter to Hon. George E Chamberlain, 15 Apr. 1916, in Carter Family Papers. Appended to the latter were copies of the Congressional Record, reflecting Chamberlain's entry on Carter's behalf. U.S. Congressional Record, 17 Apr. 1916, 7169–70.

19. Carter Diary, 13 Apr. 1916. Helen departed for Asheville on 20 Apr. 1916.

20. Carter, "Can the General Staff Corps Fulfil its Mission?" 337–51. Carter took the opportunity—without naming the protagonists—to deplore the rift between Wood and Ainsworth and to further jab at Wood for his failure to successfully lead a second round of military reform (344–47).

21. Carter, "Public Opinion and Defense," 203–10; and Carter, "National Advantage Dependent upon National Policies," 197–207. The quote is found on 199.

22. Carter, "Public Opinion," 205.

23. Carter, "National Advantage," 205.

24. Carter's nationalist interpretation shared many principles of an outlook that Samuel Huntington referred to as "Neo-Hamiltonianism." Neo-Hamiltonians, Huntington wrote, represented a school of thought that was a peculiar combination of seemingly disparate ideological traditions. They held a decidedly conservative view of human events, seeing warfare as an inevitable clash of competing interests, but deplored the immorality of crass materialism while subscribing to humanitarian notions founded on classic liberalism. Similarly, Carter's personal ideology valued foremost the national interest and believed its security was guaranteed only by physical power. But in other matters, his ideas sharply diverged from Huntington's model. Unlike the Republican leaders who Huntington believed typified Neo-Hamiltonian ideals, Carter opposed expansionism and worried that interventionist policies would surrender America's moral high ground. See Huntington, *Soldier and the State*, 270–73, and also Lane, who applies this premise to Leonard Wood in *Armed Progressive*, 152–55.

25. On Carter's increasing cynicism regarding the "preparedness" movement, see his Diary, 11 and 14 June 1916.

26. Carter Diary, 23 June 1916. The attack at Carrizal left forty Americans killed or wounded. See Ganoe, *United States Army*, 459; also Carter Diary, 26 June 1916.

27. Carter, *Adna Chaffee*, 1.

28. Carter, "Defective Military System," 363.

29. Carter, "Universal Service in War," 123.

30. Unlike the Uptonian stereotype, Carter did not attack the citizen-soldiery as a concept, but only its inability to meet professional standards in an increasingly dangerous world.

31. Carter, "Defective Military System," 365.

32. Diary entries make it clear that Carter's shift toward support for compulsory training was a carefully considered decision. See 16 July and 1 Aug. 1916.

33. William H. Carter to Secretary of War Newton Baker, 4 Apr. 1917, in ACP 1878, William H. Carter, RG 94, NARA.

34. Carter, *Memoirs*, 348.

35. Carter, "Advancing on Difficulties," 689. This article was written as the United States scurried to prepare for deployment to France. Carter once again pointed to the shortsightedness of those who opposed a more "national" military policy of the type proposed by preparedness advocates. While careful to pay homage to individual and collective sacrifices by the nation's militia, he faulted the National Guard lobby for swaying Congress to the nation's detriment.

36. On the General Staff's development during the First World War, see Hewes, *From Root to McNamara*, 21–50. Hewes provides a detailed history of the role played by the General Staff in the American war effort. It is inter-

esting to note that despite the General Staff's growth in responsibility during the war, postwar authority in the War Department was again diffused among the several staff bureaus. Carter often described the General Staff as a "harmonizing agency." See, for example, "Recent Army Reorganization," 120.

37. Pershing, *My Experiences in the World War,* vol. I, 102.

38. Joseph T. Dickman to William H. Carter, 20 July 1924, in Carter Family Papers. Dickman served as a corps commander in Hunter Liggett's First Army and published a memoir of his experiences in France, *The Great Crusade.*

39. On the wartime contributions made by "Leavenworth men," see Nenninger, *The Leavenworth Schools,* 134-51; and Coffman, "American Military Generation Gap," 35-43.

40. As he first noted in "The Army as a Career," Carter worried that the army was not representative of the population at large. When he submitted his "Study Regarding . . . Armed Land Forces" to the secretary of war in 1915, he attached a roster of recent troop transports that had arrived in Hawaii as evidence of the disproportionate number of immigrants among the ranks. He was not so much concerned that the laboring classes and immigrants were not good troops as he was appalled that the middle and upper classes were reneging on their republican obligation.

41. Carter, "Our Military Policy in Eclipse," 331; "Tinkering with the Army," 181-86.

42. William H. Carter, "Second in Command," n.d., unpublished manuscript in Carter Family Papers. To the author's knowledge, this incomplete manuscript copy remained unpublished.

43. William Crozier to William H. Carter, 27 July 1918, in Carter Family Papers.

44. The original editorial appeared in the 1 July 1918 issue of *The Military Surgeon,* 74-76. The subsequent retraction and announcement of the writer's retirement appeared in the *Army and Navy Register,* 24 Aug. 1918.

45. Root to Carter, 9 June 1923, in Carter Family Papers. On Carter's attempts to speed the publication process, see Carter Diary, 5 May 1924. The Senate referred Carter's manuscript to the Committee on Printing on 22 Jan. 1924, but it was not ordered published until 26 May 1924. Many of the original documents presented in *Creation of the General Staff* are today found in public records.

46. Maj. Gen. C. H. Martin to Carter, 1 July 1924, in Carter Family Papers; Maj. Gen. William Lassiter to Carter, 1 Aug. 1924, in Carter Family Papers; and Root to Carter, 22 Aug. 1924, in Carter Family Papers. Many other laudatory letters are maintained in the Carter Family Papers along with those quoted.

47. Carter Diary, 26 Dec. 1924.

48. James Abrahamson underlines this point in *America Arms for a New Century,* 18.

49. Lane, *Armed Progressive,* 148.

50. Zais, "20th Century Army," 279.

Bibliography

PRIMARY SOURCES

Manuscript Collections

Carter Family Papers: The Carter Papers are a private collection in the possession of the family of William Harding Carter. Their location is not disclosed in order to maintain the family's privacy at their request. The author photocopied all materials from the Carter Family Papers that are cited in this work.
Manuscript Division, Library of Congress (LOC), Washington D.C.
    William H. Carter Papers
    Henry C. Corbin Papers
    John McCauley Palmer Papers
    Elihu Root Papers
    James Harrison Wilson Papers
National Archives and Records Administration (NARA), Washington D.C.
    Record Group 94: Records of the U.S. Army Adjutant General's Office
    Record Group 107: Records of the Office of the Secretary of War
    Record Group 165: Army War College Division Files
    Record Group 393: Army Service Schools Files
    Record Group 395: Records and Returns of Overseas Departments
U.S. Army Center for Military History (CMH), Ft. McNair, Virginia
    Harold D. Cater Papers
U.S. Army Military History Institute (MHI), Carlisle Barracks, Pennsylvania
    Nelson A. Miles Papers
    Samuel B. M. Young Papers

Tasker H. Bliss Papers
Harold D. Cater Papers
U.S. Military Academy Archives and Special Collections (USMASC), West Point, New York
Peter S. Michie Papers
Eben Swift Papers
Samuel E. Tillman Papers
Annual Reports of the Superintendent
Combined Arms Research Library, Ft. Leavenworth, Kansas
John G. Bourke Diaries
Wyoming State Archives
William H. Carter Papers

U.S. Government Documents

Carter, William H. "Our Coast Defenses: A General Staff Report." Washington, D.C.: Government Printing Office, 1903.
——. *Creation of the American General Staff: Personal Narrative of the General Staff System of the American Army.* Sen. Doc. No. 119, 68th Cong., 1st sess., Washington, D.C.: Government Printing Office, 1924.
United States Congress. "Efficiency of the Army." Testimony before the Senate Committee on Military Affairs, 57th Cong., 2nd sess. In *Establishment of a General Staff Corps in the Army.* Washington, D.C.: Government Printing Office, 1902.
United States Military Academy. *Official Register of the Officers and Cadets of the U.S. Military Academy, West Point, N.Y.* Published annually.
United States Senate Committee on Military Affairs. *Hearings on Preparedness for National Defense.* 64th Cong., 1st sess., pt. 3. Washington, D.C.: Government Printing Office.
United States War Department. Annual Reports of the Secretary of War. Washington, D.C.: GPO, 1898–1916.
——. *War of the Rebellion: A Compilation of the Official Records of the Union and Confederate Armies.* 128 vols. Washington D.C.: GPO, 1880–1901.

Contemporary Periodicals

Army and Navy Journal
Army and Navy Register
Harper's Weekly
Infantry Journal
Journal of the Military Service Institution of the United States
Munsey's Magazine
The North American Review
The Outlook
Scribner's Magazine
The United Service
Journal of the United States Cavalry Association

Published Works by William H. Carter

(Note: No attempt has been made to compile a complete list of William H. Carter's publications.)

Carter, William H. *Horses, Saddles, and Bridles.* Baltimore: Lord Baltimore Press, 1906.

———. *Old Army Sketches.* Baltimore: Lord Baltimore Press, 1906.

———. *Giles Carter of Virginia.* Baltimore: Lord Baltimore Press, 1909.

———. *From Yorktown to Santiago with the Sixth Cavalry.* Indianapolis: Bobbs-Merrill Co., 1915. Reprinted with introduction by John M. Carroll. Austin, Tex.: State House Press, 1989.

———. *The American Army.* Indianapolis: Bobbs-Merrill, 1915.

———. *Adna Chaffee: Biography of a Soldier.* Chicago: University of Chicago Press, 1917.

———. *Sketch of Fort Robinson, Nebraska.* Crawford, Nebr.: Northwest Nebraska News, 1941.

———. "One View of the Army Question." *The United Service* 2 (Dec. 1889): 573–78.

———. "The Sixth Regiment of Cavalry." *Journal of the Military Service Institution of the United States* 15 (Mar. 1894): 428–46.

———. "The Infantry and Cavalry School at Fort Leavenworth." *Journal of the Military Service Institution of the United States* 15 (July 1894): 752–59.

———. "Will America Profit by Her Recent Military Lessons?" *North American Review* 174 (May 1902): 658–70.

———. "Recent Army Reorganization." *The United Service* 2, Ser. 3 (Aug. 1902): 113–20.

———. "The Training of Army Officers." *The United Service* 2, Ser. 3 (Oct. 1902): 337–42.

———. "A General Staff for the Army." *North American Review* 175 (Oct. 1902): 558–65.

———. "Post-Graduate Instruction in the Army." *Educational Review* 24 (Dec. 1902): 433–39.

———. "A General Staff Corps." *The United Service* 3, Ser. 3 (Jan. 1903): 677–81.

———. "The Organized Militia: Its Past and Future." *The United Service* 3, Ser. 3 (Feb. 1903): 791–94.

———. "The Next Head of the Army." *Munsey's Magazine* 25 (Mar. 1903): 810–11.

———. "The Passing of a High Office." *The United Service* 4, Ser. 3 (Mar. 1903): 901–8.

———. "The Decadence of the Brevet." *The United Service* 4, Ser. 3 (Apr. 1903): 1010–14.

———. "The Evolution of Army Reforms." *The United Service* 4, Ser. 3 (May 1903): 1190–98.

———. "The War Department—Military Administration." *Scribner's Magazine* 33 (June 1903): 551–73.

———. "American Cavalry." *The United Service* 4, Ser. 3 (June 1903): 1226–31.

———. "Infantry in War." *The United Service* 4, Ser. 3 (July 1903): 1–15.

——. "The New Regime at the War Department." *The United Service* 4, Ser. 3 (Sept. 1903): 309–14.

——. "The Next Head of the Army." *Munsey's Magazine* 25 (Mar. 1903): 810–11.

——. "The Evolution of a General Staff." *Journal of the Military Service Institution of the United States* 33 (Sept.–Oct. 1903): 200–206.

——. "Elihu Root: His Services as Secretary of War." *North American Review* 178 (Jan. 1904): 110–21.

——. "Economic Questions Affecting the Visayan Islands." *North American Review* 180 (May 1905): 688–93.

——. "A Meet in the Philippines: A Rational Plan of Athletic Training." *Journal of the Military Service Institution of the United States* 36 (May–June 1905): 455–66.

——. "The Army as a Career." *North American Review* 183 (2 Nov. 1906): 870–76.

——. "Comment and Criticism: National Camps of Instruction." *Journal of the Military Service Institution of the United States* 39 (1906): 464–66.

——. "A Plea for the Filipinos." *North American Review* 184 (15 Feb. 1907): 383–88.

——. "Camps of Instruction." *The Reader* 10 (July 1907): 115–21.

——. "When Diplomacy Fails." *North American Review.* 187 (Jan. 1908): 23–33.

——. "West Point in Literature." *Journal of the Military Service Institution of the United States* 43 (Nov.–Dec. 1908): 378–42,

——. "Military Preparedness." *North American Review* 191 (May 1910): 636–43.

——. "A War Organization." *Journal of the Military Service Institution of the United States* 46 (May–June 1910): 361–72.

——. "Is the Present System of Detail to Staff Departments Conducive to the Discipline and Efficiency of the Army? Should it be Revised?" *Journal of the Military Service Institution of the United States* 49 (July–Aug 1911): 15–34.

——. "Interdependence of Political and Military Policies." *North American Review* 194 (Dec. 1911): 837–47.

——. "The Border Patrol." *The Outlook* 99 (23 Dec. 1911): 973–78.

——. "The Passing of a Brigadier." *The Outlook* 100 (27 Jan. 1912): 173–74.

——. "The Charger." *Journal of the United States Cavalry Association* 23 (July 1912): 5–13.

——. "The Master of Belle Meade." *The Outlook* 101 (27 July 1912): 725–30.

——. "The Militia Not a National Force." *North American Review* 196 (July 1912): 130–35.

——. "Claude Crozet." *Journal of the Military Service Institution of the United States* 53 (July–Aug. 1913): 1–6.

——. "Intervention." *North American Review* 199 (Feb. 1914): 193–98.

——. "The Greater Leavenworth." *Journal of the United States Cavalry Association.* 25 (Oct. 1914): 173–89.

——. "Diaries." *Journal of the Military Service Institution of the United States* 56 (Mar.–Apr. 1915): 159–63.

——. "Human Element in War." *Journal of the Military Service Institution of the United States* 57 (Sept.–Oct. 1915): 177–91.

——. "Can the General Staff Corps Fulfil its Mission?" *Journal of the Military Service Institution of the United States* 58 (May–June 1916): 337–51.

——. "Public Opinion and Defense." *North American Review* 204 (Aug. 1916): 203–10.

——. "National Advantage Dependent upon National Policies." *Journal of the Military Service Institution of the United States* 59 (Sept.–Oct. 1916): 197–207.

——. "Our Defective Military System." *North American Review* 205 (Mar. 1917): 356–66.

——. "Prophets of Preparedness." *Journal of the Military Service Institution of the United States* 60 (May–June 1917): 329–44.

——. "Universal Service in War and the Taxation to Support It." *Journal of the Military Service Institution of the United States* 61 (Sept.–Oct. 1917): 123–38.

——. "Advancing on Difficulties." *North American Review* 206 (Nov. 1917): 688–94.

——. "Problems of Military Transportation." *North American Review* 207 (Jan. 1918): 52–56.

——. "Army Reformers." *North American Review* 208 (Oct. 1918): 548–57.

——. "After the War." *North American Review* 208 (Dec. 1918): 855–57.

——. "The Japanese in Hawaii." *Atlantic Monthly* 128 (Aug. 1921): 255–57.

——. "Our Military Policy in Eclipse." *North American Review* 215 (March 1922): 331–37.

——. "Tinkering with the Army." *North American Review* 217 (Feb. 1923): 181–86.

——. "A British Dragoon in the American Revolution." *Cavalry Journal* 32 (Oct. 1923): 400–11.

——. "Early History of American Cavalry." *Cavalry Journal* 34 (Jan. 1925): 7–18.

Contemporary Published Sources

Allen, Henry T. "Proposed Reorganization for Our Central Staff." *Journal of the Military Service Institution of the United States* 27 (July 1900): 26–30.

——. "The Organization of a Staff Best Adapted to the United States Army." *Journal of the Military Service Institution of the United States* 28 (Mar. 1901): 169–83.

Barry, Herbert. "In What Way Can the National Guard Be Modified so as to Make It an Effective Reserve to the Regular Army in Both War and Peace?" *Journal of the Military Service Institution of the United States* 26 (Mar. 1900): 189–231.

Bend, W. B. "In What Way Can the National Guard Be Modified so as to Make It an Effective Reserve to the Regular Army in Both War and Peace?" *Journal of the Military Service Institution of the United States* 27 (Nov. 1900): 371–79.

Bingham, Theodore A. "The Prussian Great General Staff and What It Contains That Is Practical from an American Standpoint." *Journal of the Military Service Institution of the United States* 13 (July 1892): 666–76.

Black, William Murray. "The Military Education of Army Officers." *Journal of the Military Service Institution of the United States* 32 (Mar.–Apr. 1903): 209–30.

Bourke, John G. *On the Border with Crook.* New York: John Scribner's Sons, 1891. Reprint, Lincoln: University of Nebraska Press, 1971.

Boynton, Edward C. *History of West Point, and Its Military Importance during the American Revolution: And the Origin and Progress of the United States Military Academy.* New York: D. Van Nostrand, 1863. Reprint, Freeport, N.Y.: Books for Libraries Press, 1970.

Britton, Edward E. "In What Way Can the National Guard Be Modified so as to Make It an Effective Reserve to the Regular Army in Both War and Peace?" *Journal of the Military Service Institution of the United States* 26 (Mar. 1900): 155–88.

Bullard, Robert L. "Occupying United States Soldiers." *Journal of the Military Service Institution of the United States* 54 (May–June 1914): 388–97.

Cruse, Thomas. *Apache Days and After.* With introduction by Eugene Cunningham. Caldwell, Idaho. Caxton Printers, 1941. Reprint, Lincoln: University of Nebraska Press, 1987.

Davis, Britton. *The Truth about Geronimo.* New Haven: Yale University Press, 1929. Reprint, Lincoln: University of Nebraska Press, 1976.

Dickman, Joseph T. *The Great Crusade: A Narrative of the World War.* New York: D. Appleton, 1927.

Dougherty, W. E. "The Recent Indian Craze." *Journal of the Military Service Institution of the United States* 12 (May 1891): 576–78.

Flipper, Henry O. *The Colored Cadet at West Point.* New York: Homer Lee & Co., 1878. Reprint, Lincoln: University of Nebraska Press, 1998.

Frazier, Walter. "The National Guard National in Name Only." *Journal of the Military Service Institution of the United States* 20 (May 1897): 518–23.

Garfield, James A. "The Army of the United States, Part II." *North American Review* 126 (May–June, 1878).

Giddings, Howard A. "How to Improve the Condition and Efficiency of the National Guard." *Journal of the Military Service Institution of the United States* 21 (July 1897): 61–75.

Greene, L. D. "In What Way Can the National Guard Be Modified so as to Make It an Effective Reserve to the Regular Army in Both War and Peace?" *Journal of the Military Service Institution of the United States* 27 (Nov. 1900): 340–53.

Gresham, John C. "The Story of Wounded Knee." *Harper's Weekly* 35 (7 Feb. 1891): 106–7.

Harmon, Dudley. "Bolstering Up Our Army: A Talk with Major-General Leonard Wood on the Proposed Military Reserve." *Harper's Weekly* 55 (29 July 1911).

Holloway, Laura Carter. *The Ladies of the White House.* New York: U.S. Publishing Co., 1871. Reprint, New York: Bradley & Co., 1881.

Johnston, William H. "Employment of the Philippine Scouts in War." *Journal of the Military Service Institution of the United States* 38 (Jan.–Feb. 1906): 67–77.

———. "Employment of the Philippine Scouts in War." *Journal of the Military Service Institution of the United States* 38 (Mar.–Apr. 1906): 389–98.

King, Charles. "Comment and Criticism: National Camps of Instruction." *Journal of the Military Service Institution of the United States* 39 (1906): 467.

Langdon, Russell C. "The Organization of a Staff Best Adapted for the United States Army." *Journal of the Military Service Institution of the United States* 28 (Mar. 1901): 208–20.

Latham, George E. "The Brain of the Army." *Munsey's* 29 (Sept. 1903): 900–903.

Luce, Stephen B. *Life and Letters of Rear Admiral Stephen B. Luce.* New York: Putnam Books, 1925.

Ludlow, William. "The Military Systems of Europe and America." *North American Review* 160 (Jan. 1895): 72–84.

Mason, Charles H. "The Organization of a Military Reserve Force for United States." *Journal of the Military Service Institution of the United States* 34 (Nov.–Dec. 1906): 403–16.

Michie, Peter S. "Education in Relation to the Military Profession." *Journal of the Military Service Institution of the United States* 1 (1880): 154–79.

———. *The Life and Letters of Emory Upton.* New York: D. Appleton and Co., 1885.

———. "Educational Methods at West Point." *Educational Review* 4 (Nov. 1892): 350–65.

Mooney, James. *The Ghost Dance Religion and Wounded Knee.* Washington D.C.: Government Printing Office, 1896. Reprint, New York: Dover Publications, 1973.

Moseley, George Van Horn. "A Colonial Army." *Journal of the Military Service Institution of the United States* 34 (Mar.–Apr. 1904): 242–52.

Parker, John H. "Our Army Supply Departments and the Need of a General Staff." *American Monthly Review of Reviews* 18 (Dec. 1898): 686–95.

Pershing, John J. *My Experiences in the World War.* 2 vols. New York: Frederick A. Stokes Co., 1931.

Pettit, James S. "The Proper Military Instruction of Our Officers. The Method to Be Employed, Its Scope and Full Development." *Journal of the Military Service Institution of the United States* 20 (Jan. 1897): 93–104.

Price, George F. "The Necessity for Closer Relations between the Army and the People, and the Best Method to Accomplish the Result." *Journal of the Military Service Institution of the United States* 6 (Dec. 1885): 303–30.

Remington, Frederic. "The Art of War and Newspaper Men." *Harper's Weekly* 34 (6 Dec. 1890): 947.

———. "Chasing a Major General." *Harper's Weekly* 34 (6 Dec. 1890): 946–47.

———. "The Sioux Outbreak in South Dakota." *Harper's Weekly* 35 (24 Jan. 1891): 57, 61–62.

———. "Lieutenant Casey's Last Scout." *Harper's Weekly* 35 (31 Jan. 1891): 85–87.

———. "The Galloping Sixth." *Harper's Weekly,* 36 (16 Jan. 1892): 57–58.

Rice, James M. "The New National Guard." *Journal of the Military Service Institution of the United States* 34 (May–June 1904): 467–75.

Richardson, W. P. "Some Observations upon the Sioux Campaign." *Journal of the Military Service Institution of the United States* 18 (May 1896): 512–31.

Root, Elihu. *The Military and Colonial Policy of the United States: Addresses and Reports by Elihu Root.* Edited by Robert Bacon and James B. Scott. Cambridge, Mass.: Harvard University Press, 1916. Reprint New York: AMS Press, 1970.

Schaff, Morris. *The Spirit of Old West Point, 1858–1862.* New York: Houghton Mifflin Co., 1907.

Scherer, Louis C. "The Organization of a Staff Best Adapted for the United States Army." *Journal of the Military Service Institution of the United States* 28 (Mar. 1901): 184–207.

Schwan, Theodore. "The Coming General Staff: Its Importance as a Factor in the Military System." *Journal of the Military Service Institution of the United States* 33 (July–Aug. 1903): 1–30.

Sherburne, John H. "How Far, in Time of Peace, Should the Authority of the United States Be Further Extended over the Organized Militia of the Various States and Territories?" *Journal of the Military Service Institution of the United States* 48 (Mar.–Apr. 1911): 186–99.

Sherman, William T. "The Militia." *Journal of the Military Service Institution of the United States* 6 (Mar. 1885): 1–14.

Stone, Henry. "Repelling Hood's Invasion of Tennessee." In *Battles and Leaders of the Civil War,* Vol. 4, 440–64. New York: Thomas Yoseleff, 1956.

Taylor, Daniel M. "In What Way Can the National Guard Be Modified so as to Make It an Effective Reserve to the Regular Army in Both War and Peace?" *Journal of the Military Service Institution of the United States* 26 (Mar. 1900): 233–58.

Taylor, W. Irving. "How Far, in Time of Peace, Should the Authority of the United States Be Further Extended over the Organized Militia of the Various States and Territories?" *Journal of the Military Service Institution of the United States* 48 (Mar.–Apr. 1911): 165–85.

Tillman, Samuel E. "The Academic History of the Military Academy." In *The Centennial of the United States Military Academy at West Point, New York.* Vol. 1. Washington, D.C.: GPO 1904. Reprint, New York: Greenwood Press, 1969.

Upton, Emory. *The Armies of Asia and Europe.* New York: D. Appleton and Co., 1878.

———. *The Military Policy of the United States.* Washington, D.C.: Government Printing Office, 1904.

U.S. Military Academy. *The Centennial of the United States Military Academy at West Point, New York.* 2 Vols. Washington, D.C.: GPO, 1904. Reprint, New York: Greenwood Press, 1969.

Wagner, Arthur. "An American War College." *Journal of the Military Service Institution of the United States* 10 (July 1889): 287–304.

Wellman, Walter. "Elihu Root: A Character Sketch." *American Monthly Review of Reviews* 29 (Jan. 1904): 35–44.

SECONDARY SOURCES

Books and Articles

Abrahamson, James L. *America Arms for a New Century: The Making of a Great Military Power.* New York: Free Press, 1981.

Aimone, Alan and Barbara. "Much to Sadden and Little to Cheeer: The Civil War Years at West Point." *Blue and Gray Magazine* (Dec. 1991).

Ambrose, Stephen E. *Upton and the Army.* Baton Rouge: Louisiana State University Press, 1964.

———. *Duty, Honor, Country: A History of West Point.* Baltimore: Johns Hopkins Press, 1966.

Andrist, Ralph K. *The Long Death: The Last Days of the Plains Indian.* With introduction by Dee Brown. New York: Collier Books, 1993.

Ball, Eve. *Indeh: An Apache Odyssey.* With foreword by Dan L. Thrapp. Norman: University of Oklahoma Press, 1988.

Ball, Harry P. *Of Responsible Command: A History of the U.S. Army War College.* Carlisle Barracks, Penn.: Alumni Assoc. of the U.S. Army War College, 1983.

Basso, Keith H., ed. *Western Apache Raiding and Warfare: From the Notes of Grenville Goodwin.* Tucson: University of Arizona Press, 1971.

Bernardo, C. Joseph, and Eugene H. Bacon. *American Military Policy: Its Development Since 1775.* Harrisburg, Penn.: Military Service Publishing Co., 1955.

Bledstein, Burton J. *The Culture of Professionalism: The Middle Class and the Development of Higher Education in America.* New York: W. W. Norton, 1978.

Bradford, James C., ed. *Crucible of Empire: The Spanish-American War and Its Aftermath.* Annapolis, Md.: United States Naval Institute, 1993.

Brereton, T. R. *Educating the U.S. Army: Arthur L. Wagner and Reform, 1875–1905.* Lincoln: University of Nebraska Press, 2000.

———. "James Chester and the Case against Army Reform." Paper presented at the Fifth Fort Robinson History Conference, Fort Robinson, Nebr., April, 2004.

Brown, Dee. *Bury My Heart at Wounded Knee: An Indian History of the American West.* New York: Henry Holt and Co., 1970.

Brubacher, John S., and Willis Rudy. *Higher Education in Transition: A History of American Colleges and Universities, 1636–1968.* New York: Harper and Row, 1958.

Buecker, Tom. "An Excellent Soldier and an Efficient Officer." *Nebraskaland* 67 (June 1989): 12–17.

Burrows, Robert G. "Urbanizing America." In *The Gilded Age: Essays on the*

Origins of Modern America, ed. Charles W. Calhoun, 91–110. Wilmington, Del.: Scholarly Resources, 1996.

Butt, Archie. *Taft and Roosevelt: The Intimate Letters of Archie Butt, Military Aide.* 2 vols. Garden City, New York: Doubleday, Doran, and Co., 1930.

Butts, R. Freeman. *The Cultural History of Western Education: Its Social and Intellectual Foundations.* New York: McGraw-Hill Book Co., 1955.

Calhoun, Charles W., ed. *The Gilded Age: Essays on the Origins of Modern America.* Wilmington, Del.: Scholarly Resources, 1996.

Chambers, John Whiteclay. *The Tyranny of Change: America in the Progressive Era, 1890–1920.* New York: St. Martin's Press, 1992. Reprint, New Brunswick, N.J.: Rutgers University Press, 2000.

Coffman, Edward M. "The American Military Generation Gap in World War I: The Leavenworth Clique in the AEF." In *Command and Commanders in Modern Warfare: Proceedings of the Second Military History Symposium, U.S. Air Force Academy,* ed. William Geffen, 35–43. Washington, D.C.: Government. Printing Office, 1969.

———. *The Old Army: A Portrait of the American Army in Peacetime, 1784–1898.* New York: Oxford University Press, 1986.

———. "The Young Officer in the Old Army." In *The Harmon Memorial Lectures in Military History, 1959–1987,* ed. Harry R. Borowski, 255–68. Washington, D.C.: Office of Air Force History, 1988.

———. "The Long Shadow of the Soldier and the State." *Journal of Military History* 55 (Jan. 1991): 69–82.

———. *The Regulars: The American Army, 1899–1941.* Cambridge, Mass.: Harvard University Press, 2004.

Cohen, Arthur M. *The Shaping of American Higher Education: Emergence and Growth of the Contemporary System.* San Francisco: Jossey-Bass Publishers, 1998.

Coleman, William S. E. *Voices of Wounded Knee.* Lincoln: University of Nebraska Press, 2000.

Collins, Charles. *Apache Nightmare: The Battle at Cibecue Creek.* Norman: University of Oklahoma Press, 1999.

Cooper, Jerry M. *The Army and Civil Disorder: Federal Military Intervention in American Disputes, 1877–1900.* Westport, Conn.: Greenwood Press, 1980.

———. "The Army's Search for a Mission, 1865–1890." In *Against All Enemies: Interpretations of American Military History from Colonial Times to the Present,* eds. Kenneth J. Hagan and William R. Roberts, 173–95. Contributions in Military Studies, no. 51. Westport, Conn.: Greenwood Press, 1986.

———. "The Army and Industrial Workers: Strikebreaking in the Late Nineteenth Century." In *Soldiers and Civilians: The U.S. Army and the American People,* eds. Garry D. Ryan and Timothy K. Nenninger, 136–52. Washington, D.C.: National Archives and Records Administration, 1987.

———. *The Rise of the National Guard: The Evolution of the American Militia, 1865–1920.* Lincoln: University of Nebraska, 1997.

Cosmas, Graham A. "From Order to Chaos: The War Department, the National Guard, and Military Policy." *Military Affairs* 29 (Fall 1965): 105–21.

——. *An Army for Empire: The United States Army in the Spanish-American War.* Columbia: University of Missouri Press, 1971.

——. "Military Reform after the Spanish-American War: The Army Reorganization Fight of 1898–1899." *Military Affairs* 35 (Feb. 1971): 12–18.

Cox, Jacob D. *Sherman's March to the Sea.* With introduction by Brooks D. Simpson. New York: Da Capo Press, 1994.

Cress, Lawrence D. *Citizens in Arms: The Army and the Militia in American Society to the War of 1812.* Chapel Hill: University of North Carolina Press, 1982.

Crunden, Robert M. *Ministers of Reform: The Progressives' Achievement in American Civilization, 1889–1920.* Urbana: University of Illinois Press, 1984.

——. *A Brief History of American Culture.* New York: Paragon House, 1994.

Cunliffe, Marcus. *Soldiers and Civilians: The Martial Spirit in America, 1775–1865.* Boston: Little, Brown and Co., 1968.

Curti, Merle. *The Growth of American Thought.* 3rd ed. New Brunswick, N.J.: Transaction Books, 1982.

D'Elia, Donald J. "The Argument over Civilian or Military Indian Control, 1865–1880." *The Historian* 24 (Feb. 1962): 207–24.

Dawson, Joseph G. *Army Generals and Reconstruction: Louisiana, 1862–1877.* Baton Rouge: Louisiana University Press, 1982.

DeMontravel, Peter R. "General Nelson A. Miles and the Wounded Knee Controversy." *Arizona and the West* 28 (Spring 1986): 23–44.

Deutrich, Mabel E. *Struggle for Supremacy: The Career of General Fred C. Ainsworth.* Washington, D.C.: Public Affairs Press, 1962.

Dippie, Brian W. *The Vanishing American: White Attitudes and U.S. Indian Policy.* Lawrence: University Press of Kansas, 1982.

Dunlay, Thomas W. "General Crook and the White Man Problem." *Journal of the West* 18 (April 1979): 3–10.

——. *Wolves for the Blue Soldiers: Indian Scouts and Auxiliaries with the United States Army, 1860–1890.* Lincoln: University of Nebraska Press, 1982.

Durham, Walter T. *Nashville: The Occupied City.* Nashville: Tennessee Historical Society, 1985.

Eales, Anne Bruner. *Army Wives on the Frontier: Living by the Bugles.* Boulder, Colo.: Johnson Books, 1996.

Eisenhower, John S. D. *Intervention: The United States and Mexican Revolution, 1913–1917.* New York: W. W. Norton and Co., 1993.

Elliott, Philip. *The Sociology of the Professions.* New York: Herder and Herder, 1972.

Faragher, John Mack, ed. *Rereading Frederick Jackson Turner.* New York: Henry Holt, 1994. Reprint, New Haven, Conn.: Yale University Press, 1998.

Faulk, Odie B. *The Geronimo Campaign.* New York: Oxford University Press, 1969.

Fishel, Leslie H., Jr. "The African-American Experience." In *The Gilded Age: Essays on the Origins of Modern America*, ed. Charles W. Calhoun, 137–61. Wilmington, Del.: Scholarly Resources, 1996.

Fleming, Thomas J. *West Point: The Men and Times of the United States Military Academy.* New York: William Morrow and Co., 1969.

Flint, Roy K. "The United States Army on the Pacific Frontier, 1899–1939." In *The American Military and the Far East: Proceedings of the Ninth Military History Symposium, United States Air Force Academy, 1–3 October 1980*, ed. Joe C. Dixon, 139–59. Colorado Springs, Col.: U.S. Air Force Academy, 1981

Foner, Eric. *A Short History of Reconstruction.* New York: Harper and Row, 1990.

Foner, Jack D. *The United States Soldier between Two Wars, 1865–1898: Army Life and Reform.* New York: Humanities Press, 1970.

Franklin, John Hope, and Alfred A. Moss, Jr. *From Slavery to Freedom: A History of African Americans.* 8th ed. New York: Alfred A. Knopf, 2000.

Ganoe, William A. *The History of the United States Army.* Rev. ed. Ashton, Md.: Eric Lundberg, 1964.

Gates, John M. *Schoolbooks and Krags: The United States Army in the Philippines, 1898–1902.* Westport, Conn.: Greenwood Press, 1973.

———. "The Alleged Isolation of the U.S. Army Officer in the Late Nineteenth Century." *Parameters* 10 (September 1980).

Goodchild, Lester F., and Harold S. Weschsler, eds. *The History of Higher Education.* 2nd ed. Needham Heights, Mass.: Simon and Schuster Custom Publishing, 1997.

Grandstaff, Mark R. "Preserving the 'Habits and Usages of War': William Tecumseh Sherman, Professional Reform, and the U.S. Army Officer Corps, 1865–1881, Revisited." *Journal of Military History* 62 (July 1998): 521–46.

Gray, John S. *Centennial Campaign: The Sioux War of 1876.* Ft. Collins, Colo.: Old Army Press, 1976. Reprint, Norman: University of Oklahoma Press, 1988.

Hagedorn, Hermann. *Leonard Wood: A Biography.* 2 vols. New York: Harper and Bros., 1931.

Hanrahan, Gene Z., ed. *Blood below the Border: American Eye-witness Accounts of the Mexican Revolution.* Salisbury, N.C.: Documentary Publications, 1982.

Hassler, Warren W., Jr. *With Shield and Sword: American Military Affairs, Colonial Times to the Present.* Ames: Iowa State University Press, 1982.

Hattaway, Herman, and Archer Jones. *How the North Won: A Military History of the Civil War.* Urbana: University of Illinois Press, 1983.

———. "The War Board, the Basis of the United States' First General Staff." *Military Affairs* 46 (Feb. 1982).

Hays, Samuel P. "The New Organizational Society." In *Building the Organizational Society: Essays on Associational Activities in Modern America*, ed. by Jerry Israel. New York: Free Press, 1972.

Hedran, Paul L. "Charles King." In *Soldiers West: Biographies from the Mili-*

tary Frontier, ed. Paul Andrew Hutton, 243–61. With introduction by Robert M. Utley. Lincoln: University of Nebraska Press, 1987.

————. *Fort Laramie in 1876: Chronicle of a Frontier Post at War*. Lincoln: University of Nebraska Press, 1988.

Hewes, James T., Jr. "The United States Army General Staff, 1900–1917." *Military Affairs* 38 (April 1974): 67–72.

————. *From Root to McNamara: Army Organization and Administration, 1900–1903*. Washington, D.C.: U.S. Army Center of Military History, 1975.

Higginbotham, Don. *George Washington and the American Military Tradition*. Athens: University of Georgia Press, 1985.

Hill, Jim Dan. *The Minute Man in Peace and War: A History of the National Guard*. Harrisburg, Penn.: Stackpole Co., 1964.

Hittle, J. D. *The Military Staff: Its History and Development*. Harrisburg, Penn.: Stackpole Co., 1944.

Hofstadter, Richard. *The Age of Reform: From Bryan to F.D.R.* New York: Random House, 1955.

————. *Anti-intellectualism in American Life*. New York: Random House, 1963.

————, and C. Dewitt Hardy. *The Development of and Scope of Higher Education in the United States*. New York: Columbia University Press, 1952.

Howe, Daniel Walker, ed. *Victorian America*. Philadelphia: University of Pennsylvania Press, 1976.

Huntington, Samuel P. *The Soldier and the State*. Cambridge, Mass.: Harvard University Press, 1957.

Iriye, Akira. "Western Perceptions and Asian Realities." In *The American Military and the Far East: Proceedings of the Ninth Military History Symposium, United States Air Force Academy, 1–3 October, 1980*, ed. Joe C. Dixon, 9–19. Colorado Springs, Col.: U.S. Air Force Academy, 1981.

Jessup, Philip C. *Elihu Root*. 2 vols. New York: Dodd. Mead, and Co., 1938.

Karsten, Peter. "Armed Progressives: The Military Organizes for the American Century." In *Building the Organizational Society: Essays on Associational Activities in Modern America*, ed. Jerry Israel, 197–232. New York: Free Press, 1972.

————. *The Military in America: From the Colonial Times to the Present*. Rev. ed. New York: Free Press, 1986.

Kemble, C. Robert. *The Image of the Army Officer in America: Background for Current Views*. Contributions in Military History, no. 5. Westport, Conn.: Greenwood Press, 1973.

Kerr, Clark. *The Uses of the University*. Cambridge, Mass.: Harvard University Press, 1963.

Kessel, William B. "The Battle of Cibecue and Its Aftermath: A White Mountain Apache's Account." *Ethnohistory* 21, no. 2 (1974): 123–34.

King, James T. *War Eagle: The Life of General Eugene A. Carr*. Lincoln: University of Nebraska Press, 1963.

————. "Needed: A Re-Evaluation of General Crook." *Nebraska History* 45 (Sept. 1964): 223–35.

——. "George Crook: Indian Fighter and Humanitarian." *Arizona and the West: A Quarterly Journal of History* 9 (Winter 1967): 333–48.

Kircus, Peggy Dickey. "Fort David A. Russell: A Study of Its History from 1867 to 1890." *Annals of Wyoming* 40 (Oct. 1968): 161–92.

Kohn, Richard H. *Eagle and Sword: The Federalists and the Creation of the Military Establishment.* New York: Free Press, 1975.

Lane, Jack C. *Armed Progressive: General Leonard Wood.* San Rafael, Calif.: Presidio Press, 1978.

——. "Ideology and the American Experience: A Reexamination of Early American Attitudes toward the Military." In *Soldiers and Civilians: The U.S. Army and the American People,* eds. Garry D. Ryan and Timothy K. Nenninger, 15–26. Washington, D.C.: National Archives and Records Administration, 1987.

Larson, Magali Sarfatti. *The Rise of Professionalism: A Sociological Analysis.* Berkeley: University of California Press, 1977.

Leonard, Thomas C. "Red, White and the Army Blue: Empathy and Anger in the American West." *American Quarterly* 26 (May 1974): 176–90.

Leopold, Richard W. *Elihu Root and the Conservative Tradition.* Boston, Mass.: Little, Brown and Co., 1954.

Limerick, Patricia Nelson. *The Legacy of Conquest: The Unbroken Past of the American West.* New York: W. W. Norton and Co., 1987.

Linderman, Gerald F. *The Mirror of War: American Society and the Spanish-American War.* Ann Arbor: University of Michigan Press, 1974.

Linn, Brian McAllister. *The U.S. Army and Counterinsurgency in the Philippine War, 1899–1902.* Chapel Hill: University of North Carolina Press, 1989.

——. "The Struggle for Samar." In *Crucible of Empire: The Spanish-American War and Its Aftermath,* ed. James C. Bradford, 158–82. Annapolis, Md.: Naval Institute Press, 1993.

——. "The Long Twilight of the Frontier Army." *Western Historical Quarterly* 27 (Summer 1996): 141–67.

——. *Guardians of Empire: The U.S. Army and the Pacific, 1902–1940.* Chapel Hill: University of North Carolina Press, 1997.

Lisowski, Lori A. "The Future of West Point: Senate Debates on the Military Academy during the Civil War." *Civil War History* 34, no. 1 (1988): 5–21.

Lovett, Bobby L. *The African-American History of Nashville, Tennessee, 1780–1930.* Fayetteville: University of Arkansas Press, 1999.

Machoian, Ronald G. "Peter S. Michie and West Point: Educating Professionals." Paper Presented at the Mid-American History Conference, Springfield, Mo., Sept. 1999.

Maslowski, Peter. *Treason Must Be Made Odious: Military Occupation and Wartime Reconstruction in Nashville, Tennessee, 1862–65.* Millwood, N.Y.: KTO Press, 1978.

——, and Allan R. Millett. *For the Common Defense: A Military History of the United States of America.* Rev. and exp. ed. New York: Free Press, 1994.

Milkis, Sidney M., and Jerome M. Mileur, eds. *Progressivism and the New Democracy*. Amherst: University of Massachusetts Press, 1999.

Miller, Stuart C. *"Benevolent Assimilation": The American Conquest of the Philippines, 1899–1903*. New Haven, Conn.: Yale University Press, 1982.

Millett, Allan R. *The General: Robert L. Bullard and Officership in the United States Army, 1881–1925*. Westport, Conn.: Greenwood Press, 1975.

——. *Military Professionalism and Officership in America: Mershon Center Briefing Paper Number Two*. Columbus, Ohio: Mershon Center of the Ohio State University, 1977.

——, and Peter Maslowski. *For the Common Defense: A Military History of the United States of America*. Rev. ed. New York: Free Press, 1994.

Millis, Walter. *Arms and Men: A Study in American Military History*. New York: G. P. Putnam's Sons, 1956.

——, ed. *American Military Thought*. New York: Bobbs-Merrill Co., 1966.

Monnett, John H. "The Battle of Cibicu: An Episode of the Apache Indian Wars." *Trail Guide* 14 (June 1969): 2–19.

——. *Massacre at Cheyenne Hole: Lieutenant Austin Henely and the Sappa Creek Controversy*. Niwot: University Press of Colorado, 1999.

Morrison, James L. "The Struggle between Sectionalism and Nationalism at Ante-bellum West Point, 1830–1861." *Civil War History* 19, no. 2 (1973): 138–48.

Murray, Robert A. *Military Posts in the Powder River Country of Wyoming, 1865–1894*. Lincoln: University of Nebraska Press, 1968.

Nenninger, Timothy K. *The Leavenworth Schools: Education, Professionalism, and the Officer Corps of the United States Army, 1881–1918*. Contributions in Military Studies, no. 15. Westport, Conn.: Greenwood Press, 1978.

——. "The Army Enters the Twentieth Century, 1904–1917." In *Against All Enemies: Interpretations of American History Military from Colonial Times to the Present*, eds. Kenneth J. Hagan and William R. Roberts, 219–34. Contributions in Military Studies, no. 51. Westport, Conn.: Greenwood Press, 1986.

Nenninger, Timothy K., and Garry D. Ryan, eds. *Soldiers and Civilians: The U.S. Army and the American People*. Washington, D.C.: National Archives and Records Administration, 1987.

Nobles, Gregory H. *American Frontiers: Cultural Encounters and Continental Conquest*. New York: Hill and Wang, 1997.

Ogle, Ralph Hedrick. *Federal Control of the Western Apaches, 1848–1886*. With introduction by Oakah L. Jones, Jr. Albuquerque: Historical Society of New Mexico. Reprint, Albuquerque: University of New Mexico Press, 1970.

Osborn, William M. *The Wild Frontier: Atrocities during the American-Indian War from Jamestown Colony to Wounded Knee*. New York: Random House, 2000.

Palmer, Frederick. *Bliss, Peacemaker: The Life and Letters of Tasker Howard Bliss*. New York: Dodd, Mead, and Co., 1934.

Palmer, John McCauley. *America in Arms: The Experience of the United States with Military Organization.* New Haven, Conn.: Yale University Press, 1941.

Pappas, George S. *Prudens Futuri: The US Army War College, 1901–1967.* Carlisle Barracks, Penn.: Alumni Assoc. of the U.S. Army War College, 1967.

———. *To the Point: The United States Military Academy, 1802–1902.* Westport, Conn.: Praeger Publishers, 1993.

Pavalko, Ronald M. *Sociology of Occupations and Professions.* Itasca, Ill.: Peacock Publishers, 1988.

Perkinson, Henry J. *The Imperfect Panacea: American Faith in Education, 1865–1965.* New York: Random House, 1968.

Porter, Glenn. *The Rise of Big Business, 1860–1920.* Arlington Heights, Ill.: AHM Publishing, 1973.

Porter, Joseph C. *Paper Medicine Man: John Gregory Bourke and His American West.* Norman: University of Oklahoma Press, 1986.

Powe, Marc B. "A Great Debate: The American General Staff, 1903–16." *Military Review* (April 1975): 79–82.

Reardon, Carol. *Soldiers and Scholars: The U.S. Army and the Uses of Military History, 1865–1920.* Lawrence: University Press of Kansas, 1990.

Rickey, Don, Jr. *Forty Miles a Day on Beans and Hay: The Enlisted Soldier Fighting the Indian Wars.* Norman: University of Oklahoma Press, 1963.

Roberts, William R. "Reform and Revitalization, 1890–1903." In *Against All Enemies: Interpretations of American Military History from Colonial Times to the Present,* eds. Kenneth J. Hagan and William R. Roberts, 197–218. Contributions in Military Studies, no. 51. Westport, Conn.: Greenwood Press, 1986.

Roberts, David. *Once They Moved Like the Wind: Cochise, Geronimo, and the Apache Indian Wars.* New York: Simon & Schuster, 1993.

Rudolph, Frederick. *The American College and University: A History.* With introduction by John R. Thelin. New York: Alfred A. Knopf, 1962. Reprint, Athens: University of Georgia Press, 1990.

Russell, Don. Introduction to *Campaigning with Crook,* by Charles King. Norman: University of Oklahoma Press, 1964.

Schirmer, Daniel B. *Republic or Empire: American Resistance to the Philippine War.* Cambridge, Mass.: Schenkman Publishing, 1972.

Schlereth, Thomas J. *Victorian America: Transformations in Everyday Life, 1876–1915.* New York: HarperCollins, 1991.

Schmitt, Martin F., ed. *General George Crook: His Autobiography.* With Foreword by Joseph C. Porter. Norman: University of Oklahoma Press, 1986.

Schott, Joseph L. *The Ordeal of Samar.* New York; Bobbs-Merrill Co., 1964.

Scott, Hugh L. *Some Memories of a Soldier.* New York: Century Co., 1928.

Semsch, Philip L. "Elihu Root and the General Staff." *Military Affairs* 27 (Spring 1963): 16–27.

Sexton, William T. *Soldiers in the Sun: An Adventure in Imperialism.* Harrisburg, Penn.: Military Service Publishing Co., 1939.

Shulimson, Jack. *The Marine Corps' Search for a Mission, 1880–1898.* Lawrence: University Press of Kansas, 1993.

Simpson, Brooks D. *The Reconstruction Presidents.* Lawrence: University Press of Kansas, 1998.

Skelton, William B. "The Commanding General and the Problem of Command in the United States Army, 1821–41." *Military Affairs* 34 (Dec. 1970): 117–22.

———. "Professionalization in the U.S. Army Officer Corps during the Age of Jackson." *Armed Forces and Society* 1 (Summer 1975): 443–71.

———. "Army Officers' Attitudes toward Indians, 1830–1860." *Pacific Northwest Quarterly* 67 (July 1976): 113–24.

———. "The Army in the Age of the Common Man, 1815–1845." In *Against All Enemies: Interpretations of American Military History from Colonial Times to the Present,* eds. Kenneth J. Hagan and William R. Roberts, 91–112. Contributions in Military Studies, no. 51. Westport, Conn.: Greenwood Press, 1986.

———. "The Army Officer as Organization Man." In *Soldiers and Civilians: The U.S. Army and the American People,* eds. Garry D. Ryan and Timothy K. Nenninger, 61–70. Washington, D.C.: National Archives and Records Administration, 1987.

———. *An American Profession of Arms: The Army Officer Corps, 1784–1861.* Lawrence: University Press of Kansas, 1992.

———. "Samuel P. Huntington and the Roots of the American Military Tradition." *Journal of Military History* 60 (Apr. 1996): 325–38.

Smith, Sherry L. *The View from Officer's Row: Army Perspectives of Western Indians.* Tucson: University of Arizona Press, 1990.

Spector, Ronald. *Professors of War: The Naval War College and the Development of the Naval Profession.* New Port, R.I.: Naval War College Press, 1977.

Spiller, Roger, J. "Calhoun's Expansible Army: The History of a Military Idea." *The South Atlantic Quarterly* 79, no. 2 (1980): 189–203.

Tate, Michael L. *The Frontier Army in the Settlement of the West.* Norman: University of Oklahoma Press, 1999.

Thrapp, Dan L. *The Conquest of Apacheria.* Norman: University of Oklahoma Press, 1967.

———. *General Crook and the Sierra Madre Adventure.* Norman: University of Oklahoma Press, 1972.

———. *Al Sieber, Chief of Scouts.* With foreword by Donald E. Worcester. Norman: University of Oklahoma Press, 1995.

Trachtenberg, Alan. *The Incorporation of America: Culture and Society in the Gilded Age.* New York: Hill and Wang, 1982.

Turner, Frederick Jackson. *History, Frontier, and Section: Three Essays by Frederick Jackson Turner.* With introduction by Martin Ridge. Albuquerque: University of New Mexico Press: 1993.

Twichell, Heath, Jr. *Allen: The Biography of an Army Officer, 1859–1930.* New Brunswick, N.J.: Rutgers University Press, 1974.

Utley, Robert M. "The Bascom Affair: A Reconstruction." *Arizona and the West,* 3 (Spring 1961): 59–68.

———. *The Last Days of the Sioux Nation.* New Haven: Yale University Press, 1963.

——. *Frontier Regulars: The United States Army and the Indian, 1866–1891.* New York: Macmillan Publishing, 1973.

——. *Frontiersmen in Blue: The United States Army and the Indian, 1848–1865.* New York: Macmillan Publishing, 1967. Reprint, Lincoln: University of Nebraska Press, 1981.

——. *The Indian Frontier of the American West, 1856–1890.* Albuquerque: University of New Mexico Press, 1984.

——. *Cavalier in Buckskin: George Armstrong Custer and the Western Military Frontier.* Norman: University of Oklahoma Press, 1988.

Veysey, Laurence R. *The Emergence of the American University.* Chicago: University of Chicago Press, 1965.

Wagoner, Jennings L., Jr. "The American Compromise: Charles W. Eliot, Black Education, and the New South. In *The History of Higher Education,* ed. Lester F. Goodchild and Harold S. Wechsler. 2nd ed. Needham Heights, Mass.: Simon & Schuster Custom Publishing, 1997.

Wainwright, John D. "Root Versus Bliss: the Shaping of the Army War College." *Parameters* 4, no. 2 (1974): 52–65.

Warner, Ezra J. *Generals in Blue: Lives of the Union Commanders.* Baton Rouge: Louisiana State University Press, 1964.

Watson, Elmo Scott. "The Last Indian War, 1890–91: A Study of Newspaper Jingoism." *Journalism Quarterly* 20 (1943): 205–19.

Weigley, Russell F. *Towards an American Army: Military Thought from Washington to Marshall.* New York: Columbia University Press, 1962.

——. *History of the United States Army.* New York: Macmillan Co., 1967.

——. "The Elihu Root Reforms and the Progressive Era." In *Command and Commanders in Modern Warfare: The Proceedings of the Second Military History Symposium, U.S. Air Force Academy, 2–3 May 1968,* ed. William Geffen, 11–30. Colorado Springs: U.S. Air Force Academy, 1969.

——. "The Long Death of the Indian-Fighting Army." In *Soldiers and Civilians: The U.S. Army and the American People,* eds. Garry D. Ryan and Timothy K. Nenninger, 27–39. Washington, D.C.: National Archives and Records Administration, 1987.

Wharfield, H. B. *Cibicu Creek Fight in Arizona: 1881.* El Cajon, Calif.: n.p., 1971.

Wiebe, Robert H. *The Search for Order, 1877–1920.* New York: Hill and Wang, 1967.

Wilensky, Harold L. "The Professionalization of Everyone?" *American Journal of Sociology* 70 (Sept. 1964): 137–58.

Williams, T. Harry. "The Attack upon West Point During the Civil War," *Mississippi Valley Historical Review* 25, no. 4 (1939): 491–504.

——. *Americans at War: The Development of the American Military System.* Baton Rouge: Louisiana State University Press, 1960.

Wills, Ridley. *The History of Belle Meade: Mansion, Plantation, and Stud.* Nashville, Tenn.: Vanderbilt University Press, 1991.

Wolff, Leon. *Little Brown Brother: How the United States Purchased and Pacified the Philippine Islands at the Century's Turn.* Garden City, N.Y.: Doubleday and Co., 1961.

Wooster, Robert. " 'A Difficult and Forlorn Country': The Military Looks at the American Southwest, 1850–1890." *Arizona and the West* 28, no. 4 (1986): 339–56.

——. *Nelson A. Miles and the Twilight of the Frontier Army.* Lincoln: University of Nebraska Press, 1993.

Wooster, Robert. *The Military and United States Indian Policy, 1865–1903.* New Haven, Conn.: Yale University Press, 1988. Reprint, Lincoln: Nebraska University Press, 1995.

——. *Nelson A.Miles and the Twilight of the Frontier Army.* Lincoln: University of Nebraska Press, 1995.

Worcester, Donald E. *The Apaches: Eagles of the Southwest.* Norman: University of Oklahoma Press, 1979.

Dissertations and Theses

Coates, George Y. "The Philippine Constabulary: 1901–1917." Ph.D. diss., Ohio State University, 1968.

Denton, Edgar. "The Formative Years of the United States Military Academy, 1775–1833." Ph.D. diss., Syracuse University, 1964.

Dillard, Walter Scott. "The United States Military Academy, 1865–1900: The Uncertain Years." Ph.D. diss., University of Washington, 1972.

Fitzpatrick, David J. "Emory Upton: The Misunderstood Reformer." Ph.D. diss., University of Michigan, 1996.

Griess, Thomas E. "Dennis Hart Mahan: West Point Professor and Advocate of Military Professionalism, 1830–1871." Ph.D. diss., Duke University, 1969.

Janes, William H. "Selected Writings of Eben Swift." Master's thesis, McNeese State University, 1980.

McAndrews, Eugene V. "William Ludlow: Engineer, Governor, Soldier." Ph.D. diss., Kansas State University, 1973.

Molloy, Peter M. "Technical Education and Young Republic: West Point as America's Ecole Polytechnique, 1802–1833." Ph.D. diss., Brown University, 1975.

Morrison, James L. "The United States Military Academy, 1833–1866: Years of Progress and Turmoil." Ph.D. diss., Columbia University, 1970.

Roberts, William R. "Loyalty and Expertise: The Transformation of the Nineteenth-Century American General Staff and the Creation of the Modern Military Establishment." Ph.D. diss., Johns Hopkins University, 1979.

Woolard, James R. "The Philippine Scouts: The Development of America's Colonial Army." Ph.D. diss., Ohio State University, 1975.

Zais, Barrie E. "The Struggle for a Twentieth-Century Army: Investigation and Reform of the United States Army after the Spanish-American War, 1898–1903. Ph.D. diss., Duke University, 1981.

Index

Page numbers for photographs are shown in italics. All military units are designated as U.S. units (e.g., U.S. Sixth Cavalry).